WORLD LABOUR REPORT

INDUSTRIAL RELATIONS,
democracy and social stability

1997-98

INTERNATIONAL LABOUR OFFICE
GENEVA

ILO
World labour report 1997-98: Industrial relations, democracy and social stability
Geneva, International Labour Office, 1997

/Labour relations/, /developed country/, /developing country/. 13.06.1
ISBN 92-2-110331-5; ISSN 0255-5514

Also published in French: *Le travail dans le monde 1997-98. Relations professionnelles, démocratie et cohésion sociale*
(ISBN 92-2-210331-9; ISSN 0255-5506), Geneva, 1997

In Spanish: *El trabajo en el mundo 1997-98: relaciones laborales, democracia y cohesión social*
(ISBN 92-2-310331-2; ISSN 0255-5522), Geneva, 1997

ILO Cataloguing in Publication Data

Preface

Labour relations between heads of enterprise and their associations, workers in trade unions and sometimes the public authorities traditionally perform the economic function of participating in the production and distribution of the fruits of growth. But they also perform two other functions, one democratic (giving workers a say at the workplace), the other social (ensuring that everyone in work or seeking employment is integrated into society). As the century draws to a close, we might ask whether they are still performing these functions satisfactorily, at a time when the pace of immense political, economic and social change has suddenly rushed ahead? This report seeks to elucidate that question by presenting significant facts and indicators, analysing them and highlighting future trends.

Various questions spring to mind, for example, regarding the relevance today of bilateral or trilateral collective labour relations. Do bipartite or tripartite agreements, such as those of the 1960s or 1970s, still have a future when the main concern of the industrialized countries is no longer so much a question of living and working conditions as of job creation and employment stability? This is all very reminiscent of an issue that has long been raised in connection with developing countries: is collective dialogue still an essential part of labour relations if it is no longer able to take full account of the segmentation of the labour market, the growth of precarious forms of employment, unemployment and social exclusion?

The three social partners need to come up with some answers. First, there are the public authorities, whose scope of action is curtailed by the internationalization of the market economy but who at the same time are increasingly called upon to adapt and modernize their institutions or restore stability to a severely battered social fabric.

Next come the trade unions, whose difficulties are common knowledge, stemming as they do largely from the diverging interests of the workforce. More specifically, there is a more and more noticeable rift between workers with stable jobs and the growing numbers of other, often less-skilled, workers. This crisis in worker representation, which is now all too apparent in the industrialized countries, has always existed in the informal sector of the developing countries. As that sector has grown, so too has the problem.

As things are today, the balance of power has evidently changed, and it is often the entrepreneurs' objectives that are given priority consideration. Here too, however, tensions are emerging. Small and medium-sized enterprises, whose concerns are quite different from those of larger firms, are proliferating, while the most powerful companies are increasingly clamouring for autonomy. Again, it is not easy to speak with one voice.

It is the whole concept of labour relations, of the social partners and of their scope of action that is being challenged. Are the methods that have been used so far still relevant? Must they be adapted or do we need new ones?

In industrialized countries with pluralist traditions, these changes resemble constraints which increasingly appear to stifle established systems. On the other hand, the break experienced by Central and Eastern European countries was short and sharp: there, these phenomena were amplified by the passage from one economic and political order to another. A break-up of economic structures has been witnessed in that region, the trade union movement has become fragmented and – inevitably – certain habits and methods of the old regimes have survived.

Lastly, in a whole range of developing countries, industrial relations come into play, above all, in the public sector and large-scale national or multinational enterprises. What, however, is the fate of the masses of people occupied in the informal sector?

We must bear in mind that collective bargaining first evolved in the industrial democracies, where the aim was clear: to enable the parties themselves to participate in devising and applying safeguards for the working man that were the necessary corollary of economic progress. The bargaining procedure did at least mean that the weak did not become steadily weaker. Today, that risk is again very much in the minds of all those now facing insecurity. This is all too true in the countries of the South; but it is also more and more the case in the North too. Employers' and, especially, workers' organizations must learn to cope with this fragmentation of interests and of the levels at which decisions are taken in the world of work.

If they are to succeed, workers' organizations must come to terms with social and economic change. For example, as decentralized networks gradually take over from mass production, so the possibilities for the trade unions to halt the process are diminishing. At the consumer stage, however, new means of pressure are coming to the fore, as enterprises become more and more sensitive to competition. Competition too, like the companies themselves, is gradually becoming more international, and this calls for new forms of representation.

Yet it is safe to say that there seems to be no approach other than labour relations that aims simultaneously at protecting the employed, the unemployed and the underemployed. This is especially true at a time when the State is increasingly hesitant to intervene. In any event, history has shown that it is never a good thing for the individual to have to stand alone against the State.

This is of course a transitional phase. If we are to put industrial relations back on a firm basis, we must surely look to negotiate fresh social contracts. First, then, we must make an inventory of successes and innovations all over parts of the world, and we must analyse them so that we can see what the prospects are for the future. That is what this report sets out to do.

The report will, I hope, provide food for thought for all those concerned about

WORLD LABOUR REPORT
1997-98

labour and about its future. There has, of course, always been a certain conflict between the satisfaction of immediate interests and the desire to build human relationships that are not based solely on considerations of cost or a balance of power. At the present time, however, there is a very real danger that a less egalitarian society may evolve, composed of "winners" and "losers", with all the attendant risks for democracy and for the stability of the society we live in. If that is indeed so, the social partners have a compelling duty to ensure that the changes currently taking place are directed towards a mutually acceptable synthesis of economic efficiency and social progress.

15 October 1997   Michel Hansenne

Acknowledgements

This report was prepared by a team of ILO officials headed by Jean-Michel Servais and comprising Duncan Campbell, François Eyraud, Tayo Fashoyin, Ranjana Kumari, Chang-Hee Lee, Gyorgy Sziraczki and Manuela Tomei. Research assistance was provided by Gülay Keskin, Daniela Lunardo, Sandra Parra, and Yvette Roozenbeek. Administrative and secretarial support was given by Sally Outterside, Françoise Riette and Thelma Sanitrar. Mary Hamouda provided library assistance.

During the research phase of the report, the team benefited from an exchange of views, in particular during two informal workshops when it was discussed with the following specialists from outside the ILO: Halton Cheadle, Adrían Goldín, Jean-Claude Javillier, Sanford Jacoby, Berndt Keller, Russell Lansbury, Michael Piore, Kazuo Sugeno, Robert Taylor, and Kirsten Wever.

Jelle Visser provided both data on and assistance with trade union membership statistics as well as comments on early draft chapters – which are gratefully acknowledged. The ILO's Bureau of Statistics also provided data and valuable assistance in compiling the report's statistical annex. Particular thanks are due to Alfred Pankert for his written contribution and frequent discussion of ideas and drafts prepared by the team. Thanks are also due to Miriam Golden for comments on portions of the report's themes and findings.

Other ILO staff members contributed their time and comments as work progressed. The help of Sadok Bel Hadj Hassine, Mohamed Ali Ibrahim, Jean-François Retournard, Hedva Sarfati, and María-Luz Vega Ruiz is gratefully acknowledged.

Parts of the report incorporated information from background papers contributed by the following individual authors: Nikitas Aliprantis, Silvio Feldman, Adrían Goldín, Anke Hassel, Josee Lamers, Russell Lansbury, Roger McElrath, Frank Pyke, Elżbieta Sobótka, Francisco Tapia Guerrero, Robert Taylor, C.S. Venkata Ratnam, and Kirsten Wever. Background papers providing information for the report were also jointly written by João Paulo Cândia Veiga and Marco Antonio de Oliveira, Simon Clarke and Sarah Ashwin, Peter Doeringer and Audrey Watson, and Clive Thompson and Robert Macdonald.

Contents

Introduction

Noting the drop in trade union membership in many countries and the deregulation of conditions of employment, some observers have concluded that the increasingly competitive and global economy in which we live spells the decline of collective labour relations. Yet the strong display of solidarity that has marked a number of recent labour disputes casts some doubt as to the validity of this conclusion: can we really talk of the eventual demise of collective labour relations at a time when job insecurity and wage inequality are on the increase? Although during these conflicts traditional trade unions may sometimes have faced competition from independent initiatives by employees – which raises the whole problem of union representativeness – the subsequent negotiations have made it perfectly clear that their contribution cannot be discounted.

Job insecurity and wage inequality are two symptoms of the same underlying economic trend which is pushing the wages of the least-skilled workers down, either within the country or through the relocation of production, and which requires higher skills in order to make the best use of new forms of organization and technology. In a low-growth situation, as has often been stressed, the probably lasting effects of current economic trends are threatening to undermine social cohesion even though the problem does vary from country to country. It is impossible to say at what point inequality of income or unemployment is liable to spark off serious social conflict, but their consequences in terms of crime, isolationism and marginalization are already evident. And it is quite obvious that, without reliable channels for the collective expression of grievances and fear, social movements can rapidly get out of control.

Traditionally, these channels have been the occupational organizations, but nowadays many of these are experiencing a sometimes sharp drop in membership. Again, as Chapter 1 will show, the situation varies greatly from country to country; though trade union membership is down almost everywhere, the extent of the decline and the current level of union membership differ widely, as can be seen from the table below showing how they have changed over the past ten years in the various regions of the world. The differences are equally significant when the figures are broken down by country. For example, union membership in the non-agricultural sector is 68 per cent in Denmark, 11 per cent in Spain, 32 per cent in Brazil and 16 per cent in Chile. Chapter 1 will endeavour to identify the economic, organizational, legislative or sociological factors underlying the differences among countries as well as this disenchantment with collective organization.

Region	No. of union members	Percentage change	Region	No. of union members	Percentage change
Sub-Saharan Africa	10 026 933	–	East and South-East Asia	23 930 252	+ 4.8
North Africa and Middle East	7 337 558	–	South Asia	10 445 094	+10.5
North America	20 488 500	– 1.1	Northern Europe	7 526 700	– 0.1
Central America	11 042 156	–19.0	Western Europe	23 749 071	–15.6
South America	22 430 840	– 6.1	Southern Europe	10 173 734	+ 2.0
Oceania	2 801 900	–19.4	Central and Eastern Europe	13 992 600	–35.9

Note: For the methodology used in preparing the table, see the statistical annex.

Trade unions have made a variety of efforts to recruit members. Chapter 2 reviews these efforts, focusing on the new alliances between unions and various social groups. The challenge facing the unions is how to strengthen their ability to delegate without causing a fragmentation of their sectional activity. Lastly, as international economic relations become more and more the norm, and also because economic systems themselves are becoming more and more alike, the traditional activities of the trade union movement at the international level are being completely transformed. Is effective action possible at the regional or world level? What form does it take at the moment? What impact does it have? These are some of the questions discussed at the end of Chapter 2.

Though we hear less about it, employers' organizations are also experiencing difficulties. They too represent members with divergent interests, the major difference being between small and medium-sized enterprises and large companies, which tend to have their own policies for determining terms of employment. Here again, the status of employers' organizations varies considerably from country to country, but everywhere they are a major actor in the development of labour relations. These issues are considered in Chapter 3.

Irrespective of the specific measures they are taking to reverse the downward trend in membership, occupational organizations are judged largely by what they can do for the social protection of wage-earners. However, given the constraints imposed by the intensification of competition and the need to be competitive at all costs, the question arises whether there is still anything to negotiate and how much room for manoeuvre the social partners have at the national level, which is still the natural and most realistic level for determining social protection. Chapter 4 shows that the fact that national policies are less autonomous than in the past is no reason to underestimate the scope for action. More importantly, it will be easier for States to open up their economies and enjoy the resulting benefits if they are able to provide workers with a measure of protection against the insecurity associated with globalization and technological innovation. Far from being obsolete, this function of social protection provided nationally is still both feasible and desirable for the opening up of economies. That said, it is quite clear today that national policies are more dependent on enterprises than before when it comes to reviving the economy, creating jobs and raising the standard of living, all of which were formerly assumed largely by the welfare State. The intention of this chapter is to show how the situation is changing, including the very definition of the frontiers of the enterprise and the resulting opportunity for broadening the concept of social dialogue.

The subsequent chapters examine the actual repercussions of these new developments on the institutions of social dialogue, their operation and their development and their structure and content, in industrialized countries (Chapter 5), in Central and Eastern European countries (Chapter 6) and in the newly industrialized and developing countries (Chapter 7). Is the greater importance of the enterprise partly responsible for the changing structure of collective bargaining systems? Does social dialogue still play a role in determining conditions of employment, or are they determined increasingly by personnel policy, with or without the participation of trade unions? What is the impact of the emphasis now being placed on competitiveness, and of the growing precariousness of employment? Has collective bargaining lost its influence and, if so, has this loss been proportional to the decline in union membership? Is the present trend universal, or does it vary from country to country? Such are the main questions that these chapters attempt to answer.

Because they normally have a specific structure, the practice and analysis of labour relations are generally restricted to the formal sector. Organizing workers in the informal sector has always been a major problem, and there are very few studies and data in this area. However, considering the importance of this sector, particularly in developing countries, and also its growth, an overview of the situation would seem to be in order. This means not only evaluating the role played by the traditional structures of labour relations, which are in any event poorly equipped to respond to the needs of this part of the active population, but also identifying how such a heterogeneous workforce is in fact organized. It ranges from the casual odd-job worker to the head of a small company, including the huge and very mixed group of independent workers whose interests and needs are for the most part not covered by the categories that are defined in labour relations in the formal sector. Chapter 8 focuses on the specific forms of organization and solidarity which are evolving in the informal sector and which provide a starting-point for addressing the needs and problems of workers in this sector. It is from this standpoint that the report examines the role and activities of unions and employers' organizations, so as to explain exactly what kind of strategies are needed. Lastly, the chapter looks at how some minimal protection of conditions of employment can best be brought about, i.e. by introducing a degree of regulation in a sector which, by definition, is informal.

The view that emerges from the foregoing chapters shows that labour relations are currently going through a period of considerable change. Where will this take us? What are the prospects for the future? The final chapter tries to answer these questions.

1 Trade union associations: Current issues

The revolution in communications and production technologies and in the organization of work, the political changes symbolized by the fall of the Berlin wall, the emergence of newly industrialized countries, the growing interdependence of national economies and the resulting stiffer competition have all clearly had a telling effect on States, firms and trade unions.

The impact of these changes is evident at every level, from the shop floor to the regions of the world. As will be seen below, the globalization of the economy has been accompanied by common trends in the practice of industrial relations; a good illustration of this is the greater importance often given to plant-level negotiations. However, the national institutions of some countries, and even of certain regions, are more resistant than others to these trends towards harmonization. This aspect will be examined below.

It seems advisable, however, to begin by looking at the factors determining change in the case of the two main actors in occupational life. The very real difficulties are well known and have been reported at length in the media and specialist literature. Diversification and the differing interests on both sides (the concerns of workers in stable jobs clearly differ from those of workers in precarious employment or the unemployed, and SMEs and multinational enterprises may themselves have widely divergent concerns) are affecting trade unions and employers' associations. Indeed, it is their status as single representatives which has been compromised; on the employers' side as well as on the workers' side organizations have to compete with other institutions rather than engaging in unified action. They are going through a critical period.

These trends can be found everywhere, although they are more evident in some regions or States than in others. In the developing countries, many of the points raised here are particularly applicable to the major private enterprises and the public sector. A considerable proportion of the workforce is, however, left outside this mainstream movement. There is of course just as much need for representation, but traditional methods are unable to translate this need into practice. A separate chapter will be devoted to this subject.

While the upheaval affecting employers' associations merits discussion, the thrust of the debate on the parties participating in the collective bargaining process concerns the decline in trade union membership.[1] This point will be examined in greater detail below.

This approach can be easily explained. While social issues are only a part – and economically speaking not the most important part – of managerial interests, they are normally central to workers' concerns.

Trade unionism is traditionally explained by the workers' weaker position in the employment relationship and their need to join forces with other wage-earners – union being strength – in order to negotiate their working and living conditions as a collective body.

It is generally agreed that the trade union movement has fallen on hard times. The extent of its difficulties may sometimes, of course, be exaggerated by overemphasising adverse national situations, sometimes for ideological reasons, or for the sake of convenience. None the less, as can be seen from the tables in the annex, workers' organizations are experiencing serious difficulties almost everywhere and are losing members. Some even have doubts about their future. The 1980s, it seems, were particularly bad.

Of the approximately 70 countries for which there are comparable data,[2] about half have seen a considerable drop in their membership in absolute figures over the last ten years. In several cases, it is true that this decline is linked to the shift from what was in practice more or less compulsory union membership towards truly free unionism; this is particularly true of the countries of Central and Eastern Europe, including those in the former Soviet Union (–50.6 per cent in the Czech Republic, –45.7 per cent in Poland, –38 per cent in Hungary; –71.2 per cent in Estonia, –22.8 per cent in Belarus). Mention could also be made of Portugal (–44.2 per cent). Nevertheless, the trend is also discernible across a broad spectrum of countries, including Israel (–75.7 per cent), Kenya (–28.6 per cent), Uganda (–38.3 per cent), Uruguay (–31.9 per cent), Venezuela (–32.2 per cent), New Zealand (–46.7 per cent), France (–31.2 per cent), United Kingdom (–25.2 per cent) and even Germany (–20.3 per cent between 1991 and 1995, but here much can be explained by the drop in membership in former East Germany).

On the other hand, there has been an increase in union membership in about 20 countries, first and foremost in South Africa (+126.7 per cent), Zimbabwe (+54.4 per cent), Chile (+89.6 per cent), Republic of Korea (+60.8 per cent) Philippines (+69.4 per cent), Thailand (+77.3 per cent), Hong Kong (prior to 1 July 1997, +53 per cent), Bangladesh (+57.8 per cent), Spain (+92.3 per cent) and some of the smaller Central American countries. In many of these cases the trade union movement started from a position of weakness and strengthened its position only after years of marginalization or restrictions on its freedom of action.

Among the OECD countries only two have seen a sharp increase in union membership since 1985 – Spain (noted above) and the Netherlands (+19.3 per cent); in both cases the trade union movement has managed to recover from its earlier sharp decline. In some countries union membership has remained relatively stable: Canada (+10.7 per cent), Japan (–0.1 per cent), Belgium (+5.8 per cent), Italy (–6.8 per cent), and in the Nordic countries, as well as Pakistan (+11.7 per cent), Sri Lanka (+4.8 per cent) and India (+3.1 per cent).

If these absolute figures are examined in the light of employment trends (see Annex), the situation is even more dramatic; over the last ten years the unionization rate has increased in only a few countries, in particular in South Africa, Philippines, Spain and probably Turkey (but here supplementary data are needed). However, the rate has fallen by more than 20 per cent in 35 of the 66 countries for which comparison was possible, and in particular in Argentina, Costa Rica, Mexico and Venezuela, the United States, Australia and New Zealand, Israel, France and Portugal, to say nothing of the former communist countries. While many of the East Asian and South East Asian countries have seen membership rise, the unionization rate has not significantly increased except in the Philippines and Hong Kong (prior to 1 July 1997). The rate has remained relatively stable, for instance, in Belgium, Canada, Republic of Korea and in the Nordic countries (it has even risen substantially in Finland).

Generally speaking, out of a sample of 92 countries for which figures on union membership were available (calculated on the basis of the non-agricultural workforce), only 14 had a rate of more than 50 per cent in 1995; in 48 countries, in other words more than half the sample, the rate was less than 20 per cent.

That being said, trade union influence and power cannot be measured merely in terms of the number of members, particularly if membership refers only to those who regularly pay their dues. This is an important factor in assessing their power – including financial power – and representativity: but it is not the only one. This can be seen from the success of trade union candidates in occupational elections (for example, works' committees) in Spain and in France, from the presence of trade union members in Parliament in Germany and, even more clearly in the capacity of the confederations in France to call for action, for example, during the major strikes in the public service at the end of 1995, despite the very low unionization rate. The same can be seen in Venezuela.[3] What is involved here is militant unionism rather than weight of numbers. One explanation stems from a very ideological conception of industrial relations. In France, collective agreements were for a long time seen as a temporary truce – which could always be called off – rather than as a cooperation agreement. On two occasions, first in 1971 and then in 1982, governmental programmes embodied in legislation were specifically designed to foster collective bargaining. While France thus has a fairly well developed structure for such purposes – perhaps more so than other countries of the continent – collective bargaining has never had the same importance there in practice. The collapse in Europe of the more radical political systems has led in France to a decline in support for militant trade unionism; yet the instinctive reaction is still one of protest and demands.

A dry recital of figures also masks another important trend: the emergence or reappearance of a free trade union movement in a number of countries that recently moved from a totalitarian to a democratic regime.

In the former communist countries of Europe, for example, there were close links between unions, governments and – under their leadership – the parties in power. Workers' organizations were essentially a one-way conveyor belt operating from the top downwards – encouraging wage-earners to produce more and better products in return for social benefits (they often ran the social security schemes) and fringe benefits in housing or holidays, etc.

The difficulties of all kinds besetting the trade unions in the move towards a market economy have been highlighted.[4] Trade union leaders have rapidly had to change their outlook to adjust to the ensuing changes. They have had to cope with a wide variety of economic structures, with some major State groups continuing to receive subsidies while others were privatized – in one go or in stages – with small enterprises mushrooming and foreign investors setting up new companies. In such a heterogeneous economic environment, it was no longer quite clear where the bargaining level should be. It was little wonder, therefore, that the union movements became fragmented – with the notable exception of the Czech Republic and Slovakia – although more recently, it is true, efforts to regroup have been made. Neither is it surprising to see a gradual decline in unionization rates (which were close to 100 per cent under the old regime); they remain, however, well within the average.

Throughout the world, current developments are giving rise to sometimes rather serious risks as well as opportunities – themselves not without their dangers. It is hard to separate the former from the latter, but we shall endeavour to do so here first by emphasizing the ongoing challenge, then by examining the unions' essential objectives, and finally by identifying what appear to be the basic features of a new reality.

The reasons for stagnation

Recent economic changes undoubtedly constitute basic factors affecting enterprises and thus trade unions. A second set of reasons for the adverse developments noted above has to do with social change, the attitude of the other parties, and the unions themselves. The latter reasons can be explained at least in part by the former, although there is no way of measuring their precise influence.

Economic changes

Over the long term, changes in the composition of the labour market, by sector of activity and occupation, have often reduced the traditional base of trade union membership. The manufacturing industries, for example, have for some time held a declining share of total employment. Similarly, there are fewer and fewer "blue-collar" workers and more and more "white-collar" employees. The trade union confederations often find it difficult to organize some of the recent categories of workers – women, youngsters, highly skilled persons, persons in precarious employment. Those unions that have secured a solid foothold in the public sector and in services, in particular in the new sectors of activity (state of the art technologies, where prosperity often reduces the need for the defense of interests by a union) or among women workers, have lost fewer members (in Canada, for example).

In addition to these changes in labour supply and demand, account must also be taken of globalization. The growing interdependence of national economies is undoubtedly a characteristic feature of the closing years of the century. The opening up of economies has had beneficial effects. As two recent ILO studies have shown, this openness may have a positive impact on growth, employment, earnings and equality.[5] But globalization of necessity entails adjustments, and these have a price. As will be seen, if certain paths are followed, unions may have to pay a disproportionate share of the costs; it is by no means certain, as things now stand, that globalization has had the same positive effects on union membership and action.

Many of the pressures brought to bear on unions are related to the way in which governments and enterprises are reacting to economic openness. Rapid technological change and greater freedom of choice for enterprises in deciding where to set up their business are leading to changes in production and working methods and locations. Almost all unions are having to face difficulties in adapting their structures and programmes to enterprises that are less hierarchical and more network-oriented and to economies which are less compartmentalized into country-specific sectors of activity and more integrated at the regional and world levels. At the same time, many employers are endeavouring to bring collective bargaining down to the plant level.

Several of these trends are significant enough to merit a separate chapter. Here only two aspects of the complex globalization process will be examined. First, it is often said that the integration of international capital markets – or "financial globalization" – brings with it new constraints on the autonomy of national macroeconomic policies. We shall see that the unions too are affected by this environment. Second, globalization is often described in terms of its main effect – stiffer national and international competition. This increase in competition is due to the very rapid growth in international trade. Indeed, that world trade continues to grow at a more rapid rate than world output is perhaps the most basic indicator of globalization. Once again, the unions have also been affected by this intensification of trade competition.

The new constraints on macroeconomic policies: Impact on trade unions

While there may be doubts as to the extent to which manufacturing and service companies have become fully globalized, there are no such doubts about the globalization of financial markets.[6] With the collapse of the Bretton Woods system of fixed-exchange rates in the early 1970s, and the progressive elimination of national capital and exchange controls, the world has witnessed a stunning growth in international financial markets and the proliferation of new financial instruments. Foreign assets held by banks increased threefold in the decade up to 1993, and daily transactions on the foreign exchange markets now amount to over $1.2 billion.[7]

The increase in short-term, international capital mobility has been nothing less than spectacular. Since the vast majority of these transactions are speculative in nature (for example, they are not intended to finance trade operations or long-term investments), there is a risk that they will have a destabilizing effect on the economy. Mindful of the reactions of the financial markets, States have become prudent at the fiscal and monetary level. "The essential problem posed by international capital mobility is that short-term capital mobility undermines a country's ability to undertake policies that threaten investor confidence in its economy. Countries which undertake macroeconomic policies, such as expansionary monetary or fiscal policy, or dramatic changes in tax or welfare policy, might find that investors react strongly by moving finance out of the country to invest in short-term assets abroad. When this occurs, this short-term capital flight can cause a precipitous decline in the exchange rate as well as a sharp rise in short-term interest rates as the central bank raises interest rates to try to prevent the depreciation of the currency."[8]

One of the puzzles of financial globalization appears to be that it is notably less extensive than theory would imply: "the evidence on international capital immobility is extensive, including the lack of international portfolio diversification, real interest rate differentials across countries and the high correlation between domestic savings and investment."[9] The evidence for financial globalization thus seems lacking.[10] States furthermore still have room to manoeuvre in their exchange rate policies.[11] Similarly, employers' and workers' organizations play an active part in the framing of macroeconomic policy; incomes policy, too, could be used to allay inflationary fears in international financial markets arising from expansionary monetary or fiscal policies.[12]

These arguments are not without weight, although the salient point would appear to be that capital markets have achieved a sufficient degree of international integration to place real constraints on the monetary and fiscal policies of States, which need to be mindful of their reactions. The discipline imposed by these markets leads monetary authorities and governments to the search for price stability as the principal objective of their monetary and fiscal policies. What impact do these new constraints have on trade unions?

The globalization of the financial system has shifted power to the international financial markets, which has inevitably affected worker and union strategies. Trade unions and their political allies have often been fervent advocates of expansionist macroeconomic policies to encourage full employment. But now, they find that the classic means of achieving this objective have been compromised by the new realities. Counter-cyclical government spending to stimulate the economy could trigger a devaluation and the money injected into the economy could well be wasted on the purchase of imported goods: "Speculative capital is easily swayed by short-term considerations of its best interests; anything that threatens to cheapen a currency, such as labourist economic policies, may trigger an anticipatory run".[13] This weakens the unions by undermining the political reasons on which their objectives were based. The constraints that globalization places on interventions of the Keynesian kind leave trade unions and their political allies "without a viable macroeconomic programme".[14]

The weakening of their traditional macroeconomic policy objectives is not the only challenge facing the unions as a result of financial globalization. Since the 1980s, macroeconomic policies no longer seem to be a major component of employment policy in many OECD countries. Price stability would now seem to be the objective. Policies of austerity which governments are led to introduce help reduce demand and slow down growth.

Slow growth has a number of adverse repercussions not only on employment but also on the distribution of earnings. There is a relationship between economic growth and the degree of earnings equality, albeit with a few notable exceptions. Slow growth might also be accompanied by increasing inequality.[15] In the OECD countries, macroeconomic conditions could also explain the existence of such a relationship: "The significance of the relationship between the macroeconomic environment and labour market inequality can be seen in the contrast between developments before and after 1973. The pre-1973 period recorded rapid growth of economic output and labour demand. This allowed and gave strong incentives for firms to upgrade the skills of their workforce to meet their needs. The resulting strong productivity gains allowed the real average wages to rise rapidly without increasing wage inequality among workers. The period since 1973 has witnessed a completely different macroeconomic environment that has been conducive to rising labour market inequality ... The insufficient aggregate demand linked with lower rates of growth ... led to a reduction in the rate of growth of high-paid jobs [which] tended to erode the position of less-qualified workers [which in turn] will push wages down even further."[16]

Income distribution depends not only on growth rates, but on the way industrial relations themselves are organized. The decline in unionization in the 1980s may also explain the drop in wages among low-skilled workers: "Studies which analyse the effect of de-unionization in the United States and in the United Kingdom find that around 20 per cent of the overall increase in wage dispersion can be accounted for by the decline in unionization."[17]

There is a relationship between trade union representation and collective action structures and the degree of earnings equality. Countries where the proportion of workers covered by collective agreements is greatest generally have the highest degree of earnings equality and, in these countries, inequality has increased less. In many ways, the United States and the United Kingdom are special cases, where de-unionization is higher than the OECD average. At the same time, the scope of collective agreements, unlike that of most countries, is restricted in the United States and the United Kingdom only to unionized workers. A decline in unionization may therefore more directly result in a greater dispersion of wages.

The growth rate has an effect on income distribution. High unemployment since the 1980s has also weakened the unions. Figure 1.1, which compares the change in the unionization rate in the 1980s with the increase in unemployment in the 1980s over the 1970s, clearly shows that there is a link: union membership declines when unemployment rises. There are many factors involved in the worsening and persistence of unemployment. One is the slow growth experienced in these countries since the 1970s, due in part to a macroeconomic policy of austerity. As figure 1.2 shows, there is a relationship between trends in the average unemployment rates in the 1980s compared to the 1970s and GDP growth in the 1980s. There is nothing surprising about this; higher rates of growth are generally associated with lower levels of unemployment.

Growth, union density, earnings equality: all these different observations seem to suggest a relationship between the three in the OECD countries. The accentuation of earnings inequality appears to have been caused in part (but not entirely) by the slowdown in growth since the 1970s, as well as by de-unionization, which itself has come about in part as a result of slower growth. The problem therefore seems to have originated in slow growth and, by undermining the unions' strength, has had an increased effect on income distribution by weakening wage-fixing mechanisms.

In so far as it leads to a policy of macroeconomic austerity that holds growth in check and undermines trade unions, financial globalization could be one factor contributing to the increase in such inequalities. These new circumstances are not confined to the OECD countries. As will be seen below, the current constraints of macroeconomic policies are equally felt in the developing countries.

For many of these countries, the opening up of their economies to the world market has resulted in a major reorientation of their macroeconomic policies. While this process offers promising prospects in the long term, it rarely comes without costly adaptation. The starting-point varies considerably from State to State. In Africa and Latin America, the opening up of the economy has come after rigorous stabilization and adjustment measures which have often created more difficult conditions than when the economies were more closed. Many countries in transition in Central and Eastern Europe will doubtless recover but, here again, inequalities are widening and in several cases the standard of living has fallen sharply. Empirically, it may be agreed that the opening up of the economy often initially entails adverse effects which predominate over any positive benefits. Adjustment, as noted above, almost always has its cost. If there is an exception which confirms the rule, it is Asia. While several East Asian countries have made spectacular progress, it is in part because they are exceptional. "The varied results achieved in different regions reflect differences in the timing and impact of outward- and inward-oriented development strategies. The East Asian approach was to combine export-oriented industrialization with selective forms of state intervention (export subsidies, import licenses, non-tariff trade barriers, preferential credit, privileged access to quotas, etc.), and then to roll back these policies

Figure 1.1. **The change in average unemployment between the 1980s and 1970s, and change in union density in the 1980s**

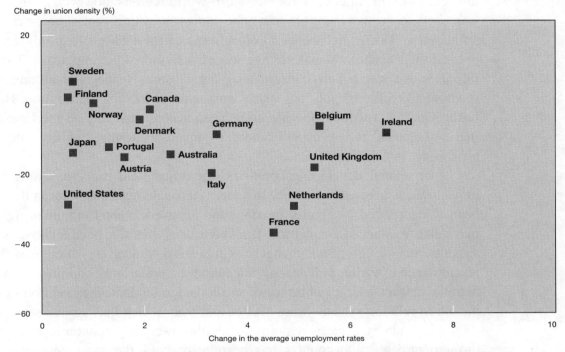

Figure 1.2. **The change in average unemployment between the 1980s and 1970s, and growth of per capita GDP, 1980-93**

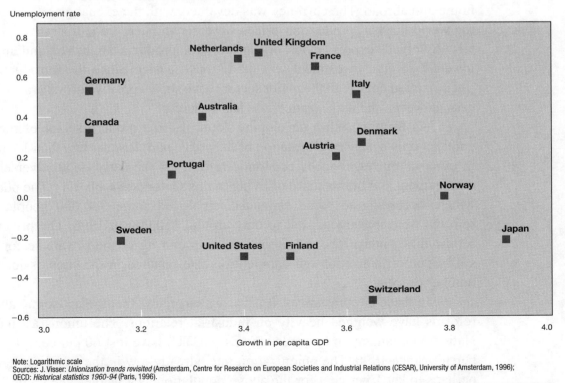

Note: Logarithmic scale
Sources: J. Visser: *Unionization trends revisited* (Amsterdam, Centre for Research on European Societies and Industrial Relations (CESAR), University of Amsterdam, 1996); OECD: *Historical statistics 1960-94* (Paris, 1996).

under internal and external pressure after successful export industries had been established. In Latin America and other Third World regions, however, state intervention was used to promote import-substitute industrialization, not export-oriented industrialization. When the liberalization reforms of the 1980s took hold, many nations opened their economies before they were internationally competitive. The resulting import surge has led to widespread plant closures (especially among small and medium-sized firms), job loss, and a worsening of income distribution. However, in Latin America, restructuring has since been accompanied by an increase in exports in new sectors, the re-establishment of macroeconomic stability and enhanced efficiency."[18]

In several developing countries, the adjustment process, strengthening the move towards greater democracy that swept through these countries in the 1980s, has been characterized by greater freedom and renewed interest in human rights, and in particular freedom of association. But that process has also been marked by new constraints because of rapid changes in industrial strategies which now bear little resemblance to earlier policies, or indeed to their underlying conditions – a protected national market, a large public sector and considerable State intervention – onto which industrial relation systems were grafted and from which they gained support.

Uganda is a case in point. After the sweeping economic reforms carried through in 1997, the country has become perhaps the most deregulated in sub-Saharan Africa.[19] The aim of these reforms was to restore competitiveness both at home and abroad. The currency was devalued, with the exchange rate determined by the world market; production prices were deregulated, trade liberalized, export cartels dissolved, export levies on agricultural products abolished and import dues lowered; foreign investment was made much easier. Since the introduction of this liberalization policy, all the major sectors have shown positive growth rates. In the process, however, the unionization rate has suffered.

As in many other developing countries, the modern sector of the economy employs only a very small fraction of the active population – less than 14 per cent. As in other countries, too, the economic reforms at the early stage adversely affected employment and the standard of living in this sector (see table 1.1). The public sector, which, according to some estimates, employed some 320,000 people when the reforms were introduced, fell to only around 150,000 in 1996. The privatization of semi-public enterprises and the major restructuring of the private sector following stiffer domestic and foreign competition also resulted in the suppression of a large number of jobs.

In these circumstances, it is hardly surprising that the economic and political reforms have weighed heavily on industrial relations. The unions affiliated to the National Organization of Trade Unions (NOTU) have lost 60 per cent of their membership since 1990. The unionization rate, already low in the small formal sector, is perhaps today 1 per cent for the active population as a whole. The unions were gen-

Table 1.1.   **Sub-Saharan Africa: Evolution of employment in the formal sector during the adjustment phase (as % of the active population)**

Country	1980	1995
Kenya	17.6	16.9[1]
Uganda	17.2	13.3
Tanzania, Republic of	7.4	8.1
Zambia	29.4	18.0[1]
Zimbabwe	34.1	25.3

[1] 1994.

Source: *Adjustment, employment and labour market institutions in Sub-Saharan Africa: An emerging consensus on consultative policy design?* (Geneva, ILO, Employment and Training Department, 1997), p. 8.

erally in favour of economic reforms, but it must be said that deregulation and privatization have impacted them unfavourably.

Trade competition and the unions

The previous section has shown how the new constraints on macroeconomic policies may have a destabilising effect on industrial relations. These constraints weaken the political channels of the unions through which employment policies used traditionally to be applied at the macroeconomic level. The macroeconomic environment, with its resulting increase in unemployment and reduction of employment in the public sector and the modern sector is also eroding the unionization rate and bargaining power. Even if these new macroeconomic constraints can in no way be seen as the sole cause of declining union membership, they are a factor. The same holds true for the increasing pressures of competition felt throughout trade.

As for globalization, one factor in particular has caught public attention: the effect of trade between the developing countries and the rich industrial countries on employment and earnings in the latter. Many studies have dealt with this subject. It is sufficient here to recall the general conclusion that can apparently be drawn, namely that the effects are not as great as sometimes imagined.[20]

That being said, it cannot be argued on the other hand that imports from developing countries have no effect on employment in the OECD countries. While, in terms of the economy, their effect on income inequality is apparently small, competition from developing country producers with low labour costs has resulted in the disappearance of low-skilled, labour-intensive jobs in the vulnerable sectors of high-wage countries. In industry, for instance, increased imports from developing countries seem to go hand in hand with a relative drop in employment in labour-intensive activities in the OECD countries (figure 1.3). In so far as union members were mostly to be found in industry, and in particular in these labour-intensive activities, there is a link between the decline in employment and the falling unionization rate. Of course, figure 1.3 does not establish any cause-and-effect relationship between imports and job losses, but the

Figure 1.3.   **Percentage change of low-wage share of total manufacturing employment against rise in LDC imports as share of total imports**

Percentage change of imports from developing countries as share of total imports

Percentage change in low-wage share of manufacturing employment

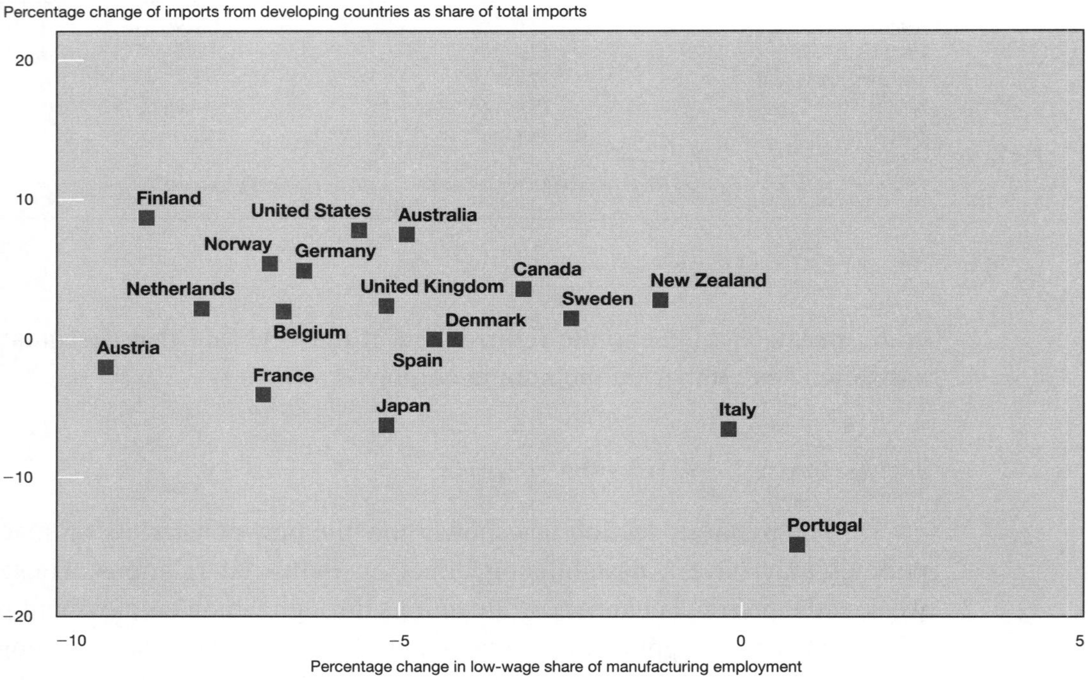

Sources: OECD: STAN Database for Industrial Analysis, March 1995; IMF: *Direction of trade statistics yearbook* (Washington, DC, 1996).

data available for some sectors, such as the garment industry, confirm that these trade developments have indeed had this sort of effect.[21]

As trade with the countries of the South seems to explain only to a very small extent the trend in earnings disparities in the countries of the North, economists have been tempted to disregard the impact of globalization and turn their attention to the internal causes of these inequalities. As a recent study shows,[22] it is possible that less attention should be paid to the effect on employment and earnings of "trade with the South" and rather more to the effects on trade in general; the bulk of world trade is made up of North-North flows, and these trading patterns probably do have an effect on the labour markets of the countries considered.

As for the impact of trade on labour demand, a distinction must be drawn between two cases.

Imports from developing countries with low labour costs are liable to cause job losses in some activities in countries where labour costs are high. The figures given earlier do not prove this but do not invalidate it either.

Trade among countries with comparable labour costs tends to strengthen internal competition. To stay competitive, enterprises have striven to reduce production costs and to be more flexible, by contracting out within the country or abroad, downsizing permanent staff and resorting to precarious forms of employment. They can no longer cope with regular pay rises that drive up unit costs. If these do increase, they now have more ways of avoiding them by transferring capital abroad. They still need staff, but the demand for labour, particularly at the lower level of skills, has become more elastic, more cost-sensitive.

Studies in the United States bear this out. Demand for production workers nowadays is much more responsive to the cost of this sort of work. This tendency, which is found in a number of activities, is particularly noticeable in those that are more exposed to international competition through foreign trade and investment.[23] Trade among the countries of the North in itself would seem to widen wage disparities.

All these factors undoubtedly have an effect on the unions' capacity to defend their members' interests. They are not the only ones, as will be seen elsewhere. Enterprise restructuring processes have also played their part. The motor industry in the United States, for instance, saw employment shrink drastically when manufacturers decided, like their Japanese competitors, to apply lean production methods.[24] It is also likely that subcontracting and relocation of production have affected union membership.

In the OECD area, it is in the private sector – especially in that part of it that is most vulnerable to international competition – that the pressure on the social partners is strongest. The OECD countries where the unionization rate has remained fairly stable are those where employment has risen in the public sector in proportion to total employment, as shown in figure 1.4. Bearing in mind the constraints affecting public finances virtually everywhere, and the provisions adopted in some countries to reduce the presence of the State (government holdings or intervention), at a time when the market economy is going global, it may seem surprising that employment in the public sector over the past 15 years has risen in most OECD countries. As there seems to be a positive relationship between this phenomenon and the unionization rate, if union membership has fallen off the shrinkage must have happened in the private sector.

In the developing countries the loss of union membership can largely be explained by the drop in employment in the formal sector, at a time when it is adjusting to the opening up of the world economy. While, with the advance of democracy, the political situation may be more favourable for unionism, the economic choices – in favour of privatization, of the opening up of the economy – may hamper union development.[25] Moreover, in some Asian countries in particular, it is possible that the rapid growth in the economy and in real earnings may have dampened the ability of unions to grow and the enthusiasm of people to join unions.[26]

The difficulties of the trade unions stems from many causes. Certainly, the opening up of countries' economies is one of the main root causes of the problems facing the unions, since unionization is far from keeping pace with employment growth in those activities that produce for the world market. It is therefore by no means sure that the unions are sharing much in the benefits of international trade, while in

Figure 1.4.   **The level of union density and share of Government in total employment in 1993**

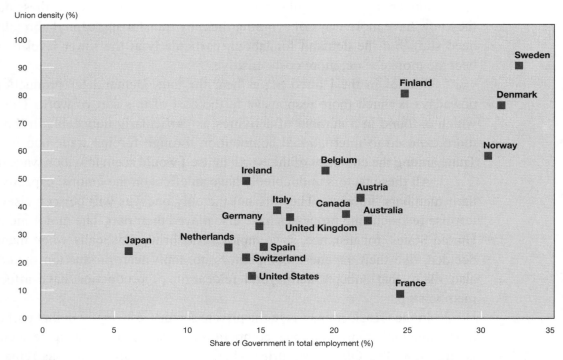

Sources: J. Visser: *Unionization trends revisited* (Amsterdam, Centre for Research on European Societies and Industrial Relations (CESAR), University of Amsterdam, 1996); OECD: *Historical statistics 1960-1994* (Paris, 1996).

other respects – capital mobility and its impact, structural adjustment, enterprise restructuring and the domestic cost it entails – interdependence poses additional problems. These issues will be addressed later, but two points may be made here and now. Firstly, while the unions are having to meet the cost of interdependence rather than reaping its benefits, the end result could well be to weaken one of the institutional channels for determining how such benefits should be shared. Secondly, there are many factors other than purely economic ones that affect the stability of unionization rates. These are discussed below.

Changing mentalities

Trade unionism has suffered from these constraints of adjustment, particularly when it has not kept sufficiently in touch with the grass roots. This is especially noticeable among young people who, as most union officials readily admit, are clearly less interested in the union movement than their forebears. There are several possible explanations for this. The first has to do with the difficulty of finding a job. Young people very often are those most likely to be among the long-term unemployed, and when they do manage to get a job there is not guarantee they can keep it. They are therefore starting their careers in the fear of being found wanting and of worsening the situation by joining an organization whose language often harks back to the concerns of their parents. It is true that the industrial culture and attitudes (if not always people's working lives) have quite changed in Europe, especially among unskilled workers; sons no longer necessarily want to follow in their father's – or uncle's or brother's – footsteps in his job, or into his factory, where he automatically takes out the same union card. These habits have disappeared with the decline in mass production and with the restructuring of enterprises. At the same time, this age group may be more sensitive to the new forms of human resource management that stresses personal responsibility; young people may feel that they are treated more as individuals and so lose something of the solidarity of the wage-earner. This reasoning of course holds good for other age groups as well, but probably not to the same extent. A trade union is even less attractive when status starts to take the place of militancy and when, as has occurred, some of the leaders seem more worried about their own personal position than about other considerations.

Wherever opposition movements – be they political, ideological or religious – become less active, the sense of solidarity on which these movements thrive also fades. The close links between large union confederations and political parties, like the resulting divisions and rivalries, may have led some people to become disenchanted with trade unionism. When membership was compulsory, in principle or in practice, under an authoritarian regime, the new confederations – sometimes unfairly – may have suffered from being assimilated to the old organizations. This is true for Spain and Portugal, which under the authoritarian regimes that lasted until the 1970s had a legal system of vertical trade unionism that was supposed to be reminiscent of the mediaeval craft guilds.

Generally speaking, the fact that workers' interests are increasingly diverse is not only a reflection of the split between long-term wage-earners and the others; their concerns seem to differ even more than before depending on the sector of activity, occupation, skill, age or sex of the people involved. Trade union federations have not always managed to embrace this growing diversity in their members' priorities; even the more decentralized relations with entrepreneurs do not completely take this panoply of interests into account. Union claims and representational structures have not always been able to adjust to more individual concerns or to the effects of the structural changes mentioned earlier. Unions that can offer attractive service in terms of social security, well-being and other benefits can, as will be seen later, sometimes survive better than others that propound a single policy line.

Attitudes of other parties to industrial relations

When an employer offers appreciable social benefits or has a dynamic human resource policy, the staff may feel less need for trade union activities. Things will change only if the enterprise engages in some fairly painful restructuring. Top management in fact has two very different approaches: some opt for stability and dialogue in their relations with the unions, others adopt strategies that are designed to undermine them. The same is true of governments, whose greater or lesser readiness to encourage unions, or simply to dialogue, can influence the unionization rate. Several States, for example, have adopted a restrictive policy with regard to recognizing unions in the hope of attracting foreign investment.[27]

The weakening of the protective legislation and institutional recognition accorded to workers' organizations in the United Kingdom, or more recently in New Zealand, has had a definite impact on union membership.

In New Zealand and in some Australian states, among others, there has been a clear move towards more emphasis on the individual in industrial relations. This can be explained in part by a fairly general disenchantment with a previous system of labour relations that was very inflexible and closed. None the less, it does often tend objectively to favour non-union workers. The legislation introducing the reforms has thus enabled some New Zealand entrepreneurs to exclude union negotiators or to insist on individual contracts (or even non-negotiated collective contracts), at the expense of collective bargaining.[28] The "solidarist associations"[29] in Costa Rica – which, whether or not this was the original intention, tend in practice to push trade union organizations into the background – are in a way all part of the same phenomenon. The same can be said about the tendency to give certain wage-earning categories of workers a kind of self-employed status – which, economically speaking, is more theoretical than anything else. Inevitably, this makes it more difficult for a union to negotiate conditions of work, a point which will be touched on later with regard to developing countries.

But that is not all. It goes without saying that legislation which infringes the principle of freedom of association or of free collective bargaining is still a serious deterrent to unionization. Safeguards on these points are included in many ILO instruments, particularly the Freedom of Association and Protection of the Right to Organise Convention, 1948 (No. 87), and the Right to Organise and Collective Bargaining Convention, 1949 (No. 98). These Conventions, of course, are not always applied as well as they should be. A recent survey by the Committee of Experts on the Application of Conventions and Recommendations, in an overview of the situation,[30] noted the following problems among others:

– restrictions on the right to establish and join workers' organizations (especially for agricultural workers, public servants and, sometimes, middle-management staff); sometimes the law requires prior authorization from the authorities;

– a limit on the number of authorized unions (the union monopoly issue) and on the possibility of forming federations and confederations, as well as joining international workers' organizations;

– suspension and dissolution of unions by administrative decision;

- obstacles to unions operating freely (free election of leaders, management of union assets, drafting of statutes and rules, as well as union activities in general);
- lack of protection against anti-union activities;
- restrictions on the right to engage in collective bargaining or to call strikes.

The numerous cases considered by the Committee on Freedom of Association of the ILO's Governing Body provide evidence, if such were needed, of how many barriers the unions still run up against day by day in their efforts to establish themselves, to defend the interests of their members and, specifically, to negotiate collectively.

These cases sometimes reveal – as in certain countries in South-East Asia – that there are cultural as well as political difficulties in accepting a union presence in an enterprise. Having unions presupposes not only the possibility of collaboration but, sometimes, of opposing the enterprise management. Moreover, it means that the authorities have to recognize the role of workers' associations in society at large, seeing them not as an obstacle to but an instrument of harmonious economic and social progress.[31] From this standpoint, what happened in the Republic of Korea in the winter of 1996-97 can be viewed ultimately as a very positive development towards more genuine social dialogue.

Another trade union vision is disappearing fast: the Marxist-Leninist tendency. The allegiance of this sort of organization of workers to the ruling Communist Party and the resulting *de jure* or *de facto* union monopoly have long been criticized for incompatibility with ILO standards. The system has now collapsed in the European and African countries that had adopted it as a official doctrine. It still has some influence in one way or another in countries such as China or Viet Nam. Elsewhere, the break with the old system is bound to have some unexpected repercussions. Several Central and Eastern European countries were not ready for a free, multi-union regime. The tensions that have emerged, for instance in Poland, among the various current components of the union movement have had serious political implications.

The liberalization of the economy has not prevented the authorities in a number of countries and in all regions from taking the initiative in determining conditions of employment for specific categories of workers (particularly, but not exclusively, in the public sector), and even restricting free collective bargaining. Some governments in European and Latin American countries have been known to prohibit wage increases completely, at least beyond a certain ceiling. Latin American countries have, in addition, a great many major restrictions on the right to strike, either in principle or in practice.

Something else that is patently obvious from the conclusions of the ILO's supervisory bodies is that there are still impediments to public fundamental freedoms which prevent the free exercise of the workers' right to freedom of association. There have been recent cases in Bahrain, Indonesia, Lebanon, Myanmar and Nigeria which have all posed a threat to the very existence of free and independent trade union organizations.

Shortcomings of some union structures

The drop in financial resources as a result in the decline in membership partly explains the many mergers among unions, which are being forced to streamline their operations. These mergers also make it easier to adjust to the restructuring of certain sectors (such as banks and insurance companies in Denmark) and to the reorganization of enterprises and of employers' associations. They do none the less raise some questions as to the relations between the central confederation and the branch unions, which in many western European countries still play a leading role in collective bargaining. Mergers also have their disadvantages, insofar as the larger unions tend to lose touch with their grass roots and, in any case, have to represent more diverse interests. Occupational or industrial unions in the countries concerned may be succeeded by general purpose unions that bring wage-earners together regardless of their job or sector of activity. There is a limit to their size, however,[32] if they want to be able to respond to the concerns we have alluded to.

It is hardly necessary to repeat how important structures are for union strategy, we have already seen that organizations whose leadership and grass roots are both strong are those that have survived relatively unscathed.[33] This is not surprising; even if the autonomy of local unions enables them to stay close to their members (and get their specific concerns across more forcefully in any decentralized bargaining), the need for central coordination, i.e. centralization, also seems quite evident. This avoids certain organizational costs and, above all, strengthens the small units which, left to their own devices, could prove to be too weak. Striking the right balance between union centralization and union democracy calls for good interfacing at all levels.

Also important is the need to adjust to the new more flexible, less hierarchical forms of enterprise organization, and particularly to the trend towards networking. The branch union is no longer necessarily the best forum for holding discussions with other parties drawn from a variety of sectors.

The fact that unions are usually still geared to mass production in very large enterprises has another drawback. It discourages workers who are spread over a large number of locations (SMEs or home workers) and wage-earners who either change jobs frequently or work only irregularly for a given enterprise (particularly those in precarious employment) from joining the union. There are three main obstacles to these people's participation in the trade union movement. The first is the high cost of a membership drive when the potential members do not work at the same place, as well as of "managing" certain types of collective agreements (settlement of grievances in Canada and the United States). The second is the difficulty already mentioned of finding a common language for people with diverging if not conflicting interests. The third is the need to identify somewhere other than the place of work for the recruitment drive. These points will be discussed later.

The fact that a very large majority of workers in precarious employment are not represented by unions has led their detractors to present unions as clubs for the privileged wage-earners whose leaders are concerned first and foremost with improving their members' already enviable conditions of employment. Whatever the merits of the argument may be, this shortcoming raises a serious problem at a time when the bulwark of trade unionism – regular employees working full time and with an open-ended contract – is crumbling. This could well further weaken the trade union movement (in terms not only of numbers but eventually of results) and thereby hasten its fall.

This phenomenon, and the generally rather low unionization rate in countries such as France and the United States and in many developing countries cast some doubt not only on the weight unions can carry and on their representativeness but even on their ability to serve as the spokesmen of workers in general and not only of their members. Are they still in a position to do anything more than voice their members' perfectly respectable but nevertheless limited concerns and continue to act as the authorized representatives of the working population? Are they still in a position to participate, as they do in Europe, in framing economic and social policies of general interest, together with government authorities and business circles? Considering that the unions are no longer really representative, is it not in fact for Parliament, as the emanation of the will of the people, to address such basic issues?

The unions' objectives: Theory and practice

To understand unions' objectives, the above-mentioned questions must consider exactly what the unions' function is in society. (As we shall see, if they did not exist they would have to be reinvented.) Let us start with a brief look at how they see their mission.

All workers' organizations try through collective bargaining, political pressure and sometimes participation in public or private bodies to defend and improve living and working conditions. Beyond this general goal, their objectives may differ greatly. Traditionally enterprise-oriented, United States unions – and to a varying extent those of other English-speaking countries – have until quite recently sought above all to defend the immediate interests of their members (and of other workers in the negotiating unit). They have wanted to control the jobs themselves, if not (with some exceptions, e.g. construction) as regards recruitment then at least in the way the job is carried out. They have thus found themselves in direct conflict with employers in matters that the latter look upon as their prerogative. This could explain why labour relations in North America have always been so antagonistic, especially as the union and the employer are face to face at the bargaining table, and bargaining, while usually restricted to the enterprise, covers a much wider area than in countries with more developed social legislation. If American unions try to intervene at the political level, they do so essentially through political channels and through electoral agreements with allied parties.

In Europe, however, the unions have always sought to represent the workers as a whole, to go beyond labour relations issues and have an influence on the actual vision of society. Very often mistrustful of governments, they present themselves as mass social and labour movements rather than just as trade unions. Their sense of solidarity is by definition broader and has prompted them, for example, to negotiate tripartite labour agreements on behalf of a country's entire workforce. Inevitably, the organization involved is more centralized at the sectoral and national level.

As we have already seen, besides their economic responsibilities unions want to play a more general role as a vehicle of democracy in all regions. They defend the share of the fruits of growth of all those who contribute to them. They insist on a consensual approach to economic progress and try to curb the headlong scramble for immediate gain. Trade union involvement in independence movements in Africa and Asia is perhaps one of the best illustrations of their broader commitment. It has even been said[34] that, having sometimes found their strength in the struggle for democracy in Africa, Latin America, Poland, etc., they have lost some of their steam once their objectives have been attained and have had to cope with the same difficulties as most other unions.

Moreover, not all unions have managed to escape the ills that are almost endemic in some societies, such as corruption, the politics of patronage and inter-union strife, which have generally worn them down in the long run. The same happens when union structures are too close to the government in a vertical corporate-style framework. This kind of system lasted long after the Second World War in Spain and Portugal. It still lingers on, in one way or another, in Argentina and Brazil, where the workers' organizations have none the less acquired a new legitimacy through their struggle against those countries' former totalitarian regimes. Be that as it may, a too close association with the power centre can be a serious handicap in negotiations, particularly at the summit, whenever government and union positions begin to diverge appreciably (on issues such as a more flexible labour market, for example).

Whenever necessary, the unions' platform for action invariably focuses on security of employment and unemployment insurance. Five of the countries with the highest unionization rates (Belgium, Denmark, Finland, Iceland and Sweden) have an unemployment insurance scheme under which the unions – alone or otherwise – handle the payment of benefits.[35] All these countries, moreover, have a large public sector and widely use the check-off system for union dues which is understandable when the unionization rate is high. It has also been pointed out earlier that medical benefits in Taiwan, China, are a major reason for joining a union,[36] also the case in Argentina. The health insurance reform in Israel, on the other hand, which prohibited the Histadrut from offering health care, immediately led to a sharp drop in union membership.[37] One senior union member found this a "no-win" situation: state control over health care benefits weakens the trade union movement, and yet when the State runs out of money control does not revert to it.

This kind of service is part and parcel of a certain image of unionism as a manifestation of solidarity and, at a deeper level, of the very nature of organizations set up to defend their members. This vision equally underlies the support that unions provide in various ways for specific groups of workers that they want to involve more closely in their movement. Women are the most striking example, but efforts are also being made to recruit young people, part-time or casual workers and immigrants. This will be discussed later.

Apart from these employment services, which only exist in a few countries, employment protection is now frequently included by unions in collective bargaining agendas. When the discussions take place in the enterprise – in Canada or the United States, for instance – they will tend to focus on "outsourcing" (i.e. subcontracting, which of course affects the union's representativeness) and how to control it. Defending jobs, including (as in Italy) efforts to curb the casualisation of labour, is also on the agenda of social dialogue at a higher level. The union confederations in Western Europe and in some Latin American countries (Argentina, Brazil, Chile, Mexico) have tried, through nationwide or sectoral joint or tripartite meetings, to go further by actively encouraging recruitment.

As we shall see later, unions have played a direct role in the conclusion of recent labour agreements in European countries – Ireland (1994 and 1997), Finland (1995), Italy (1993 and 1996), Portugal (1996), Spain (1996). These agreements have triggered an adjustment-by-consensus process in the labour market (the emphasis being on productivity) and have encouraged, for example, the strict limitation of wage increases, greater flexibility or a reduction of working time without compensation, the recruitment of long-term unemployed, the adaptation of social protection and even (Italy, Spain) the reorganization of industrial relations. Elsewhere (Belgium, Denmark, France, Germany, the Netherlands) the unions have signed interoccupational or sectoral agreements with the employers' associations that broadened the range of topics dealt with under collective agreements, at a time when pay increases or better welfare benefits are less possible to obtain. Talks on reducing working hours are taking a new turn, hinging more on flexibility.

Occupational training and retraining are increasingly regarded by unions (in Germany and Japan, for example) as fundamental issues,[38] and, in France are covered by another interoccupational agreement (1994).

Union confederations can also show through these agreements that they aware of the aspiration of skilled and highly skilled wage-earners to continue training and improve their career prospects. This is very true of women, especially when they also want to achieve a better balance between their private and working life, for example by the establishment of support services (day-care centres for children or old people) and the adaptation of work schedules to fit with family constraints (leave for family reasons, adjustment of working hours, part-time work, etc.)

Reforms in the organization of work, the introduction of new production and information technologies, even the repetition of well known experiments in industrial democracy, such as those tried in the United States motor industry, are also on the union agenda. They confirm that union attitudes have veered towards a less adversarial and more cooperative attitude. We shall see how unions participate directly or indirectly at the enterprise level in new practices designed to enhance the value of the workforce (Germany, Japan, and others). Moreover, in Northern Europe in particular, ecological demands (restrictions on smoke emissions, processing of waste, clean-up of industrial sites) are being added to the rest.

Collective bargaining has never been the sole means of union action. It has not even been the main one in France, for instance, where until the 1970s collective labour agreements played a very secondary role. The mobilization of the labour force has also – or mainly – tended to take the form of pressuring governments and the parliamentary majority or of concluding political agreements of mutual support for some cause or other with certain parties. The union organizations have thus secured the adoption of a number of labour laws. In Western Europe and Latin America, for example, labour codes or their equivalent are a very important part of the legal framework of countries of the region. Even in States where the practice of collective bargaining is extensive, unions also use political channels to pursue the same objectives.

The AFL-CIO in the United States like other national confederations pays great attention to political considerations, highlighting the pro-union stance of certain candidates for election and using political avenues to obtain satisfaction on various issues and, in particular, to seek legislative changes in conformity with union positions and in favour of worker protection. This kind of political contact is also at the heart of union activities within the European Union. Everywhere, and particularly on issues of equal treatment (men/women, minorities, etc.), the immediate interests of union members may diverge considerably and the support for certain campaigns prove less strong than expected because of internal divisions.

Writers and observers have often emphasized the advantage or "value-added" for employers of smooth relations with their unions. Unions may indeed, under certain conditions, be in favour of encouraging the workers' motivation and, consequently, their productivity. They express the collective voice of the staff. Moreover, the constraints they impose on management serve as an incentive for it to make the enterprise more productive, more innovative, more open to change. The kind of cooperative spirit that unions foster almost everywhere nowadays helps to avert social conflicts that are harmful for everyone involved. It gives firms the chance to beat their competitors by the quality of their services and products rather than by reducing costs, including earnings – a much more satisfactory arrangement for all.

This has two additional advantages. First, the sense of solidarity that it fosters helps to reduce inequalities in earnings. Second, by helping to bring about more equitable conditions of employment, it discourages social "dumping" (competition by cutting costs) and, at the international level, the drift towards protectionism.

That said, it would be very rash to try and establish a cause-and-effect link between certain labour relations practices and economic performance,[39] however plausible it may sometimes seem, particularly when labour relations break down. Anyway, practice varies too much from one country to another. If the industrial relations system is decentralized, the focus will be on whether or not enterprises have a union, and on the possible advantages of industrial-democracy schemes and their potential for innovation. In the opposite case, attention will be focused on the usefulness of centralized joint or tripartite relations at the sectoral or national level for fighting inflation and developing a real vocational training and retraining policy.

Obviously, too, union action cannot be assessed solely in terms of its ability to enhance economic performance.

The fact remains that union organizations play an important role in industrial relations and that no new institution seems able to take their place. They thus fulfil three important functions. The first is a democratic function: allowing all those who have work or want to work to have a say in their working life. The second is of course an economic function: helping to find the best possible balance in the production and the distribution of the fruits of growth. The third, which derives from the first two, is a social function: ensuring that all those who would like to work find their place in society; these organizations can certainly help to eradicate poverty, as well as to combat the social exclusion of the most vulnerable, inner-city violence, social tensions and unrest, and indeed be a contributing factor to social stability.

Notes

[1] ICFTU: *The global market: Trade unionism's greatest challenge,* 16th World Congress, Brussels, 25-29 June 1996, (Brussels, 1996).

[2] See J. Visser: *Global trends in unionization,* document prepared for the ILO (1997).

[3] E. Marín and F. Iturrape: "Perfil laboral de Venezuela", in *Revista de la Facultad de Derecho* (Caracas, Universidad Católica Andrés Bello), 1992, No. 45, p. 58.

[4] K. Tapiola: "Trade union development in CEECs" in *Transfer* (Brussels, European Trade Union Institute), July 1995, pp. 360-377.

[5] ILO: *World Employment 1995* (Geneva, 1995); and *World Employment 1996-97* (Geneva, 1996).

[6] John Evans: *Welfare, security and economic performance – Public policy overview,* document prepared for the Third International Conference on Progressive Policy, European Trade Union Institute, 2-5 March 1997 (mimeographed), p. 2.

[7] ibid., p. 3.

[8] G. Epstein: "International capital mobility and the scope for national economic management", in R. Boyer and D. Drache (eds.): *States against markets: The limits of globalization* (London, Routledge, 1996), p. 219.

[9] Gordon and A. Lans Bovenberg, "Why is capital so immobile internationally? Possible explanations and implications for capital income taxation", in *American Economic Review*, (Nashville) Vol. 86, No. 5, December 1996, p. 1057.

[10] See for example P. Hirst and G. Thompson: *Globalisation in question* (Cambridge, Polity Press, 1996), Ch. VI, pp. 129-136.

[11] Daniel Cohen: *Richesse du monde, pauvretés des nations* (Paris: Flammarion, 1997). Cohen comments on Mexico's December 1994 devaluation in the following terms: "There is a universal lesson to be drawn here: there is always an exchange rate at which the buying and selling of goods balance out, so the fear of a loss of 'global' competitiveness is therefore absurd. More specifically, as can be seen in Mexico parity imbalances are possible but they are usually quickly corrected". This seems to be largely the case; that said, it is achieved at the expense of the standard of living of the Mexican people.

[12] This is Elie Cohen's argument in *La tentation hexagonale: la souveraineté de la mondialisation* (Paris, Fayard, 1996). The implementation of national incomes policies is also considered in *World Employment 1996-97* (Geneva, ILO, 1996).

[13] S. Jacoby: "Social dimensions of global economic integration", in S. Jacoby (ed.): *The workers of nations: Industrial relations in a global economy* (New York, Oxford University Press, 1995), p. 9.

[14] ibid., p. 9.

[15] The statistics used in this report, which are based on data collected for 30 developing countries in *World Employment 1996-97* (Geneva, ILO, 1996), show a strong positive correlation between growth rate and earnings equality.

[16] ILO: *World Employment 1996-97* (Geneva, 1996), pp. 75-76.

[17] ibid., p. 75.

[18] G. Gereffi: "The reorganization of production on a world scale: States, markets and networks in the apparel and electronics commodity chains", in D. Campbell, A. Parisotto, A. Verma and A. Lateef (eds.): *Regionalization and labour market interdependence in East and Southeast Asia* (London, Macmillan, 1997), pp. 65 ff.

[19] The information given in this section is taken from T. Fashoyin: *Liberalization and industrial relations in Uganda,* document prepared for the ILO (1997).

[20] For an analysis, see ILO: *World Employment 1995* (Geneva, 1995), pp. 51-54.

[21] P. Doeringer et al., document on the apparel industry in France, United Kingdom and the United States, prepared by the ILO (1997).

[22] D. Rodrik: *Has globalization gone too far?* (Washington, DC, Institute for International Economics, 1997).

[23] M. Slaughter: "International trade and labour-demand elasticities", Dartmouth College, unpublished document, 1996, quoted in D. Rodrik, op. cit, p. 17. See also *World Employment 1995,* op. cit., pp. 58-59.

[24] Besides this, generally speaking, according to most observers, the unionization rate is roughly the same in foreign enterprises and in comparable domestic enterprises, if not higher. See *Trade, employment and labour standards* (Paris, OECD, 1996).

[25] S. Kuruvilla and C.S. Venkata Ratnam: "Economic development and industrial relations; The case of South and South-East Asia", in *Industrial Relations Journal,* (Oxford, Blackwell), March 1996, p. 18.

[26] idem.

[27] See, for instance, on Uganda, T. Fashoyin: *Contribution to the national case studies of the effects of globalization on industrial relations and adjustment at enterprise level,* document prepared for the ILO (Geneva, 1997), pp. 31 et seq.

[28] G. M. Kelly: Structural changes in New Zealand: some implications for the labour market regime", in *International Labour Review* (Geneva, ILO), Vol. 134, No. 3, 1995, pp. 333-359.

[29] ILO: *Report of the Committee of Experts on the Application of Conventions and Recommendations,* Report III (Part 4A), International Labour Conference, 81st Session, Geneva, 1994, pp. 203-205.

[30] ILO: *Freedom of association and collective bargaining,* International Labour Conference, 81st Session, Geneva, 1994.

[31] The importance of this view has been pointed out by J. Schregle in *Negotiating development: Labour relations in Southern Asia* (Geneva, ILO, 1982). See also K. Sugeno: "Unions as social institutions in democratic market economies", in *International Labour Review,* Vol. 133, No. 4, pp. 511-522.

[32] See W. Müller-Jentsch: *The new Germany under the impact of globalization: Consequences for industrial relations,* working document, 1996; J. Visser and J. Van Ruysseveld: "From pluralism to where? Industrial relations in Great Britain", in J. Van Ruysseveld and J. Visser (eds.): *Industrial relations in Europe: Traditions and transition* (London, Sage, 1996), p. 58; W. Streek: *Social institutions and economic performance: Studies of industrial relations in advanced capitalist economies* (London, Sage 1992), p. 85.

[33] A. Ferner and R. Hyman (eds.): *Industrial relations in the new Europe* (Oxford, Blackwell, 1992), p. XXIV, and the chapter in that book by A. Kjellberg: "Sweden: can the model survive?", pp. 90 et seq.

[34] A. Galin: "Myth and reality. Trade unions and industrial relations in the transition to democracy", in J. R. Niland, R. D. Lansbury and C. Verevis (eds.): *The future of industrial relations: Global change and challenges* (London, Sage, 1994), pp. 295 et seq.

[35] See in particular B. Brunhes: "Syndicats, ouvriers et organisations patronales en Europe: trois modèles de culture sociale", in *Problèmes économiques* (Paris, La Documentation Française), 20 Dec. 1989, p. 29; B. Rothstein: "Labor-market institutions and working-class strength", in S. Steimo, K. Thelen and F. Longstreth (eds.): *Structuring politics: Historical institutionalism in comparative analysis* (Cambridge, Cambridge University Press, 1992), pp. 33-53; J. Visser: "The strength of union movements in advanced capital democracies: Social and organizational variations", in M. Regini (ed.): *The future of labour movements* (London, Sage, 1992), p. 18; J. Lond: "Trade unions: Social movement or welfare apparatus", in P. Leisink, J. Van Leemput and J. Vilrokx (eds.): *Challenges to trade unions in Europe: Innovation or adaption* (Cheltenham, United Kingdom, Edward Elgar, 1996), pp. 114-116.

[36] Yueh-Ching Hwang and Cing-Kae Chiao: "The transformation of industrial relations under democratization in Taiwan, 1987-1996" in *The impact of globalization on industrial relations,* proceedings of the Third Asian Regional Congress of the IIRA (Taipei, 30 Sep.-3 Oct. 1996).

[37] A. Galin: "The difficulties of unions under democratization: The case of Israel", in T*he impact of globalization on industrial relations,* op. cit., pp. 58 et seq.

[38] See also W. Streeck: "Training and the new industrial relations: A strategic role for unions?" in M. Regini (ed.), op. cit., pp. 250-269.

[39] ILO: *Tripartite consultations at the national level on economic and social policy,* International Labour Conference, 83rd Session, Geneva, 1996, p. 33.

2 Trade unions in the throes of change

This chapter will look at the underlying processes reflected in the current strategies adopted by trade union confederations in the light of the functions referred to in the previous chapter. These strategies are still fragile, since they face difficulties of which more will be said later. The strategies focus on providing new types of services to union members, unionizing new categories of workers, opening up new areas of negotiation, and forming new alliances.

These endeavours have not always yielded immediate, or even – in some cases – significant results. But they seem to be the only viable means of achieving some kind of renewal. It goes without saying that the aim is not to replace the trade unions' traditional activities, but to complement them. An increasing number of observers, especially those directly involved, emphasize the wisdom shown by trade unions in extending their efforts to all workers, not only those with steady jobs. They add that unionism must become or go back to being a genuine social movement, or remain one if it is already, with its own resources, rather than merely grouping together shared occupational interests. As we will see, this trend is emerging within the United States confederation AFL-CIO, for example.

New services

A number of trade unions have recently made efforts to improve the direct assistance they offer to their members, whether in the form of supplementary social benefits and professional advisory services on work-related subjects (for example in the fields of law, social security, taxation and even careers, retraining and the negotiation of individual employment contracts), individual services or preferential rates. Some British trade unions offer discounts on loans, insurance premiums and credit cards, as well as running their own travel agencies or retirement homes. The AFL-CIO in the United States has even launched the Union Privilege benefit programme, offering the same kind of advantages.[1] In Japan, the "trade union identity" movement has devised "total well-being" programmes.[2]

The growing emphasis on individual services to members responds to the will to reflect the widening diversity of conditions, the increased importance attached to individual concerns and, in more mundane terms, the need to replenish trade union coffers. But this should not mean that trade union concerns are neglected. While workers' organizations in the countries in transition are quite justified in continuing to offer employees accommodation and holidays at discount rates, as they did under the communist system, obviously they must also avoid focusing too much energy on these areas where they face increasing competition, and try not to lose sight of their real objectives.

It goes without saying that trade union organizations use many other means to attract new members. Again taking the example of the AFL-CIO, whose efforts to this end have received public attention in the press, the federation launched a massive campaign entitled "Union Yes", which enlisted actors and celebrities in order to enhance the union movement's visibility and gain wider recognition of its ability to offer workers "a voice, dignity and a secure standard of living". The Confederation provided its officers with special training to enable them to express themselves clearly when they faced the media. British trade unions have sought the same kind of publicity, and those in the Netherlands have offered the same training.[3] Similar examples are to be found in the Nordic countries.

New members

Trade unions are focusing their efforts on organizing categories with low levels of unionization, such as women and young people (whose demands relate more to the elimination of discrimination based on sex or age), employees of SMEs, workers in precarious jobs, informal sector workers, the unemployed and, generally speaking, all those who are marginalized or excluded. Again, the difficulty lies in finding a common strategy for such disparate groups, whose interests differ from or even conflict with those of employees with stable jobs. It is not always easy to reconcile them.

The unionization of working women is clearly a priority. Historically, the virtual absence of women from the trade union movement has reflected their limited role in political life and the world of work. However, as they have often pointed out, the main reason why more women do not join trade unions – as is the case in most countries – is that many of them work in sectors or categories in which it is difficult for unions to recruit members (such as the private service sector and part-time or precarious jobs); another reason is that workers' organizations do not take adequate account of their specific needs and difficulties, such as the fact that obstacles to equality of opportunity and treatment are still very much a reality, and that in practice women continue to bear the main share of responsibility for their families.

Add to this the frequently chauvinistic attitudes of their male colleagues and the latter's concern to hold on to their positions of power, and it is easy to see why women have often tried to set up their own associations, even if they subsequently established more or less institutionalized relations with traditional trade union confederations. This is the case, for example, of the Coalition of Labor Union Women (CLUW) in the United States.[4] Such links also exist in the informal agricultural sector (Honduras, Costa Rica, Bangladesh).[5] In the Netherlands[6] there are separate women's trade unions which explicitly establish links with the traditional workers' organizations engaged in collective bargaining and which place equality of opportunity and treatment on the agenda.

Clearly, therefore, it is not true that women are less inclined than men to organize. According to a study on the cotton industry in Bombay before the Second World War, female workers apparently played an active part in a quarter of the strikes occurring in this sector between 1919 and 1940, and one strike in ten was carried out entirely by women.[7] More recent instances of women's militancy are the protest movements in Mexico[8] and California (San José and Silicon Valley) at the beginning of the 1980s.[9]

It may be observed that some trade unions which seem to have succeeded more than others in overcoming current difficulties have made a particular effort to organize women (Canada,[10] some American trade unions[11]), to take account of their concerns (Sweden[12]), and to integrate them into their management structures (Uganda,[13] Netherlands,[14] Germany and Sweden[15]). Several confederations now reserve certain managerial posts for women (the CTC in Canada; CFDT in France; CISL in Italy; TUC in the United Kingdom[16]) and many have even set up a department specifically for them.[17]

The fact remains that women, too, are far from being a uniform group. It is hard to find common denominators between a female homeworker in the watch-making industry and a woman supervisor of a large insurance company. Again, however, many women have in common the fact that they work in jobs in which it is more difficult to organize (for example, part-time work) and there is little or no employment stability. Their relationship with unionism therefore has to be seen in the context of this complex situation.

The relationship is further complicated by the obvious divergence of interests, mentioned above, between employees with stable jobs and workers in precarious situations. In this connection, there has been a change in the trade unions' attitude to the latter: traditionally, they advocated equality of treatment (i.e. extending coverage of labour laws or collective agreements), which reflected a concern for social justice and, at the same time, preserved job stability by denying employers the advantages of recruiting precarious workers. However, in most cases this strategy does not meet the wishes of those concerned, who want a job more than anything else. Trade union programmes today take better account of their specific needs. This shift in attitude is quite clear in the case of part-time workers (in Germany,[18] France,[19] Japan[20] and the United Kingdom,[21] for example) and homeworkers. The latter have been targeted by trade union campaigns in Australia, Canada, the Netherlands and the United Kingdom.[22] "The Clothing and Allied Trade Union (CATU) in Australia began a campaign in 1986 within the union and then nationally. They put out information which made people more aware of homeworking. The union also employed outwork project officers who held meetings with outworkers and liaised with local community groups and migrant organizations. Over 6,000 outworkers contacted the union in one year of the campaign and some joined the union."[23]

Depending on the country and its trade union tradition, greater emphasis may be placed on the need to protect the most vulnerable categories, or to increase membership by focusing on these other occupational groups.

It is certainly no easy task to integrate into the trade union movement such widely dispersed and vulnerable individuals as these precarious workers. However, although they are not in the majority, at least in the industrialized countries, these workers currently represent a significant minority who often find themselves in conditions comparable to those of yesterday's proletariat. The problem is compounded by their heterogeneity and by the often highly personalized nature of relations between the partners – for example, in SMEs – which inhibits recourse to a third party, whether a union delegate or an external body. These workers are less likely to perceive themselves as sharing common interests with their fellow workers, much less with those holding steady jobs.

Nevertheless, trade unions have concluded collective agreements for workers sent on assignment by temporary work agencies or for other casual workers (in Germany,[24] Canada,[25] France[26] and the Netherlands[27]). Organizations have been set up to defend their interests in Chile,[28] the Republic of Korea[29] and Peru.[30] Efforts at unionization have been made in the United States.[31] However, little progress has been achieved.

Sometimes migrant workers have formed their own trade unions, having been unable to obtain the type of services they needed from the large confederations, and because the atmosphere of trust conducive to solidarity had not been created.[32]

Another case, which will be dealt with in a separate chapter, is that of all the men and women whose employment relationships lie outside the usual employer/employee pattern. In some developing countries, they are in the overwhelming majority (up to 92 per cent in India). For them, the traditional concepts of wage-earners, entrepreneurs and workers are blurred. Rather than trying to work out whether the relationship between the partners is one of wage employment, it should be defined in economic terms (perhaps as one of economic dependence). These workers, too, have set up associations to defend their interests. When the main purpose of these associations is to improve productivity, they are more akin to employers' associations. If on the contrary they aim to protect the working and living conditions of their members, they are in fact workers' organizations. It is true that the distinction can often seem tenuous.

Again, the situation varies considerably from one country or sector to another. In Canada, for example, the well-developed system of representation for the purposes of collective bargaining, in principle, only covers persons in wage employment. However, exceptions have been made for workers in the grey areas between a dependent employment relationship and self-employment. Recent legislation, including at federal level, classes, for example, artists' and performers' associations with employees' trade unions to enable them to bargain collectively on their working and living conditions.[33] In France, non-wage workers have made extensive use of the right to bargain collectively,[34] resulting in collective agreements between oil companies and the tenant managers of service stations; interoccupational agreements for commercial travellers and sales representatives; collective agreements between authors and composers, through the agencies that collect their fees, and user enterprises (television companies, record manufacturers, publishers), as well as agreements between the latter and performers; and collective agreements between doctors' associations and the organizations administering social security funds (relating mainly to the fees applicable to patients covered by social security).

In some countries, for example Argentina and Pakistan, the law limits the possibilities for self-employed workers to join the same trade unions as employees. More often than not this is because their concerns are different. They tend to have their own special occupational associations in India (for example, the SEWA for women) and many Latin American countries (Argentina, Brazil, Chile and Peru for example). But they may join traditional trade unions if they stand to gain something specific from it: in Taiwan, China, for example, this gives them access to the occupational insurance scheme.[35]

Other categories find it difficult to organize, such as retirees, whose specific problems are now receiving more coverage, and especially the unemployed, who are often trapped in exclusion and isolation. Chilean law prohibits them from joining trade unions.[36] All the organizations affiliated to the European Trade Union Confederation (ETUC) allow workers who have lost their jobs to continue to be members, and more than half of them report that these persons have in fact retained their membership. This observation is especially true of the north European countries, where the trade unions administer unemployment benefit funds and other services for the jobless.[37] Confederations in several European countries have set up departments specifically to meet the needs of the unemployed and have launched special programmes for target groups such as young people, women, the long-term unemployed and migrants. They have also tried to stay in touch with their retired members.[38] By contrast, the associations for the unemployed set up in France, for instance, have failed to attract many members.[39]

However successful some of these efforts have been, the fact remains that so far the results have been modest.[40]

The more robust organizations of atypical workers have, for the most part, been formed around a single occupation; for instance, artists and performers (musicians or composers, for example) have formed influential associations in countries as diverse as Canada, France and Japan. Other examples include translators and taxi drivers.

As has already been pointed out, trade union structures centred on the workplace, whether at the enterprise or industry level, are often not suited to new forms of work organization. An alternative focal point for organization other than the enterprise therefore needs to be found. It may be the worksite, as stipulated by the French

Act of 28 October 1982,[41] which is apparently only rarely applied. It may also be the area where the worker lives, a solution which seems appropriate for those in precarious jobs.

The problem is compounded in the case of systems such as that in North America, where a single majority trade union has exclusive bargaining rights in an establishment (bargaining unit). The same is true of the unwillingness of many SME employers to negotiate with a trade union representative from outside the enterprise. In Italy, the insertion of a clause to remedy this problem in the national collective agreement for workers in the small-scale textile, clothing and footwear industry, signed in 1987, was seen as an important step forward.[42] In 1997 the AFL-CIO launched a massive campaign focusing on local communities aimed at setting up labour councils at this level and paying special attention to working women and minorities.

Another point worth mentioning is that for these groups recourse to the methods generally used in industrial relations is limited. There is no need to emphasize here that there is often no point in calling a strike, although this is certainly a unifying event if ever there was one – provided it succeeds. In many cases – though not in all, as will be seen below – collective bargaining, too, is still a risky undertaking.

Sometimes the conditions laid down by national legislation for setting up an organization prevent certain groups from organizing, even if that is not the intention. To the examples already given, one might add the requirement that a worker have a certain amount of seniority in the enterprise in order to be eligible for trade union office (in Chile and other Latin American countries), or that a minimum number of workers be employed at the same workplace (Kuwait, Nigeria, Panama). Similarly, the law may provide for a system of collective bargaining centred mainly, if not exclusively, on an enterprise or one of its units (Brazil, Canada, United States, Peru, Dominican Republic). These legislative provisions, rooted in the history of each country's labour relations system, can seriously hamper these workers' efforts to organize. Lastly, certain groups may be excluded altogether, as is the case of homeworkers or agricultural workers in Canada.[43]

All the problems which trade union confederations face with respect to precarious workers are greatly magnified in the case of people in developing countries who work in the informal sector. In addition to the factors already mentioned, these countries have their own constraints, which are linked to poverty and underdevelopment.

In view of the considerable difficulties experienced by trade unions in dealing with these workers, special organizations have been set up. More will be said about them below; suffice it here to make the following remarks.

These organizations provide the people concerned with information and advice on the legislation in force and try to improve their protection by introducing reforms, drafting legislation or even signing collective agreements. But they usually have little bargaining power or means of bringing pressure to bear in the political arena. They can offer greater assistance by helping to establish mechanisms for participation or consultation with the public authorities or the partners in the working relationship, thus contributing to improving interpersonal relations (which affects both working conditions and output). They also try to obtain recognition from the public authorities (initially, they do not have the same kind of political support as most trade unions), to make them aware of the problems of the informal sector and to enlist more active support (not to mention curbing authoritarian measures such as the discretionary relocation of the workplace).

In more general terms, these organizations have to take account of the problems stemming from underemployment and of the development policies aimed at overcoming them. They may prompt or encourage national administrations to establish an enabling environment for qualitative economic progress in the informal sector. They help to abolish restrictive regulations and practices (such as those pertaining to registration and licensing requirements), and to promote access to facilities such as funding, premises, water and electricity supply, sewerage, health services, basic education and training, raw materials and basic tools, and advice on opportunities. They push for public subsidies and tax exemptions, and fight to eliminate usury. They help to clarify the rights (especially property rights) and obligations of the persons concerned. They require heads of small establishments to provide sanitary installations and basic catering facilities at the workplace. They may also protect their members against abuse and acts of violence such as those committed by unscrupulous middlemen.

New frontiers: Transnational trade union activities

It is true that cross-border cooperation between workers' organizations is nothing new. The trade unions have been an internationalist movement from the outset. But with the emergence of multinational enterprises, they have made every effort to step up this aspect of their activities. They have responded to the increasing globalization of the economy by opening up their strategies, activities, procedures and structures to a new international dimension. However, there are many legal and practical obstacles to international collaboration between trade unions.

The rocky road to international trade union cooperation

The most obvious difficulties stem from specific legal provisions which either prohibit (Nigeria) or hamper the affiliation of national workers' organizations to international confederations (for example, in Cameroon and Kenya the public authorities must give their prior authorization). More frequently, it is participation in international trade union activities which raises problems, as is clear from the cases handled by the ILO Governing Body Committee on Freedom of Association.[44] These cases relate for example to the possibility for national federations to maintain contacts with international trade unions, to participate in their activities, meetings and conferences, to exchange publications and to benefit from the services and advantages – including financial ones[45] – arising out of their membership.

In addition, there are the more general limitations imposed by the legislation of many countries on even the most essential principles of freedom of association and collective bargaining. These restrictions are sometimes confined to free zones; more often, they apply to the entire national territory. Reference has already been made to them above. It is an understatement to say that such provisions hamper the free development of the international trade union movement. What is more, other problems that are equally serious – if not more so – stem from the (mis)application of the law, including the violation of fundamental rights (such as the right to life and personal safety), and from the lack of adequate enforcement of protective provisions.

In addition to these infringements of the ILO Conventions on freedom of association and collective bargaining, the very diversity of the legal systems covering industrial relations can sometimes hinder international trade union activity. France and the United Kingdom, for instance, have opposing concepts of the right to strike: in the former it is a constitutional right, while in the latter it is a freedom that guarantees participants protection against legal action (unless accompanied by punishable offences), but not against dismissal. Recourse to direct action coordinated on an international scale is also ruled out by the restrictions imposed in certain States on sympathy and solidarity strikes. The same is true of legislation limiting recourse to secondary boycotts (in Brazil, the United States and the United Kingdom). Recognition of a trade union takes place at enterprise level in the United States and in countries with a similar legal system, while it is based on the law and pre-established objective criteria in several European countries. There are many examples of such differences: the legal force of collective agreements and the possibility, especially in Europe, of using extension procedures, legal provisions fixing the usual bargaining level(s), etc. Such divergences, even if they can be overcome, clearly inhibit transnational collective bargaining.

These legal barriers are not the only obstacles in the way of cross-border solidarity between workers. Others, just as formidable, stem from the differences in languages and all the cultural, religious and social diversity they reflect. Moreover, the structures and, as we have seen, the very concept of trade unionism vary from one country to another. Workers' economic interests also differ: opposition to lay-offs in an industrialized country can obstruct the transfer of activities to and the resulting job creation in a developing country; pressure for substantial improvements in worker protection in the latter can be interpreted there as an indirect means of avoiding competition from a cheaper workforce. Generally speaking, it appears to be part of human nature to put one's own concerns before those of the workers of other countries.[46] Lastly, when it becomes institutionalized cooperation can also mean a shift (even to a limited extent) of authority and resources to supranational bodies, and this is not what national leaders necessarily want.

What transnational trade union cooperation has to offer

The fact remains that the globalization or regionalization of enterprises has certainly prompted them to take a broad view of the constraints specific to a particular country. They are more willing to transfer activities abroad and even encourage competition between sites. The phenomenon of the relocation of production should not be overestimated: most of the major multinationals still achieve a large share of their turnover in their country of origin,[47] labour costs are rarely a central concern of their policies and they do not wish to destabilize their workforce to an excessive degree.[48] And workers and their representatives have learned to respond to employer strategies involving relocation.

These strategies have nevertheless helped change the attitude of trade unions, making their leaders more cautious and prompting them to seek support from their fellow organizations in other countries. They have strengthened their common structures and refined their working methods.

The International Confederation of Free Trade Unions (ICFTU) and the International Trade Secretariats (ITS) for the different branches of economic activity are well known for their international role. Neither is there any need to recall the importance of another organization, the World Confederation of Labour (WCL) and its sectoral federations. Both maintain close contacts with regional workers' organizations, such as the European Trade Union Confederation (ETUC). Coordination between the MERCOSUR federations was initiated by the ICFTU and its regional branch, the Inter-American Regional Organization of Workers. Other regional federations have no institutional links with these two confederations. A third international organization, the World Federation of Trade Unions (WFTU), has been in decline since the events symbolized by the fall of the Berlin Wall.

The main task of all these organizations is to gather information and documentation on subjects of common interest and to disseminate them among their members. They also facilitate bilateral relations between national trade unions and represent the latter in international institutions such as the ILO. They coordinate their activities, and it is this last point that will be examined here.

The ITSs in particular have recently expanded their capacity to bring together the unions of the subsidiaries of multinationals, such as Mitsubishi, Honda, Fiat, Mazda and SKF, into committees of a formal or informal nature in order to exchange experience or prepare for talks with the central management of the company concerned. European enterprise committees have set up special facilities for such

Box 2.1.   international trade union partnership in the Dominican Republic

On 22 July 1994, workers at the Bibong Apparel Corporation in the Dominican Republic won the first collective agreement in the long history of that country's export processing zones (EPZs). On 22 November 1995, workers at the Bonahan Apparel Company, another factory in a Dominican Republic EPZ, signed a collective agreement following a successful and legal strike.

An international partnership, consisting of the ICFTU-affiliated National Confederation of Dominican Workers (CNTD) and its affiliate, the Federation of Free Zone Workers (FENATAZONAS), the ITGLWF and its inter-American regional organization FITTCC-ORIT, the AFL-CIO, its institute, the AIFLD, and two AFL-CIO affiliates (which have since merged to form UNITE) developed and implemented a well-planned and coordinated organizing strategy.

The strategy was based on the following elements: applying pressure to targeted companies and the Government of the Dominican Republic, and direct support to a trade union organization on the ground by trained organizers, followed up with trade union education of new members. The partnership contributed support for union organizers, legal assistance and other technical advice and training. The organizing campaigns were supplemented by pressure on the United States-based corporate customers of the targeted companies and by the use of the workers' rights provisions in the Generalized System of Preferences (GSP) section of the United States trade law. The Government of the Dominican Republic reformed its Labour Code so as to allow trade unions in the EPZs. In the organizing campaign at Bibong, the threat of GSP sanctions probably encouraged the parties concerned to enforce the new Code.

Source: ICFTU: *The global market: Trade unionism's greatest challenge,* 16th World Congress of the ICFTU, Brussels, 25-29 June 1996 (Brussels, 1996).

consultations, and similar structures have been created outside Europe. More loosely structured workers' organizations have also emerged. Some have been set up in large multinationals in the automobile, food and chemical industries.[49] Others, known as "transnational networks", link national, or more often local, groups of vulnerable workers. These networks operate along similar lines as some environmental or consumer movements or inter-union "coordination" bodies bringing together several unions (for example in France); they are not limited to trade unions (and sometimes do not even include them), but also comprise representatives of churches, foundations, political movements or academic institutions; their social vision may be very radical.[50]

International trade union activity consists either in assisting an affiliate union (see box 2.1), and sometimes coordinating local demands, or in conducting a truly international campaign (for the elimination of child labour, for example). As might be imagined, it can take a wide variety of forms. First, politicians or even members of the government may be approached. For instance, as part of the action referred to in box 2.2, the Postal, Telegraph and Telephone International (PTTI) denounced the activities of the Sprint company, which it considered to be anti-union, to the United States and Mexican labour ministers. Lobbying can also be aimed at achieving a majority vote within the governing bodies of the OECD, the ILO or other international institutions on a given policy or draft instrument.

Public opinion campaigns are also waged with a view to enlisting support for a given cause from enterprises, consumers, politicians and the public in general. The IUF (International Union of Food, Agricultural, Hotel, Restaurant, Catering, Tobacco and Allied Workers' Associations), for example, pressurized companies such as Pepsi-Cola, Heineken and Carlsberg into refraining from setting up joint ventures in Myanmar in view of the working conditions prevailing there. Such campaigns can also aim to find a solution to a local dispute. For example, in March 1997 Renault factories experienced their first "Euro-strike" (i.e. a strike in their factories located in the European Union) following the firm's decision to close a plant in Vilvorde, Belgium. Other forms of pressure include calling for boycotts of the firms concerned. Examples of this may be found in box 2.2. Consumers are the focus of attention. In the past the power of trade unions has been centred on production centres and their capacity to mobilize workers. We have seen how new methods of labour organization, including outsourcing, and the increase in unemployment have brought about tangible, though limited, changes in this state of affairs. At the same time, consumer pressure is becoming increasingly important and enterprises are more aware of their image in the face of fiercer international competition.[51]

Campaigns are often accompanied by coordinated letters of protest to target companies, articles in the press, radio and television interviews, and, lately, the use of information technology (the Internet), as well as work stoppages if necessary and the provision of financial assistance to national trade unions taking action.

Should it succeed, a campaign with international objectives leads to discussions at that level with the enterprises concerned or with employers' organizations, to negotiations and sometimes to more or less formalized agreements such as that concluded in November 1996 with Bridgestone, a multinational tyre manufacturer. UNICE (the Union of Industrial and Employers' Confederations of Europe) and the ETUC, or their sectoral organizations, have concluded some 100 joint declarations at European level, including those signed by EuroCommerce and Euro-FIET (International Federation of Commercial, Clerical, Professional and Technical Employees) for the abolition of child labour (8 March 1996), with a view to combating violence in commerce (9 March 1995), and the joint document on future social dialogue in commerce, presented to the Intergovernmental Conference on the Revision of the Treaty on European Union (27 October 1995).

Box 2.3 shows that protest movements can also lead – in the same way as the pressure of public opinion – to the implementation of codes of conduct which an enterprise, or group of enterprises, undertakes to observe in its subsidiaries and even to impose on subcontractors. In April 1997, several major American clothing firms (Nike, Reebok, L.L. Bean) concluded an agreement with trade unions and human rights movements in which they agreed to implement basic rules governing wages and working conditions in the workshops they used throughout the world. The agreement provides that these companies attach a special label on the clothes manufactured and

Box 2.2. The growth of international campaigning

There are a growing number of examples where trade unions have taken the offensive against what they see as abuses of labour rights by global corporations. A recent case has concerned the Teamsters Union and the Finnish food conglomerate Huhtamaki which wanted to close a plant in Illinois and transfer production to a non-union facility. The Union mobilized a coalition of the local community involving other business people, community groups and politicians and then took the campaign to Finland where it succeeded in securing the company's agreement to hold an independent inquiry into its plant closure decision.

The Postal, Telegraph and Telephone International is involved in global action against Sprint, the United States company, after it dismissed Hispanic workers in San Francisco for allegedly wanting to organize themselves in a trade union. The plant was also closed down. Deutsche Postgewerkshaft, the German telecommunication union, has indirectly pressurized Sprint to negotiate with its fired workers, demanding that Deutsche Telekom, the German state-owned company, introduce a code of basic labour standards as part of its planned £2.7 billion joint venture with Sprint. French workers demanded the same from France Telecom and Sprint, while STRM, the Mexican telecom company, has drawn up charges against Sprint, which it alleges is in breach of the labour provisions of the North American Free Trade Agreement (NAFTA).

Widespread trade union mobilization was established by both the International Metalworkers' Federation and the International Federation of Chemical, Energy, Mine and General Workers' Unions (ICEM) against the anti-union behaviour of Bridgestone, the Japanese tyre manufacturer, at its United States subsidiary, Firestone, where striking workers were replaced with a substitute workforce. The unions claimed that the company intends to destroy union organization in its United States facilities and reduced the terms and conditions of employment of their workers. Bridgestone had refused to accept a pattern agreement on the lines of those signed by its Goodyear and Michelin competitors and instead demanded a number of concessions from their employees, including reduced health care coverage, the introduction of 12-hour shift working, the removal of cost-of-living allowance payments, a requirement to work scheduled holidays at reduced pay and lower wages and conditions for newly recruited workers. In 1994 and 1995, Vic Thorpe, ICEM's General Secretary, made several trips to Japan to discuss the situation with the Japanese Rubber Workers' Federation, which is an ICEM affiliate. The company refused to meet him. It would not even see Robert Reich, the United States Labor Secretary, to discuss the Firestone dispute, while President Bill Clinton criticized the company for "flagrantly turning its back" on United States labour traditions. ICEM has established a network of trade unions at national, regional and local levels to negotiate with Bridgestone around the world. The United States steelworkers' union (USWA), which amalgamated with the United Rubber Workers' Union, had circulated stickers, badges and other campaign material, expressing support for the company's United States workers. ICEM used the Internet to increase its impact and linked up with the AFL-CIO.

In April 1995, rubber workers' union leaders from 22 countries met at an ICEM conference in Istanbul. The Turkish Union Lastik-IS has taken a particularly vocal part in the campaign against Bridgestone by mobilizing its members in the Turkish facilities of the company. Locked-out United States workers have visited Turkey, as well as Italy, Spain and Bulgaria, to seek solidarity. The USWA has organized a number of marches and street demonstration in Japan in front of the company's corporate headquarters.

In January 1996, Centrale Générale/Algemene Centrale, Belgium's largest trade union covering the rubber and chemical industries, leafleted Brussels commuters explaining why it was wrong that American workers could be permanently dismissed from their jobs for exercising their right to strike.

This was followed by the decision of the ICFTU Executive Board to condemn Bridgestone's violations of workers' rights. Efforts to reach an agreement with the company in mid-January 1996 had failed to achieve a breakthrough. A conference organized by the USWA and ICEM was held in Nashville in March 1996 to plan further international action against Bridgestone.

Finally, an agreement meeting the USWA's demands was reached with Bridgestone in November 1996.

Source: R. Taylor: *Trade union strategies in the global economy* (Geneva, ILO, 1996).

Box 2.3. Just one of many codes of conduct

When workers at the Korean-owned Mandarin clothing factory in El Salvador sought to put an end to harsh and degrading treatment that included being forbidden to talk while working, beatings and sexual abuse, their attempts to form a union were suppressed. Over 350 workers, most of whom were women, were fired.

In the United States, a pressure campaign directed at Mandarin's biggest customer, the United States retailer The Gap, was mounted by trade unions and religious, consumer, women's and students' organizations. At first, The Gap, which is one of the largest apparel companies in the world, sought to deny that its subcontractor was guilty of such acts. But in the face of overwhelming evidence that the

charges were true, and mounting pressure including from shareholders and politicians, The Gap announced that it would pull out of El Salvador. The campaigners demanded that The Gap reconsider this decision and instead use its influence to ensure that workers' rights were protected.

The Gap agreed to remain in El Salvador, to translate its hitherto ignored code of conduct into the languages of the 47 countries where clothing is produced for the company and to make sure that the code is posted prominently in each factory. The Gap also accepted responsibility for the working conditions where its products are made and agreed to the independent monitoring of its subcontractors by a third party.

Source: International Textile, Leather and Garment Workers' Federation (ITLGWF), in ICFTU: *The global market: Trade unionism's greatest challenge,* 16th World Congress of the ICFTU, Brussels, 25-29 June 1996 (Brussels, 1996).

---

that an association be set up to verify implementation. One need hardly point out that merely drafting rules is not enough. It is clearly also necessary – and this is a much more complex task – to ensure that their actual implementation is monitored. This point is emphasized in the C&A code of conduct.

Sometimes these campaigns also aim to compel enterprises to inform consumers of the conditions in which products are manufactured. This was the case of operation Clean Clothes, launched recently in several European countries (Belgium, France, Germany, the Netherlands, Switzerland and the United Kingdom). It was backed by trade unions, charities and support groups. Furthermore, the idea has been floated,[52] and in some cases put into practice, of awarding a "social label" to enterprises that prove that certain minimum rules are observed in their manufacturing processes. Again, the system's credibility depends on the actual implementation of these rules, and hence on effective verification procedures.

In the best of cases – which are, however, rare – negotiations lead to formal agreements, such as those concluded since 1988 between the IUF and the Danone company. The agreements cover the following areas: skills training and development; access of trade unions to information; promotion of equality between women and men; and union rights.[53] On 9 June 1995, the same ITS signed an agreement with the Accor hotel group guaranteeing the full exercise of freedom of association in all establishments belonging to the group (Novotel hotels, for example). On the question of the abolition of child labour, the IKEA company, a Swedish trade union affiliated to FIET and an association importing carpets into Sweden recently set up a joint committee to examine the conditions in which carpets are manufactured in certain Asian countries and identifying those made by children in order to withdraw them from sale.

There are also examples of agreements concluded not at the enterprise, but at the sectoral level. In 1995, for example, the ETUC organization for the textiles, clothing and leather sector and the European Confederation of the Footwear Industry signed a charter on child labour: member companies of the Confederation undertook not to employ children in manufacturing, in any area of the world, either directly or indirectly (i.e. through subcontracting arrangements).[54]

Such transnational sectoral agreements remain limited in number, however, since employers' associations appear to be more reluctant than their trade union counterparts to conclude formal arrangements at this level. Arrangements often focus more on relations between the parties than on fundamental issues.

Lastly, at the interoccupational level, on 14 December 1995, UNICE, the ETUC and the European Centre of Enterprises with Public Participation (CEEP) signed a framework agreement on parental leave, whose area of application was extended by a European Union Council Directive of 3 June 1996. On 14 May 1997, they concluded another agreement on the promotion of part-time work.

However, it should be pointed out once again that transnational collective agreements are rare. They apply essentially to the European Union, which is much further along the road to integration than other regional groups. Even in this area it is more a case of social dialogue than genuine collective bargaining. And, as often happens when centralized consultation does not go far enough, lobbying flourishes as a means of making up for its deficiencies.

New alliances?

It has been observed that workers' organizations are both seeking and finding new alliances, sometimes on a one-off basis, sometimes over a longer period. It is with this in mind that we will now return to two oft-discussed aspects of the trade union movement; its place in the public sector and its link with political groups. These will not be analysed as such, but only as they relate to the perspective on new alliances. These new partnerships and their future prospects will then be discussed.

The example of the public sector

Very often, unionization rates are much higher in the public than in the private sector. This is true of most European States, the United States and Japan; the rate has also increased in the public sector in Canada and the Netherlands, for example, which helps explain the growth in trade union membership in these two countries.

A drop in the number of new members often occurs with privatization. This observation is particularly valid in the former communist countries of Central and

Eastern Europe;[55] it also applies to the developing countries of Asia and Latin America (Argentina), but here the data are more difficult to verify. The same situation occurs in OECD countries such as Australia, the Netherlands or the United Kingdom.[56]

Trade unions in the public sector sometimes face serious obstacles stemming from an excessively rigid view of these workers' functions, and in particular the fact that they are in the service of the State and its government, and that they often carry out duties considered to be in the public interest. It is on these grounds that national legislation still denies, whether explicitly or otherwise, state employees (Bolivia, Ethiopia, Liberia, Chad) or certain categories of them (Malaysia, Panama, Nigeria) the right to join trade unions. Sometimes, however, organizations are set up on the basis of general legislation on freedom of association, where these are unable to benefit from the specific provisions applicable to trade unions (Bangladesh, Ecuador). More often, there are restrictions on the right of some or all state employees to negotiate formal collective agreements with the State that employs them (Colombia, Iraq, Pakistan), and especially the right to strike (Germany, the Republic of Korea, Japan).

All the more reason for protest movements in the public sector, if they are to succeed, to take account of users' concerns and the public interest (and this includes the efficiency and management of public services); if they fail to do so, they risk losing the support of public opinion, which is all the more valuable given that the position of their employer is largely dependent on it. Strategies should therefore be envisaged with a view to forming alliances.

An author[57] who has analysed several trade union campaigns in California (San Francisco area) in the 1980s emphasizes the extent to which public opinion is a vital element for success. The campaigns for female municipal employees in San José and district nurses in San Francisco owed their success to scrupulous consideration for users' needs. The campaigns also sought the necessary support of public opinion by forging an alliance with women's organizations (by emphasizing how the campaigns could help promote gender equality) and by joining forces with groups sharing similar social concerns, such as janitors.

The conclusions to be drawn from these examples go beyond the public sector. Particular reference could be made to a 1987 campaign which became famous, launched in support of janitors, under the slogan "Justice for Janitors". "The Justice for Janitors campaign of SEIU (Service Employees International Union) [...] effectively bypasses the rules regulating union organizing that are established by the National Labor Relations Act (NLRA), targeting labour markets in geographical areas rather than individual employers. The building services industry, in which cleaners and janitors are for the most part employed, is now dominated by contractors who often have less control over the nature and cost of service delivery than the building owners who hire them. Competition on the basis of low wages has long been the norm in this sector. Organizing contractors one by one, and gaining contracts that increase wages and improve conditions, would drive individual contractors out of business. Workers are not only low paid, but often part time, and have little attachment to a particular employer. Turnover is high. The campaign has been tremendously successful in certain cities (Seattle, Denver, Portland, Los Angeles, among others), where citywide bargaining structures have been created with the aid of significant support from local communities. The union must begin by representing workers in the absence of a collective bargaining contract – a circumstance not foreseen or addressed by current labour law, and not widely embraced by more traditional US unions. Once enough workers have joined, as many contractors as possible are approached simultaneously, and various pressures – from community pressure and corporate campaigns to worker walk-outs – are applied in the interest of gaining a geographically encompassing contract. Organizers involved in this campaign praise many of its innovative aspects, but emphasize especially emphatically their successes in organizing 'outside the law'."[58]

Here again, a movement which was essentially concerned with workers of Mexican descent emphasized the civil liberty dimension of the protests (including equality) and forged links with human rights organizations, religious and women's groups and other community institutions. Launched at a time when work had become increasingly subcontracted, the movement succeeded in reaching groups of contractors, as well as the companies using them. The success achieved surpassed all expectations. This and the cases mentioned above prompt further discussion of the links between unionism and politics, in the broad sense of the word.

The labour movement and politics

In many African and Asian countries, the trade union movement has played a part in the struggle for independence, as has been pointed out. However, once independence has been attained, relations with the party in power have sometimes led to excessive symbiosis, with the result that trade union confederations have lost their autonomy. Elsewhere the situation has turned to conflict. Rarely has a return to the normal functions of trade unionism been achieved without upheaval.[59] In Asia, the fear of communist subversion has led more than one country (the Republic of Korea, Malaysia, Singapore) to exercise control, in one form or another, over the trade union movement. In many cases, the end of the Cold War brought with it a more flexible attitude, where this had not already occurred.

On the other hand, since the end of the Second World War but especially since the late 1960s, governments in Western Europe in particular have increasingly involved representative employers' and workers' organizations in economic and social policies. They have done so by concluding tripartite agreements, of which more will be said later, as well as by allowing them to participate in various public or semi-public bodies. The political role of the social partners has developed in the same way in Canada.

Currently, however, situations are evolving in different ways. The ties between trade union confederations and political parties have loosened recently in several

Western European countries – Spain, France, the United Kingdom and Sweden, where the collective affiliation of LO members to the Social Democratic Party ceased in 1990-91 – as well as outside Europe (South Africa). The conclusion of social pacts has been made more difficult as a result. In Latin America, however, close political ties apparently still prevail (Mexico and Venezuela), although tensions do arise from time to time (Argentina).

The fall of the communist regimes unleashed much more radical transformations in Central and Eastern Europe. However, in many cases the trade unions retained their political influence,[60] with former workers' organizations generally breaking away from Marxist-Leninist ideology. In some cases, their role even increased in the absence of political parties representing workers. The decline of the trade union Solidarity in Poland has been attributed by some to its broad support for government policy in 1989 and thereafter.[61]

Relationships between the trade unions and politics have evolved. The question now is whether other alliances will emerge.

Unusual partnerships

Whatever its causes may be, the diversification of interests is a reminder that working people do not identify themselves completely with their job or with the production relationship. They also define themselves in terms of their national, social or ethnic origin, philosophical, religious and political views, age, sex and often also as consumers. In France, in particular,[62] as well as in other countries,[63] the scarcity of jobs has sparked off a debate on the place of work in society, on the possibility of separating income from work, and on the concept of a career comprising periods spent at work, training, on leave, or other social or political activities, for example. Specifically, the employment crisis has prompted a rethinking of the role of other actors in society (trainers, those responsible for developing social skills and reintegration, social workers and charities), and has raised the question of more innovative approaches (for example, making people more responsible, and focusing more on personal concerns while taking individual characteristics into account). The broader sensitivity to individual concerns obviously affects interpersonal relations and is sometimes translated into the formation of influence groups in defence of a particular cause. However, there is inevitably a certain amount of overlap between new social organizations and trade unions; in a way they even compete with each other. Hence the dilemma: competition versus coalition.

In order to gain some idea of future prospects, we therefore have to place trade union confederations in the context of civil society, and see them in relation to these other groups. With this in mind, a distinction can be drawn between three kinds of groups: the first correspond to genuine workers' organizations, even if they differ somewhat in structure from traditional trade unions; the second are social associa-

Box 2.4.   Trade union initiatives for the most vulnerable workers

The Tennessee Industrial Renewal Network (TIRN), created in 1989, is engaged in an effort to identify the specific needs and characteristics of temporary workers, and to develop legislative and union organizing and representational strategies that will meet these needs.[1] It is still too early to evaluate the success of this project in which community involvement (which includes churches and other local groups) plays a critically important role, as do long-term relationships – and trust building. Like about half of the states in the United States, Tennessee is a "right-to-work" state, i.e. the right of workers to work without joining a union. Employers' opposition to unionization in such states tends to be particularly fierce, and often fire employees who express an interest in unionizing (even though this is technically illegal). The task of the trade unions is therefore particularly difficult.

The Carolina Alliance for Fair Employment (CAFE) in South Carolina is another effort to assist temporary workers.[2] An ongoing community-building initiative, its focus is on the development of a campaign to pressure temporary agencies. The initiative targets particular employers identified as exploiting or bypassing workers' (limited) rights and meets with friendly agencies to try to obtain voluntary compliance with basic employment standards.

The Massachusetts Community Care Workers' Campaign (MCCWC) has similar aims, though on a larger scale.[3] Its aim is to organize contingent (contract, leased, temporary and part-time) workers employed by private companies who contract health-care services to the State. Twenty thousand workers are the target of this campaign. Most are low-wage women employees, working for multiple small companies that would be extremely difficult to organize in the traditional way (through the National Labor Relations Board's supervised elections at separate bargaining units). Hence, the campaign bypasses labour law. It is particularly innovative, and in some ways resembles the French and Canadian temporary industry initiatives in that it is an effort to engage firms in multi-employer bargaining, ultimately taking the cost of labour out of competition. It seeks voluntary recognition by employers, and has begun informal consultations with willing companies. At the same time, this effort entails legislative reform initiatives, trying to get the State of Massachusetts to help create a bargaining structure that would cover these workers. Success cannot be measured at this time.

Home health-care workers are the target of a recent organizing campaign on the part of the United States service union (SEIU)[4] in California. In order to keep down the costs of health care, the State employs 160,000 home health-care aides – untrained minimum wage workers who care for patients at home. These workers cost the State about $7,000 per year, while placing a patient in a nursing home would cost more than four times that amount. The SEIU, one of the most innovative American unions, especially in the area of organizing, has had considerable success with such workers in the past decade. Employer resistance is minimal (unlike in most private sector organizing drives), since the employer is the State of California. Given the health-care crisis in the United States, the SEIU is likely to continue to gain members from among other workers in this industry, many of whom already are, or may soon become, contingent workers of one kind or another. SEIU campaigns to organize emergency medical service workers have also been successful in the San Francisco Bay Area of California.[5]

[1] S. Putz and N. Gregg: *Organizing contingent workers in a right-to-work state: Steps toward an agenda for action,* paper prepared for Workplace 2000: Women's rights, workers' rights, New York, Cornell University, NYSSILR, May 1995.

[2] F. Gardner and J. McAllister: "Temporary workers: Flexible or disposable?", in *Poverty and Race,* PRRAC (Poverty and Race Research Action Council) research report, Vol. 4, No. 6, Nov.–Dec. 1995, pp. 9-14.

[3] F. Carré and L. Dougherty: *Improving employment conditions for contingent workers: The Massachusetts Community Care Workers' Campaign,* working paper (Radcliffe Public Policy Institute, Harvard University, 1995).

[4] P.T. Kilborn: "Strategies changing for union: Home care aides are fresh target", in *New York Times,* 20 Nov. 1995.

[5] A. Shostak: "Contracting out of management services: A unique opportunity for labor unions", in *Proceedings of the Industrial Relations Research Association Annual Meetings* (Madison, Wisconsin, IIRA, 1993).

Source: K. Wever: *Unions adding value: Addressing market and social failures in the advanced industrial countries* (Geneva, ILO, 1996), pp. 52 ff.

tions, with which the trade unions have every interest to cooperate; the third are non-governmental organizations (NGOs), which, in supporting specific causes, do not take the form of associations of members.

Almost all parts of the world have registered successful attempts to defend and promote the interests of the least protected segments of the population, including homeworkers. The ETUC has observed and analysed a significant number of such segments in the area it covers.[64] Several initiatives have recently been taken in the United States to support the most vulnerable workers (see box 2.4), or to guarantee an adequate income ("living wage campaigns"). Reference has already been made to such movements in support of people working in the informal sector in developing countries[65] in Africa,[66] Latin America,[67] and Asia, especially in India.[68] These will be examined in greater detail in Chapter 8.

These movements are often the result of gradual grass-roots mobilization efforts culminating in the establishment of occupational or other associations (more will be said about this later), which normally operate in such a way as to enable all their members to express their opinions freely. They are community-based rather than centred on the workplace, and often act in close cooperation with institutions providing support services (local authorities, churches, charities, organizations assisting the unemployed, technical cooperation bodies, and those providing training or assistance to jobseekers). Sometimes they have also taken on board the concerns of environmental and consumers' associations.

It should be recalled that the concept of workers' organization, as it is used by the ILO, in particular in Conventions Nos. 87 and 98, and in many other instruments (such as the Rural Workers' Organisations Convention, 1975 (No. 141)), is broad in scope, referring to any kind of organization of workers that aims to promote and defend the latter's interests. It therefore covers, at least in principle, the associations referred to here. The idea has developed[69] of enlisting these dynamic new forces, using the possibilities now offered by networking, or simply of achieving better coordination with these important social movements. The unions have much to learn from their working methods, which are often less standardized and more individualized, and place greater emphasis on each person's initiative and responsibility. After all, history shows that trade unions have kept pace with change. Those in the United States, for example, succeeded in combining the new movement born of mass production and federated in the CIO with the traditional craft-based unionism represented by the AFL.

Again, the fact remains that it is difficult to organize these disparate categories of workers, whose interests vary greatly; it is also difficult to reconcile their concerns with those of employees who have steady jobs, who are more easily unionized and hence more readily heard by management.

The second type of organization consists of associations pursuing social aims but set up with other – and usually narrower – objectives than those of trade unions.

In the same way as workers' confederations, they act as an interface between their members and civil society. They include environmental groups, those set up to defend civil rights or local interests, or to protect a particular ethnic minority, cooperatives, and of course women's and consumer movements. The latter are sometimes highly skilled at using means of action such as boycotts, and have succeeded, for instance, in ensuring that specific information appears on product labels. Trade union federations now often seek to adopt similar means of action.

These organizations share several features with the new kind of trade union associations described above. Having said that, in most cases their specific aims objectively rule out their being integrated wholesale into the trade union movement – nor, of course, is it clear that this is what their members want. As has already been pointed out, however, "political" alliances – in the broad sense of the term, which encompasses local community issues – have been concluded during protest movements and have contributed to their success. Many examples of these can be found in the United Kingdom,[70] Hong Kong (prior to 1 July 1997),[71] Taiwan, China,[72] and Brazil. "From the late 1970s, vigorous new trade unions succeeded in sidestepping the tightly controlled trade unions system set up under Getúlio Vargas and preserved by the military. Metal workers in the São Paulo agglomeration defied labour laws and national security legislation in order to demand wage increases from the large industrial firms in the area. Labour demands gradually evolved into open criticism of the trade union system and of authoritarian politics. [...] the movement also developed close links to the new urban movements and to massive popular mobilization in favour of democracy and social reform."[73] Another example is Zimbabwe.[74] Several authors, and in particular Mr. Piore, in his book *Beyond individualism: How social demands of the new identity groups challenge American political and economic life,*[75] have emphasized the potential benefits of this kind of social interaction.

Again, it goes without saying that the development of a joint programme and agreement on the specific services to be provided to the targeted community – even if the programme is limited in time, space and content – have proven to be more difficult to bring about in practice than they are to recommend; trade union members in particular may have misgivings regarding some of these groups' demands. Notwithstanding, these new-style coalitions do exist; they have been successful and many feel the future looks promising.

Like the socially oriented groups referred to above, trade unions are non-governmental organizations. However, the NGOs that make up the third category are not fundamentally based on associative principles. They comprise various kinds of institutions ranging from churches, charities and institutions providing support services (in particular for the unemployed), to technical cooperation, development assistance and occupational safety and health projects. This is where we find the men and women field workers whose job it is to train the people faced with social exclusion and help them find jobs or re-enter the labour market (the long-term unemployed, the homeless, welfare or social assistance recipients, indebted households, illegal immigrants, drug addicts or people who are just poor and have no resources). Often these institutions cooperate with the local authorities and their staff and social workers.

Obviously, these organizations cannot replace trade unions or their specific role, and neither can those in the second category. Clearly, however, they can prove to be useful partners in the attainment of common objectives. The frequent cooperation between informal sector associations and local churches in Latin America is just one of many examples.

An entirely different matter – and one which should not be confused with the above – is the extension of the traditional cooperation between employers, trade unions and, in some cases, the authorities to include some of the social groups referred to here. The idea is not entirely new.[76] Major advisory bodies have long included representatives of self-employed persons (in the agricultural sector and craft industries in particular), and of cooperatives, family associations or persons appointed as experts or spokespersons for the general interest. Occupational categories not represented by employers' or trade union organizations have also participated in central negotiations. The employment crisis, however, seems to have afforded more opportunities for putting this idea into practice, whether at the central level, as in Quebec (1996), or at different levels, as in Ireland since 1994.

One further point may need to be made clear: these new partnerships do not in themselves affect the traditional cooperation between employers and trade unions. Furthermore, some of these groups (as has already been pointed out in the context of the informal sector) are mainly concerned with improving productivity. They are therefore more reminiscent of small entrepreneurs' associations. On the smallest scale, the distinction between employers and workers sometimes becomes blurred since, after all, the activities of both are centred on work.

Initial conclusions

Many trade unions have made a strong commitment to reform and modernization. The main forms these have taken have been examined above. First, though, they had to face the reality of the crisis they were going through. It goes without saying that this was a difficult but necessary step to take if the collective representation of workers was to recover its momentum. For after all, what would have become of collective representation if the trade unions lost their influence? The natural alternatives (failing which it would still be possible in some cases for exploitation to reappear) are direct (elective) representation at enterprise level and, obviously, political representation. These forms of representation certainly serve a purpose, but as history and empirical observation show, they cannot fully replace collective labour relations without endangering society and, ultimately, human beings themselves.

So it is most reasonable to assume that trade unions will change as well. However, it is a well-known fact that social institutions based on associative principles need more time to transform themselves than do economic institutions. This of course is not to justify any delays in making the adjustments required by changing times, for such delays could admittedly be very dangerous.

Assertions, recommendations and publications abound in these times of uncertainty. New visions of social relations are proposed, examined and debated. They recommend that citizens be helped to manage the increasingly varied and individual career paths they take in their professional lives. This is not without implications for the organizations referred to above. But it is also essential for this ferment of ideas to spark off real discussions among employers and trade unions and for the conclusions to be widely supported. This means that all workers, including the most vulnerable, must be able to express their opinions through genuine representatives and that trade unions, if necessary by forming alliances, must demonstrate the ability to speak on behalf of all those concerned. And this in turn calls for genuine and efficient union participation in the three functions – democratic, economic and social – of industrial relations, and their adaptation, in line with the strategies analysed above, to a world which has probably become harsher for a lot of people. But it also requires appropriate instruments for dialogue and structures which provide the three functions with a lasting framework. This will be the subject of another chapter. First, however, other issues need to be examined in more detail, beginning with the specific constraints of employers' organizations.

Notes

[1] See A. Pankert: "Adjustment problems of trade unions in selected industrialized market economy countries: The unions' own view", in *The International Journal of Comparative Labour Law and Industrial Relations* (The Hague and Cambridge, Massachusetts, Kluwer Law International), Vol. 9(1), Spring 1993, p. 14; S. Olney: *Unions in a changing world: Problems and prospects in selected industrialized countries* (Geneva, ILO, 1996), pp. 79-81.

[2] H. Fujimura: "New unionism: Beyond enterprise unionism?", in M. Sako and H. Sato: *Japanese labour and management in transition: Diversity, flexibility and participation* (London, Routledge, 1997), p. 309.

[3] S. Olney, op. cit., p. 84.

[4] A. Trebilcock: "Strategies for strengthening women's participation in trade union leadership", in *International Labour Review* (Geneva, ILO), Vol. 130, No. 4, 1991, p. 418, note 37.

[5] See M. Breedveld and M. Endeveld: "Women's organizations and trade unions in the agricultural sector", in M. Mulders and Th. Van Osch (eds.): *New trade union perspectives: Organizing women workers in the agricultural sector, export processing zones, informal sector* (Amsterdam, FNV-CNV, undated), pp. 37-48.

[6] K. Wever: *Unions adding value: Addressing market and social failures in the advanced industrial countries* (Geneva, ILO, 1996), p. 15.

[7] R. Kumar: "Women in the Bombay cotton textile industry, 1919-1940", in S. Rowbotham and S. Mitter (eds.): *Dignity and daily bread: New forms of economic organizing among poor women in the Third World and the First* (London, Routledge, 1994), p. 59.

[8] S. Tirado: "Weaving dreams, constructing realities: The 19th of September National Union of Garment Workers in Mexico", in S. Rowbotham and S. Mitter, op. cit., pp. 100 ff.

[9] See P. Johnston: *Success while others fail: Social movement unionism and the public workplace* (Ithaca, New York, ILR Press, 1994).

[10] G. Murray and P. Verge: "Trade union representation in Canada: Current situation and future prospects", in *Modern unionism and its future,* International colloquy held in Łódź from 25 to 27 October 1993 by the Faculty of Labour Law and Social Security of the University of Łódź (Łódź, Wydawnictwo Uniwersytetu Łódzkiego, 1995), p. 135.

[11] K. Wever, op. cit., p. 14.

[12] W. Higgins: "The Swedish municipal workers' union: A study on the new political unionism", in *Economic and Industrial Democracy* (London, Sage), Vol. 17, 1996, pp. 167-197; S. Nelander: *The trade union as a popular movement* (Oslo, LO, 1996), pp. 28 ff.

[13] T. Fashoyin: *Contribution to the national case studies of the effects of globalization on industrial relations and adjustment at enterprise level,* paper prepared for the ILO (1997), p. 15.

[14] K. Wever, op. cit., p. 25.

[15] A.H. Cook: "Women and minorities", in G. Strauss, D.G. Gallagher and J. Fiorito: *The state of the unions* (Madison, Wisconsin, IRRA Series, 1991), pp. 246 and 248.

[16] K. Wever, op. cit., p. 58.

[17] ibid., pp. 15-16.

[18] M. Weiss: "Challenges for and future of trade unions in Germany", in *Modern unionism and its future,* op. cit., p. 40.

[19] S. Boyer: "Les syndicats peuvent-ils être des partenaires?", in J.P. Durand (ed.): *Le syndicalisme au futur* (Paris, Syros, 1996), p. 242.

[20] M. Iwamura: "Rapport japonais", *Travaux de l'Association Henri Capitant,* Vol. XLV (Paris, Litec, 1996), p. 603.

[21] S. Olney, op. cit., p. 23.

[22] S. Rowbotham: *Homeworkers worldwide* (London, The Merlin Press, 1993), pp. 86 ff.; J. Tate: "Homework in West Yorkshire", in S. Rowbotham and S. Mitter, op. cit., pp. 193-217; J. Tate: "Organizing homeworkers in the informal sector: Australia, Canada, the Netherlands", in M. Hosmer-Martens and S. Mitter (eds.): *Women in trade unions: Organizing the unorganized* (Geneva, ILO, 1994), pp. 67 ff.

[23] S. Rowbotham, op. cit., p. 59.

[24] K. Wever, op. cit., p. 17. "White-collar" temporary workers are covered here by collective bargaining contracts negotiated with the associations of temporary employment agencies.

[25] ibid., p. 50. In Quebec, multi-employer sectoral negotiations have led to an increase in the basic wage of temporary workers.

[26] ibid., p. 50. *Le Monde,* 5 Feb. 1997, Employment supplement, p. I. Sectoral negotiations for workers in irregular employment involve two employers' associations representing temporary work agencies and the main trade union federations.

[27] L. Delsen: "Atypical employment and industrial relations in the Netherlands", in *Economic and Industrial Democracy* (London, Sage), 14(4), Nov. 1993, pp. 591 ff.; see also IDS (Income Data Services, London), No. 421, Jan. 1997, pp. 6–7.

[28] T. Galvez and R. Todara: "Chile – Women and the unions", in E. Jelin: *Women and social change in Latin America* (London, Zed Books, 1990), pp. 118 ff.; F.J. Tapia Guerrero: *Efectos de la globalización en las relaciones industriales: el caso chileno,* paper prepared for the ILO (1996), p. 14.

[29] Ho-Hwan Park: "Crossfire ahead: Where to go?", in *The impact of globalization on industrial relations,* document of the Third Asian Regional Congress of the IIRA (Taipei, 30 Sep.–4 Oct. 1996), Vol. 2, p. 236.

[30] I. Yépez del Castillo: *Les syndicats à l'heure de la précarisation de l'emploi* (Louvain-la-Neuve, Academia-L'Harmattan, 1993), pp. 243 ff.

[31] K. Wever, op. cit., pp. 52 ff.; P. Doeringer et al.: *Industrial relations and production channels in apparel: A comparative study of labour, management and industry,* paper prepared for the ILO (1997).

[32] ILO: "Protecting the least protected: Rights of migrant workers and the role of trade unions", in *Labour Education* (Geneva), No. 103, 1996, pp. 17 and 38.

[33] Status of the Artist Act of 23 June 1992. See also, for Australia, R. Markey: "Marginal workers in the big picture: Unionization of visual artists", in *Journal of Industrial Relations* (Sydney, Industrial Relations Society of Australia), 38(1), Mar. 1996, pp. 22-41. In Japan, a decision has classed musicians performing in restaurants with employees for the purposes of the law on trade unions.

[34] G. Lyon-Caen: *Le droit du travail non salarié* (Paris, Sirey, 1990), para. 148.

[35] J.S. Lee and Young-Bum Park: "Employment, labour standards and economic development in Taiwan and Korea" (Proceedings of the 10th World Congress of the IIRA, Washington, DC, 31 May-4 June 1995), in *Labour* (Oxford, Basil Blackwell), p. S241, note 2.

[36] ILO: 241st Report of the Committee on Freedom of Association, *Official Bulletin,* Vol. LXVIII, Series B, No. 3 (Geneva, 1985), Case No. 1285, para. 213.

[37] G. Fonteneau and A. Meunier: *Les syndicats face à l'exclusion et aux précarités sociales. Bilan des actions de la Confédération européenne des syndicats et de ses organisations* (Brussels, ETUC, 1995), p. 18.

[38] See for example, for the TUC, R. Taylor: *The future of the trade unions* (London, A. Deutsch, 1994), p. 64.

[39] D. Demazière: "Des chômeurs sans représentation collective: une fatalité?", in *Esprit* (Paris), Nov. 1996, pp. 12-32. The author attempts to identify the numerous causes of this phenomenon, which appears to be the result of the fragmentation of the problems of the unemployed, their tendency to isolate themselves and the fact that they are more united by a lack (of work) than by the emergence of collective identities.

[40] For people faced with social exclusion, see P. Rosanvallon: *La nouvelle question sociale. Repenser l'Etat-providence* (Paris, Le Seuil, 1995), pp. 202 ff.; R. Castel: *Les métamorphoses de la question sociale. Une chronique du salariat* (Paris, Fayard, 1995), p. 441.

[41] In establishments with fewer than 11 employees, but whose activities are conducted on a site where at least another 50 people are employed on a regular basis, the departmental director for labour may order the election of staff delegates – this institution differs from trade union representation in the strict sense of the term – if problems common to the enterprises working on the site justify it: new section L421-1(5). The site can be an industrial estate, shopping mall or centre, or a construction site set up for a certain period: see J.M. Verdier: *Droit du travail* (Paris, Dalloz, 10th edition, 1996), p. 122.

[42] V. Franzinetti: "The informal sector in an industrialized country: Textile and garment workers in Northern Italy", in M. Hosmer-Martens and S. Mitter, op. cit.

[43] F. Morin: *The future of collective bargaining and new forms of employment,* Third American Regional Congress of Labour Law and Social Security (Montreal, 24–27 May 1995) (Cowansville, Quebec, Yvon Blais, 1995), pp. 93 ff. See also, for Canada, A. Sims, R. Blouin and P. Knopf: *Seeking a balance* (Ottawa, Ministry of Public Works and Government Services, 1995), pp. 47 and 239 ff.

[44] ILO: *Freedom of association: Digest of decisions and principles of the Freedom of Association Committee of the Governing Body of the ILO* (Geneva, 4th ed., 1996), paras. 622 ff.

[45] See ILO: *Freedom of association and collective bargaining,* International Labour Conference, 81st Session, Geneva, 1994, para. 197 and note 20.

[46] See M. Rothman, D.R. Briscoe and R.C.D. Nacamulli (eds.): *Industrial relations around the world: Labor relations for multinational companies* (Berlin and New York, W. De Gruyter, 1993).

[47] P. Marginson, P. Armstrong, P. Edwards and J. Purcell: "Facing the multinational challenge", in P. Leisink, J. van Leemput and J. Vilrokx (eds.): *The challenge to trade unions in Europe: Innovation or adaptation?* (Cheltenham, United Kingdom, Edward Elgar, 1996), pp. 188-189; P. Marginson and K. Sisson: "The structure of transnational capital in Europe: The emerging Euro-Company and its implications for industrial relations", in R. Hyman and A. Ferner (eds.): *New frontiers in European industrial relations* (Oxford, Blackwell, 1994), pp. 23 ff. and pp. 37 ff.; C. Erikson and S. Kuruvilla: "Labour cost incentives for capital mobility in the European Community", in S.M. Jacoby (ed.): *The workers of nations: Industrial relations in a global economy* (Oxford, Oxford University Press, 1995), p. 50; K. Dörre: "La fin du pacte de croissance en Allemagne, la crise du modèle de production et ses incidences sur les relations professionnelles", in *Travail et Emploi* (Paris, Ministère du Travail), No. 67, 2/1996, p. 13.

[48] K. Dörre, op. cit.

[49] See M. Martinez Lucio and S. Weston: "Trade unions and networking in the context of change: Evaluating the outcomes of decentralization in industrial relations", in *Economic and Industrial Democracy* (London, Sage), 16(2), May 1995, p. 235.

[50] T. Kidder and M. McGinn: "In the wake of NAFTA: Transnational workers' network", in *Social Policy* (New York), 25(4), Summer 1995, pp. 14-21.

[51] See also, in a different context, ILO: *The ILO, standard setting and globalization,* Report of the Director-General to the International Labour Conference, 85th Session, Geneva, 1997, pp. 30 ff.

[52] ILO: *Defending values, promoting change. Social justice in a global economy: An ILO agenda,* Report of the Director-General to the International Labour Conference, 81st Session, Geneva, 1994, p. 65.

[53] ICFTU, *The global market: Trade unionism's greatest challenge,* op. cit., p. 52.

[54] *European Industrial Relations Review* (London, Eclipse), Mar. 1996, p. 25.

[55] K. Tapiola: "Trade union development in the CEECs", in *Transfer* (Brussels, European Trade Union Institute), pp. 374-375.

[56] S. Olney, op. cit., p. 12.

[57] P. Johnston, op. cit.

[58] K. Wever, op. cit., p. 31.

[59] For a comparison of the development of the trade union movement in Zambia and Zimbabwe, for example, see H. Thomas (ed.): *Globalization and Third World trade unions: The challenge of rapid economic change* (London, Zed Books, 1997), Ch. 9, by P. Mihyo (pp. 221 ff.), and Ch. 10, by F. Schiphorst (pp. 226 ff.).

[60] A. Tyomkina: "The problem of advancing industrial democracy in a post-socialist society", in E. Klopov and C. von Otter (eds.): "The Russian labour market and the beginnings of an industrial relations system", in *Economic and Industrial Democracy* (London, Sage), Vol. 14 (Suppl.), (Nov. 1993), pp. 32 ff.

[61] M. Weinstein: "From governance to ungovernability: The reconfiguration of Polish industrial relations, 1989–1993", in K. Wever and L. Turner (eds.): *The comparative political economy of industrial relations* (Madison, Wisconsin, IRRA, 1995), pp. 151–179.

[62] See A. Supiot: *Critique du droit du travail* (Paris, PUF, 1994); D. Méda: *Le travail. Une valeur en voie de disparition* (Paris, Aubier, 1995); see also the report of the Commission (Government Economic Advisory Committee) chaired by Jean Boissonnat: *Le travail dans vingt ans* (Paris, O. Jacob, La documentation française, 1995).

[63] U. Mückenberger, C. Stroh and R. Zoll: "The challenge of modernisation: Towards a new paradigm for trade unions in Europe", in *Transfer,* Vol. 1, 1995, pp. 23 ff.

[64] G. Fonteneau and A. Meunier, op. cit.

[65] See for example M. Hosmer-Martens and S. Mitter (eds.): *Women in trade unions: Organizing the unorganized* (Geneva, ILO, 1994).

[66] T. Fashoyin, op. cit., p. 15.

[67] See also I. Yépez del Castillo, op. cit.; S. Feldman: *La organización y representación de quienes desarrollan actividades en el sector informal en Argentina, Brasil y Perú,* paper prepared for the ILO (1996).

[68] See also C.S. Venkata Ratnam: *Non-governmental organisations and trade unions* (New Delhi, APRO/ICFTU, 1996).

[69] See ICFTU, op. cit., p. 81; N. Aliprantis: *Relations professionnelles transnationales,* paper prepared for the ILO (1997).

[70] J. Tate: *Homework in West Yorkshire,* op. cit., pp. 193 ff.

[71] D.A. Levin and S. Wing-Kai-Chiu: "Industrial relations and democratization: The case of Hong Kong", Proceedings of the Third Asian Regional Congress of the IIRA (Taipei, 30 Sep.-4 Oct. 1996), Vol. 1, pp. 209-210.

[72] See Yueh-Ching Hwang and Cing-Kae Chiao: "The transformation of industrial relations under democratization in Taiwan, 1987-96", Proceedings of the Third Asian Regional Congress of the IIRA, pp. 73-74.

[73] K. Koonings, D. Kruijt and F. Wils: "The very long march of history", in H. Thomas, op. cit., p. 108.

[74] F. Schiphorst: "The emergence of civil society: The new place of unions in Zimbabwe", ibid., p. 230.

[75] Cambridge, Massachusetts, Harvard University Press, 1995.

[76] ILO: *Tripartite consultation at the national level on economic and social policy,* International Labour Conference, 83rd Session, Geneva, 1996, pp. 37 ff.

3 Employers' organizations

The employers' confederations, too, are having difficulties. One basic problem that has arisen in some countries is that free autonomous employers' organizations are in fact only a recent phenomenon. These organizations have little power in most of the former communist countries (see box 3.1), for instance, whereas enterprises obviously have an important role to play in the transition to a market economy. Despite the wide diversity of these countries, they face many common obstacles to the development of strong independent employers' organizations.[1]

In these countries the public enterprises continue to represent an important share of the economy, since the privatization process is still generally fairly slow. Consequently, to exclude these enterprises from the employers' associations would amount to weakening the position of the employers in the collective bargaining context. To integrate them, on the other hand, would be an excellent opportunity to strengthen these associations. However, this will only be the case if the latter retain full independence. This means that the public enterprises which become members of employers' associations need to have sufficient autonomy vis-à-vis the government authorities to run their businesses on market economy principles.

A further obstacle is the fact that the respective roles of the social actors, and particularly of employers, in this transition period do not always seem to be well understood. This is especially evident in the Russian Federation and in the other countries of the Community of Independent States (CIS), but it is also evident, although to a lesser extent, in Central Europe. Old habits and ways of thinking and acting which hark back to the past often persist, whereas employers' interests now clearly differ from those of the State and of the people who formerly managed state-owned enterprises.

The legal framework frequently works against employers' associations. The absence of any appropriate legislation actually perpetuates the imbalances of the previous regime to the advantage of the trade unions in terms of influence and resources.

The situation has favoured the emergence of a variety of groupings which are supposed to represent entrepreneurs, whereas actually very few of them can rightly claim to do so; even the former chambers of commerce and industry sometimes retain their previous attributions, laid down in obsolete legislation; and the agricultural sector does not always find its place in this chorus of diverging voices. Hence the further delay in the necessary coordination of interests and the doubts that are expressed as to the ability of these organizations to speak for the employers. What is more, the payment of contributions comes up against all sorts of legal and fiscal red tape. In

Box 3.1.　Employer interest representation in Central and Eastern Europe

Central and Eastern Europe has been caught in the turmoil of transition for some considerable time. Have the seven lean years passed and is the end of chaos and privation in sight? Have the many nations born of the New Order acquired sufficient infrastructure and legal foundations to finally take off? What of organized interest groups and especially the employers, who are new on the scene?

The ILO stands for certain basic rights – among which freedom of association – and was created to introduce institutional pluralism as an alternative to the domination of civil society by one group only, embodying the principle of tripartism. The countries of Central and Eastern Europe are all ILO members and so these principles are fully applicable to them. Previously, there were trade unions of a kind, but no recognized and organized employers – and no proper social dialogue between independent partners. The situation is finally improving for the employers, even if much remains to be done.

Countries in the region are extremely diverse. Some have got off to a better start than others, but by and large there has been definite progress. Political democracy is taking root; legal reforms and institutions are largely in place and most basic human rights and freedoms are being upheld; the decline of industrial production seems to have bottomed out, although large groups and whole regions remain very hard hit; privatization, though shaky, is now past the half-way mark and free enterprise well established.

The main challenges facing employers' organizations remain the lack of experience and tradition; the insufficient legal basis of established ownership rights and conditions for free enterprise; corruption and the informal economy; crude taxation practices and high social contributions; and negative attitudes towards and lack of understanding of employers in certain quarters.

In the first years of transition, the ILO's Bureau for Employers' Activities was able to supply the emerging employers' organizations with information, advice and some training. Gradually its contacts have become more focused as its constituents have developed longer term strategic plans. Today, the ILO continues to help them to train staff, develop materials and meet to exchange experiences – and advises them generally. Such support naturally commenced in Central Europe, but has gradually expanded, with an active programme for the Russian Federation, a second in the Baltic republics, and assistance to Ukraine and the Balkan countries.

Organized employers generally have good relations with trade unions, though the employers are most active in the private sector and the unions tend to be concentrated in the public sector, leaving the government as the main counterpart of both. In many countries employers have managed to coordinate all or most of their interest representation into one national confederation, joint council or "umbrella" association. These are then representative enough to facilitate national relations and have also been recognized by the International Organization of Employers. In six other countries, however, coordination processes are under way but have not yet stabilized. In Belarus the three main employers' organizations (EOs) formed a joint confederation two years ago, but initially had some difficulties getting it accepted. Estonia and Lithuania each have two employers' organizations that are seriously contemplating closer cooperation. Moldova has about ten, half of which earlier this year formed one confederation and the others a looser group; these two are now discussing how best to go ahead. Albania – which has just established a Tripartite Council – has four recognized employers' organizations that are cooperating but are not yet ready for joint action. Ukraine now has one dominating League of Industrialists and Entrepreneurs, plus an active Entrepreneur's Union. In war-torn Bosnia-Herzegovina and the Former Yugoslav Republic of Macedonia, the Chambers of Commerce have undertaken to organize the employers by forming an association that functions as a separate department handling employer issues. There are also several groups of private entrepreneurs, but to our knowledge no independent employers' organizations have yet been established.

every case, these countries suffer from a flagrant lack of experience in formulating and implementing policies to promote these organizations, essential though they are.

More basically, the enterprises in the countries concerned need to plan if they are to prosper. They expect energetic action on the part of their associations to secure the social, political and economic stability that is essential to their development.

The implementation of a strategy of that nature presupposes non-conflictual industrial relations. It also requires that entrepreneurs be fully aware of their duties with regard to their personnel. But there are also specific obligations which devolve upon the public authorities. The first is to consult the employers' associations whenever they are drafting laws and regulations concerning enterprises; it will be necessary, for example, to arrive at a precise concept of ownership and to guarantee absolute equality of treatment for all undertakings. The second relates to the definition and application of policies which ensure economic stability; the public authorities must focus on bringing inflation under control, developing a capital market, devising a clear and coherent taxation system, and hunting down corruption; they must also attend to the quality of the education system.

It goes without saying that it is the national institutions which are primarily responsible in these various areas. Nevertheless, international aid can provide valuable support for the proposed reforms.

Employers' organizations also carry too little weight in many developing countries, mainly because of the difficulty of coordinating the action of the various sectors of the economy and in uniting diverging interests. Such is the case, for example, in Burkina Faso, Ethiopia, Mozambique, the Libyan Arab Jamahiriya, the Syrian Arab Republic and Yemen, the Lao People's Democratic Republic, Myanmar and Thailand. Sometimes, the membership of the employers' organizations comprises mainly branches of multinational companies.[2] Moreover, the relatively small size of the modern sector manifestly impedes the development of employers' organizations. There are also divisions amongst such organizations which have not yet been entirely overcome. This is the case in India, Mexico and Paraguay.

Furthermore, the lack of social, political and economic stability which has already been mentioned in the case of the transitional economies is here again proving at times to be a considerable obstacle to the development of free enterprise and of the organizations which represent it. Several developing States adopted for example a Soviet-style organization of power, if not necessarily the Soviet doctrine itself. Some authors explain the propensity of the public authorities to substitute themselves for private initiative – in Africa from the sixties onwards, for example – or the drift towards dictatorial regimes by the relative absence of a middle class of independent national entrepreneurs.[3] The refusal of those regimes to accept the expression of independent views, let alone the free collective negotiation of wages and other employment conditions, has certainly also contributed to the weakness of employers' associations.

Box 3.2.   SMEs and employer's organizations

In most countries a majority of small enterprises are not members of representative organizations. In developing countries the membership levels are particularly low. This partly reflects entrepreneur's lack of awareness of benefits and maybe their lack of time and resources to become involved, but also in some cases a slowness by existing employers' organizations to broaden their membership base. Employers' organizations can make an extra effort to attract small-scale entrepreneurs, possibly including the self-employed and those located in the informal sector.

The representation of entrepreneurs' interests vis-à-vis government has long figured high among the activities of employers' organizations. In some places, such as in certain regions of Italy, small-firm employers' organizations are strong and governments consult them closely. In many countries, however, small firms do not have strong representation, which goes against the interests of both small enterprises and government policy-makers, who may be denied valuable inputs to their deliberations. Employers' organizations may play an advocacy role towards government by voicing the concerns of small and medium-sized enterprises regarding policy and regulatory questions.

Low level of productivity and low awareness of quality concepts and tools are often serious constraints on SME growth and competitiveness. The tripartite National Productivity Board in Singapore, with the active support of the private sector, has run television shows with well-known music bands and other entertainment, skilfully integrated with information and case stories on quality-control circles, teamwork and similar productivity and quality-related tools. Such campaigns can play an important role in raising the general awareness of such concepts and facilitate their introduction into the workplace. Employers' organizations can become involved in such campaigns to raise quality, productivity and ethical standards.

Employers' organizations may, and in many cases already do, develop the capacity to provide direct support services to the SME sector in such areas as training, consultancy, access to credit, information, linkages with larger enterprises, marketing and export support and advising members on legal and social responsibilities.

There are many examples of employers' organizations that have extended their traditional roles to providing direct support services to their members. In India, the Mahratta Chamber of Commerce and Industry provides a range of services to small enterprises, including: consultancy services (for example, in respect of quality management and labour relations); information (in respect of, for example, rules and regulations pertaining to small enterprises); training; organizing exhibitions; and shared use of fax and other communication equipment.[1]

In Colombia, a dynamic leather industry association, ASOCUEROS, offers members a wide variety of courses, sponsors technical consultants and, in general, encourages networking and information sharing among firms.[2] Around Guadalajara and León in Mexico, the small-firm footwear industry has been significantly assisted by entrepreneurial associations providing services like fiscal and labour consultancy, commercial assistance, managerial training and the organization of trade fairs.[3]

Employers' organizations may also become involved, along with workers' organizations, in the governance of decentralized public and public-private SME support institutions, including business start-up incubators, quality testing centres and training institutes.

The involvement of employers' organizations in such activities has increased strongly over recent years. In countries like Spain, Italy and Pakistan entrepreneurial associations in footwear, furniture, textiles, food and other sectors are involved on the boards of technical centres which provide the firms with services such as marketing, training, technological information, research and development and quality testing.[4]

Employers' organizations can be important vehicles for rapid dissemination of information on best practices. This can be done through publications or through specially convened experience-exchange groups and training sessions. The existence of associations which bring entrepreneurs into contact with one another can provide significant advantages for launching further cooperative projects (see earlier references to credit associations and other organizations, such as those in Benin, that have progressed to a range of collaborative activities). Employers' organizations may thus act as vehicles for collaborative action and mutual learning processes among small and medium-sized enterprises.

Employers' organizations may also participate with workers' organizations and other interest groups in councils, task forces and other bodies at the central and local level established to deal with important economic and social issues, including policies and programmes affecting the SME sector.

South Limburg in the Netherlands is an example of a region of declining heavy industry that underwent extensive restructuring. During the 1960s and 1970s all of its 12 coalmines were closed, causing high unemployment and a shortage of employment opportunities. In a concerted effort involving the national Government, the Provincial Government of Limburg, the municipalities and the employers' and workers' organizations, a reorganization plan was produced. Today, the economic structure, previously entirely dependent on mining, is much more diversified and resilient.

[1] B.R. Sabade: "The case of the Mahratta Chamber of Commerce and Industries, Pune (India)", in ZDH (German Federation of Small Business): *The growing involvement of private sector institutions (PSIs) in small and medium enterprise development and their support by donor agencies - Strategic options for Technonet Asia,* paper and proceedings of the ZDH/TA Conference, Singapore, November 1993.

[2] B. Levy: *Successful small and medium enterprises and their support systems: A comparative analysis of four country studies,* report prepared for World Bank Conference: "Can intervention work? The role of government in SME success", Washington, DC, February 1994.

[3] R. Rabellotti: *Footwear industrial districts in Mexico and Italy: A comparative study,* Discussion Paper No. 65 (Geneva, International Institute for Labour Studies, 1994).

[4] F. Pyke: *Small firms, technical services and inter-firm cooperation,* IILS Research Series No. 99 (Geneva, International Institute for Labour Studies, 1994).

Source: ILO: *General conditions to stimulate job creation in small and medium-sized enterprises,* Report V(I), International Labour Conference, 85th Session, Geneva 1997, pp. 76-78.

As the result of the recent trends towards democratization, employers' associations in several of these countries have also been enjoying full freedom of action. However, the difficulties encountered in the employers' organizations of the European nations in transition are frequently also found in those of the developing countries (including the fact that there is no single confederation covering all employers).

Small and medium-sized enterprises (SMEs) form the overwhelming majority everywhere, in both industrialized and other countries. The proportion even seems to be growing and many authors stress how they are contributing to job creation.[4] Production and services centres are multiplying; many establishments are "externalizing" part of their activities, which they subcontract out to independent entrepreneurs; competition is sometimes becoming stiffer even within a firm or group.

Most small enterprises do not join the representative employers' organizations despite the services that they can provide (see box 3.2), for example by relieving them of administrative tasks. Affiliation rates are still particularly low in developing countries. There is a clear divergence, not to say conflict of interests between the major firms and the others. Even in industrialized countries many SMEs balk at having to follow rules which are accepted at the sectoral or national level. They sometimes very openly voice their doubts as to the ability of the employers' confederations to reflect their specific problems. Often they have their own groupings which may belong to the general employers' organizations (Belgium, Ireland, the Netherlands, Spain), but not necessarily (France, Italy). The associations of micro-entrepreneurs that one finds in developing countries (Argentina, Brazil, Peru and India too) generally lack organic links with the other employers' organizations.

At the other end of the spectrum, the biggest undertakings are also inclined to go it alone and to opt for bargaining at the enterprise level. The tension apparent in German employers' circles and in the BDA (following IBM's withdrawal from Gesamtmetall) is a typical symptom of this trend. Enterprises are particularly tempted by this approach when they cover several sectors. Firms which work in networks encounter specific obstacles that make it difficult for them to take part in sectoral or intersectoral negotiations, with which employers' organizations dealing with labour issues which are mainly concerned.

The membership of some employer associations is dwindling, but there is too little information on the subject to generalize. That said, the history of enterprises and their representative associations have always been marked, where labour issues are concerned, by tension between two opposing currents of opinion. The first, which is very much apparent in Canada and the United States, for example, advocates the widest possible freedom for employers themselves to organize industrial relations within their own firms. The second is in favour of regulating conditions of employment, and even other conditions of production, at a higher level (sector, region, even the whole country). The objective here is to avoid unbridled competition, which is often to everybody's disadvantage, and to ensure the kind of stability and forward-looking management that is necessary for long-term investment and, hopefully, training. This is manifestly the approach favoured by European employers. The most delicate issue is of course determining what might be acceptable for all enterprises, from the most competitive to the least.

In Malaysia and Singapore, too, power is still essentially in the hands of individual enterprises, particularly as far as collective bargaining is concerned. Some observers[5] consider that one of the reasons for this is the multiplicity of firms of different national origin. Still, among other activities, the National Federation of Singapore Employers runs courses in collective bargaining and provides technical assistance for its members.

In the current context of fiercer competition though, employers everywhere are very much inclined to favour autonomous action especially in the export business. This would seem to be a significant factor in the change of attitude of some Swedish employers who now favour decentralized collective bargaining.[6] More generally, the adoption of directives by the European Union prohibiting agreements on prices and products also contributes to this trend, which is inevitably accompanied by a change in relations with the trade unions and the public authorities and in the collective bargaining structure: asserting their freedom, employers will opt as far as possible for discussions at the plant level.

In many employers' associations, particularly in Europe, internal relations – and internal means of action – are evolving and tending ultimately towards a new balance of power arising out of the trend toward decentralization. The centre of gravity does seem to be moving from the central interoccupational federations and confederations

– the level at which decision-making power had been concentrated – towards the sectoral organizations (as reflected, for example, by mergers in the financial and industrial sectors in Denmark in the late eighties) or regional organizations (Flemish and French-speaking, in Belgium), or even a combination of the two. Decentralization would thus seem to be limited and to be accompanied in some cases by recentralization at sectoral levels. Elsewhere, the phenomenon is more significant and more thorough, the power going essentially to the enterprises themselves, leaving the federations and confederations without any real decision-making role (United Kingdom).

The world of the enterprise is consequently very disparate. The traditional divergences of opinion amongst sectoral organizations (for example, between the metallurgical industry and the services)[7] add to the diversity, as does the continued existence of a large public sector in several countries. It certainly is not easy to find a common denominator, a common vision going beyond a few fundamental principles (such as entrepreneurial freedom, etc.) and uniform solutions to diverse concerns. But there is some degree of *rapprochement* on one point: although public enterprises sometimes retain their own representation, private sector employer structures are tending to integrate them, as is the case in Italy. The emphasis on the qualities of private management has definitely been a contributing factor here.

And yet, although employers would like to have more flexibility and, in many cases, simplified collective labour agreements (as we shall see in Germany, with the exemption clauses for undertakings in difficulty), they do not all necessarily want more competition between enterprises where wages, new technology, working time and training are concerned. Many – in Belgium, France, Germany, Italy, Spain, and even to some extent in the United Kingdom, according to a recent survey[8] – continue to think that this strategy of "going it alone" has more drawbacks than advantages and prefer bargaining to be centralized at the sectoral level and/or at the regional level.

In the Republic of Korea the Korea Employers Federation (KEF) has been officially representing employers' interests with regard to wages since 1970. The KEF is currently a central national organization which is composed of 13 regional employers' associations, 20 economic and trade associations, and 4,000 major manufacturing enterprises in the building, transport, banking and insurance sectors as well as several services industries. The KEF is the mouthpiece of organizations of all sizes, from the largest down to the smallest. Its staff and functions have been reinforced since 1987 due mainly to the need to face trade union challenges. The number of companies which are directly affiliated has thus increased by 15.9 per cent since 1987.

Since most collective bargaining takes place at the enterprise level, neither the sectoral associations nor the KEF engage in these discussions directly. The Federation proposes guidelines in this field for its member companies. However, since the Confederation of Korean Trade Unions (KCTU), which won *de facto* recognition at the beginning of 1997, has stepped up its efforts to build up an industrial trade union movement in sectors such as hospitals and the metal trades (including shipbuilding and the auto industry), the functions of the sectoral employers' associations concerned might be affected by these new developments. It is of course difficult at this stage to predict what the outcome will be.

Mention must be made of the most influential of the employer associations, the Federation of Korean Industry (FKI), which was founded in 1961. This organization covers virtually all of the big conglomerates in the country, the *chaebols*. It has a major impact not only on national economic policy but also on industrial relations, as it demonstrated during recent events connected with labour law reform. The KEF played an active role in promoting the recognition of the CKTU, whereas the FKI has been against opening up to trade union pluralism. The persons responsible for strategic planning and coordination in each *chaebol* take part in the FKI's working groups, whereas the KEF meetings at the same level are attended by the heads of personnel of the major companies; the latter carry comparatively less weight than the former.

Even if undertakings – particularly the largest ones – retain their freedom at the general level, they are evolving some more or less formal networks. Industrial relations may well be included on the agenda of the meetings of the managing directors of very large firms, or of a "business council". It is common knowledge that the managements of the major Japanese undertakings hold informal coordination meetings at the sectoral, inter-sectoral or industrial-group level in order to respond to the spring offensives *(shunto)*.[9] Going a step further, enterprises form alliances amongst themselves, establish more or less permanent interactive vertical or horizontal links. This is the case with garment manufacturers and distributors.[10] It is then in their interest to have not only one industrial and commercial strategy but also one social strategy. All this is, however, liable to weaken the traditional employers' associations, which have responded either by transforming themselves completely, for example (the New Zealand Employers' Federation has turned itself into an organization that is more for providing its members with services – training, legal advice, strategic planning – than for representing them), or by adjusting to the new context and improving the quality and relevance of their services.

More and more mergers are taking place between employers' organizations with economic objectives and those concerned with social and labour issues. In Finland, Ireland and Norway, for example, pressure from the grass roots to streamline (or even to have to pay only one subscription) has led to the unification of both types of organization. This phenomenon is observed both in the central associations and in those operating at the sectoral level. Elsewhere (Germany, Sweden, Switzerland), however, this trend has not been in evidence (or at least not as yet) for various reasons (the special nature of Switzerland's multicultural environment being no doubt one of them).

Where industrial relations are decentralizing, the importance of the traditional public relations, lobbying and representation functions of employer associations is growing in proportion. Even in the industrial relations sphere, the organizations operating at a higher level frequently retain an important role in providing advice, coordination and support.[11] Added to this are other services which they already provide or could develop in the future (see box 3.3). If a single organization deals with both economic and labour issues, the assistance it provides will cover both of these fields. As far as labour issues are concerned, assistance will relate in particular to the applicable legislation (including European law in the case of the European Union), education and training, wages and other conditions of employment (including occupational safety and health), recruitment, and the social consequences of planned privatization moves.[12] The organization can still offer opportunities for supranational, regional and international cooperation without having to establish the more formal structures which entrepreneurs do not always want. However, more than ever, it must justify its existence by the quality of the services offered otherwise members are likely to be disenchanted and withdraw their affiliation.

Enterprises and their associations are also becoming increasingly involved in social integration or reintegration. Some participate along with worker representatives in joint committees for improving vocational skills; this is the case in Canada's steel sector, for instance, where a programme has been launched for retraining the victims of redundancy. National and international groupings of entrepreneurs such as the *Union internationale chrétienne des dirigeants d'entreprise* (UNIAPAC) are furthermore endeavouring to take measures to promote employment and combat social exclusion.[13] The same obviously applies to the firms themselves, particularly the large ones.

One further point: we have mentioned the current trend in some trade unions to form alliances with other social organizations with a view to achieving common objectives. Without drawing any unwarranted parallel, it could be noted that undertakings also entertain relations with other groups. Apart from the links with other professionals in their particular branch, with suppliers and clients, and apart from the development of networking, there is fairly intensive contact with shareholders, depending on the individual undertaking, the country (it would seem to be more frequent in Anglo-Saxon countries) and the circumstances. Similarly, relations with the local, regional or national authorities and personalities are often a significant feature of their promotional activities. Moreover, employers' organizations have themselves established links with community groups (women, young people, educational institutions). The Employers' Federation in New Zealand, for example, has set up actual partnerships with schools and training centres to organize in-company training courses for students. All this inevitably influences how industrial relations are conducted – though it is easier to state the fact than to measure its impact.

What is more, employers' associations are anxious to coordinate their action at the supranational level and have thus set up structures at that level. The most extensive of these is beyond any doubt the International Organization of Employers (IOE),

---

Box 3.3. Organizational and functional complexity

Members of employers' organizations are major companies and small individual enterprises. By nature, employers' organizations are alliances of competitors and commercial decision-making structures. This explains to a large extent why employers' organizations are usually very complex. They operate at local, regional, national and international levels, and may be concerned specifically with an industry or a sector. They can be highly centralized, as in Scandinavia until recently or be more similar to loose federations, as in the United States and Australia. Their ultimate structure is often the result of a delicate balance between partly overlapping and partly competitive aims.

The market economy and free enterprise are the indispensable framework within which employers' organizations take shape and evolve. This has been clearly demonstrated in Central and Eastern Europe, where the demise of the centrally planned and controlled economies has been a powerful stimulus to the spontaneous creation and growth of new but already active employers' organizations.

Elsewhere, too, with today's greater emphasis on privatization and the market economy, countries with traditionally highly centralized economies or state control of industrial relations have seen the emergence of increasingly assertive employers' organizations. In others, long marked by oligarchic structures and highly protected markets, employers' organizations are undergoing an agonizing reappraisal of their structures and policies.

Historically, many employers' organizations were initially established in response to pressure on businesses from the trade unions to come to the bargaining table. At the national level, experience until recently has shown that the creation of umbrella bodies for broad representational, political and legislative purposes lagged behind the rise of national trade union centres by roughly ten to 20 years.

No less complex than the structures are the functions of employers' organizations, but there tend to be three main functions common to all: defence of the enterprise and its image and, more generally, of the market economy; representation of the enterprise in industrial relations; and provision of services to the members. As a rule, representation and service functions are conditioned by the level at which negotiations with trade unions take place. If they occur at the industry or national instead of just the plant level, the organizational structure of an employers' organization automatically becomes more elaborate.

Source: ILO: *World Labour Report 1994* (Geneva, 1994), pp. 43-44.

---

whose headquarters are in Geneva and which currently groups together national confederations from more than 100 countries. Its main activity consists of presenting employers' views on social problems before the ILO's deliberative bodies, where it coordinates the positions of employers on standard-setting policy, the social dimension of international trade, and any other issue under debate.

The Union of Industrial and Employers' Confederations of Europe (UNICE), for its part, organizes the employers' contribution to the ongoing European social dialogue. There is currently some conjecture as to the likelihood of similar institutions evolving within the other regional groups, in South-East Asia (with ASEAN) or in North America (with NAFTA, the free trade agreement concluded between Canada, the United States and Mexico). An industrial council and a council of chambers of commerce have already been set up within the framework of the common market of the southern cone of Latin America (MERCOSUR).

Notes

[1] ILO: *Conclusions of the International Round Table on the New Role of Employers' Organizations in Countries with Economies in Transition* (Geneva, 29-31 May 1995), doc. GB.264/LILS/10 (Geneva, 1995), appendix.

[2] A. Etukudo: "Reflections on the role of African employers' organizations in tripartism and social dialogue", in *International Labour Review* (Geneva, ILO), Vol. 134, No. 1, 1995, p. 53.

[3] Etukudo, op. cit., pp. 51 ff.

[4] ILO: *General conditions to stimulate job creation in small and medium-sized enterprises,* Report V(I), International Labour Conference, 85th Session, Geneva, 1997, pp. 9 ff.

[5] S.B. Chew and R. Chew: *Employment driven industrial relations regimes: The Singapore experience* (Aldershot, Avebury, 1995), pp. 84-106.

[6] Ch. Berggren: "Sweden: A fragile but still innovative system", in E.M. Davis and R.D. Lansbury (eds.): *Managing together: Consultation and participation in the workplace* (Melbourne, Longman, 1995), p. 198.

[7] J. Bunel: "France: les dilemmes de l'action patronale", in *Problèmes économiques* (Paris, La documentation française), No. 2.482, 21 Aug. 1996, pp. 9-17.

[8] *European Industrial Relations Review* (London, Eclipse), No. 250, Nov. 1994, pp. 18 ff.

[9] M. Sako: "Shunto. The role of employer and union coordination at the industry and intersectoral levels", in M. Sako and H. Sato (eds.): *Japanese labour and management in transition: Diversity, flexibility and participation* (London, Routledge, 1997).

[10] F. Palpacuer: *Stratégies compétitives, gestion des compétences et organisations en réseaux: étude du cas de l'industrie new-yorkaise de l'habillement,* unpublished thesis, University of Montpellier-I, Company Management and Law Faculty, Nov. 1966, Ch. 1; P. Doeringer et al.: *Industrial relations and production channels in apparel: A comparative study of labor, management and industry,* document prepared for the ILO (1997).

[11] S.R. de Silva: *Employers' organizations in Asia in the twenty-first century* (Geneva, ILO, 1996), pp. 29-39.

[12] J.-J. Oechslin: "Employers' organizations", in R. Blanpain (eds.): *Comparative labour law and industrial relations in industrialized market economies* (Deventer, Kluwer, 1993), pp. 37 ff.

[13] UNIAPAC: "Engagement entrepreneurial contre le chômage", in *Cahiers socio-économiques,* No. 8 (Brussels, 1996).

4 The new features of production and industrial relations

Economic globalization and technological innovation appear to have considerably reduced the manoeuvrability of States. At the same time, as we have just seen, there has been a drop in union density – and employers' organizations are not without their difficulties either. The usefulness of collective bargaining is being challenged. As a result of this decline, industrial relations no longer seem able to function properly – income disparities are growing and poverty, unemployment and underemployment are leading to social exclusion.[1]

Globalization and technological change are clearly proving disruptive for national industrial relations' systems and national redeployment and growth support policies. This can lead to resistance to the process of economic openness in spite of its associated gains. For this reason, the extent of the loss of state autonomy and its implications require careful examination. We will address this issue in the first part of the chapter.

The unquestionable decline in national policy autonomy, while still leaving a certain manoeuvrability, is prompting States increasingly to transfer to enterprises functions previously largely performed at the national level, giving rise to a corresponding increase in enterprise autonomy. But what exactly does this autonomy consist of, and is there any chance of reaching a "social compromise" at this level which would reconcile labour and capital interests? These questions will be answered in the second part of the chapter.

Opening national borders: What effects for industrial relations?

Interdependence and autonomy of national policies

As widespread inequality and unemployment go hand in hand with economic interdependence, it is no surprise that in some people globalization has aroused considerable mistrust which is reflected, in public debates, by doubts as to its advantages and wariness as to its cost. The truth is that we still face many unknowns. Differing and sometimes contradictory views can contain elements of truth. Some aspects do seem clear, however, in particular the fact that for countries, enterprises and individuals alike, economic openness means adjusting to change. It is not unusual for such adjustments, regardless of their benefits, to involve certain costs. What are these adjustment costs at the national level and what are their causes?

First, as pointed out in Chapter 1, in contrast to the immobility of States and peoples, capital has become extremely mobile – at least in theory. This mobility may appear to be a rather abstract concept; but, as we shall see, its implications for industrial relations are both multiple and direct. The reason for this is that capital mobility affects behaviour. Some indications give the impression that, because it changes attitudes, the mere possibility of transferring capital is a more potent influence on behaviour than actual transfers themselves.

Before the advent of globalization there were a number of formerly stable relationships which many now believe are coming unstuck. One sign of this is that capital mobility is placing new constraints on the Keynesian inspired system which came into being after the Second World War. This, however, is simply one effect of capital mobility. It is also true that the liberalization of investment regimes and the ability of firms to raise and spend money anywhere in the world increase the locational freedom of firms and thereby shift the balance of power away from labour to capital. This same freedom could shift the balance of power to the mobile factor – capital – and away from the tax and regulatory authority of the State.

Capital mobility and state immobility

Today capital is mobile in an interdependent world. States, for which it is a source of revenue and an object of regulation, are enclosed within their borders. This situation provides an incentive for them to lighten the tax and regulatory burden faced by firms within their borders. In short, "competitive detaxation" and "competitive deregulation" are plausible policies in a world of mobile capital. But taxes and regulations form part of the overall social pact that the industrial relations actors have a hand in shaping. If both lose their importance, the burden of adjustment could be felt more by the workers themselves.

Two other factors also apply here. First, locational choices are increasing – consider the proliferation of export processing zones (EPZs) – which can be a compelling reason for States to engage in competitive underbidding. Second, if governments can no longer engage in counter-cyclical spending, they become even more reliant upon firms for job creation and perhaps more reluctant to tax or regulate the sources of job creation.

This having been said, some doubts exist as to whether taxes or regulations strongly influence business location decisions. For example, since tax jurisdictions vary on a state-by-state basis in the integrated market of the United States, this should afford a natural test ground for the theory that differences in taxation matter in firm location. Despite highly publicized tax concessions given to such companies as Toyota, however, one study finds that locational choice seems little affected by differences in state tax regimes. It is possible that taxes fund services that are appreciated by enterprises – and thus could even be a reason for business location.[2]

Economic integration in Europe means that European Union firms no longer need to serve the local market from behind nationally fragmented tax, tariff and regulatory boundaries, but now have far greater locational choice from which to serve the European market. But there is little evidence of massive relocation in the European Union.

A look at foreign direct investment also inspires a certain scepticism as to the role to be played by tax and regulatory policies in investment decisions. First, while the world stock of such investments doubled in real terms between 1985 and 1990, a substantial share of new investment was destined for Europe in anticipation of economic and monetary union.

Second, as an investment destination for foreign capital, Germany, a country where production costs can be said to be high, has slipped in its European Union ranking (from the point of view of total volume of investment), but only from second place in 1980, to third place in 1994.[3] Second place was taken not by Greece or Portugal, countries where costs are low, but by France, a medium- to high-cost country – and one which does not score at the bottom of the league either in terms of corporation taxation, payroll taxes or labour market regulation.

Third, it is true that the outflow of German capital has markedly increased in the 1990s. But it was exceeded by France, the United Kingdom, Japan and the United States. The total level of German outward investment, as a share of its GDP, is about average, less than one would expect for a country of its size and wealth.[4]

Fourth, there is no obvious inverse relationship between the level of labour costs in the European Union and the volume of investment attracted from abroad. Foreign investment has grown throughout the European Union since 1980. It rose considerably (in total volume) between 1980 and 1994 in relatively high-cost, high-regulation countries such as Belgium, France, Finland and Sweden.[5] This is not surprising, as labour costs are rarely the sole criterion in the locational choices of multinational firms.

Fifth, it is not certain that high taxes on capital discourage savings and investment. European investment rates compare favourably with those of the United States, and have done so since the 1960s. European savings rates, meanwhile, are far higher than those seen in the United States. Finally, the capital share of national income in Europe has actually increased, from 31 per cent in the 1970s to the current level of 38 per cent.[6]

In spite of all these observations, there would appear to be no consensus on these issues. This is not surprising. The setting up of a business or the opening of a plant is a long-term investment decision. One should not expect to see the theoretical mobility of capital result in the massive uprooting of established business. Nevertheless, the relative immobility of existing capital says nothing about future location decisions. Although the evidence presented above suggests that there are other, more important criteria in a firm's location decision than taxation rates, it is still possible that taxation and regulation could be of rising importance in location decisions. To take an example, a study shows that in the United States the differences in taxation rates do influence American enterprises in their decisions to invest in one state or another.[7] Another study gives more weight to the idea that the location of recent investments by Japanese and European firms in the United States have been in states characterized by their low levels of unionization and that many of them have been accompanied by major tax concessions.[8] Firms intending to set up foreign affiliates may become more responsive to taxation and regulatory problems in the future, especially when market integration further broadens their locational possibilities.

Although foreign investment in Europe does not entirely obey this logic, it is clear that Spain and the United Kingdom are relatively attractive to investors – and it cannot be ruled out that labour costs and other features of their tax or regulatory regimes have a part to play in this regard. Spain, which ranked seventh in the list of European countries in terms of total inward foreign investment in 1980, had climbed to fourth position, just behind Germany, by 1994.[9] There are certainly prima facie grounds for assuming that some diversion of foreign investment to lower cost locations within the European Union has occurred. Finally, investment inflows into Germany have been weak. At least one study finds that investors do respond to high nominal wage costs, and Germany's are the highest.[10]

In a related vein, one study finds that the location decisions of United States multinational enterprises in Europe are sensitive to labour-market regulation. They avoid setting up affiliates in locations where such regulation would restrict their organizational freedom, such as stringent provisions on dismissals or the existence of collective bargaining frameworks beyond the level of the enterprise. In a subsequent study, the same author finds that the locational choices of multinational enterprises from the United States and other countries are sensitive to taxation rates in locations where they envisage establishing affiliates.[11]

In any case, enterprise behaviour is only half the picture. How governments behave is an even more decisive factor. And States are not immune to the implications of capital mobility. As figure 4.1 shows, corporate taxation burdens have been lightened in the majority of OECD countries since 1990. The OECD, concerned by the "revenue consequences of tax competition", has recently established a task force to look into the matter as it recognizes that capital mobility "opens up the risk of competitive bidding between countries for mobile business".[12] This is not just a risk, and lively competition should be expected, in the form of tax and regulatory concessions, from capital-poor countries seeking to attract investment by offering the most favourable conditions.

Payroll taxes have also been the subject of considerable debate. In theory, and in accordance with general observations, payroll taxes do not usually constitute a

Figure 4.1. **Basic rates of central government corporate income tax (%)**

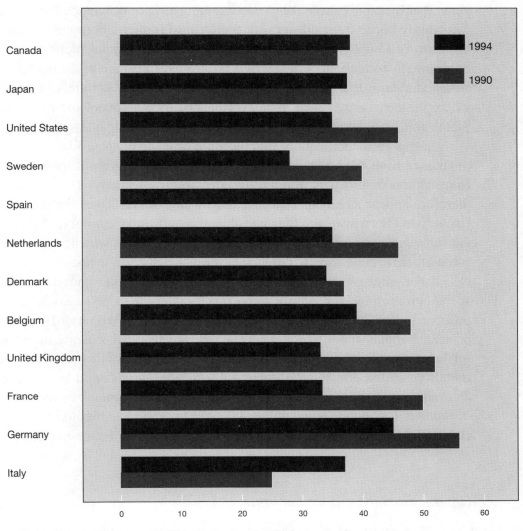

Source: D. Carey, J. C. Chouraqui et R. P. Hageman: *The future of capital income taxation in a liberalized financial environment,* Working Paper No. 126 (Paris, OECD, 1993).

major barrier to job creation since non-wage costs are, to some extent at least, paid for by employees in lower wages. Consequently, if there is an argument for cutting payroll taxes, it is primarily for cases in which they are "regressive" – that is where they account for a disproportionate share of the wage bill at the lower income levels and where minimum wages or negotiated wage floors limit downward wage adjustments.[13] This view of payroll taxes seems to fit a closed economy, not one where capital is mobile. Here too, the fact that payroll taxes might act as a locational disincentive also poses a problem.

Payroll taxes are exposed to downward pressure as a result of the competition generated by capital mobility. When capital was less mobile the cost of payroll taxes was jointly borne by employers (in the form of higher labour costs) and workers (in the form of lower wages). The main implication of capital mobility is that it is the immobile factor, labour, which will pick up a greater share of the tax bill. The level of labour standards that payroll taxes help to finance could certainly be maintained, but, where these standards used to be co-financed by employers and employees (and the State), it is now the employee who would have to pay the bill.[14]

It appears, incidentally, that there are limits to the payroll taxes that can be used to finance high labour standards,[15] since the burden, even in the situation resulting from capital mobility, is never fully borne by the workers. These payroll taxes can therefore appear as labour cost increases which would lower the competitiveness of firms. Two alternatives are thus possible: the outflow of capital (a disincentive to foreign inward investment) or a reduction in payroll taxes which, if not offset through some other revenue source, could also mean a reduction in social protection.

For some observers, the main implication of capital mobility is to undermine social compromise, the "implicit contract" – a contract shaped essentially by national postwar industrial relations systems. Globalization "makes it difficult to sustain the postwar bargain under which workers' pay and benefits steadily improved in return for labour peace and loyalty".[16] Capital's potential mobility may exceed its actual mobility, but the effects are the same. Firms are less able and less willing to sustain their share of financing the welfare State than when capital was more immobile and economies less open. This applies not only to who pays the non-wage cost bill, but also to the full scope of collective bargaining, to which discussion now turns.

Capital mobility and labour immobility

The reality of capital mobility enhances the credibility of threats to exercise that mobility. As Werner Stumpfe, head of Gesamtmetall, Germany's largest employers' federation for the engineering and electrical sectors, remarked: "In the old days, employers asked themselves: 'How bad is this wage agreement for me?' Today they say, 'I don't care about the agreement any more, because I have four or five excellent exit routes. I may simply relocate 10,000 jobs to the Czech Republic. Or I may outsource'."[17] Exit routes really do exist, and they may well increase in significance in years to come, even if the evidence to date suggests that outbound exit routes can scarcely be described as crowded. On the other hand, it may matter less whether mobility is acted upon; it is the exit potential that produces real outcomes in collective bargaining.

There is substantial theoretical support for the proposition that potential capital mobility is one factor inducing change in bargaining behaviour and outcomes. "Union wage premia are driven down by the openness of the world financial system and the ability of capital to move offshore really does pose limits on the wage-setting or wage-bargaining strategies of trade unions which are restrained in their wage demands by the higher elasticity of labour demand."[18] The demand for labour was less elastic – that is to say, less sensitive to its cost – when capital, like labour, was immobile. With greater locational choice, the cost of labour is back on the table; wages, once taken out of competition, are now back in the competitive sphere. For highly skilled, specialized labour, this is less of a problem. Low-skilled labour, however, becomes readily available to enterprises once they have a certain degree of locational freedom.

Studies on collective bargaining systems and their macroeconomic effects demonstrate the point. A relationship has been observed between these effects – on wages, prices and employment – and the degree of centralization or coordination of collective bargaining.[19] In the period of stagflation arising from the first oil supply shock, the empirical observation was that the most centralized (national level) and most decentralized (enterprise level) bargaining structures appeared to produce the best macroeconomic outcomes. Where industry-level bargaining prevailed, however, inflation and unemployment results scored the worst.

The explanation for this trend was that in the most decentralized systems, market competition obliged the unions to act with a certain degree of restraint, an approach they were also led to take in the very centralized systems, due to the need to anticipate the consequences of their claims on their members (such consequences being "internalized"). Only in an intermediary situation, where industry-level bargaining prevailed, was there less cause for concern (the consequences of the unions' demands became an "external" risk, essentially transferred to the rest of the economy). The result of these "middle" systems was higher wage increases, a factor in inflation and unemployment. But these outcomes and the explanations assigned to them assumed a relatively closed economy. With trade liberalization and capital mobility, even industry-level arrangements would have to internalize the consequences of excessive wage increases.[20]

Capital mobility destabilizes the sheltered structure of wages that national industrial relations systems produced when market competition was largely a national matter. A recent study shows that the liberalization of the financial system increases income inequality. Capital mobility rewards very qualified workers, since mobile capital seeks them out and bids up their wages, but the contrary is true for the less skilled, who used to be protected from wage competition.[21]

Capital mobility, which makes firms more sensitive to labour costs – although, as we have seen, it is not the only factor involved – can also make them more sensitive to union organizing campaigns. One recent study examined employer strategies in over 600 United States establishments. In 50 per cent of cases, the employer used the threat of closure to oppose the unions wishing to represent the staff (and, in 10 per cent of cases, they threatened to transfer production to Mexico); in 12 per cent of cases where the trade union won the election actual closure did occur. Unions tended to fare poorly in these bargaining rights elections, leading the authors to conclude that the credibility of the mobility option effectively swayed voter opinion against the desire for representation.[22]

Exit options may induce important behavioural changes in the exercise of freedom of association or in the industrial relations climate. Capital mobility can produce similar effects in countries seeking at all costs to attract capital. Examples abound and this could explain some of the difficulties that freedom of association often encounters in export processing zones.

With the inflow of Japanese investments into the United Kingdom in the 1980s, a form of pre-investment bargaining occurred which had the effect of transforming traditional industrial relations practices. While in the traditional British system the workers were represented at the enterprise level by several unions, the Japanese firms negotiated single-union recognition arrangements and no-strike clauses in collective bargaining agreements. This situation initially triggered inter-union rivalry as individual unions competed against each other to obtain recognition rights. Mutually destructive disputes within the Trades Union Congress (TUC) ultimately resulted in inter-union agreement on the procedure to adopt in such cases.[23]

Similar "entrance option" effects of capital mobility are in evidence in the car industry in Latin America in which foreign car manufacturers' locational decisions have been made contingent on prior trade union assent to conditions demanded by firms. This is true for over 50 per cent of the cases shown in box 7.1 (Chapter 7).

Trade competition and capital mobility have the effect of dividing workers at the national level. Demand for the most highly skilled (who, in any case, tend to be the most highly mobile), may be less sensitive to their earnings. The wages of the less skilled, however, are bid downward as a result of market forces, an effect which is further reinforced when collective agreements provide less protection.[24] It could be that "trade impinges on domestic society in ways that can conflict with long-standing social contracts to protect citizens from the relentlessness of the free market".[25]

The discussion of these three shifts in the balance of power suggests that capital is less mobile than its theoretical potential. But it is the potential for speculators to trigger a run on the currency that disciplines monetary and fiscal policies. It is the potential for firms to disinvest that triggers favourable tax and regulatory treatment. It is the potential for firms to relocate or outsource that dampens wage bargaining or even union organization. In short, capital may well be less mobile than its potential, but it is the potential for mobility that determines real outcomes, and that is a destabilizing factor for industrial relations systems.

In some ways, the outcomes described above are paradoxical. In fact, as countries open their borders, their governments appear to contract – although, in the past, the opposite tended to be true; government size increased as the economy became more open. In a similar vein, the trade unions appear to be affected by globalization, while traditionally they have not been opposed to the expansion of the international economy. We will discuss these two issues in more detail in the following section.

A certain degree of labour market regulation promotes economic openness

A popular view of globalization has tended to equate the process with the triumph of free markets. It is often perceived as reflecting the supremacy of liberal thinking – as seen since the end of the 1970s and more dramatically since the fall of the Berlin wall – over more regulated or managed approaches to the economy. There is some truth in this view. The opening of borders and deregulation have been the concomitant policy choices which have contributed most to the growth of world markets. As such, the free-market assumptions that underlie globalization are real. Does this mean that this recognition of the benefits of openness reserves little space for institutions that intervene in the market, such as trade unions, collective bargaining and governments, and that they only have a diminished role to play in an open world economy? This is doubtful.

A recent study using data relating to over 100 countries finds a strong, positive correlation between countries' exposure to trade and the level of government spending (measured as government consumption)[26] (figure 4.2). Countries more open to trade may be exposed to greater external risk. Government spending could thus play a role in mitigating that risk by compensating those negatively affected by exposure to trade. Indeed, in the industrialized countries, one function of the welfare State has been to compensate workers through increased welfare protection for the risks inherent in greater economic exposure. In a world of growing external risk, this role is increasingly important. "With rising competition and job insecurity, workers will rely more on state resources for unemployment insurance, education and training in the coming years. In the absence of these government policies and programs, political support for globalization would erode."[27] This is certainly the context framing national debate and negotiation in many European countries.

Evidence for the same countries confirms the relationship between economic openness and welfare State expenditure. Both rising trade and capital mobility were "generally associated with greater spending on income transfer programmes" over the years 1966-90.[28] Figure 4.3, relating to OECD countries, compares the level of economic openness (the trade ratio as a percentage of GDP) with the level of social transfer payments (also as a percentage of GDP), and the association is both clear and positive. In an era in which the efficiency of large governments has been called into question in many countries, it is useful to recall the importance of government spending in sustaining a climate of openness to trade. "Economists tend to think of governments and markets as substitutes. Most types of government intervention [...] are viewed as inimical to the operation of markets. The expansion of markets, on the

Figure 4.2. **Partial relation between openness and government consumption in 115 countries**

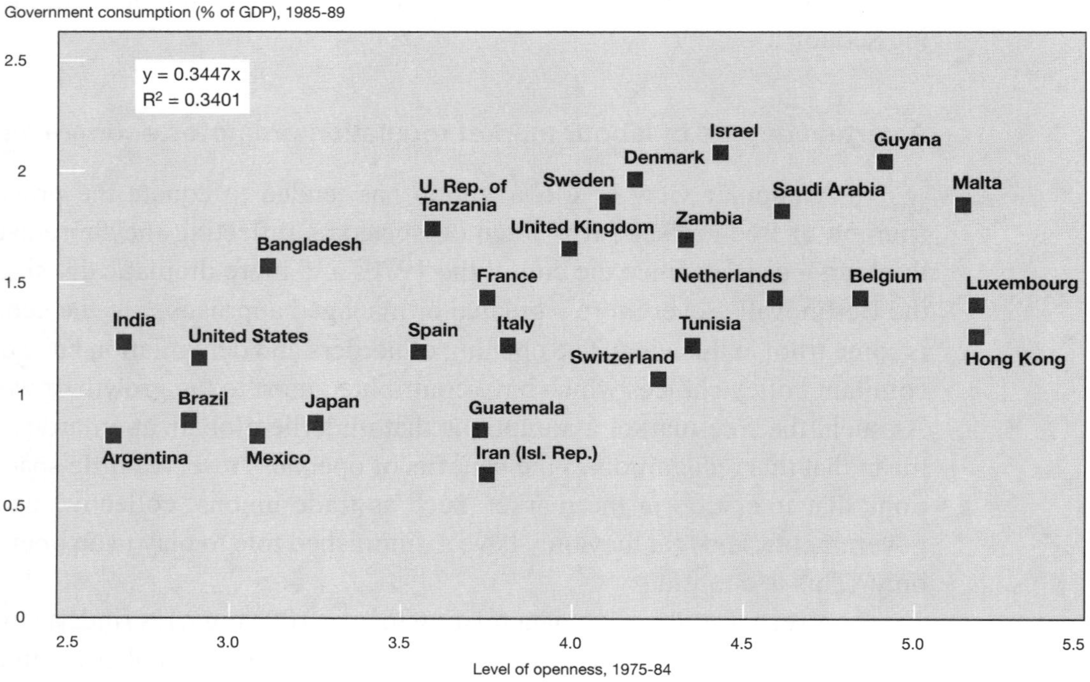

Government consumption (% of GDP), 1985-89

Note: Logarithmic scale.

Source: D. Rodrik: *Has globalization gone too far?* (Washington, DC, Institute for International Economics, 1997).

other hand, is perceived as undercutting the effectiveness of governmental action, both in macroeconomic and microeconomic areas. [But] contrary to what most economists would expect, the scope of government has been larger, not smaller, in economies taking greater advantage of world markets. Indeed, governments have expanded fastest in the most open economies [...] Scaling governments down – which is the trend of the 1990s – may actually harm the prospects of maintaining free trade on a global scale. Globalization may well require big, not small government."[29]

Of course, not everything that government does is what it ought to do. The world abounds with examples of inefficient government sectors and public-sector companies that misallocate resources and are a brake on growth.[30] In this case the government does not contribute to economic performance. But just as there is no necessary link between public ownership and inefficiency, so too, as one recent study shows, is there no inverse relationship between large government and economic performance. It is the quality of interventions that matters. Some government interventions can hamper economic performance, but size alone would not appear to be the issue.[31] Other recent evidence confirms the same for OECD countries.[32]

A further point to have emerged is that, historically, trade unions have not gen-

Figure 4.3. **Level of openness and welfare transfers as a percentage of GDP in 1993**

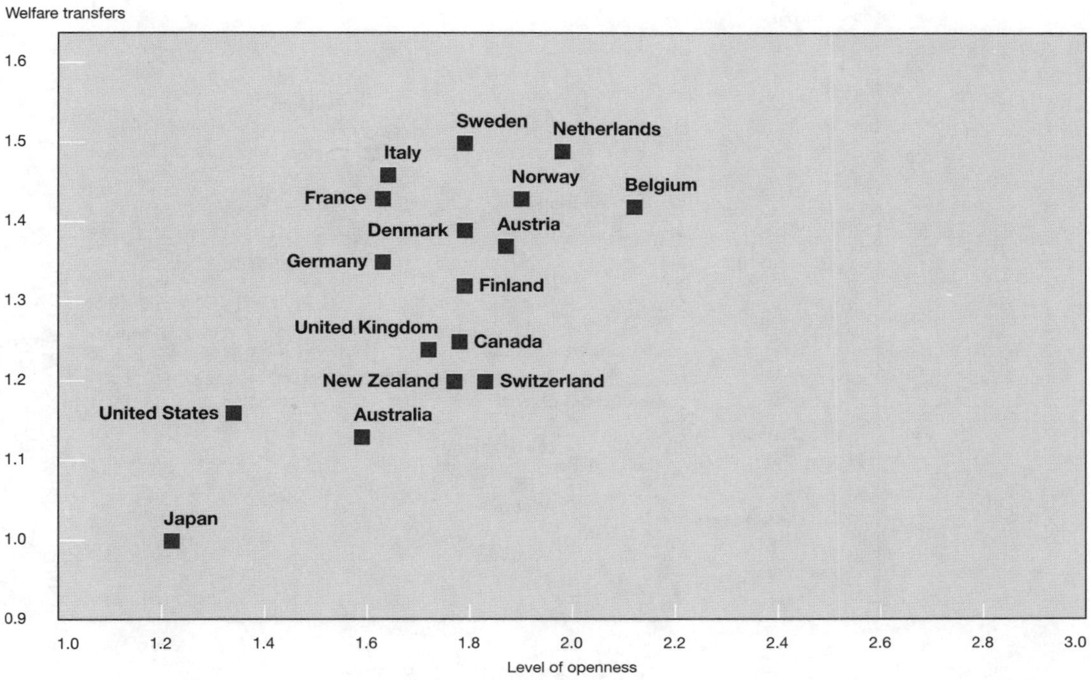

Welfare transfers

Note: Logarithmic scale.

Sources: IMF: *International trade statistics yearbook* (Washington, DC, 1996); World Bank: *World Development Report 1995* (Washington, DC, 1995).

erally been agents of protectionism or obstruction of the expanding international economy, but have instead been strongly and positively associated with economic openness, as demonstrated in a study carried out at the end of the 1970s.[33] Figure 4.4 shows this still to be true – it shows a clear relationship between the strength of the national trade union movement and the degree of economic openness to trade. It may be thought that this relationship (were one to be wary, given that small countries tend to be more densely organized than large ones and also tend to be more open to trade) is no mere coincidence since there also appears to be a relationship between trade unions and government spending.

Social transfer payment programmes seem to be more strongly developed in countries with weaker right-wing parties and larger trade union movements.[34] Figure 4.5 gives the impression, for a broad set of countries, of a relationship between trade union density and the volume of these transfer payments. The demand for welfare protection could arise from the greater economic insecurity in those countries exposed to greater external trade risks. Trade unions and their political allies, traditional advocates of welfare spending, have thus contributed to influencing government action and spending in a manner conducive to sustaining openness to trade.

Figure 4.4. **Union density and level of economic openness in 1993**

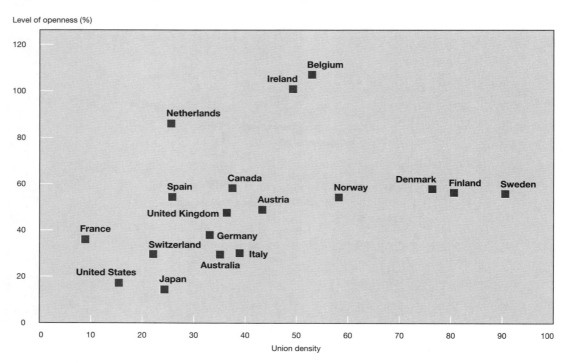

Sources: J. Visser: *Unionization trends revisited* (Amsterdam, CESAR, University of Amsterdam, 1996); IMF: *International financial statistics yearbook* (Washington, DC, 1996).

The trade unions contribute to a more even distribution of economic gains, and the question that must be asked is what would happen to trade expansion in the absence of the transfer payments that have served the function of redistributing the gains and losses which go along with external exposure. It is clear that both economic openness – and globalization in general – are something more than the spontaneous and anonymous interplay of market forces; they seem strongly rooted in national policy and may equally strongly require national political action for their continued sustenance. Deregulation and liberalization have been required for market expansion. But the government must also address any negative effects. If openness is good for growth and employment, then so is government spending. However, in this area the government's role not only requires the resources but also the political will to raise and spend these resources. And this is not evident in the current economic environment.

In any case, whatever the opinions on government size may be, the empirical record for the OECD shows a relative stability in the level of government spending as a share of GDP.[35] But the relative stability of government spending can mask significant changes in the functions of government. "In 1979 real general government spending in the UK accounted for 42.5 per cent of GDP, almost exactly the same as in

Figure 4.5.   **Union density and welfare transfers as a percentage of GDP in 1993**

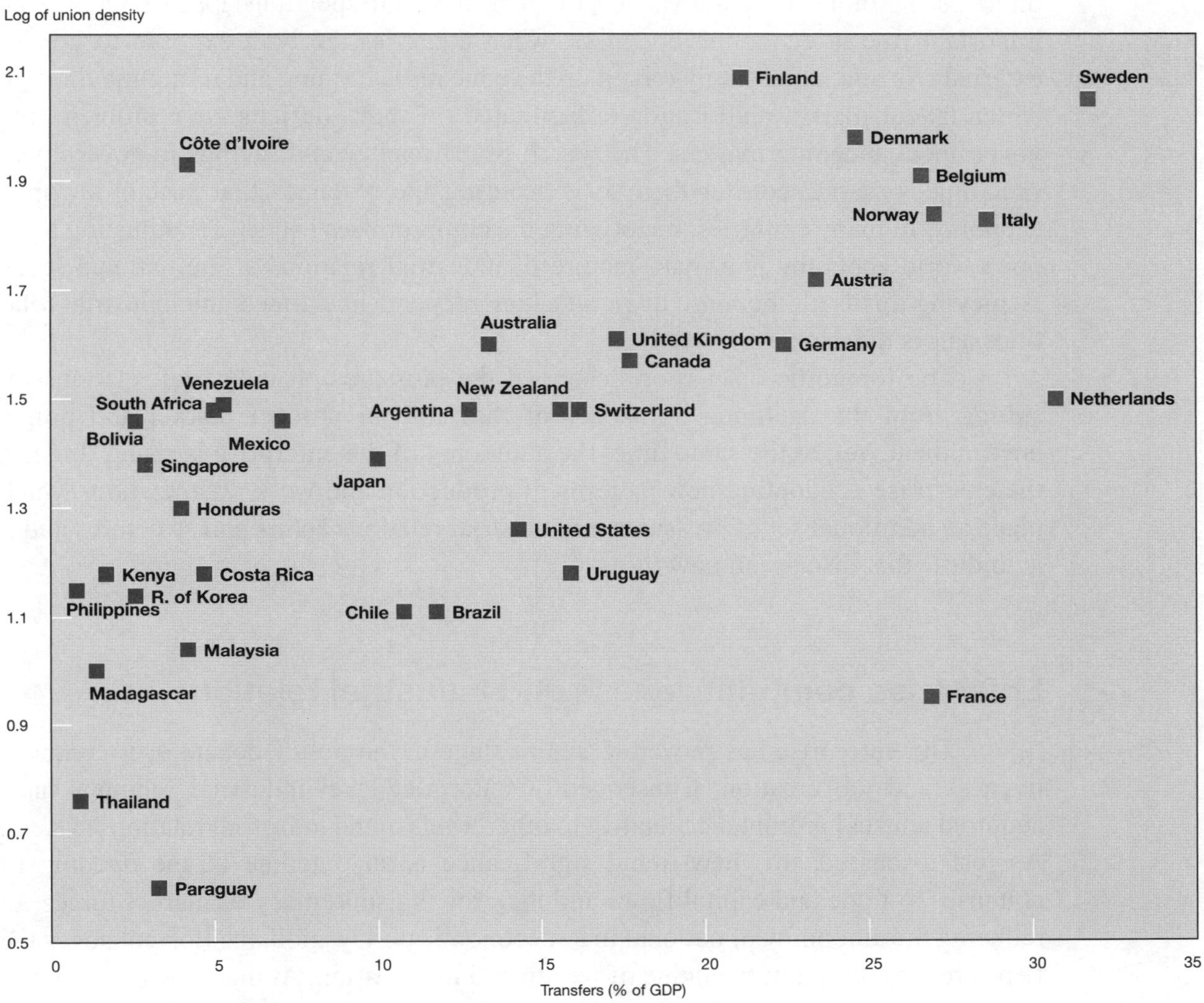

Log of union density

Sources: World Bank: *World Development Report 1995* (Washington, DC, 1995); S. Kuruwilla and C.S. Venkata Ratnam: "Economic development and industrial relations: The case of South and Southeast Asia", in *Industrial Relations Journal* (Oxford, United Kingdom, and Cambridge, United States, Blackwell Publishers), Vol. 27, No. 1, 1996; M. Rama: "Do labour market policies and institutions matter? The adjustment experience in Latin America and the Caribbean", in *Labour* (Rome, Fondazione Giacomo Brodolini, E and L Publications), special issue, 1995.

1995-96. But clearly the State then had a very different impact on the economy. Indeed, large chunks of industry were in the public sector. Roughly 30 per cent of the employed workforce was working for either central or local government or for a state-owned corporation, compared to about 16 per cent today."[36]

As we have already said, the size of government spending would appear to be less an issue than the quality and direction of that spending. The material fact is that governments everywhere are under pressure to shrink and often face substantial public budget deficits. If government size is no particular handicap, budget deficits can be;

they crowd out private-sector investment and thus slow job creation. Cutting expenditure is therefore a well-advanced trend. But social spending appears to play an important role in economic openness, when countries are both exposed to greater external risk and increasingly reliant on the education, training and retraining through which labour market reallocation is facilitated. In short, deficits are a problem, but government spending matters. The search for efficiency and savings in government spending is warranted, but then so is securing the revenues that sustain an open economy. In many countries, negotiating the compromises needed for adjusting to an open world economy is a main feature of industrial relations at the national level. Achieving this is all the more difficult as interdependence affects the industrial relations actors themselves.

The foregoing discussion described the pressures on industrial relations resulting from the declining autonomy of the national product market and policy environment. Yet, at the same time, the autonomy of the enterprise is rising. Indeed, the enterprise is adopting new patterns of production and work organization, which place an additional set of pressures on industrial relations actors and structures and it is to these that discussion now turns.

Enterprise competitiveness and industrial relations

The enterprise has moved to centre stage in the policy debate over competitiveness and job creation. Consequently, enterprise-level industrial relations have acquired unusual prominence relative to other levels of the industrial relations system. As just discussed, this new-found significance is an outcome of the opening of countries to trade and capital flows and the growing supremacy of market forces. In reducing the autonomy of national macroeconomic policy, globalization enhances the firm's role as the primary engine of wealth and job creation. At the same time, globalization and market forces expose the firm to heightened competition. They erode the shelter in which firms used to operate and make flexibility at the enterprise level essential for responding to rapid product market changes. Enterprises have responded by transforming how they organize work and production. In the process, industrial relations structures have come under pressure to adapt.

Is the autonomy of the enterprise rising or declining?

In the new competitive context of the enterprise, globalization naturally plays a major role. It shapes enterprise strategies and, in so doing, induces changes in how work and production are organized. These changes derive in part from the manner in which enterprises are responding to rising autonomy. Indeed, by reducing national autonomy, globalization has increased the autonomy of the enterprise, which was formerly sheltered by national borders and national institutions but is now open to greater external pressures.

The increased autonomy of the enterprise induces a parallel need for greater enterprise flexibility. Conversely, greater enterprise flexibility is also likely to increase the autonomy of the enterprise. The need for flexibility and the form it takes are partially determined by the specific product market conditions facing the enterprise.

How do enterprises gain the flexibility that their greater exposure to competition requires? One way is through changes in the organization of work. As we shall see later in the text, there is a clear trend in the workplace away from fragmented, narrowly defined tasks, toward multiskilled, interdependent work. This trend is borne out by the new emphasis that firms are placing on human resources and their management. The diffusion of work organization and human resource management innovations – which is very uneven not only across countries but also types of enterprises – places pressures on trade unions and industrial relations systems. The question also arises of whether industrial relations and human resource management are distinct or complementary systems. We shall return to this key issue.

Reorganizing work inside the enterprise is, however, not the only way to attain greater flexibility. This can also be achieved when the enterprise contracts for work it formerly undertook "in-house". The "externalization of production" has been a major trend in recent years, as we shall see in a subsequent section. Here, too, rising enterprise autonomy has been one of the determining factors. Again, as national boundaries recede, the enterprise is exposed to greater competition. The search for new ways to protect itself against that exposure often leads it to find ways to reduce its newly found autonomy. In short, heightened competition has blurred the boundaries of firms and encouraged the creation of activity networks. This can mean considerable repercussions for the sphere we are looking at, as these new interfirm dependencies do not necessarily conform to industrial relations structures that assume the independence of the individual firm.

Before discussing these organizational changes in more detail, we shall look at a factor which has greatly facilitated them – technological advancement. To survive in an increasingly integrated and interdependent world, many firms have moved away from mass production. The new bases of competition emphasize integrated production, quality products, the capacity to meet particular customer demands and adaptability to rapidly changing market conditions. Considerable technological advances have brought about these changes. New information and transportation technology has enabled the coordination of production activities to encompass more extensive areas and this has resulted in a considerable increase, both in number and size, of multinational, and even global, enterprises. Furthermore, it is technological change which, along with policy liberalization, market integration and the heightened domestic and international competition that it generates, has resulted in the important qualitative changes seen in the international organization of production.

Technology, by shortening product life cycles, has increased both the uncertainty of product markets and the costs and risks of research and new product development. It enables the divisibility of production – the firm's value-added chain – and the identification, for the various activities, of the most advantageous locations. Further, it gives enterprises the choice of either performing those activities themselves in their own factories, or of contracting out for them. The rise in a range of international alliances is a consequence of these new organizational options.

Substantial doubt surrounds the assumption that technological change has a purely domestic influence on work and production organization.[37] It is hard to believe that the heightened competition associated with globalization has not quickened the pace of the reorganization which new technologies enable. Reorganization would probably occur anyway, even if economies were less open, but not in such an extensive or rapid way. It is thus difficult to dissociate globalization and the information technology revolution.

The restructuring of purely domestic firms is not unrelated to a reorganization of production in which the world market plays a deciding role. These firms are just as likely to face import competition and can also have commercial links to multinational firms. To be players in the new organization of production, they must conform to general standards of quality.[38]

In other words, widespread corporate restructuring is a feature of globalization in which technology is playing a major role. Thinking that the effects of trade and technology are entirely separate is quite misleading.[39] "The current trade-versus-technology debate obscures a more fundamental question about how firms respond to import competition." In consequence, "statements of the sort 'trade has been of secondary importance compared with technical change' are therefore inaccurate".[40]

New interfirm dependencies and integration within the multinational enterprise

The nature of new interfirm dependencies

The various forms of organization behind the production and distribution of goods for the world market often involve complex, hierarchical networks of interfirm relations. The tendency toward rising interdependence in the organization of production is manifested in two ways. First, activities ranging from the conception, production and distribution of the final product come increasingly within the framework of an interfirm organization of production. Second, the intrafirm organization of production within multinational enterprises also shows signs of rising interdependence or, indeed, integration across affiliates.

Of course, inter-enterprise linkages are in one sense not at all new: enterprises have always contracted with each other for product and service inputs. Recent trends, however, suggest at least three ways in which the present differs from the past. First, international subcontracting has grown relative to other types of commercial relations.[41] Thus, trade in "intermediate goods and services" – inputs not destined for final consumer markets – constitutes a rising share of total international trade.[42] Contracting with enterprises in wealthy consumer markets is a major way that developing countries participate in world markets. Second, domestic subcontracting is on the rise as firms "externalize" or "outsource" activities they once undertook in-house. Third, while commercial links between firms have long been a feature of the organization of production, qualitative changes are changing the intensity of these linkages with implications for the autonomy of the enterprise.

International subcontracting and industrial relations

The trend toward subcontracting is driven by competitive "push" and technological "pull" factors. Heightened competition has inclined firms to focus on their core competencies and to contract for activities they once undertook themselves.[43] The evidence is not comprehensive, but the subcontracting of activities or the carrying out of operations by the offshore affiliates of multinational firms seems to have greatly increased since the 1970s. For a broad sample of United States industries, imported intermediate inputs on non-energy materials rose from just 5.3 per cent of purchases in 1972 to 11.6 per cent of purchases in 1990. United States imports from offshore assembly plants in Mexico accounted for almost half (42.2 per cent) of all imports from that country in 1990.[44] This partial outsourcing is one way in which firms have responded to increased competition.

The main implication of these mechanisms is that a major share of trade and production occurs not in the market at large, but within the internal – or intermediate – market that firms construct. In certain sectors, such as garments, international trade should best be thought of as the organized outcome of lead firms and their suppliers. This may even take the form of the regionalization of North-South trade. Box 4.1 deals with the new economics of proximity which underlie this trend.

Some production chains are "buyer-driven", that is, controlled by the buyer (by commercial capital).[45] This is especially the case in many labour-intensive industries such as garments, toys and footwear. In these industries it is the buyer, in other words the retail trade, which increasingly governs the activities of manufacturers and their suppliers. For example, "One of the main characteristics of the firms that fit the buyer-driven model, including retailers like Wal-Mart [...] [and] [...] athletic footwear companies like Nike and Reebok [...], is that these firms design and/or market, but do not make the brand-named products they order. They are part of a new breed of 'manufacturers without factories' that separate the production of goods from the design and marketing stages of the production process".[46]

As it is the production strategies of lead firms that organize activity,[47] it is inappropriate to think of the individual firm as an autonomous actor in the market. The

Box 4.1. The advantage of proximity

The industrial migration of manufacturing jobs to countries where labour costs have been a significant source of comparative advantage has been a key trend in the international division of labour. The improving speed and declining costs of transportation and communication resulting from technological change have reduced the importance of proximity to the final market. For more and more services, too, proximity is irrelevant. For example, software development in Bangalore, India, has sky-rocketed in a brief, ten-year period. The engineers are highly skilled, earnings are a fraction of United States or German salaries, and the "product" – software – can be delivered anywhere in the world in real time at the push of a button.

For some industries, however, the pendulum may be swinging back in favour of proximity. Technological change has reduced the labour-cost component of many manufacturing processes and thus the lure of low labour-cost locations. Also, product-market changes resulting in shorter product life cycles and new interfirm production strategies both tend to favour proximity to final consumer markets. Apparel manufacturing is the quintessential competitive industry – easy entry due to low capital requirements, relatively few economies of scale and scope, and low concentration. Because of this, it has become the most geographically dispersed of all industries producing for the world market. Now, however, there are signs that the advantages of proximity may be rising.

Mass-producing manufacturers used to set the pace in the United States garment industry. Since the 1960s, however, much has changed. Reduced transportation costs, changes in clothing tastes, and new information technologies facilitated the entry of non-union competition, first from domestic firms and then increasingly from foreign production. Jobs and wages both declined and foreign competition from developing countries has been mostly to blame. Import penetration grew from about 10 per cent in 1970 to more than 50 per cent in the 1990s. In 1965, unions organized 66 per cent of the domestic industry; in 1995, they organized only 33 per cent.

The 1980s and 1990s also saw a shift in economic power from producers to buyers. As retailers became more concentrated and developed lower-cost sources of clothing, their power over manufacturers rose. Increased foreign and domestic competition had broadened contracting and sourcing options for retailers. Then the advent of "lean retailing" further consolidated their power. Used by mass retailers, lean retailing employs information technology in an attempt to allow manufacturers to respond to retailers' needs as sales occur. "Rapid response" means that lean retailers demand more frequent replenishment of products and faster response to orders. As a result, retailers are able to reduce inventory holdings and markdowns. Rapid response itself has been triggered by an increase in style proliferation. Not only does an increasing proportion of manufacturers' product lines consist of new styles for which no demand history exists, but at the same time the number of selling seasons per product has increased. Product life cycles have become shorter. All this adds to product-market uncertainty and increases the pressure on manufacturers for quick response – and technology enables it: information linkages between retailers and manufacturers have grown sharply. Purchase orders and product sales data are sent electronically to manufacturers in real time.

These major changes in the United States garment industry seem to be changing the "economics of proximity" of international outsourcing for the United States market. In the past, most imports traditionally came from Asia's "Big Four": China, Hong Kong, the Republic of Korea and Taiwan, China. However, United States firms have increasingly resorted to outsourcing closer to home, in the Caribbean and Latin America. Imports from the Caribbean and Mexico have risen from 7 per cent of total imports in 1984 to 29 per cent in 1995, while the share of the traditional "Big Four" has fallen from 63 per cent to 28 per cent. Trade policy toward Latin America and rising Asian labour costs have played a role. But the new competitive dynamics of the product market may be the biggest factor. The increased demand for rapid response has been hailed as a boon for domestic manufacturers who, in theory, can respond to retailers' needs more quickly than foreign producers. And since the global production channel is moving closer to home, this may also reflect the rising comparative advantage of proximity. Firms source from Latin America to combine their labour cost advantages with the quick response capacity of domestic production, something that is not possible when sourcing from Asia.

contracting firm's dependence on the buyer could make it more sensitive to labour costs and pose an obstacle to trade union organization. International subcontracting chains give rise to two additional industrial relations related concerns.

First, concerns over wages, working conditions and the autonomy of industrial relations actors have mostly arisen in relation to buyer-driven production chains. As we have said, these chains are often found in labour-intensive, low-skilled industries, where labour costs can play a predominant, if fleeting, role in comparative advantage. In these industries barriers to entry are also low, as the capital investment and equipment requirements to enter the market are minimal. Evidence from a comprehensive analysis of enterprise-based trade patterns shows that the relocation of production in buyer-driven chains, such as garments, has been far greater than in capital-intensive industries which, on the contrary, show considerable locational stability.[48] When dealing with buyer-driven chains, because labour costs play a predominant role, both governments and unions may be left with less room to manoeuvre than when dealing with activities which obey a more balanced array of considerations.

Second, as shown in box 4.1 on the economics of proximity, offshore contracting has clearly been a factor in the decline of the unionization rates in the United States garment industry – and the same also holds true for other national garment industries.[49] International subcontracting has thus affected union membership in labour-intensive, low-skilled production jobs in high-wage countries.

The externalization of production and industrial relations

Even on the domestic front, large corporations are changing their production structures to concentrate on core activities in which their high value-added is, and outsourcing their ancillary activities or subcontracting them to smaller firms. Evidence for the prevalence of "production externalization" is available not only for the United States, but also from a major, recent survey of large Australian enterprises.[50] Corporate restructuring involving the outsourcing of activities formerly undertaken in-house topped the list of organizational changes in these firms in the mid-1990s. Domestic outsourcing to non-union firms has, for example, been one of the most hotly contested industrial relations issues in the United States in recent years.[51] The trend toward outsourcing is also a factor behind the proliferation of small and medium-sized enterprises (SMEs); furthermore, a widespread empirical finding is that, relative to large firms, SMEs are far more likely to be non-union.[52] Outsourcing of a purely domestic nature could thus be a factor in the decline of trade union organization in some countries.

Partly because small enterprises are less likely to be organized by trade unions, wages and working conditions in the small-firm sector are often inferior to those proposed by large firms. The externalization of production is therefore a source of widening labour market segmentation in some settings.[53] In addition, some evidence

---

Box 4.2.   The factory of the future?

Radical changes are sweeping through the auto industry. From Stuttgart to Detroit, car makers are racing to reduce factory costs through ever closer partnerships with component makers. Since the late 1980s, such auto makers as Ford and Chrysler have handed over responsibility to suppliers for complete modules of parts. In a traditional factory, however, suppliers deliver parts to the loading dock or occasionally to the assembly line, but final assembly is done by the car maker's own workers. Volkswagen's new US$250 million truck plant, which was opened in November 1996 at Rensende, a rural town close to Rio de Janeiro, made the biggest leap. In this plant, seven main suppliers make components using their own equipment, then their own workers actually assemble the components together into finished trucks and buses. Improvements by the suppliers in the assembly process are expected to cut work hours in the plant by 12 per cent as compared with the traditional auto factory. But the approach has other attractions too. First, Volkswagen capital investment drops. While Volkswagen provides the building and the assembly line conveyors, suppliers put in their own tools, fixtures and workers. Second, if sales of trucks and buses run significantly below the planned annual capacity, all the partners are affected, not just Volkswagen. Since parts arrive just an hour or so before they are needed, inventory costs plummet. And third, with a multiple workforce in the same factory but belonging to different companies, it is harder for unions to gain strength. Of the expected total 1,400 workers when the factory is in full operation, just 200 will be direct VW employees.

The approach may be a blueprint for the new auto factories springing up all over the developing world. However, in Western Europe and the United States, where the industry faces overcapacity, change will come slowly because new factories are not needed, and unions resist allowing suppliers into assembly plants. But in developing markets, such as China and South America, this radical new way of making vehicles could quickly become the norm.

Source: "VW's factory of the future", in *Business Week,* 7 Oct. 1996, pp. 18-19.

---

shows that there has been an increasing segmentation of the labour force, not only between core companies and their small-firm suppliers, but also within core companies themselves. This occurs, for example, in the car industry, where a new method of work organization sometimes results in the subcontractors themselves managing production (see box 4.2). Such a situation makes it harder to organize unions and to promote dialogue and collective bargaining at the level of the enterprise.

From purely commercial links to organizational links between firms

A feature of the modern organization of production has been the diffusion of "just-in-time" linkages between supplier and assembly firms.[54] Such relations introduce a qualitative change in the traditional ways in which enterprises have engaged in commercial relations. Indeed, the relationship between firms engaged in just-in-time production goes far beyond mere commercial links and is more in the nature of an intense, interorganizational relationship. In the process, the effectiveness of enterprise-based worker representation might be altered. In traditional industrial relations systems, employees are represented and trade unions are organized on the basis of the relative independence of the employer – independence as concerns key elements of the terms and conditions of work at least. The more intense linkages between firms could limit management's scope for action which, in turn, would leave workers' representatives little room for manoeuvre. For example, the management of a supplier firm may no longer be able to decide independently on the use of technology, work organization, production methods, qualifications, operating hours and personnel management practices. Even in larger German enterprises with traditionally strong worker representation, constraints on the autonomy of the works council have arisen.[55] The dilemma created by the erosion of the boundaries of the enterprise is that new points of reference are needed for union strategy. In some cases, trade unions may need to bring their structure of worker representation into line with the new networks of enterprises.

Where trade unions are organized along industry lines, and where collective bargaining occurs at industry level, adjusting to the new, more organizationally based forms of inter-enterprise relations may be made easier. For instance, the German IG Metall Union started to organize meetings of works councils from the producer and supplier firms in the car industry to promote their cooperation. In Japan, company unions have developed structures along the lines of the new corporate groupings, enabling them to coordinate their activities (see figure 4.6).

Today, the success of an enterprise, be it a multinational or an SME, is increasingly influenced by the quality of its network of relationships with other enterprises. Greater integration across units of production – whether between enterprises or within the same enterprise – can favour the diffusion of new human resource management practices. As we shall see later in the text traditional industrial relations structures could be a factor in that diffusion – either where they fail to adjust and thus encourage management initiatives or, on the contrary, where they facilitate needed adjustment.

Integration within the multinational enterprise

The rapid expansion of world trade is closely linked to the development of multinational enterprises. It has been estimated that no less than one-third of trade occurs within multinational enterprises, either between the mother company and its foreign affiliates, or among the affiliates themselves. Trade among multinational enterprises constitutes a further third. Only a small share of international trade – some say no more than 25 per cent – represents trade conducted in conditions of true independence.[56] In other words, the bulk of global trade appears to be the result of the international organization of production and trade which is governed by the multinationals.

The challenges introduced by multinational enterprises to "local" trade unions and collective bargaining are neither new nor unrecorded in the literature. In purely quantitative terms, the rapid increase in foreign direct investment (FDI) can be expected to magnify these challenges, all the more as the growth of multinational en-

Figure 4.6.   **Main activities of union organizations at the level of company groupings in Japan (%)**

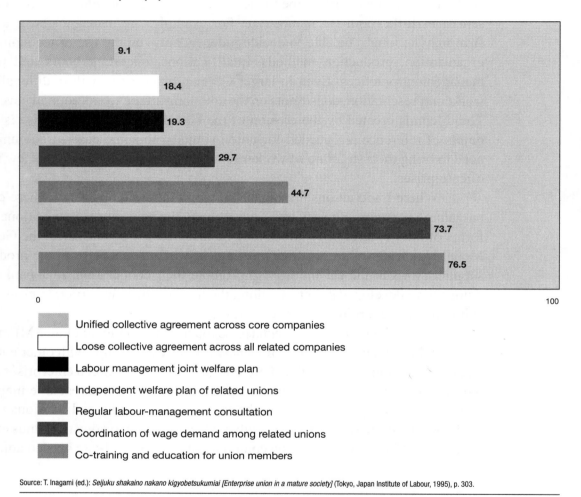

Source: T. Inagami (ed.): *Seijuku shakaino nakano kigyobetsukumiai [Enterprise union in a mature society]* (Tokyo, Japan Institute of Labour, 1995), p. 303.

terprises from non-traditional countries is also pronounced.[57] The present discussion will not review this literature; rather, the focus here is on qualitative changes within the "intrafirm" organization of production. These changes do not apply to the full range of multinationals,[58] but address only the most globally integrated enterprises competing in the most global of product markets.

The activities of some multinationals show signs of greater integration at the regional or global level. By rationalizing their production lines, they are progressively entering into a context of global integration and their technological and employment needs are becoming increasingly homogeneous. They are adopting global strategies and international structures that reduce the autonomy of their national affiliates.[59]

Multinationals are opting for this approach because, with the dismantling of formerly sheltered national markets, firms no longer seek to replicate the whole of their value chain in each of their locations. Instead they prefer to set up establishments specializing in specific intermediate phases of production in different places. This process of integrating operations is confirmed in various studies, although great diversity prevails in enterprise strategies. Those enterprises which, due to their particular features, must replicate the same chain of operations with the same jobs in each location, are less subject to integration.[60] In manufacturing, however, there are clear opportunities for specialization within an integrated production strategy. An indication of deeper integration would be the degree to which multinational parents and affiliates trade predominantly among themselves (and with allied supplier firms); such trade has risen in both absolute and relative terms (with respect to the total volume of group exports),[61] as has affiliate-to-affiliate trade.[62] The increase in integration can also be seen in the size of affiliate exports, which have risen in relation to their volume of sales.[63]

The rise in intra-affiliate trade would appear to be particularly marked in the electronics industry. But a trend toward intra-affiliate specialization and integration can also be noted in other industries, including the food industry, where, however, the perishable nature of products and the wide variance in tastes argue in favour of local market presence.

"In Europe, the Nestlé group has reduced the number of manufacturing units while increasing its volume of sales during 1989-94. Production has become increasingly specialized and flows of goods and services among affiliates have increased, with some facilities catering to the entire European market. Economies of scale and other restructuring in Europe are expected to create cost savings of around $750 million."[64]

Additional evidence comes from the relationship between FDI flows and trade flows themselves. If the FDI flows were largely substitutes, then this would be an indication of the setting up of relatively autonomous affiliates in host countries to work predominantly for the local market. If they both tend to develop together then this could be an indication of deeper integration.[65] Evidence on bilateral trade and FDI flows for Germany, Japan and the United States suggests that FDI is both a complement to trade and a vehicle for integrating a cross-border organization of production.

The integration of operations could also be a factor in the convergence of work and production organization across borders within certain multinational enterprises in which the autonomy of affiliates has been reduced.[66] However, the general rule still appears to be that the local setting distinctively shapes key features of the employment relationship, in spite of the growing convergence seen in relation to the organization of work and remuneration.[67]

While recognizing differences among multinational enterprises and the contexts within which they operate, there are common trends. The internationalization of markets and the greater integration of production in a global economy have increased the need of some multinational enterprises for cross-national coordination of indus-

---

Box 4.3.   Labour standards and performance competition

AusCo, with 500 workers in Sydney, is one of the three companies that have dominated the home appliances market in Australia. When the Australian Government deregulated manufacturing and reduced tariff protection for home appliances from 35 to 5 per cent, the increasing foreign competition induced all three Australian companies to look overseas and to establish joint ventures in China. Though AusCo retained its production base in Sydney, it set up a Chinese joint venture in 1992 with a Hong Kong home appliance manufacturer, GES, which already had an operation (GES Shenzen) in China. The Australian company provided technical assistance in the organization of production and allowed its product designs to be manufactured in the GES Shenzen plant and marketed under different names. There were striking differences, as shown below, in wages, benefits, working time and trade union bargaining rights between the GES Shenzen plant and AusCo's Sydney plant:

Working conditions	AusCo (Sydney)	GES (Shenzen)
Monthly base wage		
Starting wage rate	A$1,580	A$34
Highest wage rate	A$2,472	A$81
Working hours per week	38	60
Labour rights	Right to bargain collectively; shop-floor representation	No collective bargaining rights; "negotiate" only individual contracts with employer
Dismissal procedure	Unfair dismissals defined; established procedures; notice periods 7-21 days depending on length of service	7-days notice; no rights; worker liable for registration fee on labour contract; residency revoked upon dismissal, then becomes an illegal worker
Labour market	Legally "free" labour	Restricted access to jobs through permit system

The huge difference in labour costs exerted immense pressure on the Sydney plant, threatening it with closure. The China factory became the benchmark and the "negotiating lever" in the enterprise bargaining for a new arrangement and in the process of reorganization of the Sydney plant. To save the Australian plant, an alliance was formed between middle management and the workforce. The overriding objective was to increase productivity in the Sydney plant up to the level where it would counterbalance the wage and benefits differentials. The management adopted a more open, information-sharing managerial style, sourced material inputs competitively and introduced teamwork and continuous improvement techniques in production. In addition, between 1992 and 1994, employment was cut by 50 per cent and the assembly line was speeded up. A substantial increase in productivity was achieved through work teams which met every week to discuss how productivity could be increased. This process resulted in a partnership between assembly line workers and the technical staff, with significant innovations on the assembly line and cost savings to the point where the unit cost of production in Australia is now competitive with that in China, despite the vast wage and benefit differentials.

Source: Rob Lambert, "Global dance – factory regimes, Asian labour standards and corporate restructuring", paper presented at the Conference on Globalization and Labour Regulation, Warwick University, 11-13 Sep. 1996.

---

trial relations and human resource management policies and practices. They have therefore developed cross-border organization-based systems of employment and human resource management (HRM).[68] These structures create common attitudes and values among managers and help to sustain a decentralized grouping of subsidiaries. They sometimes also imply that multinationals seek to free themselves from the constraints posed by sector bargaining. Such a trend is already in evidence in the German engineering industry where some multinationals are leaving sectoral bargaining.

Advances in information technology and communications now allow multinationals to compare the performance of their different units. A survey of 176 multinationals headquartered in the United Kingdom showed that 70 per cent of them make comparisons of this kind.[69] Information gathered in this way could be used to exert pressure on the management of individual units or to extract concessions in employment and work practices from the local workforce, keen to prevent plant closure or to attract future investments. For multinationals they constitute "a powerful mechanism to discipline the bargaining behaviour of local managements as well as workforces".[70] On the basis of this information, enterprises such as Digital, IBM and Analog Device have adopted a corporation-wide approach to the management of human resources and Ford has introduced employee-involvement programmes in many of their European affiliates. Another striking example is AusCo, a medium-sized Australian corporation that set up a joint venture in China and then used the results of this operation to challenge existing practices and performance standards in its home-based plant (see box 4.3). The employment policy of multinationals is increasingly influenced by the conditions seen in its affiliates operating in different countries.

The enterprise and collective labour relations

As mentioned earlier, enterprises have seen an increase in their level of autonomy and responsibility as a result of the constraints being placed on national policies. This change has ushered in far-reaching changes in forms of work organization, the acquisition of skills, the performance of duties and remuneration – although this trend is certainly not a uniform one.

A variety of new forms of work organization have been introduced, variously termed "flexible specialization", "high commitment organization", "high performance work system", and so on. To promote flexibility and "lean" production, firms have reduced the number of management layers and decentralized many responsibilities by transferring them to the workplace, often involving the use of autonomous work teams. Thus, the average number of management layers in large British companies decreased from seven in 1986 to fewer than five in 1996.[71] In Germany, a recent survey of medium-sized and large enterprises reflected a similar, if less marked, trend: 4 per cent of firms (employing 26 per cent of the workforce surveyed) reported that they had reduced the number of hierarchy levels between 1993 and 1995.[72] The low percentage may be explained by the already fewer hierarchical levels in German industry relative, say, to the United Kingdom. Indirect evidence of "delayering" comes also from the United States: 18.6 per cent of the positions phased out since 1988 were in middle management, although such employees only make up 5 to 8 per cent of the workforce.[73]

At the same time, the nature of employment has also been changing as technological innovations and new information systems have automated jobs and streamlined operations. Within firms work processes have been re-engineered for cross-functional teams. The traditional system of highly segmented jobs and rigid job descriptions and work rules has been unable to cope with the evolution of consumer demand which has become changeable and diversified. To meet such demands effectively, a production line should be able to produce a wide range of products, and workers need multi-functional skills and greater adaptability. Jobs are more complex, involving more tasks, multiple skills and greater interaction among workers, between workers and employers, and with suppliers and customers. With the quality of products increasingly representing a core determinant, the task of quality inspection must be incorporated into the production line, involving the need to broaden job definitions.

The rapid expansion of teamwork has been one of the most prominent changes during the last decade. When this form of work organization first became popular in the 1970s, the aim was to improve the quality of working life, humanize the content of work and increase productivity. The development of teamwork stopped with the onset of recession and the strong rise in unemployment in the 1980s. Since then it has been resumed, with the primary focus now on increasing productivity and competitiveness.[74] It still offers certain advantages to workers in the form of greater autonomy, responsibility and decision-making power.

The question to be asked is whether the effective implementation of these changes requires that industrial relations be managed in accordance with the rules of the market or whether they can, or in fact should, be regulated collectively.

Over the past decade employment security has waned and the array of employment contracts has broadened. The proportion of full-time workers with prospects for career development and lifelong employment in a firm is falling in relation to that of casual workers. The employment situation today is characterized by a reduced core labour force – a small number of highly skilled and valued employees – and a growing percentage of peripheral workers on casual, temporary, part-time or fixed contracts.[75]

From a different angle, a growing number of enterprises have, since the beginning of the 1980s, introduced human resource management practices – evidence that the above changes often require the upgrading of workers' skills and measures to retain them within the enterprise. As we have seen, the trends are contradictory. It is therefore necessary to consider the features of these policies more closely and to identify their similarities and differences with traditional industrial relations systems.

The principal features of human resource management policies

Human resource management (HRM) is often regarded as equivalent to personnel management or as a catch-all term to encompass the whole field of people management. Some enterprises have simply renamed their personnel department without making any real change in the way they manage their employees. Others, however, see HRM as a radically new approach to managing human resources. They emphasize the need for adopting an internally consistent bundle of HRM practices and the integration of HRM into business strategy ("strategic HRM"). The "hard" HRM model stresses such aspects as just-in-time production, flexibility, strong management control, individualism and cost minimization. In contrast, the "soft" HRM model regards employees as valued assets and as a source of competitive advantage. This model includes a decentralized organizational structure, semi-autonomous work groups, enhanced communication between management and labour, employee motivation, a qualified and adaptable workforce, and a set of pèople-centred labour policies and practices.[76]

Reality is more complex than this abstract distinction. Enterprises often "muddle through" difficult times adopting a stance one researcher has named "pragmatic eclecticism".[77] It is not rare, for example, for the very same company adopting the "soft" HRM approach to implement corporate restructuring involving drastic downsizing and the increasing use of contingent workers. Nevertheless, insofar as HRM policies represent an effort to realign people management with new corporate strategy, they may redefine traditional social relationships and culture at the workplace.

These policies encompass a number of elements including training, compensation, communication between employees and management and employee involvement in problem-solving and decision-making. They place considerable emphasis on training. Training programmes must support functional flexibility by enhancing the spectrum and quality of skills production workers possess and expanding the range of tasks they can perform. Technological advances and the incorporation of quality control into the production line mean that workers must have specific analytical and behavioural abilities. A 1994 national employer survey in the United States identified education and training as the most important factors for increasing productivity and competitiveness (see figure 4.7).

Another aspect of HRM concerns salaries. It relates to the setting up of pay systems linked to performance at the level of the individual, work group, plant or firm, providing incentives for higher productivity. Profit-sharing is also increasingly popular and seeks to align employees' interests with those of management, by establishing a closer linkage between income and the company's fortune. There has also been a trend towards compensation based on skills and abilities, rather than on seniority or job content. According to one recent survey, for example, 70, 65 and 51 per

Figure 4.7.   **Factors for increased productivity in the United States, all establishments (%)**

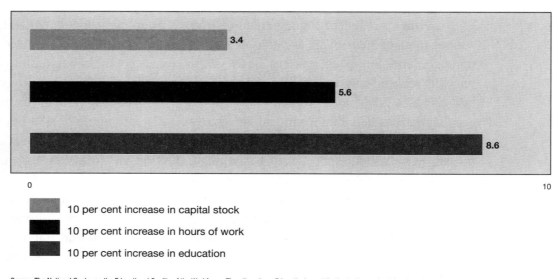

Source: The National Center on the Educational Quality of the Workforce: *The other shoe: Education's contribution to the productivity of establishments: A second round of findings from the EQW National Employer Survey* (Philadelphia, University of Pennsylvania, 1995), p. 2.

cent of French, British and Irish firms, respectively, are implementing merit-related pay systems. In addition, 54, 49, 40 and 38 per cent of Danish, German, French and British firms, respectively, report that there have been increases in the share of variable pay in the total remuneration package.[78]

HRM also incorporates various schemes of direct employee participation in problem-solving and productivity improvements, and endeavours to promote closer communication between management and employees. Quality circles have gained popularity.[79] Through them employees are encouraged to participate in the process of continuous improvements to production, and, more than previously, in decision-making. The objective is to enhance job satisfaction and to share common interests with management.

Each HRM element may be analysed and evaluated separately. However, "it does not make sense to isolate one rule [of internal labour markets] and ignore the others".[80] It is the synergistic effect of the different elements that creates competitive advantage. It is essential to ensure that work organization and human resource management form a cohesive framework which is consistent with the enterprise's competitive strategy. Organizational effectiveness is more doubtful when there is random adoption of particular practices or when there are ad hoc responses to problems as they arise.[81]

The advantages and disadvantages for industrial relations

Factors detrimental to collective regulation

Work organization innovations, including the shift from vertical and hierarchical organization to flatter structures and the decentralization of responsibility and decision-making, have been transforming social relationships in the workplace. To take an example, the introduction of the teamwork system impacts on industrial relations. It enhances workers' autonomy but also erodes the traditional prerogatives of management – which is why management frequently opposes it. The enhanced autonomy of workers also affects the traditional functions of trade unions and representative institutions. In some countries, such as the United States and the United Kingdom, teamwork with the integration of broader job content and flexible work organization is posing a challenge to traditional job-control unionism. Furthermore, a critical issue is whether functional flexibility through teamwork means simply the ability of management to move employees around at will between jobs requiring little skill, or whether it implies a general upskilling of the workforce so that employees are able to move between a range of tasks requiring ability and autonomy.

With enterprises' increased manoeuvrability in wage determination, the new individual compensation schemes affect various aspects of traditional industrial relations. They enhance the scope for management control through the leverage of personnel assessment and foster individualism. As a consequence they call into question, at least in part, the traditional industrial relations settings. One survey showed that the widespread merit-based payment scheme in Japan has weakened the perceived necessity of unionization among employees.[82] Likewise, profit-sharing wage schemes, by forging a closer linkage between employees' income and corporate fortunes, tend to alter their attitude towards unionization.

Policies that promote direct participation in the workplace aim to increase employee involvement in improvements to production, increasing common interests with the management. This is a positive development because it provides workers with the opportunity to go beyond the simple execution of duties and to use all their abilities. However, this identification with the interests of management might distance the workers from the trade unions and erode the traditional forms of participation, collective bargaining and consultation with workers' organizations or representative bodies. It is not surprising that union leaders have at times opposed such policies.

The degree of this opposition varies, however, according to circumstances. Human resource management policies may undermine existing industrial relations where labour-management relations are prone to conflict. In this case they might be used as a corporate strategy of union avoidance and combined with enterprise paternalism. For instance, Samsung and POSCO, two Korean companies that are well known for their practices in this sphere, have established a well-developed corporate

---

Box 4.4. Paternalism and unionization

POSCO in the Republic of Korea is the second largest steel corporation in the world. Since its inception in 1968, it has introduced all elements of Japanese-style HRM practices, including lifetime employment, a highly developed in-house training system, teamwork and quality circles. The managerial philosophy can be summarized as follows: We do not need unions in order to provide benefits. This paternalistic philosophy has led the personnel to identify with the enterprise and to reject unionization. It is true that the benefits provided by the enterprise are not negligible. Among other facilities, the company provides almost all employees with housing, and provides for the education of employees' children from kindergarten to university.

Given the tight housing situation and the heavy burden of education in the country, POSCO's corporate welfarism is considerable.

Before political democratization and the renaissance of the union movement in 1987, labour-management relations were dealt with through a labour-management committee. In 1987, a company union was organized and in 1990, militant leadership took over the union. When the union tried to engage in solidarity action with other companies, employees withdrew from it, which led to its *de facto* dissolution. Today, labour-management committees and workplace councils operate as a close communication channel between employees and managers.

Source: J. Park: *Saengsanen Jeongchiwa Jakupjong Minjujuen [Politics of Production and Workplace Democracy]* (Seoul, Manwol Academy, 1996), pp. 202-234.

---

welfare system which has essentially had the effect of ousting the trade unions (see box 4.4).

Less extreme examples can be found in India where the introduction of certain techniques – quality circles, total quality management – has diminished the role of trade unions by enhancing direct communications between management and workers.[83] In Latin America, management has sometimes introduced quality circles and other similar practices not only to increase productivity, improve workplace atmosphere and reduce the inevitable tensions found with authoritarian management styles, but also to undermine the power of the trade unions, opposed to enterprise restructuring.[84] In these cases, the new forms of direct participation have weakened the role of trade unions as the representatives of employees; they have been introduced in order to defuse adversarial relations and replace them with consultative relations controlled by management.[85] This trend is all the more marked when the enterprise is dealing with job-control unionism which tends to be incompatible with flexible work organization and related human resource management practices. By favouring direct participation, management may also seek to avoid problems arising from inter-union rivalries.

Another scenario occurs where the enterprise adopts a "greenfield strategy". Profound departures from traditional industrial relations practices tend to be most evident in high technology industries. Relocation to a greenfield site provides companies with opportunities to introduce innovative work reorganization, new technologies and new relationships with workers. Furthermore, the mere threat of relocation to a greenfield site could serve to contain union demands, allowing management to gain concessions and exercise greater control over work organization. This strategy can therefore lead to a decline in industrial relations, particularly when relocations take enterprises to countries where the industrial relations framework is less rigid. Last but not least, these practices are associated with a growing diversity of contractual relationships – and the individualization of labour conditions has meant that there is less coalescence of interests. Individual workers may find it more advantageous to negotiate their own terms and conditions. The increasing heterogeneity of employees in the workplace creates an identity problem for unions, which normally cover permanent, full-time workers.

The synergies between human resource management policies and industrial relations

The race for flexibility and competitiveness has increased the importance of such issues as technological change, work organization – including teamwork, training, payment systems, employee participation and personnel policy – all of which are issues best resolved at the level of the individual firm. The growing importance of these issues provides an opportunity for trade unions and employers to broaden the agenda of bargaining and consultation at both the level of the enterprise and beyond. The challenge for trade unions is to try to enhance the competitiveness of the firm while ensuring workers benefit from organizational changes. In this context, the relationship between collective representation and management-driven HRM policies is a key issue.

HRM policies are sometimes introduced in collaboration with trade unions. In this case various historical, institutional and cultural conditions must be met. In Japan a variety of factors – strong employment security based on legal guarantees, a management culture, government policy and collective bargaining at the enterprise level[86] – mean that instead of opposition there is in fact complementarity between these policies and the actions of enterprise unions. Outside Japan, Japanese-style management and HRM practices often face different constraints.

Where relations between employers and workers are relatively free of conflict, where employees have the right to consultation and unions exert a relatively high level of influence, the introduction of HRM policies generally does not seek to bypass the traditional system of industrial relations. When employee co-determination rights on personnel and production matters are well established, as is the case in Germany, HRM tends to be mediated through the traditional collective industrial relations channels. This is especially true in the HRM areas relating to decentralization and development, pay flexibility, enterprise-based training, employee communications, teamwork and working time arrangements. The results of a Price Waterhouse Cranfield survey show that in most European countries the introduction of direct labour-management communications goes hand-in-hand with an increase, albeit a small one, in communication through the traditional channels.[87] A study of personnel management practices in the German chemical industry found that the new practices, by focusing on individual issues and creating a more cooperative environment, have in fact helped improve traditional industrial relations within enterprises.[88]

HRM mechanisms and unions might provide distinct channels of communication, fulfilling different functions. According to one survey, while Swedish workers usually prefer to handle group-level matters themselves without union involvement, especially where the direct communication mechanisms available to them are advanced, the majority favour union mediation in management-level issues such as the pace and design of production.[89] Surveys conducted in Belgium, Italy and Austria reached a similar conclusion – that direct participation is not an alternative but rather a complementary model of employee involvement.[90] Another survey showed that in the German car industry, introducing teams on the assembly line does not cause divisions among workers. They still see themselves as a collective group, even in their relations with management.[91] The results of these different surveys suggest that, given their multiple needs and concerns, employees' commitment to the enterprise, which is fostered through HRM, does not necessarily conflict with their commitment to unions.

The experience of the United Kingdom and the United States with regard to the relationship between unions and HRM appears to differ from that of Japan and Europe. In the context of a traditionally adversarial collective bargaining culture, this relationship has been more confrontational. However, a survey found that in the United States the new practices have spread more widely in the union than in the non-union sector of employment.[92] The same is true for the United Kingdom.[93]

These developments can be interpreted in two ways: either that the union presence facilitates the introduction of these methods, or that they are used to counter the influence of the unions. Whatever the case may be, the most essential aspect, as revealed by recent research in the United States, is that the diffusion of workplace level innovations is influenced less by the mere presence or absence of unions than by the actual role they play. When unions play a consultative role in decision-making the new practices expand more rapidly.[94] This finding suggests that it is the quality of labour-management relationships and not the mere existence of a union that has a positive impact on the productivity of enterprises. To introduce workplace innovations, employers can either restrict union involvement, if they consider it to be a hindrance or constraint, or build alliances with unions if they think that changes can be more easily achieved with union cooperation than in an atmosphere of tension, especially in particularly critical restructuring periods.

Trade unions in many countries are becoming increasingly aware that they should make the most of the management-initiated innovations to enhance the competitiveness of enterprises, thereby improving the quality of work and strengthening the influence of workers. In Europe in the 1980s, direct participation was primarily seen as a threat to trade unionism. Today's approach is a more pragmatic one, with the accent being placed on complementarity. In the United Kingdom the TUC has recognized the need for enterprise-level reforms and has called for more constructive union responses, although the politicization of some affiliated trade unions makes their position more ambiguous.[95] The AFL-CIO in the United States has opted for the approach of negotiated participation.[96] Lastly, human resource management policies and industrial relations perform, on a certain number of points, different functions. As far as redistribution is concerned, opposition continues between employees and management and compromises must be sought in this area through collective bargaining rather than in the framework of cooperation-based policies.

On the basis of these elements, the prospects for enterprise-based industrial relations can be specified. Their importance, while undeniable, must be put into context for a number of reasons.

The first is that the practices that focus on the dedication and commitment of employees and hence on the need for the enterprise to ensure a certain level of employment stability, only relate to part of the workforce. As we have seen, they exist alongside increased recourse to precarious forms of employment, in the same and other enterprises, and especially in the growing number of small and medium-sized enterprises where collective representation is hard to achieve. It is difficult for workers with a precarious status to gain the same competence as permanent employees and to upgrade their skills. Although the enterprise remains undeniably at the heart of industrial relations, this does not exclude recourse to other fora.

A second reason is that these innovations have so far been diffused in a restricted and uneven manner. In some countries, flexible work organization and human resource management have become relatively commonplace, while others have taken longer to adopt them due to strong resistance from both employees and management. In some branches and sectors more than others, enterprises have been forced to innovate as a result of particularly vigorous competition. Some enterprises are more inclined and more able than others to adjust and adapt. While there is a widespread trend for employers to achieve greater flexibility because of pressures linked to competition and technology, these common factors are shaped by different historical circumstances, the roles of the social actors and their evolution, national laws and practices and institutional mechanisms. This means that the results obtained and the changes implemented vary greatly from country to country.

Finally, as we shall see, occupational organizations – workers' organizations in particular – frequently have to confront issues which extend beyond the boundaries of the enterprise, whatever its size may be. These concerns must also be given a forum for expression.

Notes

[1] See, for example, ILO: *World Employment 1995* (Geneva, 1995) and *World Employment 1996/97* (Geneva, 1996).

[2] M. Sawicky: *Monti on European tax reform* (Washington, DC, Economic Policy Institute, 1997), duplicated document, p. 12.

[3] Calculations made on the basis of Table 3 of the Annex to the *World investment report,* 1995 (Geneva, UNCTAD, 1995), p. 401.

[4] Calculations made on the bases of Tables 2 and 6 of the Annex to the *World investment report, 1995,* op. cit., pp. 397 and 421.

[5] Calculations made on the basis of Table 1 of the Annex to the *World investment report, 1995,* op. cit, p. 391.

[6] Sawicky, op. cit., p. 17.

[7] J. Hines Jr.: "Altered States: Taxes and the location of foreign direct investment in America", in *American Economic Review* (Nashville), Vol. 86, No. 5, Dec. 1996, p. 1076.

[8] See for example: *Multinationals and the national interest: Playing by different rules* (Washington, DC, the United States Congress, Office of Technology Assessment, 1993).

[9] Calculations made on the basis of Table 3 of the Annex to the *World investment report, 1995,* op. cit.

[10] P. Raines: *Labour market regulation and foreign direct investment* (Glasgow, European Policies Research Centre, University of Strathclyde, 1996).

[11] See W. Cooke: *The influence of industrial relations factors on US foreign direct investment abroad* (Detroit, Michigan, College of Urban, Labor and Metropolitan Affairs, Wayne State University, 1996), duplicated document. W. Cooke and D. Noble: *Industrial relations systems and US foreign direct investment abroad,* ibid., duplicated document.

[12] Quoted in D. Rodrik: *Has globalization gone too far?* (Washington, DC, Institute for International Economics, 1997), p. 81.

[13] The question of payroll taxes is considered in *World Employment 1995,* op. cit., Ch. 4.

[14] Rodrik, op. cit., p. 19.

[15] ibid., p. 45.

[16] ibid., p. 19. See also E. Kapstein: "Workers and the world economy", in *Foreign Affairs* (New York, Council on Foreign Relations), Vol. 75, No. 3, May-June 1996 and S. Jacoby (ed.): *The workers of nations: Industrial relations in a global economy* (New York, Oxford University Press, 1995).

[17] "Stumpfe shakes pillar of labour law", in *Financial Times,* 21 Aug. 1996. Rodrik, op. cit., makes much the same point: "Far-sighted companies will tend to their own communities as they globalize. But an employer that has an 'exit' option is one that is less likely to exercise the 'voice' option", p. 70.

[18] J. Sachs: *Globalization and employment* (Geneva, International Institute for Labour Studies, 1997), p. 10.

[19] A prolific literature on this subject emerged in the 1980s; see, for example, M. Bruno and J. Sachs: *The economics of worldwide stagflation* (Oxford, Blackwell, 1985) or D. Soskice: "Wage determination: The changing role of institutions in advanced industrialized countries", in *Oxford Review of Economic Policy* (Oxford University Press), Vol. 6, 1990. The question of which institutional variables appear to matter in producing specific macroeconomic outcomes was also much debated. In "The dynamics of trade unionism and national economic performance", in *American Political Science Review* (Menasha, Wisconsin, American Political Science Association), Vol. 87, No. 2, June 1993, Miriam Golden argues convincingly that union monopoly may be more important than the centralization or coordination of bargaining, and that to a large extent it is due to union fragmentation and competition that the "Swedish model" stopped producing its positive macroeconomic results.

[20] L. Calmfors: *Centralisation des négociations de salaires et performances macro-économiques: une analyse* (Paris, OECD, 1993).

[21] D. Quinn: *Some consequences of international financial liberalization* (Washington, DC, 1996), duplicated document.

[22] The 1996 study entitled "Plant closings and labor rights", coordinated by Kate Bronfenbrenner (head of workers' education research at Cornell University), was carried out on the request of the secretariat of the Commission for Labor Cooperation, the body responsible for monitoring the application of the provisions relating to the rights of workers in the North American Free Trade Agreement (NAFTA). The information obtained on the content of the study were taken from a press release "U.S. Labor/Suppressed study says NAFTA used against workers", in *Inter Press Service,* 27 Jan. 1997.

[23] L. Rico: "The new industrial relations: British electricians' new-style agreements", in *Industrial and Labor Relations Review* (Ithaca, New York State School of Industrial and Labor Relations), Vol. 41, No. 1, Oct. 1987.

[24] It is clear that market forces have a greater influence on wages and employment conditions in countries where, like the United States, the employment market institutions are less developed. On this subject, see P. Cappelli: "Forces driving the restructuring of employment", in *Looking Ahead* (Washington, DC, National Planning Association), Vol. XVI, No. 2-3, 1994, pp. 5-12.

[25] Rodrik, op. cit., p. 26.

[26] D. Rodrik: *Why do more open economies have bigger governments?* (Cambridge, Massachusetts, National Bureau of Economic Research, 1996), working document No. 5537.

[27] E. Kapstein: "The welfare State? An economic cornerstone, not a luxury", in *International Herald Tribune,* 26 Nov. 1996.

[28] G. Garrett and D. Mitchell: *Globalization and the welfare State: Income transfers in the industrial democracies, 1966-1990* (Wharton School, University of Pennsylvania), unpublished document, Aug. 1996, p. i.

[29] Rodrik: *Why do more open economies have bigger governments?*, op. cit., pp. 25-26.

[30] See, for example, M. Rama: "Do labour market policies and institutions matter? The adjustment experience in Latin America and the Caribbean" in *Labour* (Oxford, Basil Blackwell), special edition, 1995.

[31] J. Slemrod: "What do cross-country studies teach about government involvement, prosperity and economic growth?", in *Brookings papers on economic activity* (Washington, DC, Brookings Institution), Vol. 2, 1995.

[32] These are the conclusions of the recent study by R. Layard, cited by Stephanie Flanders in "Rethinking the State", in *Financial Times,* 3 Mar. 1997.

[33] D. Cameron: "The expansion of the public economy: A comparative analysis", in *American Political Science Review* (Menasha, Wisconsin, American Political Science Association), Vol. 72, No. 4, 1978.

[34] Garrett and Mitchell, op. cit., p. i.

[35] G. Thompson: "What kinds of national policies?: Globalization and the possibilities for domestic economic policy", in *Internationale Politik und Gesellschaft* (Bonn, Friedrich-Ebert Stiftung), forthcoming.

[36] Flanders, op. cit.

[37] This is the view of A. Wood *in North-South trade, employment and inequality* (Oxford, Clarendon Press, 1994) who considers that commercial competition has encouraged enterprises to invest in new technology in order to save on labour costs.

[38] The problems encountered by foreign affiliates in the countries where they are set up are often cited as one of the main obstacles to their integration into the local economy, because national enterprises are not in a position to adequately fulfil their needs. The fact that they are obliged to upgrade is an example of the impact that the international organization of production can have on national enterprises and on seemingly purely national restructuring measures.

[39] Several recent studies seeking factors to explain the growing income inequality in OECD countries have tried to distinguish between the impact of globalization linked to trade and to technology, usually considered as a purely internal influence.

[40] The first quotation is taken from R. Feenstra and G. Hanson: "Globalization, outsourcing and wage inequality", in *American Economic Review* (Nashville, American Economic Association), Vol. 86, No. 2, May 1996, p. 240. The second is from Rodrik: *Has globalization gone too far?*, op. cit., p. 16.

[41] Feenstra and Hanson, op. cit.

[42] See, for example, J. Cantwell: *The relationship between international trade and international production* (University of Reading, 1991).

[43] For an exhaustive study of published work on enterprise strategy and the outsourcing of production, see F. Palpacuer: *Stratégies compétitives, gestion des compétences et organisations en réseaux: étude du cas de l'industrie new-yorkaise de l'habillement,* unpublished thesis, University of Montpellier – I, Faculty of management and enterprise law, Nov. 1996, Ch. 1.

[44] Feenstra and Hanson, op. cit., p. 242.

[45] For the distinction between buyer-driven and producer-driven chains see G. Gereffi: "The reorganization of production on a world scale: States, markets and networks in the apparel and electronic commodity chains", in D. Campbell, A. Parisotte, A. Verma and A. Lateef (eds.): *Regionalization and labour market interdependence in East and Southeast Asia* (London, Macmillan, 1997).

[46] H. Figueroa: "In the name of fashion: Exploitation in the garment industry", in *NACLA Report on the Americas* (New York, North American Congress on Latin America), Vol. XXIX, No. 4, Jan.-Feb. 1996, p. 34.

[47] In more technical terms, in production chains power is situated at the point in the chain where access

is the most difficult. In clothing, for example, it is often the large retailers that control the manufacturing operations from above. In the retail trade there is also evidence of a concentration tendency which further increases the power of the large buyers (Marks & Spencer, Nike). A background paper commissioned for the present report documents this trend: P. Doeringer, B. Courault, L. Oxborrow, E. Parat and A. Watson: *Industrial relations and production channels in apparel: A comparative study of labor, management and industry* (1997).

[48] *International trade and employment: An analysis of international trade patterns in selected industries characterized by different types of commodity chains* (Geneva, International Institute for Labour Studies and International Trade Centre, UNCTAD/WTO, 1996), unpublished draft.

[49] Doeringer et al., op. cit.

[50] See R. Wandersee and A. Griffiths: *The changing face of organizational change* (Sydney, Centre for Corporate Change, 1996), p. 5.

[51] T. Kochan and M. Weinstein: "Recent developments in U.S. industrial relations", in *British Journal of Industrial Relations* (London, London School of Economics and Political Science), Vol. 32, No. 4, Dec. 1994.

[52] W. Sengenberger, G. Loveman and M. Piore (eds.): *The re-emergence of small enterprises: Industrial restructuring in industrialized countries* (Geneva, International Institute for Labour Studies, 1990).

[53] Feenstra and Hanson, op. cit.

[54] The way in which just-in-time production has spread, particularly in the car industry, is explained in *World investment report, 1995,* op. cit.

[55] J. Sydow: "Enterprise networks and co-determination: The case of the Federal Republic of Germany", in D. Campbell and W. Sengenberger (eds.): *Is the single firm vanishing? Inter-enterprise networks, labour and labour institutions* (Geneva, International Institute for Labour Studies, 1992), p. 57.

[56] An estimate of the importance of multinational enterprises in the world trading system can be found in *World investment report, 1993* (Geneva, UNCTAD, 1993).

[57] For example, several developing and newly industrialized countries have become investment capital exporters in their own right. Foreign direct investment (FDI) outward stock from developing countries increased 24-fold from 1980 to 1994, six times the rate of growth of FDI from OECD countries (derived from data in Table 4 of the Annex to the *World investment report, 1995,* op. cit., p. 407). The new multinational enterprises might adopt distinctive approaches of their own to labour-management relations. One survey of nine Korean affiliates in South-East Asia showed that none of them had a union. Korean firms, with their own labour traditions, tend to consider unions as an obstacle to their financial objectives. The survey also shows that industrial relations and human resource management practices in these foreign affiliates are similar to those seen in Korean enterprises before 1987. At that time unions were prohibited and employers had entire freedom to control the workforce by way of pay and employment systems. See Y. Park: *Industrial relations and human resource practices in Korean manufacturing firms in selected Asian countries,* unpublished report, 1996.

[58] P. Hirst and G. Thompson: *Globalization in question,* op. cit. The authors argue, for example, that the majority of multinational enterprises are not truly global firms but retain strong ties to their home-country location and markets. See also R. Lipsey, M. Blomström and E. Ramstetter: *Internationalized production in world output* (Cambridge, Massachusetts, National Bureau of Economic Research, 1995), Working Paper No. 5385.

[59] S. Frenkel and C. Royal: *Globalization and employment relations,* document prepared for the East Asia Multidisciplinary Team (Bangkok, 1996), p. 19.

[60] International hotel chains are a good example. Hotel services are not affected by trade and are consumed in the same location that they are provided. Enterprises must therefore provide the same, or almost the same, activities in all the locations where they establish themselves. Activities across affiliates may in consequence be less integrated; on the other hand, the sort of services available or quality of staff could be relatively homogeneous across different affiliates in the same international hotel chain (or same fast-food restaurant).

[61] *World investment report, 1995,* op. cit., p. 196.

[62] ibid., p. 199.

[63] B. Burger and R. Jungnickel: *Relocation outside the union* (Hamburg, HWWA, 1996), p. 10.

[64] *World investment report, 1995,* op. cit., p. 200.

[65] E. Gundlach and P. Nunnenkamp: "Globalization and labour markets in the triad: Different adjustment patterns", in *Transnational Corporations* (Geneva, UNCTAD), forthcoming.

[66] S. Frenkel: *Patterns of workplace relations in the global corporation: Towards convergence?* (Sydney, University of New South Wales, 1991), duplicated document.

[67] On remuneration linked to results in the large European multinationals, see R. Taylor: "Employment flexibility 'common across EU'", in *Financial Times,* 2 Apr. 1997.

[68] P. Marginson and K. Sisson: "The structure of transnational capital in Europe: The emerging Euro-company and its implications for industrial relations", in R. Hyman and A. Ferner (eds.): *New frontiers in European industrial relations* (Oxford, Blackwell, 1994), p. 23.

[69] P. Marginson, P. Armstrong, P.K. Edwards and J. Purcell: "Extending beyond borders: Multinational companies and international management of labour" in *International Journal of Human Resource Management* (London, Routledge Journals), No. 6, Sep. 1995. P. Marginson and K. Sisson: "Multinational companies and the future of collective bargaining: A review of research issues", in *European Journal of Industrial Relations* (London, Sage), Vol. 2, No. 2, July 1996.

[70] P. Marginson: "EWCs – opening the door to European bargaining?", in *European Works Councils Bulletin* (University of Warwick, Eclipse), No. 1, 1996, p. 11.

[71] *Financial Times:* "The UK cut down to size", 10 Mar. 1997, p. 15.

[72] L. Bellmann et al.: *Patterns of enterprise flexibility in Germany: Results of the IAB establishment panel, 1993-95,* contribution to the OECD's "Flexible Enterprise" project (Nuremberg, Institute for Employment Research, 1996), p. 69.

[73] *Guide to responsible restructuring* (Washington, DC, United States Department of Labor, Office of the American Workplace, 1995), p. 9.

[74] M. Ozaki: "Labour relations and work organization in industrialized countries", in *International Labour Review* (Geneva, ILO), Vol. 135, No. 1, 1996, p. 37.

[75] In the United States, for instance, the number of temporary and contract workers has increased dramatically during the last decades and currently accounts for a quarter of the total workforce. Highly skilled professionals account for approximately 24 per cent of contract workers, including lawyers, doctors, scientists, computer analysts and financial auditors. The number of persons working for personnel supply agencies increased from 250,000 in 1975 to 1.9 million in 1993. The major recent change has been in the development of subcontracting in the public sector of a number of countries. In the United Kingdom, for example, subcontracting of the public sector functions has gone far beyond its traditional domain such as refuse collection, catering, cleaning and maintenance, and currently involves various high-skilled occupations, such as accountancy, legal, architectural, and administrative occupations. See ILO: *Contract labour,* International Labour Conference, 85th Session, 1997, Report VI(1), pp. 17-19.

[76] For overviews of the various concepts of HRM, see: J. Storey (ed.): *Human Resource Management:* "Human resource management: Still marching on, or marching out?" (London, Routledge, 1995), and J. Kitay and R. Lansbury: "Human resource management and industrial relations in an era of global markets: Australian and international trends", in *Human Resource Management and Workplace Change,* proceedings of an EPAC roundtable held in Canberra on 6 Feb. 1995 (Canberra, Economic Planning Advisory Commission, 1995), pp. 17-70.

[77] See K. Sisson "Change and continuity in British industrial relations: 'Strategic choice' or muddling through?", in R. Locke, T. Kochan and M. Piore (eds.): *Employment relations in a changing world economy* (Cambridge, MIT Press, 1995). M. Regini: "Human resource management and industrial relations in European companies", in *International Journal of Human Resource Management* (London, Routledge Journals), No. 3, 1993.

[78] C. Brewster and A. Hegewisch (eds.): *Policy and practice in European human resource management: The Price Waterhouse Cranfield Survey* (London, Routledge, 1994), Tables 4.2a and 4.3a.

[79] Available surveys show that only 19 per cent of German companies had quality circles in 1992 (ibid., table 6.6) while 52.1 per cent of Japanese employees surveyed replied that their companies were implementing small group activities such as quality circles in 1994. See *Survey on labour-management communications* (Tokyo, Ministry of Labour, 1994). According to a 1994 United States survey, 37 per cent reported that they had adopted a formal total quality management programme: *First findings from the educational quality of the workforce national employer survey* (Philadelphia, University of Pennsylvania, 1995), p. 3.

[80] P. Osterman: "How common is workplace transformation and who adopts it?", in *Industrial and Labor Relations Review* (Ithaca, New York State School of Industrial and Labor Relations), Vol. 47, No. 2, 1994, p. 306.

[81] A study of steel mills in the United States revealed that a coherent and integrated system of innovative practices, including extensive recruiting and careful selection, flexible job definitions and problem-solving teams, gains sharing-type compensation plans, employment security, and extensive labour-management communications, substantially improves productivity and quality outcomes. In contrast, the adoption of individual work practice innovations has no effect on productivity. See C. Ichniowski, K. Shaw and G. Prennushi: *The impact of human resource management on productivity* (Cambridge, Massachusetts, National Bureau of Economic Research, 1995), Working Paper No. 2333.

[82] T. Noda and T. Tachibanaki: "Misosiki rodoshato noryokushugi" [Non-unionized workers and meritocracy], in *Rodokumiaino Keizaigaku [Economics of Trade Unions]* (Tokyo, Toyokeizaishimposha, 1993).

[83] V. Ratnam: *Indian industrial relations,* document prepared for the ILO (1996).

[84] R. Dombois and L. Pries: "Structural change and trends in the evolution of industrial relations in Latin America", in *Avances de Investigación* (University of Bremen, 1995), No. 1, p. 68.

[85] See for example J. Carrillo: "La experiencia latinoamericana del justo a tiempo y el control de calidad",

in *Revista Latinoamericana de Sociología del Trabajo* (Mexico, Asociación Latinoamericana de Sociología del Trabajo), No. 1, 1995. C.M. López: "Programas de calidad total: Un camino hacia la democracia industrial en Colombia?", in R. Dombois and C. M. López (eds.): *Cambio Técnico, Empleo y Trabajo en Colombia* (Fescol, Bogota, 1993).

[86] M. Morishima: "Embedding HRM in a social context", in *British Journal of Industrial Relations* (London, London School of Economics and Political Science), No. 4, 1995, p. 636.

[87] C. Brewster et al.: "Employee communication and participation", in Brewster and Hegewisch, op. cit.

[88] H. Weibrecht and S. Fisher: "Individualism and collectivism: The dimension of human resource", in *Industrielle Beziehungen* (Mering, Rainer Hampp Verlag), No. 2, 1995.

[89] C. Berggren: *Alternatives to lean production. Work organization in the Swedish auto industry* (Ithaca, ILR Press, 1992), pp. 228-229.

[90] D. Frohlich and U. Pekruhl: *Direct participation and organizational change fashionable but misunderstood: An analysis of recent research in Europe, Japan and the USA* (Dublin, European Foundation for the Improvement of Living and Working Conditions, 1996), p. 153.

[91] T. Murakami: "Introducing team working: A motor industry case study from Germany", in *Industrial Relations Journal* (Oxford, Basil Blackwell), Vol. 26, No. 4, Dec. 1995, p. 302.

[92] C. Ichniowski, J. Delaney and D. Lewin: "The new human resource management in U.S. workplaces: Is it really new and is it only non-union?", in *Relations industrielles* (Quebec, Faculty of Social Sciences), Vol. 44, 1988.

[93] N. Millwards, S. Stevens, D. Smart and W. Hawes: *Workplace industrial relations in transition: The ED/ESRC/PSI/ACAS Surveys* (Dartmouth, Aldershot, 1992).

[94] T. Kochan and P. Osterman: *Mutual gains enterprise: Forging a winning partnership among labor, management and government* (Boston, Harvard Business School Press, 1994), pp. 106-107.

[95] K. Wever: *Negotiating competitiveness: Employment relations and organizational innovation in Germany and the United States* (Boston, Harvard Business School Press, 1995), p. 24.

[96] *The new American workplace,* Report by the AFL-CIO Committee on the Evolution of Work (Washington, DC, AFL-CIO, 1994).

5 The instruments of social dialogue in the industrialized countries

Introduction

All countries are currently experiencing a trend towards an increasing autonomy of enterprises and an individualization of labour relations, albeit to differing degrees. It has even been suggested that, in the future, worker protection could be provided on a purely individual basis through the courts, while enterprises would be directly responsible for collective labour relations through their personnel management policies. Simultaneously, however, it is equally apparent that a considerable proportion of workers are subject to exclusion, whether on account of marked inequality in wages and social protection, unemployment, or increasing casualization of jobs. The resultant problems of social cohesion have become a major source of concern in most countries. While the crisis of solidarity experienced by the social actors and the precedence given to the pursuit of competitiveness might have been expected to weaken the different forms of social dialogue, in many countries the reverse phenomenon is occurring. The following chapters will demonstrate that the various social pacts negotiated in Central and Eastern Europe, Latin America and South Africa have proved to be the most effective means of preserving social cohesion and of introducing vital reforms during these periods of great instability. Western Europe has a tradition of highly structured instruments of social consultation which continue to be invoked, on occasion very intensively, by governments. In Canada, in 1996, a working group set up by the Government drew up a series of proposals designed to enhance the effectiveness of collective bargaining.[1] In the United States similar concerns were expressed in the Dunlop Commission report, almost three years ago. Some would doubtless consider that the outcomes of these various initiatives have not lived up to expectations. Obviously, the obstacles encountered by national policies, outlined in previous chapters, also have a bearing on the results of social dialogue. But is there any other way to respond today to the dilemma facing most countries of how to reconcile the decentralization and individualization which accompany more intense competition, and the competitiveness imperative, with labour regulations which reduce insecurity and inequality, as well as the pressures they exert on social integration and economic development? Such regulation is precisely the objective of industrial relations and of collective bargaining, its principal institution, taken in its broadest sense to include not only the negotiation of formal collective agreements but also the different channels of consultation and social dialogue. Responses vary in accordance with the nature of the social relations and institutions in different countries. This chapter will examine these responses.

In the context of industrialized countries, a comparison is traditionally made between a "voluntarist" model which originated in England, but of which the United States is today the main proponent, and a European model. The first model features decentralized bargaining which focuses on the economic protection of workers, with minimal state intervention. In the second, collective bargaining is coordinated at a more centralized level and seeks to promote both economic protection and a model of social solidarity, with considerably more extensive state intervention. These two models were subsequently joined by a third which is based on the Japanese situation. Here, collective bargaining is decentralized but less conflictual than under the voluntarist approach and is coordinated at the national level; while state intervention is not ruled out, it is of a considerably less formalistic nature than in Europe. The Japanese case illustrates the impact of a country's particular social structures on the evolution of industrial relations, given that this system was originally based on the American model. Figure 5.1 compares the first two groups. It may be seen that, in countries with a voluntarist system, collective bargaining coverage corresponds fairly closely to the level of trade union membership. In countries with a "coordinated" system, it is markedly higher. The fact that bargaining continues to be conducted outside the enterprise means that the representativeness of the social partners as bargaining agents does not reside exclusively in the number of trade union members, although a drop in numbers would necessarily undermine their effectiveness. It will become apparent that the nature of industrial relations has an impact on the way in which the growing role of the enterprise in social regulation, identified in the previous chapter, is accommodated.

In the light of these differences industrial relations in industrialized countries will be presented in a manner that distinguishes those countries with a coordinated bargaining system (primarily those in Western Europe) from those with a decentralized bargaining system (United States, United Kingdom and, more recently, New Zealand and Australia), and the principal characteristics of each group will be outlined. Japan will be dealt with separately.

While all economies obviously seek to bolster their competitive position, the means to achieve this end is by no means obvious, despite numerous studies on the subject.[2] A familiar fascination exists regarding the successive economic miracles brought to the public's attention the moment a country's growth rate remains a few points above the average for any length of time. Often, the most miraculous aspect of these cases is that they are wholly unexpected. *A posteriori* explanations vary considerably. On occasion, good economic performance is attributed to deregulation. Cases in point are the United States and the United Kingdom where, judging by unemployment indicators, the voluntarist model based on enterprise bargaining appears to be the most effective system under current conditions. But good performance is also sometimes due to sound regulation backed by broad social consensus. Such was the

Figure 5.1. **Unionization and collective bargaining coverage rates, 1994-96**

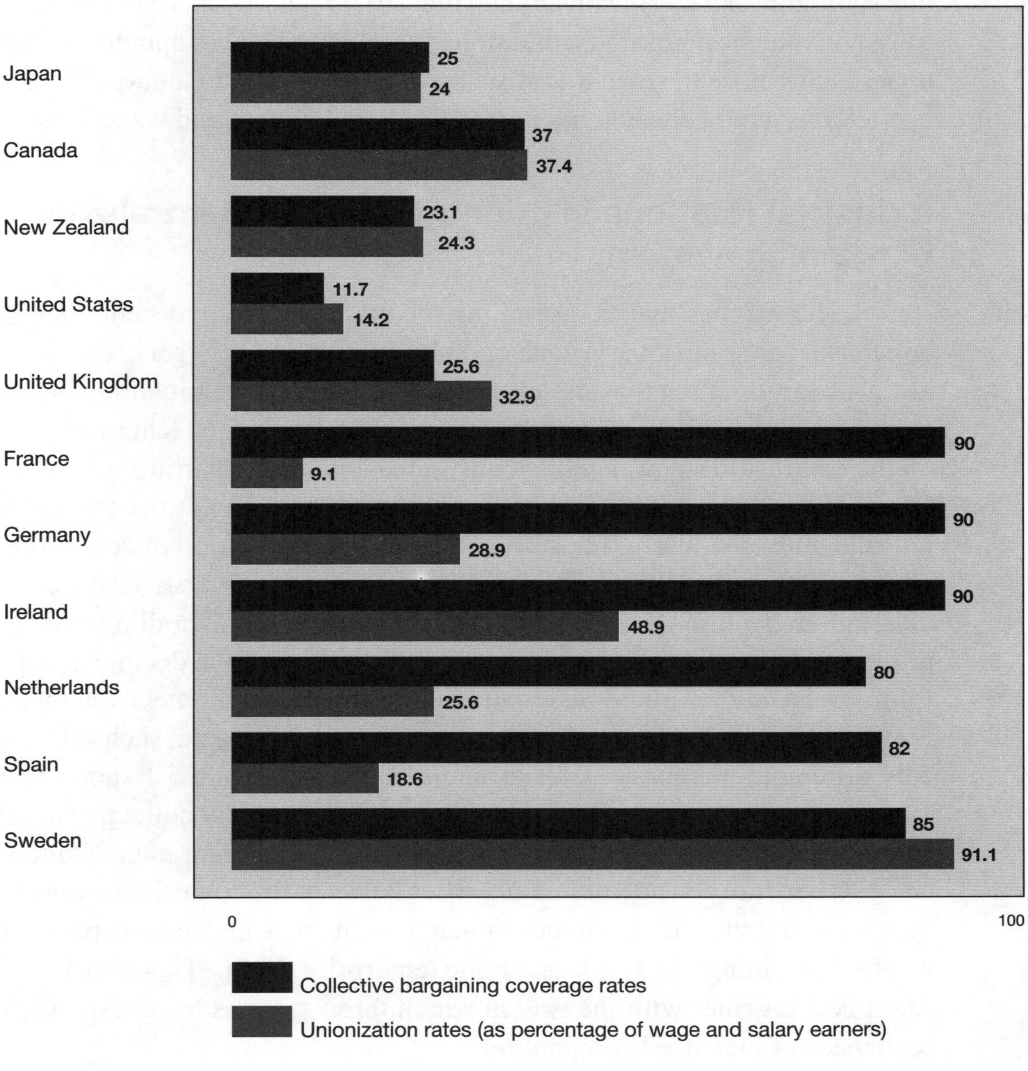

Country	Collective bargaining coverage rates	Unionization rates
Japan	25	24
Canada	37	37.4
New Zealand	23.1	24.3
United States	11.7	14.2
United Kingdom	25.6	32.9
France	90	9.1
Germany	90	28.9
Ireland	90	48.9
Netherlands	80	25.6
Spain	82	18.6
Sweden	85	91.1

0　　　　　　　　　　　　　　　　　　　100

■ Collective bargaining coverage rates
■ Unionization rates (as percentage of wage and salary earners)

Source: See the technical notes in the Statistical Annex.

case, in the past, in Sweden and Japan. It also applies, today, to Ireland and the Nether-lands which employ highly centralized collective bargaining systems and currently display particularly enviable economic indicators. Indeed, the role of industrial rela-tions is to contribute to the implementation of policies which, in the context of the specific economic conditions existing in a given country, take account of the social balances to be maintained if social cohesion is not to be jeopardized. In short, it is not possible to formulate a single, ideal model of industrial relations that is more condu-cive to economic growth than any other. In demonstrating their effectiveness in maintaining or strengthening social cohesion, and in finding solutions which reconcile economic and social constraints, industrial relations serve in a democratic society to provide the best possible conditions for economic development. The question that arises is therefore the extent to which social dialogue can, today, counter the pressure exerted on social cohesion by increased unemployment and wage inequalities.[3]

Industrial relations in countries with decentralized bargaining systems

The circumstances prevailing in countries with decentralized systems of collective bargaining vary considerably. In some cases, such decentralization has always been dominant, while centralized or sectoral negotiations have held a very uncertain status, if they existed at all (United States, United Kingdom). In other cases, on the contrary, decentralization constituted a radical departure from earlier practices (New Zealand, Australia). In some countries, bargaining at the enterprise level does not rule out sometimes quite substantial national regulation of conditions of employment. In other cases, it is the main source of collective social protection. Finally, although trade union membership levels in general are dwindling, particularly in the private sector, as was shown in Chapter 1, the extent of the decline is not comparable, for instance, in the United States and in the United Kingdom. Given that unionization is a pillar of the bargaining process in a decentralized system, such a decline has markedly different repercussions for different countries. Figure 5.1 shows that while only 14 per cent of workers in the United States are covered by collective agreements, this figure stands at over 37 per cent in Canada and 33 per cent in the United Kingdom.

There are considerable differences between the countries of Europe, as we will see below, but they are not to be compared with those that exist between the countries where bargaining takes place at the enterprise level. These differences will be examined, together with the way in which these systems have responded to the consequences of increased competition.

Social protection in the voluntarist system of industrial relations

Under the voluntarist system, which is applied in its purest form in the United States, it is left to the social partners to define their labour relations, while the prime function of legislation is to organize collective bargaining and lay down the rules of social dialogue. Thus, the collective bargaining process lies at the heart of American labour legislation.[4] Although a number of federal and state laws do deal with retirement, minimum wages, occupational health and safety or discrimination at work,[5] such legislation is more limited than in European countries. It is illegal, for instance, for an enterprise to provide medical insurance to men but not to women, but it is not illegal to fail to provide any medical insurance whatsoever.[6] This voluntarism has achieved a degree of consensus, as evidenced by the fact that the efforts of American trade unions in the legislative sphere have sought (without success) to enhance their bargaining powers rather than to improve the legal protection of workers. Two examples of this are the proposal submitted in 1976-77 which sought to facilitate the establishment of trade unions in enterprises and that put forward in 1989, intended to prevent employers from permanently hiring workers to replace strikers. Currently, however, the substantial weakening of collective bargaining coverage has prompted the AFL-CIO to support the introduction of stronger legislative protection, as shown by its support of Clinton's health insurance bill.

The voluntarist principle is also practised in Canada and, of course, in the United Kingdom, where it originated, although in a far less stringent manner. In Canada, voluntarism came to the fore in legislation drafted in 1994 along similar lines as the United States' Wagner Act. But it is not applied in the same way, in that state intervention at both the federal and provincial levels is markedly more extensive and social protection legislation is therefore considerably more developed than in the United States. One of the major differences lies in the fact that the responsibility for protection in the areas of health and education resides in the public sector. And in the United Kingdom, although legislative regulation regarding conditions of employment is virtually non-existent, in keeping with the voluntarist principle, the existence of a national system of medical protection sets it apart from the United States. More recently, despite government reluctance, European regulations have required the United Kingdom to break with many aspects of voluntarism, for example requiring mandatory consultation on collective dismissals and working hours, as well as the establishment of works councils.

Until recently, the voluntarist principle was applied in Australia and New Zealand in a particularly unorthodox manner. Although their legislation governing conditions of employment is less extensive than that existing in Europe, these conditions were for a long time fixed in a highly centralized manner, with extensive involvement of the State through arbitration tribunals. In this respect, decentralization of collective bargaining introduced in 1991 in New Zealand, and beginning in 1987 in Australia, represented a more marked break with the past than in other countries, despite the fact that Australia had undergone some measure of decentralization during the 1950s and 1960s. None the less, the fact that these countries have national coverage in the areas of health and other social benefits clearly sets them apart from the United States.

The voluntarist system and the decline in collective bargaining coverage

Conditions of employment are protected in the United States primarily through collective agreements. These strictly binding agreements function as a labour code, setting down all aspects of conditions of employment for the workers they cover. Thus, potentially, they represent a substantial additional cost for unionized enterprises. This applies not only to wages, as demonstrated by numerous statistical analyses of the subject, but also to other conditions of employment. These costs were managed within a system of industry-wide bargaining ("pattern bargaining") through the application of homogeneous conditions of employment to all unionized enterprises in a given sector. This homogenization was extended also to non-unionized enterprises – at least to the largest among them – wishing to recruit quality labour and to preclude the establishment of a trade union. With the weakening of pattern bargaining which accompanied the deregulation of the early 1980s, enterprise-level collective agreements lost their main source of strength.

Since such agreements involve an additional cost to an enterprise relative to non-unionized competitors, employers obviously endeavour to weaken them, either by union avoidance or by seeking concessions from unions. A third course, which is complementary to the latter, is to enlist worker cooperation, although trade unions in the United States are not unanimous in their view of the matter, for reasons that will be discussed below. All this has the obvious result of markedly reducing the number of workers covered by collective agreements and of substantially weakening collective forms of social protection as a result. In a voluntarist system such as that in the United States, a decline in unionization levels therefore raises social protection problems that are very different from those arising in European countries where, in addition to legislation, homogeneous social coverage is extended to all enterprises through centralized national or industry-wide agreements. Although many non-unionized American enterprises provide the same level of benefits without an agreement as they would if an agreement existed, none the less the absence of collective protection tends to increase workers' sense of insecurity.

This phenomenon has been less extensive in Canada and the United Kingdom. Despite a decline in unionization rates, a substantial number of workers are still covered by collective agreements. The success of collective bargaining in Canada may no doubt be attributed in part to its favourable legislation. In the United Kingdom, although bargaining coverage and unionization levels did decline in recent years, the fact that there was not a sharp drop is remarkable, given the particularly unfavourable economic and political climate. It is true that in both countries employer opposition to trade union presence has been considerably less than in the United States. In the United Kingdom, procedures for derecognition of trade unions as bargaining agents have been limited to only one or two sectors and a few large enterprises.[7] There is no doubt an economic reason for this, namely the fact that the existence of state regulation, for example concerning health insurance, makes enterprise agreements less costly, both individually and in relative terms. It is also worth noting that trade unions in the United Kingdom have successfully maintained a degree of industry-wide coordination on non-wage-related matters such as annual leave, working time, etc.[8] In general, in these countries, a greater readiness exists to recognize collective bargaining as a mechanism of social regulation.

Over and above direct financial costs, intense deregulation and competition have affected collective bargaining all the more since agreements in the United States traditionally contain clauses which specify job structures. Therefore, enterprises embarking on job re-engineering must enter into lengthy negotiations at a time when the new economic situation makes it necessary continually to seek more productive ways of organizing work. It is interesting to note that these practices were originally intended to protect jobs, which would be less likely to be cut if their content were controlled. Regardless of whether or not these clauses really are effective in protecting jobs, workers' feelings of insecurity are heightened when they are challenged, including in the agreements concluded in many enterprises.

Such trade union control of job content occurs, in different forms, in other Anglo-Saxon countries. In Australia, it was partly the desire to restrict these practices and to reduce the number of job definitions that led the social partners to decentralize wage bargaining, in order to make wage increases conditional upon the patterns of work organization intended to boost productivity. Trade union control of job content is rooted in a tradition of craft-based unionism which has long sought to ensure that the specific tasks corresponding to the trade that a given union represents are not carried out by other categories of workers. In the United Kingdom, these "restrictive practices", which were not prescribed in written form but were customarily applied, were a longstanding leitmotif of collective bargaining, particularly during the 1970s, and led to the conclusion of what came to be called "productivity agreements" negotiated at the enterprise level. However, they never acquired the "legalistic" nature that existed in the United States. Even in Canada, which has a similar job definition system, it does not seem to be as rigid.[9]

Decentralization or decline of collective bargaining?

To talk of decentralization in countries where bargaining is centred on the enterprise might seem paradoxical. But decentralization is in fact taking place, as evidenced by the virtual disappearance of pattern bargaining in the United States, and to a lesser extent in Canada, and also of industry-wide agreements in the United Kingdom. This process is by no means recent, however, and in fact began some 15 years ago. It should further be borne in mind that, in the United States, industry-wide bargaining never became as prevalent as in Europe, while enterprise bargaining has always occupied a particularly prominent position. In contrast, decentralization is a major phenomenon in Australia, and to an even greater extent in New Zealand. In Australia, decentralization occurred gradually, with the participation of employers' and workers' organizations. It does not, however, rule out central bargaining, since there are still "agreements" at that level fixing minimum conditions of employment, a function which appears to have been institutionalized by the Workplace Relations and

Other Legislation Amendment Act, adopted in November 1996. It would, however, be premature to venture a definitive assessment of the evolution of the Australian system that is currently being implemented amidst a great deal of controversy. It is apparent, then, that the nature of decentralization varies from country to country. In addition, judging by the decline in collective bargaining coverage, the prevailing trend in countries such as the United States and New Zealand, and possibly Australia in the future, is the waning influence of collective bargaining.

A debate is at present taking place in the United States regarding the possibility of negotiating conditions of employment in non-union enterprises. Under current legislation, this is not possible since, as in many other countries, a collective agreement must be signed by a representative trade union. There are two ways of looking at this. On the one hand, collective representation could be provided where trade unions have not been established, thereby improving the protection of workers. In the longer term, this might give new impetus to the trade union movement. But on the other hand, it might forestall the establishment of trade unions, since collective protection would thereby be afforded without their intervention. While it is difficult to predict the long-term outcome, the examples of Australia and New Zealand, where this possibility is enshrined in legislation (the Industrial Relations Reform Act 1993 in Australia and the Employment Contracts Act 1991 in New Zealand), offer some indication for the short and medium term. Studies show that in Australia, three years after the law was passed, only 181 such agreements had been signed, compared to 6,269 agreements signed with unions.[10] In New Zealand, five years after the reform, collective agreements signed with trade unions apply to 85 per cent of workers covered by collective agreements.[11] These figures indicate that, under current circumstances, collective bargaining continues to be associated with the presence of traditional trade unionism. If a similar reform were to take place in the United States, what future would there be for collective bargaining in a context of sharply declining unionization rates and decentralized bargaining? This question may best be answered by looking at the way in which the content of collective agreements has evolved.

Changes in the content of collective bargaining

The purpose of concession bargaining, which began ten years ago in the United States, was to save jobs. Initially, concessions mainly involved wage increases. For the most part, it was more a matter of wage moderation than wage cuts, except in the case of newly hired workers for whom some trade unions accepted a reduction in wages and related benefits. Agreements intended to curb the cost of health insurance were also concluded from the outset. Over time, the job protection clauses were fine-tuned. Those which occur most frequently, for instance in agreements signed in 1994, involve early retirement, increased compensation for voluntary separation and continued health coverage for a given period after redundancy.[12] An increasing number of agreements also contain measures intended to promote training to help workers either to get another job in the same enterprise or to search for another job outside it. The most remarkable feature of these clauses, when compared to the European bargaining that will be examined in the following section, lies in the fact that they seek first and foremost to protect workers while they are unemployed rather than to keep them employed. The European rationale of work-sharing does not prevail in the United States. A rare exception to this is the agreement signed between the NYNEX telephone company and the industry trade unions, which includes a measure to this effect.[13]

Interpretations of how concession bargaining has affected the evolution of industrial relations have always diverged. Some hold the view that it was a temporary phenomenon triggered by a situation of economic depression and that, once the economy had recovered, trade unions would regain their strength and collective bargaining would revert to its traditional concerns. This view was partially borne out by negotiated wage levels which rose after 1989 (but, after 1992, although still fairly high, these increases were none the less lower than in previous years). Others considered that the change was more deep-rooted, with new technologies and increased competition and productivity requirements exerting a far-reaching effect on labour relations and conditions of employment. If trade unionism was to survive under these circumstances, it would have to undertake radical reforms.[14] This view is borne out by concession clauses affecting control of job content.

As mentioned previously, together with the seniority rule, the formal job descriptions contained in collective agreements provided American trade unions with a powerful means of controlling personnel management by the enterprise. Indeed, a substantial part of a trade union representative's functions consisted in resolving disputes in this area through existing grievance procedures. Just as the objective of wage concessions is to reduce production costs, so concessions on job content seek to enhance productivity by allowing greater flexibility in the allocation of human resources in the production process. The number of grades at which such flexibility is permitted is generally reduced under these agreements, while at the same time they facilitate the implementation of cooperation programmes, at the enterprise and shop-floor levels, intended to boost productivity. As stated in the previous chapter, such programmes are not confined to non-union enterprises, but have been introduced in unionized firms as well.

These experiences of participation constituted a radical departure from the United States' tradition of trade union activity founded on economic opposition to employers, in defence of wages and jobs. As stated by the Dunlop Commission, this situation was reflected in the highly conflictual climate surrounding the election of representatives.[15] It was therefore considered that any participation in management would inevitably lead to sell-out agreements. The recent agreements thus represent a new departure, both as regards control of job content and in terms of opposition between unions and employers, and this explains why the trade union movement is sharply divided on this issue.

Collective bargaining and social integration

One of the main conclusions of the Dunlop report is that, if the current situation persists, the American system will inevitably move towards an increasing opposition between workers and employers, thereby perpetuating a cycle of disputes and mistrust, with harmful repercussions for innovation and productivity.[16] While the decline in collective bargaining coverage does appear to confirm this increasing opposition, the reality of the situation is somewhat more complex. Numerous studies carried out in large enterprises in the automobile, telecommunications, rubber and steel industries reveal a by no means insignificant number of conflictual situations, but also point out that traditional relations have been maintained, while new machinery for dialogue has been established, with or without trade unions. While it is limited in scope, one study on bargaining in small enterprises identifies three models: traditional, conflictual and cooperative. The authors suggest that the latter two models are gaining ground.[17] Case-studies of enterprises engaging in cooperative relations show that tangible advantages are obtained by workers (in terms of social protection, vocational training) with no concomitant deterioration in the enterprise's competitive position, which in some cases even improves. Of course, enterprises without social dialogue can also achieve a positive economic performance. But what these examples show is that social dialogue is compatible with sound economic management of enterprises. Therefore, the choice is based on altogether different criteria.

The paradox of the situation in the United States is that, notwithstanding very low unemployment levels, opinion polls reveal a widespread feeling of job insecurity. This lies at the centre of the social debate in that country, on a par with income inequality, which is clearly borne out by the figures. This sense of insecurity was no doubt engendered by the mass lay-offs attending the restructuring of major American enterprises, particularly since they occurred for the most part in domestic markets where job security had appeared to be protected under collective agreements. Subsequently, as enterprises became convinced that they had to restructure continually in order to maintain their competitive edge, lay-offs came to be considered to be a normal element of personnel management practices.[18] Mobility has always been particularly high in the United States, but it has today acquired the peculiarity of most often leading to a lower-paid job than that held previously. A survey has shown that 65 per cent of workers who are made redundant subsequently accept a lower-paid job.[19] Workers' sense of insecurity is exacerbated by a voluntarist system of social protection, which becomes particularly vulnerable in a context of declining unionization rates.

Job insecurity and the growing wage disparities affecting low-skilled workers result in a polarization of the American workforce which undermines social integration. This rift will inevitably widen in response to the weakening of trade unions and the resultant substantial reduction in collective bargaining coverage. The phenomenon is less marked in other countries with decentralized bargaining systems, where statutory protection exists for health, for instance, and where unionization levels and collective bargaining coverage have retained some measure of critical mass. It should also be noted that the increased earnings differential is not as marked in the United Kingdom as in the United States, since the real income of the lowest-paid workers is dropping in the United States, while in the United Kingdom the rate of increase is simply lower than for other categories.[20] As it has been pointed out, in these countries the trade unions still have a recognized role in social regulation and stability. In Canada, national tripartite bodies, as well as bipartite sectoral committees, engage employers and trade unions in social dialogue on matters of national interest, vocational training or employment.

In the United States, it is the wage-earning population that is liable to experience social fragmentation, which might therefore be combated effectively through social dialogue within the enterprise. Indeed, collective bargaining, by its very nature, involves people at work, and is therefore not best equipped to deal with that sector of the population which is excluded from the labour market. The traditional collective agreement in the United States certainly lays a particular burden on individual enterprises because of the structure of the industrial relations system, in which the collective regulation of conditions of employment takes place essentially through collective bargaining. Hence, in the context of fiercer competition, the absence of a system ensuring minimum homogenization of conditions of employment (a function which was carried out in part by pattern bargaining) and which requires individual enterprises to bear the cost of social protection, contributes to the decline in collective bargaining coverage, which can be expected to continue. One way to remedy the situation would be to draw up federal regulations, as has been done for retirement pensions. But the health protection reform backed by the trade unions, for example, failed, and this highlights the obstacles lying in the way of such an approach under the American system, with the exception of particular periods in its history. A second, possibly more realistic course would be to alter the forms of collective bargaining in such a way as to make agreements less legalistic and detailed, and providing a greater flexibility in human resource management, in exchange for collective protection of general conditions of employment (wages, social benefits, leave, training). This approach at the micro level does not imply that trade unions must necessarily be replaced by other forms of collective representation, such as works councils, as has been suggested by some American specialists, although it does entail a new style of bargaining. It is a more lengthy process and requires that a climate of mutual confidence be gradually built up. In the United States and Canada, instances of local bargaining have occurred, as described in Chapter 2, which will be further discussed at the conclusion of this chapter.

This analysis of countries with decentralized systems shows that the approaches adopted and the solutions implemented regarding labour matters are strongly influenced by national circumstances. This is reflected in differing levels of solidarity (unionization rates, attitudes towards social dialogue) and in particular institutional arrangements (forms of social protection) which combine to create different lines of resistance that must be taken into account by national policies. Moreover, an analysis of the content of bargaining in the United States, and indeed in other countries, shows that the process clearly seeks solutions above and beyond the application of market mechanisms alone, and is based on specific economic and social realities. Mobility, for instance, has always been high in the United States and collective bargaining seeks to provide some attendant measure of security. This is the case of agreements which promote training to improve workers' future job prospects. It is none the less true that such a highly decentralized system is particularly vulnerable when competition becomes fiercer. The system can and should be rebuilt along lines that are appropriate to the country's situation, because a society is exposed to considerable risk if it is managed solely on the basis of the laws of the market.

Industrial relations in countries with coordinated bargaining systems

Currently, in most of Western Europe, the issue of employment has come to take precedence over the combat against inflation waged during the 1970s. At that time, incomes policy was the order of the day. It has been superseded by the concept of the employment pact. While at that time it was believed that efforts to reduce inflation by holding down wage increases might be more efficient if carried out through centralized collective bargaining, the cornerstone of corporatism, today it is thought that unemployment can only be effectively combated through initiatives at enterprise level. The circumstances and the issue are, of course, very different. At that time, the objective was to prevent enterprises from granting the high wage increases (which they could now afford thanks to sustained economic growth) dictated by the shortage of labour. Trade unions had to moderate their demands in exchange for a fairer redistribution of productivity gains and improved qualitative benefits. In contrast, as a result of globalization, and in a context of heavy competition, low growth and high capital intensity, the aim is to get enterprises to maintain and, where possible, to increase their workforce. One possible course is to "deinstitutionalize" the economy, and as far as possible to create the theoretical conditions for pure and unhindered competition. Another option is to seek alternative forms of institutionalization, which is the course favoured by most European countries.

Clearly, the new economic, organizational and social circumstances analysed in the preceding chapters also have an impact on coordinated bargaining systems. However, the fact that collective bargaining structures are firmly established at the different levels in all these countries means that the upheavals occurring in industrial relations are not affecting social dialogue to the same extent as in countries with a decentralized system. They are reflected in two tendencies. The first is to look at the role that should be played by enterprise in dealing with the effects of the new forms of competition. The second, at the opposite extreme, is to seek solutions at the national level through the support offered by a number of governments in drafting centralized bi- or tripartite agreements. In a sense, these agreements have a political dimension in that they aim both to legitimize innovative solutions and to maintain a stable framework, while ensuring the solidarity necessary to tackle certain issues at a time of rapid transformation, and hence instability. In other words, these national pacts seek to provide a framework for change in order to mitigate the attendant insecurity, for the fact remains that this appears to be a situation of radical transformation during which countries are experimenting with many different options in order to find the most appropriate institutional combinations.

Experimenting with enterprise bargaining

In the countries with coordinated bargaining systems a trend is apparent towards decentralization, while national and industry-wide bargaining are losing ground. In Sweden, where centralized industrial relations have long been the norm, the employers' confederation recently gave up its seats on a number of central tripartite advisory bodies and ceased signing national bipartite agreements with trade unions. Similarly, in Germany, which has a long tradition of industry-wide bargaining, some employers, particularly in the metalworking sector, have recently begun to question the desirability of continuing this practice. Their main argument was that industry-wide bargaining could no longer give enterprises the flexibility they needed to adapt to continually increasing competition. Moreover, today, German industry-wide agreements increasingly include an "opening clause" which allows works councils and employers to negotiate amendments to these agreements at the enterprise level. For instance, the 1994 agreement in the metalworking branch on job security allowed the local social partners to modify the working time stipulated in the collective agreement in order to save jobs. More recently, the agreement signed in the chemical sector in June 1997 provided for the possibility of enterprise negotiation of a variable portion of wages which may be increased or reduced according to local economic conditions. Such exemptions are currently more frequent in countries such as Germany, where enterprise-level bargaining is subject to legal restrictions, Austria and the Netherlands. In France, the number of enterprise agreements has increased since the early 1980s, and especially since 1990, rising from 6,496 to 8,550 in 1995.[21] In this country, however, while industry-wide agreements are a linchpin of the collective bargaining system, with the exception of a few branches they have often had less impact on enterprises than that in other European countries, particularly as regards wages.

But decentralization is still limited in these countries. In 1995, enterprise agreements covered only 8 per cent of the private sector in the Netherlands (compared to 75 per cent for industry-wide agreements), 14 per cent in Spain (compared to about 70 per cent for industry-wide agreements) and 25 per cent in France (compared to over 80 per cent for industry-wide agreements). Moreover, while the reappraisal of industry-wide bargaining in Germany should certainly not be underestimated, it would none the less be premature to conclude, as some already have, that the German system of industrial relations, which had previously been considered one of the most solid bastions of the "European model" of industry-wide bargaining, is on the way out. In this connection, it should be pointed out that, while such a reappraisal is the subject of heated debate among employers in the metalworking sector, the German employers' organization in the chemical sector has published an official position paper supporting industry-wide bargaining, and the same view is held by the regional affiliates of the employers' organization in the metal industry.[22] Similarly, in Sweden, while central wage agreements are no longer the order of the day, bargaining at industry level remains a current practice. Indeed the wage agreement signed in March 1997, which covers a dozen branches of economic activity, shows that the social partners still desire some measure of centralization.

Entrenched traditional bargaining structures alone cannot account for the enduring presence of bargaining levels outside the enterprise. The countries with coordinated bargaining systems have a historical tradition of maintaining the neutrality of the enterprise as a bargaining level, regardless of the degree of opposition between employers and trade unions, which varies a great deal from country to country. This tradition is apparent in legislation of the type existing in Germany, which keeps the trade unions, in their function as bargaining agent, outside the enterprise. This practice of neutralizing the enterprise is particularly prevalent in France, where trade unions have always feared that enterprise-level bargaining might lend itself too readily to cooperation with management and to the development of enterprise corporatism. It is significant, in this connection, that it has proved so difficult for enterprise bargaining to gain ground in this country, despite the stimulus introduced by the Act of June 1971 and strengthened by the Act of November 1982, which made the practice mandatory.

Works councils were set up in these countries in order to develop institutions within enterprises focusing on dialogue and cooperation as opposed to confrontation, even though the elected representatives are generally trade union activists (see box 5.1). As was pointed out in the previous chapter, the implementation of human resource development policies is easier in these countries than in those without joint bodies for dialogue. Indeed, matters relating to the organization of work in the broadest sense have, on the whole, been dealt with in a non-conflictual manner, allowing the employer a great deal of room to manoeuvre, or through dialogue within works councils. This model is therefore, to a large extent, the reverse of the voluntarist model.

Box 5.1. Main features of works councils in European countries

The works council is the main institution for participation in Europe. It is a representative body at the establishment, enterprise or group level; its members are, in principle, elected by all the workers, whether or not they belong to a trade union. Works councils have the right to be informed and consulted on matters including those relating to production and jobs; in some cases, they have the right to participate in decision-making on personnel issues. Over the last ten years, they have proliferated and their influence has increased following the adoption of legislation, and also because of the growing importance attributed to qualitative factors in improving enterprise competitiveness. Greek legislation created works councils in 1988; Switzerland introduced mandatory participation in the private sector in 1994; and France, Austria and Spain have recently widened the remit of works councils. In the Netherlands, in April 1996 an Act respecting works councils extended worker representation to the public sector.

All the countries of continental Europe now have works councils, with the exception of Sweden and Finland where it is the local trade unions that have the right to be represented in the enterprise. However, the structure, activities and decision-making powers of works councils vary considerably. The matters they deal with generally exclude those already covered by employers' and trade union organizations. Their main function is cooperation, and most are not authorized to initiate or to participate in strikes. Spanish legislation differs in that it authorizes councils to negotiate wages and call strikes. Similarly, in Italy, councils have both a consultation/information and a bargaining function. In general, works councils have more extensive consultation rights in Austria, Denmark and the Netherlands than in Belgium, France, Greece or Portugal, for instance. It is in Germany, however, that they are most influential, as they have powers of co-determination on a number of matters affecting workers, including methods of remuneration, working time, leave, hiring, movement of personnel and dismissals.

In countries where works councils have clearly defined powers and functions, as in Germany, they serve as a forum for consultation and decision-making not only on wages, but also on qualitative issues such as technological change, work organization, training and personnel policy, which can generally be dealt with most effectively at the enterprise level, and which are proving to be increasingly decisive in boosting competitiveness. The works councils' job is made easier by the fact that the European system of collective bargaining deals with the potentially conflictual redistribution issues.

Joint management institutions also exist. During the 1970s and 1980s, eight European countries adopted legislation introducing worker representation on boards of directors. While legislative provisions vary from country to country, it would appear that, with the possible exception of the metalworking industry in Germany, the influence of worker representatives on boards is limited.

Given these characteristic features, decentralization clearly takes on an entirely different aspect in countries with a coordinated bargaining system. On the one hand, employers in these countries have had more leeway than those in voluntarist systems as regards decision-making on the organization of work; on the other, aside from formal agreements, works councils mostly play a quasi-bargaining role.

However, the growing importance of the enterprise as a bargaining level is increasingly offsetting the tendency towards neutralization mentioned above. This is borne out by the "opening clause" of German industry-wide agreements, or the French agreement of October 1995, followed by experimental legislation which, under certain conditions, allows agreements to be signed with works councils. Indeed it would appear that any real measures to combat unemployment must involve the enterprise. But the social partners are embarking upon this course very gingerly, most often on the basis of industry-wide or national agreements. A few significant examples of bargaining will provide an insight into the reasons why caution is advisable.

With a few exceptions, collective bargaining in Europe focuses primarily on the issue of working time (taken here in the broadest sense: reduction, organization, job-sharing, retirement, etc.) and related means of saving jobs. An analysis of the content of industry-wide and enterprise agreements shows that the most frequent job-related topics are as follows: (i) wage moderation, or even reduction (generally on an annual basis); (ii) reduction in working time with a corresponding drop in wages; and (iii) payment of overtime at the base rate or in the form of compensatory leave. These provisions are accompanied by a number of measures to facilitate access to employment, such as hiring at a reduced wage rate and, especially in Germany but also in the Netherlands, an increase in the number of apprenticeship places or a commitment to hiring a given percentage of apprentices.

Demands for a reduction in hours of work in order to enhance workers' well-being have apparently not been dropped by trade unions, as is clear from the 1995 agreement in the German metalworking sector. However, the focus on well-being, which dominated the large-scale campaigns of the late 1970s and early 1980s, has subsequently been increasingly replaced by a desire to use reduced working time as a tool for creating jobs. Consequently, the content of bargaining has become more complex, in social as well as technical terms. The trade unions' response to the meagre results achieved in creating jobs through the limited reductions in working hours that were characteristic of the previous generation of agreements, has been increasingly to consider that only substantial reductions in hours of work will lead enterprises to take on more workers. This has caused a shift towards bargaining focused on work-sharing, including part-time work, with more or less radical proposals being put forward. This is a technically complex issue, since it is difficult to ascertain how far working time must be reduced in order to trigger job creation. In addition, there are various alternatives, including a reduction in overtime, parental or sabbatical leave, partial retirement, etc. And can agreements of this kind really yield a firm commitment by enterprises to hire more workers? This type of bargaining is also complex in social terms, since it calls for strong solidarity among the workers who must accept a reduction in pay under such arrangements. Lastly, these negotiations generally mean that the trade unions have to make concessions on flexibility of working time.

In France, in 1993, following numerous unsuccessful attempts to reduce unemployment, the Government launched a five-year plan for employment which, among other things, allowed working-time arrangements on an annual basis. The results of the plan were equally inconclusive and the social partners, in turn, embarked on national negotiations regarding working time and job protection, which led to an agreement in October 1995. The agreement did not break new ground in terms of concrete measures and appeared to be intended primarily to get a message across to the negotiators' constituents. The trade unions signalled that they were not opposed to

more flexible working-time arrangements, while the employers recognized that reducing working hours might be a means of creating jobs, and reminded enterprises
that they should take an active part in combating unemployment. This interoccupational agreement provided that the ways in which these principles were to be applied
would be determined through industry-wide bargaining. However, only a limited
number of agreements have been concluded within this framework, mainly because
trade unions cannot obtain firm commitments to create jobs from employers' organizations at the branch level. And how can enterprises be encouraged to make this
commitment? Finally, the few agreements that were concluded traded a certain reduction in hours of work without loss of wages for greater flexibility in working time,
without any specific or significant job creation measures.

   This relative failure of industry-wide bargaining is not surprising if it is borne
in mind that it is obviously difficult for employers' organizations at this level to
compel enterprises to take on workers. Conversely, trade unions are unlikely to make
significant concessions (such as time off to compensate overtime) in exchange for
unsubstantiated promises that jobs will be created. And so they fall back on the traditional demand of a limited reduction of working hours without loss of wages. It is very
different within the enterprise, where the real scope for protecting jobs may more
readily be assessed. At this level, employers and trade unions do in fact commit themselves to clearly defined measures for maintaining and creating jobs in exchange for
more substantial concessions, such as a significant reduction in working hours (by
four or five hours) with a cut in wages. This kind of bargaining does of course threaten
deep-rooted standards (such as the standard of living) and calls for a degree of solidarity that not everyone may be willing to accept. It may also open the way to a broad
reappraisal of acquired benefits. Dealing with these issues at the enterprise level
makes it easier to ascertain the state of mind of the workers involved and to monitor
the effects of the concessions granted.

   A similar question arose in 1994 in Germany when the metalworkers' trade
union concluded an innovative agreement encouraging enterprises to negotiate their
own agreements to reduce working time substantially (from 36 to 30 hours per week),
with a proportional cut in wages, in exchange for a commitment on their part to refrain
from lay-offs during the term of the agreement. In addition to the wage reduction, the
agreement broke new ground in that the trade unions accepted more extensive enterprise bargaining. None the less, the following year, the same trade union reverted to
the most traditional practices, demanding and obtaining an industry-wide reduction in
working time (from 36 to 35 hours), without concessions in terms of either wages or
flexibility.

   This return to classical trade union positions is no doubt to be attributed to the
trade union's fear that its proposals had overstepped the bounds of what the body of
its members could accept in exchange for uncertain results. The metalworkers' union's
call for tripartite discussions (which are unusual in Germany) on job issues might

therefore be interpreted as a desire to acquire broader legitimacy before embarking upon "innovative" negotiations in a climate of rising unemployment coupled with an increasingly inflexible attitude on the part of employers in response to the 1995 agreement. Contrary to the impasse in the metalworking sector, 1996 saw the successful conclusion of a number of agreements in other sectors, encouraging enterprises to negotiate a substantial reduction in working hours with corresponding wage cuts, the elimination of overtime rates of pay and increases in the number of apprenticeships. The industry-wide agreement tends to provide a framework for enterprise bargaining, particularly where new or difficult issues are involved. The above-mentioned agreement in the chemical sector, concluded in June 1997, is a case in point. Under this agreement negotiated wage reductions should go to protect jobs and should be backed up by economic and financial data made available to local trade unions.

Experiences such as these in bargaining on jobs issues should give a clearer idea of the changes occurring in enterprise bargaining and thus help to sort out the contradictions between analyses claiming that decentralization is gaining ground, and those which disagree. First and foremost, it should be borne in mind that, at the present time, industry-wide bargaining, whether at the national or regional level, is still a very important component of the different national systems of industrial relations. Industry agreements are concluded on a very regular basis in most branches of economic activity in the countries of Europe, and continue to exercise a degree of influence on enterprise bargaining.

The change that has occurred is the fact that industry-wide bargaining now offers much more scope for enterprise negotiation, as pointed out above with regard to agreements on jobs. In Germany, for instance, industry trade unions are now more willing to accept the growing prevalence of enterprise bargaining. The reason for this, as mentioned above, lies in the fact that real commitments regarding job creation can only be made by each enterprise. The increased autonomy accorded to enterprises also affects other areas. This is the case of wages, as is clear from the agreement signed in Italy in 1993, which allows enterprises to fix wage increases linked to productivity, or the above-mentioned German agreement of 1997 in the chemical industry. A trend is thus emerging towards the redefinition of functions at each bargaining level, whereby the industry agreement increasingly serves as a framework laying down minimum standards while providing guidelines for enterprise negotiations. This is a radical transformation, since it affects not only the content but the structures of collective bargaining. The enterprise is emerging as the level at which arrangements concerning production methods, as well as new labour-management relations, are taking shape. Action taken at this level is aimed at adjusting to the new competitive environment and takes the place of adjustment through market forces. Centralized bargaining is keeping pace with this trend.

Centralized bargaining

Although major differences certainly exist between countries with coordinated bargaining systems, they are none the less remarkably homogeneous in their approach to the jobs issue, and in the importance consequently attributed to the question of maintaining social cohesion. Certainly, as elsewhere, the welfare State has been obliged to find a *modus vivendi* with the market economy, but in most of these countries social dialogue at both national and industry levels, and state intervention, have very successfully resisted pressures towards decentralization.

Criticism has often been levelled against centralized bargaining for failing to produce tangible results in terms of jobs. This section will show that the fact that these negotiations are so complex, as regards both the subject-matter dealt with and the objectives pursued, means that eventual judgements cannot be confined to a single criterion, even one as important as the level of unemployment. Such prominent subjects as vocational training or indexation of wages have been dealt with effectively through centralized bargaining. Moreover, where jobs are concerned, such bargaining has made it possible to open up new prospects at other levels of negotiation, in particular at the enterprise level, as we have just seen.

The endurance of centralized bargaining

Collective bargaining is indisputably most active in European countries, notwithstanding a decline in trade union membership levels. National bargaining may have lost its authority, particularly regarding wages, but centralized bargaining has been given a new impetus in recent years. For the most part, central industrial relations are not being dismantled. Consultation and central bargaining continue to take place, albeit with varying degrees of success.

This is particularly true for most of the countries which have a tradition in this regard, such as Austria and Ireland. The Austrian system, which affords greater importance to in-depth and regular consultation on major economic and social issues than to the conclusion of formal agreements, continues to function without any major problems. By way of example, mention may be made of the extensive consultations surrounding the 1996 budget, and the adoption in March 1996 of a detailed joint position of central employer and worker organizations on matters relating to the future development of the European Union. Going back a little further in time, reference may also be made to the adoption, in 1992 and 1993 respectively, of a declaration of principle on social partnership (bipartite) and a stability pact (tripartite), which both reflect the social partners' concern that requirements arising from globalization of the economy and Austria's accession to the European Union should be taken into account. In Ireland, initially bipartite and subsequently tripartite central negotiations took place throughout most of the 1970s followed by a return to decentralized bargaining between 1980 and 1987, and a subsequent shift back to central tripartite bargaining after 1988. Since that date, the partners have concluded four major agreements. The first three – the National Recovery Programme (1988-90), the Programme for Economic and Social Progress (1991-93) and the Programme for Competitiveness and Work (1994-96) – contain extensive economic and social measures. A further tripartite agreement, Partnership 2000, was signed on 30 January 1997. It puts forward a series of provisions intended simultaneously to maintain the country's financial equilibrium and to ensure a fair distribution of the fruits of growth in such a way as to benefit the most disadvantaged groups, particularly the jobless. The agreement also establishes a rate of wage increase in the private and public sectors. It should be emphasized, finally, that this was the first time that community and social entities had participated in such negotiations. These major tripartite agreements are generally considered to have been decisive in the remarkable improvement registered in Ireland's economic indicators.

Elsewhere, central industrial relations have generally lost more ground than in Austria and Ireland. Despite these difficulties, however, central consultations and bargaining remain a key element in the industrial relations systems of most of the countries in question. Hence, in Italy, central agreements were concluded in July 1992, July 1993 and September 1996. The agreement of July 1993 contained major provisions seeking, primarily, to introduce a non-inflationary wage policy and to establish a system of structured bargaining. It is widely held that these provisions have not so far proved effective in achieving these undeniably ambitious objectives.

It may also be noted that centralized consultation and bargaining continue to fulfil a specific function in countries as different as Norway, the Netherlands and Spain. In Norway, as in Denmark, where centralized bargaining formerly played an important role, industry-wide bargaining regularly continues to be closely coordinated by central employer or worker organizations. In Denmark, for instance, employers' organizations are required to subject their draft industry-wide agreements to their central organization for approval. This is no mere formality, since the central organizations have been known to withhold approval. In Spain, a marked return to centralized bargaining began in 1996 with the signature of agreements on subjects ranging from the settlement of labour disputes, the prevention of occupational hazards, retirement and rural employment. The same phenomenon has occurred in Portugal and Finland where central agreements were concluded, in 1995 and 1996 respectively, following a period of several years during which there was no centralized bargaining at all. In both countries, in fact, industrial relations are in the process of being recentralized to a certain extent. A similar trend has been apparent in Belgium since the early 1990s, with regard to wages. The framework law of 1996 on wages – which was closely modelled on the draft interoccupational agreement which had been rejected by one of the trade union confederations – specified that the brackets for maximum wage increases would in future, where possible, be established centrally through bargaining or, failing that, by governmental decision.

It may therefore be concluded that, although consultation and bargaining procedures at central level have been subject to considerable difficulties and failures, they remain firmly entrenched. Indeed, it would appear that there are very few countries in which an appeal has not been made in recent years for a "social pact" to tackle current burning issues – usually made by the government, but also, on occasion, by employers or workers. This also applies to countries which have traditionally shown reservations regarding the various forms of central industrial relations. Here again, the example of Germany may be raised, where attempts to conclude a "pact for employment" were initiated in 1995. The endeavour was not ultimately successful, but it did have a number of spin-offs which will be analysed subsequently. In addition, this tripartite dialogue was revived in 1997 for the purpose of devising ways to combat unemployment in the eastern regions of the country.

This overview of experiences in European countries clearly demonstrates the vitality of centralized social dialogue, although it is not without its weaknesses. The most frequent are, on the one hand, that they currently fail more often than they used to and, on the other hand, that they sometimes lead to opinions or commitments that are insufficiently specific, thereby making it unlikely that concrete results will be achieved. In order to assess the degree of effectiveness of centralized bargaining, the field they cover must first be clearly identified, distinguishing negotiations which focus on particular topics, which are often of a technical nature, from those connected with jobs and competitiveness. Results may then be assessed on the basis of criteria adapted to the nature of this type of bargaining, including the job indicator.

The complexity of centralized bargaining

Centralized bargaining on "technical" subjects

The extensive media coverage devoted to the negotiation of major national agreements has distracted attention from a series of central agreements bearing on specific matters that are frequently of decisive importance and success.

By way of example, an interoccupational agreement was signed in France in 1994, on the subject of vocational training, and a further three interoccupational agreements were concluded in 1996 on the financing of supplementary pensions. In Spain, a number of tripartite agreements have tackled the subjects of occupational safety and health. Also in Spain, in October 1996, the Government and the most representative trade unions signed an agreement under which a series of measures intended to consolidate and streamline the system of social security pensions and their financing would be submitted to Parliament. In such cases, central agreements have proved effective in regulating matters which call for joint, coordinated administration.

It should also be mentioned that some central agreements deal with industrial relations questions where the intention is frequently to provide a framework within which enterprise bargaining can proceed more smoothly. The Italian agreement of July 1993 introduced a new, highly sophisticated system which listed the topics to be negotiated at each level of bargaining, complete with respective timetables, and stipulated that wage increases would be linked primarily to inflation forecasts and productivity increases within the enterprise. The agreement also outlined a mechanism for temporarily modifying wage levels, for use in cases when bargaining was not concluded within the expected time-frame, together with a correction mechanism for use when forecasts of price increases proved inaccurate. The above-mentioned Belgian framework laws of 1996 on wages and employment – which are broadly based on an unsigned central agreement – also provide for the introduction of a new bargaining system which, in some regards, is similar to the Italian system; it is certainly as sophisticated and ambitious as the latter. Among the numerous examples that might be mentioned are the above-mentioned Spanish agreement of 1995 on the settlement of labour disputes and the French agreement of 31 October 1995 on collective bargaining policy. The French agreement was followed by an experimental law which established that, in enterprises in which there was no trade union presence, agreements might be concluded, under certain conditions, with the works council or with worker representatives appointed by the trade unions. In conclusion, it should be added that the various Irish central agreements were drawn on extensively during the drafting of the new legislation on industrial relations (1990), and made a substantial contribution to a number of "codes of conduct" dealing specifically with the settlement of labour disputes in essential services, and with the rights and duties of workers' representatives within enterprises.

Particular mention should here be made of the fact that a number of difficult problems, extending far beyond the purely technical sphere – and, in some cases considered to be totally "intractable" – have been "settled", in full or partially, through central agreements. The provisions of the Italian agreement of July 1993, which sought to introduce a non-inflationary wage policy and to institute a system of structured bargaining, are generally held to have been effective. The central level also played a decisive role in gradually removing the "taboo", as it was considered in Italy, on automatic wage indexation. Finally, the 1995 Italian agreement on pensions (which was at the end of the day not signed by employers who considered that it did not go far enough) made considerable savings in the financing of pensions which no government had ever until then been able to impose unilaterally.

This ability, if not to resolve, at least to facilitate the solution of complex problems is also demonstrated by central agreements on jobs and competitiveness, despite the fact that these issues are of an extremely technical and, more particularly, social complexity.

Centralized bargaining on jobs and competitiveness

Given the present economic climate, an increasing number of problems related to employment can only be dealt with by state intervention. Suffice it to consider the range of issues for which the solution lies in amending legislation (for instance, regarding flexibility of the labour market) or in state funding (for instance, occupational integration). One possible approach is to dissociate action by the social partners from that of the public authorities: the former might negotiate anything still left to be negotiated – generally at the enterprise level – while the public authorities enact the necessary legislation to enable enterprises to adapt and, ultimately, to protect some individual rights of workers in a context in which collective bargaining no longer fulfils this function as effectively as in the past.

However, although the State in most countries does not rule out this approach, the preferred attitude is to support collective bargaining at a time when it is experiencing particular difficulties. This support is, on occasion, so marked that it leads to situations that may appear somewhat contradictory. For instance, the large-scale state intervention in industrial relations that generally follows the failure of ambitious tripartite bargaining projects does not necessarily imply – as one might suppose – the termination of all bargaining, at least for some time. To return to the example of Belgium, it might be noted that the failure of central tripartite negotiations in 1993, and the Government's enforcement of a "global plan", did not prevent the Government from persevering in its attempts to engage the social partners in consultation on the ways and means of implementing the plan. Similarly, despite the failure of tripartite negotiations in 1996, the Government wrote into the framework law on wages that maximum wage increase brackets would be decided through central negotiation, and that the public authorities would impose a decision only if negotiations failed. The situation becomes more confusing still when employers' organizations and trade union confederations negotiate a bipartite agreement on measures to facilitate integration into employment, to be funded by the government, which subsequently also agrees to bear the cost of implementing the agreement. An example of such a procedure was the agreement on the entry of young people into working life concluded in France on 13 June 1995.

Although the public authorities do sometimes assume the role of the social partners, this is rather an exception. It is more usual for state intervention in industrial relations to take the more moderate form of dovetailing governmental and collective bargaining initiatives. Fundamentally, there is nothing new in such interaction in that collective bargaining has in effect always served to develop the channels for implementing legislation and adapting its substance to the specific situations in individual branches of activity or in individual enterprises. Collective bargaining has always helped pave the way for certain laws; either they are the direct or indirect outcome of negotiations with employer organizations and trade union confederations, or they merely endorse solutions previously embodied in the collective agreements of certain branches of activity or large enterprises. Today, such complementarity between legislative action and collective bargaining is probably far more common than in the past. One reason for this situation is that an increasing number of problems cannot be resolved without legislative amendment or financial intervention by the State which, in turn, wishes to involve as many social partners as possible in resolving these problems. In this context, particular attention should be drawn to the fact that a number of recent laws permit exceptions that are "unfavourable" to workers, provided that certain limits are respected and that these exceptions are submitted to collective bargaining in order to ensure minimum guarantees. Numerous examples could be mentioned, including the Netherlands Act on hours of work which came into force on 1 January 1996.

Where substance is concerned, bargaining in connection with jobs is further complicated by the fact that the three objectives of promoting the competitiveness of enterprises, combating unemployment and ensuring fair income distribution must be simultaneously met. Central consultations and bargaining generally cover five subject areas. The first involves measures intended to boost macroeconomic stability, consisting primarily of provisions seeking to keep down wage bills, together with provisions regarding budgetary, fiscal and monetary policies. The second includes arrangements connected with the flexibility of the labour market, where the most frequent topic is that of the flexibility of hours of work, although numerous provisions also exist to increase flexibility in the areas of wages and organization of work, as well as in the nature and regulation of individual labour relations. The third revolves around combating inflation and job creation, primarily involving measures connected with training, redistribution of work, the integration into employment of unemployed workers (for instance, by means of training courses on subsidized contracts) and tapping the source of labour at the local level (for example, through local and community development and neighbourhood services). The fourth and fifth involve, respectively, the fine-tuning of social security systems and support for economic activities.

An examination of the substance of central consultations and bargaining reveals that the differences between countries lie essentially in the number of issues dealt with, rather than in the manner in which they are approached. Hence, depending on the country, the area covered by central consultation and bargaining may include only a few of the issues raised above, or it may include them all. But, at the end of the day, issues are dealt with in a similar manner, and no country appears to set itself apart with solutions that are fundamentally different from those applied elsewhere. Boxes 5.2 to 5.5 illustrate the substance of such central job-related bargaining in several countries, together with the procedures involved and the extent of the central role played by the State.

Box 5.2.   Collective bargaining and state intervention in Belgium

State intervention has unquestionably been more extensive in Belgium than elsewhere. The Government has exerted a particularly strong influence on a number of issues relating to economic and social policy, following the breakdown of tripartite central bargaining in 1993, and again in 1996. In 1993, following the initial failure of an ambitious tripartite social pact, the Government imposed a "global plan" which placed a number of restrictions on the system of automatic wage indexation – which had long been considered to be "out of bounds" in Belgium – and practically froze real wages for a period of three years. The plan also included numerous detailed measures designed to introduce greater flexibility in the labour market, to improve the social security system and to protect and increase jobs through a series of measures to promote entry into employment and the redistribution of work. When bargaining broke down once more in 1996, the Government passed a framework law on wages and another on job creation measures. The law provides for the application, by 2002, of a highly sophisticated system of bargaining, under which the maximum and minimum brackets

for wage increases will be set every two years at the central level. The lower end of the scale corresponds to the increase in the cost of living in Belgium, while the upper limit will be determined on the basis of the evolution of wages in France, Germany and the Netherlands, Belgium's three most direct competitors. Should employers and workers fail to reach an agreement within the National Labour Council regarding this band, the Government will attempt conciliation, failing which it will take the decisions it considers appropriate and require the parties to abide by them. The framework law on job creation measures provides for a similar mechanism, and likewise contains a reference to the situation in France, Germany, and the Netherlands. However, should conciliation attempts fail, the Government might assess on a case-by-case basis whether or not it would be desirable to impose its own decisions. Although the first negotiations held on wages and jobs do not bode well for a successful conclusion, the Belgian case reveals an enduring desire to keep the door open to negotiation.

A number of lessons may be learned from these experiences of centralized consultation and bargaining. It may be noted, first, that vocational training, retirement and legislation pertaining to industrial relations are among the issues that can be tackled in an effective manner through centralized bargaining. Such topics, which call for either solidarity (retirement), coordination (vocational training) or broad involvement (legislative amendments), must be dealt with at the central level – provided, of course, that social dialogue is still considered essential in implementing reforms, which is true in most European countries.

Results are frequently more mixed in the case of social pacts with more ambitious objectives. But should they be dismissed out of hand for that reason? Beyond their success or failure, one effect of this type of bargaining, which is generally taken for granted but rarely acknowledged, is that it changes perceptions and alters principles, thereby making way for new practices at other levels of decision-making. The Belgian Government's decision to end indexation was no doubt facilitated by the ultimately inconclusive negotiations of 1993. Central agreements on flexibility made it possible to explore new spheres of negotiation, on which a number of social partners, at the branch and enterprise levels, might have hesitated to embark. A classic example is offered by the Spanish agreement of April 1997 which exchanged greater stability

---

Box 5.3.   Social dialogue in Spain

Although national negotiations produced agreements in Spain in the early 1980s, such as the 1981 National Agreement on Employment, and the 1984 Economic and Social Pact, they did not culminate in 1994 in the signature of a social pact desired by the Government. In the absence of an agreement, the Government submitted to Parliament its own measures to amend the Workers' statute. This did not, however, signal the end of all bargaining since, first, these amendments included some of the measures submitted for tripartite discussion and, second, they contained provisions to replace Francoist edicts by collective agreements, on the basis of a tripartite accord. Moreover, such fundamental labour issues as the extension of fixed-term contracts, and hours of work would be negotiated collectively. More recently, in order to forestall a recurrence of the unilateral action taken in 1994, the trade union bodies adopted a more active stance and negotiated a new plan for rural employment in the provinces of Andalucia and Extremadura. This plan provides for the creation, in these regions, of an integrated service for promoting jobs, jointly administered by the town councils, trade unions, the National Employment Institute and agricultural enterprises. Tripartism in Spain has more recently tended to focus on topics that are more specific, although no less essential, such as the agreement signed in April 1997 which lightened restrictions on redundancy, while encouraging employers to hire more extensively under permanent contracts. The agreement introduced a new work contract of four years' duration, in exchange for a reduction in redundancy compensation (33 days' pay for every year of service in place of the previous 45 days). As in Belgium, collective bargaining has not been pushed aside as a result of a permanent state presence.

---

in employment contracts for less advantageous regulations on redundancy (see box 5.3). These central consultations and bargaining processes clearly show that the State and social partners, in their attempt to find ways to deal with the problem of employment (and, more broadly, that of exclusion resulting from a drop in wages and social protection, or from unemployment), try to find solutions which depart from the strict application of the laws of the market. While social dialogue may not create jobs, it certainly does seek alternatives to prevent redundancy and unemployment. Central agreements do not offer a ready-made solution – which does not exist – to employment problems, but they do make it clear that possibilities must also be sought outside market mechanisms. In conclusion, it would appear that employment matters cannot be viewed – and subsequently dealt with – in strictly economic terms, unlike the attempts to curb inflation. Were that the case, lay-offs could simply be allowed to do their work of restoring equilibrium. In Europe, there is a whole social and political aspect to the issue of employment and centralized bargaining contributes towards trying to find a new mode of regulation which conciliates economic and social constraints. The enterprise, with its resources and its limitations, must occupy a central position within this framework because it is at this level that concrete decisions regarding the preservation and creation of jobs may be taken. While the trend clearly lies in this direction, we have already seen that the extent of the changes required is equalled only by that of the obstacles in their way.

Box 5.4.   Collective bargaining and state intervention in the Netherlands

In the Netherlands, the 1996 Act on working time bears witness to the interaction between the Government and collective bargaining initiatives. This Act replaces a law of 1919, as required by the European directive of 1993, and takes up a number of provisions previously contained in collective agreements – such as those pertaining to standard working time. This legislation simultaneously serves as a framework law, and provides a broad margin of manoeuvre for collective bargaining. This way of dovetailing governmental and collective bargaining action is likewise apparent in the State's frequent endeavours to encourage the social partners to negotiate on the basis of these proposals, a procedure which could be described as two-stage tripartism. The bipartite

agreement signed in 1993, which restricted wage increases and made modes of remuneration more flexible in exchange for a commitment by employers to try to create jobs, was strongly promoted by the Government which urged the social partners to conclude a solidarity pact to combat unemployment, while reserving the possibility of intervening in the event of an impasse. The Government had used the same model in 1993 to encourage the social partners to reduce minimum wages in collective agreements to the level of the national minimum. It would appear that its appeal was heeded in 1996 when a significant number of industry-wide and enterprise agreements incorporated such a measure.

Source: Ministry of Social Affairs and Employment of the Netherlands: Document cited in IDS-E (Incomes Data Services), No. 415, July 1996, pp. 18-19.

The case of Japan

The system of enterprise-level bargaining introduced in Japan was based on the postwar American model but, evolving as it did in a context of cooperation, it employed very different mechanisms. While disputes, particularly those occurring during the 1970s, were certainly severe, they were in no manner comparable to the antagonistic tradition of American industrial relations. Moreover, the decentralized Japanese system features highly influential forms of national coordination, which have prompted reference to a Japanese neo-corporatism. Finally, the State is a major protagonist in industrial relations. Its intervention is apparent in its legislative action, whether in connection with the reduction of hours of work after 1987, or reforms of the pension system in 1986 and 1996. It also intervenes through measures to promote, for instance, the implementation of employment policy benefiting industries, regions or categories of workers which have been placed in jeopardy by restructuring. The State also participates, usually in an informal manner, in the national coordination process.

The most prominent form of national coordination is the *shunto,* which organizes annual wage bargaining. This system is well-known and will therefore not be described in detail, although several comments should be made. Although this coordinated bargaining directly affects only 25 per cent of employees,[23] it serves as a benchmark for wage increases in small and medium-sized enterprises. Moreover, not only are the results of the *shunto* applied in drafting recommendations for wage

---

Box 5.5. The "pacts for employment" in Germany

In Germany, the State was slower to act, and less energetic than its counterparts in other European countries. It did not introduce legislation to facilitate the use of temporary contracts or amend the Hours of Work Act until 1994. Even then, its action was prompted by new European directives. Therefore, job-related initiatives originated rather in collective bargaining, in particular the chemical sector agreement of 1993, and the metal trades sector agreement of 1994, in which trade unions accepted wage restraint and a reduction in hours of work, with wage cuts, in exchange for job protection measures. This is doubtless to be attributed to the specific nature of the German system, as well as to the fact that the unemployment problem came to prominence later here than in other countries. Moreover, the action of the federal Government acquired greater momentum from that period onwards, as demonstrated by its participation in tripartite meetings on employment with a view to concluding a "pact for employment". These meetings were requested by the trade union confederation in the metal trades sector, which embarked upon negotiations with German employers in the industry on job security. Although these two initiatives did not produce any final conclusion, a number of the proposals submitted during discussions were taken up in other forms. Indeed, they paved the way for the conclusion, in February 1996, of a central tripartite agreement – which subsequently became law

– on the introduction of a system of part-time jobs for older workers if new workers were hired simultaneously; in addition, a tripartite "pact for employment" was successfully concluded in Bavaria in June 1996; finally, the "philosophy" underlying endeavours to achieve a central pact – namely, wage restraint in exchange for job protection measures – made a significant contribution to a number of industry-wide agreements, particularly those concluded in 1996 in the chemical and textile sectors. It should also be noted that, although the Government took a highly controversial step in reducing payment of sick leave, the measure will not truly come into effect, where applicable, until the social partners re-negotiate industry-wide agreements – thereby confirming the strategic position of collective bargaining by branch of activity in Germany.

In May 1997, at the Government's instigation, a new tripartite pact came into being, entitled "A joint initiative for more jobs in Eastern Germany". This pact aims to create 100,000 jobs per year through more flexible wage agreements, increased investment and purchases by enterprises in the western regions of the country. The pact followed the traditional approach adopted by such agreements in seeking to create a national consensus regarding the potential threat to social cohesion of an unemployment rate of over 17 per cent in the eastern regions of Germany.

---

increases in the public sector, but the conclusion of the *shunto* is signalled when the Tripartite Central Minimum Wage Commission determines the new minimum wage. Thus, the State is by no means indifferent to the results of the bargaining process and participates in it indirectly, particularly during the tripartite advisory forum it organizes to discuss economic forecasts. These details highlight the importance of this form of coordination of negotiations as well as the extensive role of the State. Tripartism is also practised in a more formal manner though a large number of national and local consultation committees. Within these committees, trade unions, employers and ministries discuss matters of a social nature, in addition to questions relating to industrial and economic policies.[24] These national consultation and bargaining activities, particularly at the sectoral level, are most frequently held on an informal basis, as preferred by employers. This does not, however, detract from their importance in defining the conditions of economic and social regulation.

Meanwhile, bargaining at the enterprise level continues to be a cornerstone of Japanese industrial relations. It was given increased momentum, following the first oil shock in 1973, by the newly established worker/employer cooperation committees, which a number of non-Japanese enterprises subsequently sought to imitate. However, in Japan, bargaining at this level does not encounter the same legal and sociological obstacles as in the United States. As in other countries, Japanese trade unions are present primarily in the larger enterprises. In 1993, the level of trade union membership in enterprises with over 1,000 workers stood at 58.2 per cent, compared to only 1.8 per cent in enterprises with less than 100 employees. This situation may be expected to continue, given the difficulties encountered by trade unions in attracting new members as the result of the increasingly precarious nature of jobs, compounded by a loss of interest by Japanese workers who are becoming increasingly individualistic. A little under half of all small and medium-sized enterprises have alternative forms of representation for determining conditions of employment.[25] In this connection, it should be noted that although joint committees, which are responsible for consultation and exchange of information and which exist in 56 per cent of enterprises (1994 figure), occur more frequently where trade unions are present (81 per cent), they also exist in a substantial proportion of non-union enterprises (32 per cent). Furthermore, *shunto* wage increases serve as a benchmark for fixing wages in non-unionized enterprises. National coordination therefore, whether formal or informal in nature, exerts a regulatory effect on the economy as a whole, over and above direct trade union representation. An enterprise's size does not preclude the existence of strong national coordination by means of which social protagonists have acquired a recognized status within the Japanese economy and society.

Comments on the public sector

It is apparent, therefore, that conclusions regarding collective bargaining may vary widely. The practice continues in Europe where social consultation institutions are firmly entrenched and play an active role in organizing civil society. There is, however, cause for concern that the considerable decline in trade union membership rates may undermine the functioning of these institutions. In other countries, meanwhile, membership rates remain at satisfactory levels, although a certain downward trend, including in Japan, is none the less disquieting. In contrast, collective bargaining has lost ground in countries with a voluntarist tradition, where its fortunes are closely linked to those of trade union membership. Consequently, the notable endurance of the trade union movement in the public sector suggests that the means to rebuild industrial relations might be sought in the public sector's own practices.

It has sometimes been concluded that strong mobilization and high levels of trade union membership among public sector employees is to be attributed to the solid protection they enjoy. The strong support forthcoming from private sector workers for a number of public sector strikes suggests that they were perceived as proxy strikes in which public sector workers who were secure in their jobs expressed the discontent of private sector workers who could not mobilize as readily on account of the instability of their situation. However, an analysis of this nature fails to take account of the essential point that the mobilization occurring today in the public sector is frequently directed towards defending jobs. Privatizations, opening up to competition (for instance, in telecommunications), and budget-cutting policies obviously do not foster a sense of impunity among public sector employees where their jobs are concerned. A recent OECD study emphasizes the importance of this "uncertainty and insecurity among public sector employees regarding staff reductions and programme cutbacks".[26] The higher level of mobilization in the public sector is in fact the result of some of its particular features. The first, which applies equally to large private enterprises, is related to the size of units of production and the homogeneity of occupational status which facilitates trade unionization. The second revolves around the fact that a large number of employees work for a single employer, which is conducive to the delegation of authority to trade unions. Obviously, there are exceptions, as identified in the previous chapter, but on the whole the existence of trade unions is fully acknowledged in the public sector. The third feature relates to the centrality of the idea of public service in employer-employee relations, which serves to strengthen solidarity. This, combined with the fact that funds are of public origin, encourages consultation which, in a number of countries, takes the place of collective bargaining; consequently, considerable restrictions are sometimes accepted in connection with bargaining and strikes which would be less readily accepted in the private sector. In conclusion, it might be added that these various features lend a political dimension to mobilization, even when it is directed towards obtaining economic benefits, which it less frequently acquires in the private sector. Suffice it to consider the disputes in the health sector. Certainly, in recent years, the public sector has undergone far-reaching changes in most countries, whereby it has grown closer to the private sector. Market constraints have made their appearance in the form of privatizations or the introduction of competition between some services and the private sector, as well as cost cutting. Worker training policies have been introduced, in conjunction with a decentralization of decision-making in some spheres.[27] None the less, the distinctive characteristics listed previously will continue to be a feature of the public sector; namely, occupational status which, although it has been diversified to some extent, still affects a considerable number of workers, budgetary ceilings continue to be fixed at the central level and the idea of public service is a principle which may be expected to grow stronger. Therefore, the model of industrial relations in the public sector would not appear to be readily applicable to a private sector whose share will, on the contrary, continue to increase. Obviously, this does not rule out alliances between trade unions from the two sectors, as outlined in Chapter 2.

Towards a diversification of the levels of social dialogue

This analysis demonstrates that systems of social dialogue and, hence, the way in which employment conditions are regulated, vary from country to country, although several general models may be identified, for instance distinguishing between the voluntarist system and the coordinated system. These differences are the product of each country's history, since the features of industrial relations systems are likewise those of the society to which they are applied. If they are to function effectively, they must be applied to a homogeneous whole in both economic and social terms. While all must accept the growing importance of the enterprise as a point of decision-making, the way in which this is accommodated is by no means universal. The autonomy of national industrial relations policies is today only partially affected by the globalization of trade.

However, it would appear that a move is occurring towards arrangements where the international and regional levels, on the one hand, and the local and enterprise levels on the other, are acquiring greater importance, although they continue to revolve around the hub of national systems. Chapter 2 demonstrated that, at the international level, useful and necessary initiatives are being introduced to deal with specific problems. But, they focus on national or local units that are too heterogeneous to be expected to be applied, or become more widespread – they will none the less be all the more effective if they reside on the springboard of solid national systems which respond to the economic and social constraints existing in the societies where they are applied.

However, the degree of homogeneity increases at the regional level. Firstly, an economic interdependence exists which currently makes this level the focus of globalization. Figure 5.2 shows that regional trade has grown more rapidly than interregional trade. In other words, a shift towards regionalization is currently occurring in the increasingly close relationships of interdependence resulting from globalization.

This is of course true of the European Union, but also of MERCOSUR, the common market of the southern Latin American countries. In both cases, this homogenization of economic constraints is accompanied, with a few exceptions, by a degree of similarity in the national systems of industrial relations, suggesting that it might ultimately prove possible to construct a consistent system at the regional level. However, considerable caution is called for, as demonstrated by the difficulties encountered by the process in the European Union, which is the region that has gone furthest along this road. This, in turn, emphasizes the key position that continues to be held by national systems.

At the other extreme, enterprises have clearly acquired increasing importance in the regulation of labour relations. They occupy very different positions in national industrial relations systems, although a measure of unanimity exists in as much as the

Figure 5.2.   **Regionalization of trade percentage in three major regions**

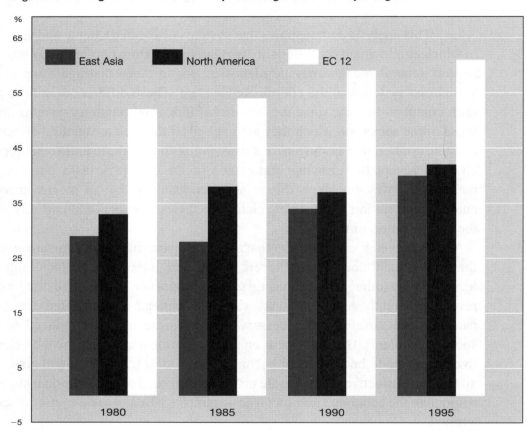

Note: East Asia: Indonesia; Japan; Republic of Korea; Malaysia; Philippines; Singapore; Thailand; Hong Kong; Taiwan, China.
North America: Canada; Mexico; United States.
EC 12: Belgium; Denmark; France; Germany; Greece; Ireland; Italy; Luxembourg; Netherlands; Portugal; Spain; United Kingdom.

Source: C. Primo Braga and G. Bannister: "East Asian investment and trade: Prospects for growing regionalization in the 1990s", in *Transnational Corporations* (New York and Geneva, UNCTAD), Vol. 3, No 1, Feb. 1994. The data for 1995 are taken from the *Direction of trade statistic yearbook* (IMF, Washington, DC, 1996); they do not include Taiwan, China.

position they occupy is central. The substance of industrial relations could be expanded, at this level, to cover matters of organization of work, technical advances, training, new employment practices and manpower development. And it is at this level that national systems of industrial relations could now most rapidly accommodate the international dimension. The same applies, of course, to multinational enterprises, although the practice of collective bargaining continues to be most unusual at this level. The most notable development has occurred at the European level with the creation of European works councils (see box 5.6). It is as yet too early to assess how satisfactorily these bodies function. None the less, an analysis of the works councils created voluntarily by some 250 multinational enterprises before the directive came into force showed that, overall, workers and employers were satisfied with the expe-

---

Box 5.6.   European works councils

The first multinationals to establish European works councils – during the second half of the 1980s – were three enterprises based in France: Thomson, BSN and Bull. During the early 1990s, their example was followed by over a dozen major enterprises. They subsequently proliferated throughout the European Union, particularly following the introduction of measures to promote "social dialogue". A decisive influence was brought to bear by the adoption, in 1994, of the European Union directive introducing European works councils. It should be noted that this directive was not applicable to enterprises that had already created such bodies, provided that they fulfilled the information and consultation function.

Indeed, the key words of the directive are information, consultation, exchange of views and dialogue. It contains no reference whatsoever to participation or collective bargaining, thereby dissociating the right to information and to consultation from collective bargaining. This dissociation reflects the fundamental distinction, in several European countries, between consultation structures based on elected representation, on the one hand, and bargaining structures based on trade union representation, on the other.

The European Union directive is flexible and accords with the trend towards decentralization. It is basically a framework law instituting an information and consultation mechanism close to the central administration of multinational enterprises. But it gives Member States considerable leeway in adapting this mechanism to their national systems. For instance, it does not specify who should represent workers. Neither does it define what is to be understood by a information and consultation mechanism. It allows workers and employers to set up a system in keeping with the management structures of multinational enterprises and of industrial relations. Thus, the directive does not imply that there should be a standard European system of industrial relations.

The directive is applicable to all enterprises with at least 1,000 employees in Europe, and a minimum of 150 employees in each of at least two Member States. It is applicable to both the public and private sectors, regardless of whether their headquarters are in Europe. Multinational enterprises whose central administration is located outside Europe should appoint a representative agent in one of the Member States with responsibility for setting up the European works council. The directive covers 17 European countries, of which 14 European Union Member States and three members of the European Economic Area.

The European Trade Union Institute estimates that the directive is applicable to some 1,200 multinational enterprises, of which almost 70 per cent are German, French, British or Dutch. These 1,200 multinational enterprises employ approximately 14 million people, which is almost 10 per cent of the European Union's working population. By the end of the century, the number of workers covered by the directive is expected to rise to 20 million.

---

rience and held a positive opinion of exchange of information and consultation at this level. The councils are not intended to serve as bargaining fora (only Danone has given its European works council that competence), but information exchange and consultation are a minimum basis for coordinating national bargaining policies.

Side by side with the company level, a local level of bargaining is developing which takes into account increasingly diversified situations – particularly workers in precarious employment and the unemployed; moreover, it appears more geared to the development of social dialogue in the growing number of small and medium-sized enterprises where the level of trade unionization is low. The wide-ranging objectives, forms and origins of the experiments conducted in this framework are described in previous chapters. Some are designed to return the unemployed to work, with emphasis on the hard-core unemployed – these are particularly common in the European countries and Canada. In other countries, the aim is to organize workers in casual employment, while simultaneously boosting the local industrial sector (one such example is the textile sector in a number of urban areas in the United States). Finally, in the well-known case of the industrial districts of northern Italy, such local bargaining is the "spontaneous" product of pre-existing local social cohesion, serving as the basis of consensus whereby strong economic vitality has been combined with decent social protection within the small enterprise sector.[28] To conclude, it may be noted that, in the informal sector of developing countries, the forms of organization and bargaining that are encountered are frequently the result of local initiatives (see Chapter 8).

In Europe and Canada, the initiative has often been taken at national level. For instance, in Belgium in 1987, the Minister of Labour introduced a measure to create local employment agencies set up on a voluntary basis and administered by representatives – who might or might not be elected – of the local community, trade unions and employers. The objective was to facilitate the return of the unemployed to working life by offering them, at the request of users, activities "which are not offered by regular work circuits" (domestic help or administrative assistance, etc.). Under this system, the unemployed received pay but did not lose their unemployment benefit. The initiative was extended in 1994, following its initial success, although it is no longer voluntary. This point will be discussed later in the text. In Ireland, numerous local programmes were set up at the instigation of the national tripartite agreement of 1990 and with assistance from the State and the European Community.[29] A case in point is the "Contact Point" programme, inspired by the Netherlands experience, which seeks to promote contacts between the unemployed and local enterprises. Other local projects aim to boost local industry, following the example of northern Italy. Hence, initiatives and funding frequently originate at the national level – but this is not always the case. The Italian example bears this out, as does the experiment conducted in Normandy, France, where trade unions (CFDT, CGC, CFTC) and the employers' union, with the participation of the local authorities, set up a plan of action, named "Cap sur l'Emploi", to identify job openings in small and medium-sized enterprises, and inform and advise them on appropriate ways of meeting their needs. Experiments mounted in the United States seek likewise to boost the small enterprise sector, in order to create jobs and improve qualifications, and simultaneously coincide directly with the new forms of collective bargaining on protection of workers' employment conditions. One of the best-known examples here is that of the garment industry in San Francisco, or in New York (see box 5.7). In Milwaukee, a group of trade unions and local employers in the metal trades sector signed an agreement designed to improve worker training.

Any number of examples may be given to confirm that dialogue at the local level is certainly a reality, though it may not be universal. Will this trend prove to be the way of the future for collective bargaining? Numerous arguments suggest that this

---

Box 5.7. Cooperation between employers' organizations and trade unions at the local level: The example of *Garment 2000* in San Francisco

The need for the garment industry in San Francisco to compete with low-wage countries, particularly Mexico, prompted unprecedented co-operation among previous adversaries: small and medium-sized enterprises, contractors and organized labour. In 1994, these groups came together within a consortium called *Garment 2000* which aimed to restructure the industry by moving it away from mass production towards high-quality production, with "just-in-time" production capabilities.

This consortium, which includes the Mayor's Office of Community Development, the District Office of the United States Department of Labor and several colleges and schools, is funded by public and private supporters at local, state and national levels. Its programme activities include: workshops in business management and state-of-the-art technology; training sessions in production-related areas, such as equipment repair, productivity, supervision and modular manufacturing; demonstration projects featuring best industry practices; on-site customized technical assistance services for small and medium-sized enterprises; and assistance in accessing capital. *Garment 2000* has trained workers and management on such issues as costing garments, compliance with labour law and quality control.

Source: F. Pyke: *Small firms, industrial relations and new roles for employers' and workers' organizations,* document prepared for the ILO (1996).

---

will be the case: the increase in small and medium-sized enterprises in the new production context, the demands by workers in precarious employment and by the hard-core unemployed for more specific attention and, in developing countries, the desire to organize workers in the informal sector whose conditions of employment are particularly poor. However, the main reason for the success of these programmes lies in the fact that they are voluntary, bureaucracy is limited and they show great inventiveness. Therefore, efforts to apply them more widely, which would involve greater institutionalization and heavier constraints, would probably render them less effective. For instance, the extension of coverage of local employment agencies in Belgium under the Act of March 1994 simultaneously made registration of the long-term unemployed automatic and penalized the failure to respond to a second summons by the possible loss of entitlement to unemployment benefits.

If such local initiatives are to retain their effectiveness, they must remain flexible in terms of both their initial objectives and their functioning. This does not, however, mean that they should be totally divorced from the institutionalized collective bargaining system. A two-way relationship may be established. Traditional collective agreements could promote such initiatives, as was the case of the national tripartite agreements in Ireland, and local initiatives may play a part in adapting the collective bargaining system by forging new links between the social actors themselves and between them and the people they are supposed to represent. It would be desirable in the future to increase the number of initiatives at the local level (including personnel management policies) to cater for a growing and rapidly changing range of situations and expectations. Indeed, the same stakes exist for enterprise negotiations.

However, it is vital that the process should not be allowed to run out of control, and this calls for the maintenance of a degree of coordination as it is practised in many countries, including those such as Japan which engage in decentralized bargaining.

Conclusions

There is no escaping the fact that today economies must endeavour to make themselves more competitive. However, the ways and means to achieve this are by no means as certain. By undermining social protection, enterprises can no doubt adapt more readily to changing situations, but this approach is not guaranteed to improve the productivity of labour – and in some countries less than others. The contradiction has been mentioned, in this regard, between a trend towards the increased casualization of labour and that of seeking to involve workers more closely in their enterprise. Economic performance depends on numerous factors, and it is difficult to prove that one particular system of industrial relations is more effective than another in this regard. This chapter has sought to demonstrate that the form and content of collective regulations is certainly linked to demands for national social cohesion that vary in time and space. And it is through their effectiveness in this sphere that they demonstrate their effectiveness, in turn, on the economic front. In all events, social dialogue, whatever form it takes, is not an end but a means. It serves collectively to regulate relations between those participating in the world of work. Under certain conditions, it may contribute to improving performance by encouraging a closer involvement in collective work. At the very least, it is preferable to keep it functioning in order to have an effective remedy at hand for situations in which dissatisfaction reaches such a pitch that it spills over into serious social upheaval – which might otherwise be uncontrollable.

Notes

[1] A.C.L. Sims, R. Blouin and P. Knopf: *Seeking a balance,* Canada Labour Code, Part I: Review (Ottawa, Ministry of Public Works and Government Services, 1996).

[2] For a summary of such studies, see C. Dell'Aringa and M. Samek Lodovici: "Industrial relations and economic performance", in T. Treu (ed.): *Participation in public policy-making: The role of trade unions and employers' associations* (Berlin and New York, Walter de Gruyter, 1992), pp. 26-58.

[3] See in particular ILO: *World employment 1996/97,* (Geneva, 1996).

[4] A.L. Goldman: "United States of America", in R. Blanpain (ed.): *International encyclopaedia for labour law and industrial relations* (The Hague, London and Boston, Kluwer, 1996), p. 44.

[5] For a summary of the most recent legislation in this area, see R.N. Block, J. Beck and D.H. Kruger: *Labor law, industrial relations and employee choice: The state of the workplace in the 1990s* (Kalamazoo, Michigan, W.E. Upjohn Institute for Employment Research, 1996), p. 46.

[6] ibid., p. 41.

[7] Institute of Personnel and Development: "The United Kingdom", in *Industrial Relations and Collective Bargaining* (London, Incomes Data Services, 1996), p. 343.

[8] ibid., p. 349.

[9] R. Locke, T. Kochan and M. Piore (eds.): *Employment relations in a changing world economy* (Cambridge, Massachusetts, and London, MIT Press, 1995), p. 118.

[10] A. Coulthard: "Non-union bargaining: Enterprise flexibility agreements", in *Journal of Industrial Relations* (Oxford, Basil Blackwell), Vol. 38, No. 3, Sep. 1996, pp. 339-358.

[11] K. Hince and R. Harbridge: "The Employment Contracts Act: An interim assessment", in *New Zealand Journal of Industrial Relations* (Wellington, Industrial Relations Society of New Zealand), Vol. 19, No. 3, 1994, pp. 235-255.

[12] L. Williamson and P. Brown: "Collective bargaining in private industry, 1994", in *Monthly Labor Review* (Washington, DC, Department of Labor), Vol. 118, No. 6, July 1995, pp. 3-12.

[13] M.H. Ciminu and C.J. Muhl: "Labor-management bargaining in 1994", ibid., Vol. 118, No. 1, Jan. 1995, pp. 23-29.

[14] For a summary of this debate, see J. Cutcher-Gershenfeld, P. McHugh and D. Power: "Collective bargaining in small firms: Preliminary evidence of fundamental change", in *Industrial and Labor Relations Review* (Ithaca, New York State School of Industrial and Labor Relations), Vol. 49, No. 2, Jan. 1996, pp. 195-212.

[15] Commission on the Future of Worker-management Relations: *Fact-finding report* and *Report and recommendations* (Washington, DC, Department of Labor and Commerce, 1994).

[16] ibid.

[17] J. Cutcher-Gershenfeld, P. McHugh and D. Power, op. cit.

[18] For a discussion of this issue, see "Does America still work? On the turbulent energies of the new capitalism", in *Harper's Magazine* (New York), May 1996, p. 41.

[19] E.B. Kapstein: "Workers and the world economy", in *Foreign Affairs* (New York, Council on Foreign Relations), Vol. 75, No. 3, May-June 1996, p. 26.

[20] D. Leslie and Y. Pu: "What caused rising earnings inequality in Britain? Evidence from time series, 1970-1993", in *British Journal of Industrial Relations* (London, London School of Economics and Political Science), Vol. 34, No. 1, Mar. 1996, p. 112.

[21] Ministère du Travail et des Affaires Sociales: *La négociation collective en 1995*, Vol. I (Paris, La documentation française, 1996), p. 12.

[22] "Allemagne. Remise en cause de la politique contractuelle dans la métallurgie", in *Social International* (Paris, Union des industries métallurgiques et minières), No. 541, July 1995, p. 5.

[23] M. Sako: "Shunto. The role of employer and union coordination at the industry and inter-sectoral levels", in M. Sako and H. Sato (eds.): *Japanese labour and management in transition. Diversity, flexibility and participation* (London and New York, Routledge, 1997), p. 252.

[24] K. Sugeno: *The three faces of enterprise unions: The status of unions in contemporary Japan,* JILL Forum Paper No. 6, Feb. 1996, p. 24.

[25] C.H. Lee: *Recent changes in Japanese industrial relations,* document prepared for the ILO (1996), p. 27.

[26] OECD: *Integrating people management into public service reform* (Paris, 1996), p. 24.

[27] OECD: op. cit.; T. Olsen (ed.): *Industrial relations system in the public sector in Europe* (Norway), Fafo Institute for Applied Social Science for the European Public Service Committee, 1996.

[28] A number of studies have been published on this subject; for the most recent, see: F. Cossentino, F. Pyke and W. Sengenberger: *Local and regional response to global pressure: The case of Italy and its industrial districts* (Geneva, International Institute of Labour Studies, 1996).

[29] OECD: *Ireland: Local partnerships and social innovation* (Paris, 1996).

6 The instruments of social dialogue in the countries of Central and Eastern Europe

In industrialized countries where there is a tradition of pluralism, change occurs more or less gently, only gradually making its influence felt on established systems; but in countries in transition, it is abrupt and brutal. What is particularly striking in these countries is not merely that new actors and institutions are emerging, but that many of these are acquiring a clearly identifiable shape and direction which will constitute the industrial relations systems of tomorrow. Although it is possible with some certitude to predict the way in which several of the aspects of these systems will evolve, this is not true in the case of others – which are unprecedented in the history of industrial relations.

The breakaway from the old systems has obviously been total; nevertheless the basic components of the new structures bear the imprint of the past, resulting in evident similarities between the countries. It is, however, equally important to consider the conditions in which the transition to the market economy is taking place, for these are far from uniform. The extent to which countries have broken away from previous modes of trade union organization and activity and developed their private sector varies considerably. In some instances structural adjustment reforms have been introduced overnight; in others, they have been implemented gradually. Consequently, despite their similarities, the industrial relations systems in various countries are not – and never will be – interchangeable. The differences are particularly marked between the countries of Central Europe and Eastern Europe.

These differences notwithstanding, it is the basic components they have in common which are the most obvious at present. Most noteworthy is the fact that, in many countries, trade unions are at once political movements and labour rights advocates. In addition, they are the only actors in civil society with any degree of organization; indeed they are, along with deeply divided political parties, the social actors best able to shape the building of the new societies. And the unions are very present in the political and economic debate, as was shown in Chapter 2, the prime example being *Solidarity* in Poland. During the drafting of the Gdansk Agreements, in 1980, which played an essential role in the construction of democratic Poland, as well as the Round Table Agreements concluded in 1989, the unions intervened as representatives of civil society in its broadest sense. Thus, even though in time the more traditional elements of the trade unions' role may come to the fore, it seems unlikely that they will adopt a purely "economic" approach. By contrast, employers as a group are poorly organized and fundamentally heterogeneous. There is little community of interest between the employer-owners of small and medium-sized enterprises, who see little advantage at present in being more organized, and the managers of state enterprises who have often much to gain from being on good terms with the unions. The most one can expect is that employers' organizations will become stronger with the emergence of a significant number of large private enterprises. At present, the trade unions, along with the State, are the dominant actors in industrial relations.

One final common point is the dichotomy which exists in the institutions of social dialogue, where collective bargaining is being developed, with a great many difficulties, in a compartmentalized fashion: at the national level, on the one hand, and at that of the enterprise, on the other. The weak link between these two levels seriously hampers the effectiveness of the system of negotiation. Bargaining at enterprise level is, as we shall see later in the text, developing in accordance with a somewhat different logic from that seen in relation to the countries examined in the previous chapter. At the other extreme, while their progress has sometimes been very uneven, centralized tripartite agreements have assumed special importance, in terms both of their ability to maintain social cohesion, which has been undermined by the transition process, and of the reforms which they have made possible. For all its successes and failures, collective bargaining, especially centralized bargaining, is playing a key role in the process of building these new democracies. This will be illustrated in the paragraphs which follow.

Collective bargaining at enterprise level: Real but uneven progress

The vast majority of these countries now have legislation, often based on the model of Western European countries, which authorizes collective bargaining at various levels – namely enterprise, industry-wide and interoccupational level (see box 6.1). In reality, however, the development of collective bargaining is proving problematic, particularly at industry-wide level. There are many reasons for this. The weakness of the social actors is the one most often cited. The unions' authority over their members is uncertain – but this is also the case in some Western European countries, without that preventing the development of collective bargaining. As we have already stated, the real problem today is the representativeness of the employers' organizations. In the first place, state-owned enterprises constitute a large proportion of the economic sector, which, in the eyes of the unions, justifies a government presence at the negotiating table – against the latter's will in certain countries, notably in the Czech Republic and Bulgaria.[1] In the second place, small and medium-sized private sector firms very often see little advantage in regulating conditions of employment. Moreover, employees themselves show a certain indifference towards collective agreements. In the private sector, this may be explained by the fact that workers either enjoy a regular salary, often higher than the national average, or else their situation is so precarious that they would not dream of taking collective action. This is particu-

---

Box 6.1.   New legislation on collective bargaining in Central and Eastern European countries

Mechanisms and institutions of collective bargaining vary substantially from one country to another and are in general determined by law. Current legislation regulating the conduct of negotiations and the conclusion and validity of collective agreements often dates back to the beginning of the economic transition in Central and Eastern Europe. In the Czech Republic, the Collective Bargaining Act of 4 December 1990 regulates collective bargaining mechanisms, while, more recently in the Slovak Republic, the new Act No. 54/1996 has introduced some changes to the regulation of these mechanisms. In other countries, changes have been made as the result of the adoption of new Labour Codes. In Hungary, the Labour Code of 1992 regulates the conclusion of collective agreements under Chapter II (sections 30-41). In Bulgaria, the various amendments made to the Labour Code (in force since 1 January 1993) have created a new legal framework for the conduct of collective bargaining and the conclusion of collective agreements. In Poland, changes have also been introduced to the Labour Code of 1974. In this country, the Act of 26 October 1994 now provides the legal framework for collective bargaining and the conclusion of collective agreements. It replaces Title Eleven of the Labour Code and introduces important changes in the industrial relations system of the country, inter alia, the principle of free collective bargaining between the parties.

The regulation of collective bargaining and collective agreements has also been on the agenda of many other countries in the region, which have had to update their legislation. For example, in Romania the Parliament adopted a new law regulating collective labour agreements on 23 September 1996. This law redefines the legal structure within which the functioning of institutions and mechanisms of collective bargaining at the various levels should take place. In

this respect, one major issue is the adoption of new criteria for the determination of union representatives for consultation and negotiation at the various levels of the economy.

Changes to labour law have also been introduced in the three Baltic States. For example, in Lithuania, Act No. I-1202 of 4 April 1991 introduced new and substantial changes to the legal framework of collective bargaining. This law was also amended in 1994. In Latvia, the Labour Code has been amended during the past few years, including its Chapter Two on collective labour agreements. These changes specifically involved a series of sections regulating the role of the parties to collective agreements and their conclusion. Finally, in Estonia, trade unions, employers' associations and representatives of the Ministry of Social Affairs are holding discussions on the various reforms needed in the collective bargaining sphere.

In some other countries, such as the Russian Federation and Ukraine, where the respective Parliaments are in the process of revising their current labour laws, much discussion is taking place on the reform of collective bargaining and the introduction of new legal measures for the settlement of labour disputes. In the Russian Federation, Act No. 2490-1 of 11 March 1992 "respecting collective agreements and accords" is in force, while in Ukraine the "Act respecting collective contracts and agreements" of 1 July 1993 regulates the same subject. These two laws are very similar with respect to procedures, rules and terminology – and both establish the legal framework for the regulation of collective bargaining and the conclusion and implementation of collective agreements. It should be noted that in both countries, many draft laws concerning industrial relations are being examined by Parliament. In the Russian Federation, new laws have already been introduced as a revision of the 1992 Act.

Source: G. Casale: *Collective bargaining and the law in Central and Eastern Europe: Some comparative issues* (Budapest, ILO (Central and Eastern European Team), 1997).

---

larly true of Eastern Europe. A survey carried out in the Russian Federation revealed that one-third of employees in small firms did not even have a contract of employment.[2] Furthermore, whatever the type of firm, many employees in these countries are afraid that in these troubled economic times, negotiations conducted outside the enterprise might set conditions which would result in their firm going bankrupt and, ultimately, to the loss of their jobs.[3] Finally, the new unions believe that industry-wide negotiations might well consolidate the position of the unions created under the previous regime, which are traditionally well established at this level, even though the purpose of these negotiations is now very different.

Thus, although industry-wide agreements gained momentum in the early nineties, today they are experiencing a marked decline. In the majority of the countries of Central Europe, this level tends to be neglected. In Hungary, for example, 24 sectoral agreements were registered in 1992. In 1995, there were just seven.[4] In Poland, by September 1996, only ten collective agreements had been concluded above enterprise level (at sectoral, occupational, regional or national level). In countries such as the Russian Federation, where industry-wide negotiation has continued, it is of a very formal nature. The unions have always attached great importance to this level of bargaining but the interlocutor on the employers' side remains ill-defined. With the abandonment of the central planning system, the obligations of the ministries responsible for each branch have become unclear. For instance, typical industry-wide agreements merely reiterate legal obligations and recommend that additional benefits be determined in regional or enterprise-level agreements – if the economic situation so allows. Employees must therefore look to the enterprise for an improvement in their working conditions.

The prominent role accorded to firms is not merely the result of a deliberate political choice based on liberal principles, even if, as in the Czech Republic, the Government explicitly favours this level of bargaining. Indeed, already under the previous regime, a certain amount of informal bargaining took place, especially between workers and foremen. There is therefore a tradition of sorts, even though, at that time, the unions' role was mainly to organize social activities rather than to negotiate with the employers. Studies undertaken demonstrate that nowadays the unions have adapted to their new role and are negotiating, within firms, workers' wages and conditions of employment. The number of enterprise-level agreements is growing. In Hungary, registered agreements increased from 391 in 1992 to 816 in 1995.[5] In the Czech Republic, it has been estimated that 30 per cent of employees are covered by enterprise wage agreements.[6] In Poland, the Ministry of Employment put the number of enterprise-level agreements in September 1996 at 6,128, of which 2,337 were new ones, concluded after September 1994.

A study conducted in the Russian Federation in 1995 amongst 246 firms in five regions[7] revealed that two-thirds of firms were covered by collective agreement: 93 per cent in the transport sector, 86 per cent in industry, 73 per cent in the civil service, 57 per cent in construction, 50 per cent in the social services, but less than 10 per cent – one out of 11 firms – in the financial sector, despite increasing union membership rates in this sector. The vast majority of these agreements were only valid for one year, although they could legally have been concluded for three years. The same survey found that in one-third of the enterprises not covered by agreements, unions were nevertheless present. It is interesting to note that, in the social services sector, only half of the unions wished to have an agreement. This no doubt implies that the definition of collective agreements remains vague. In the private sector, collective bargaining has made very little progress. It is concentrated in large enterprises, leaving small and medium-sized firms without any collective regulation.

Other forms of worker participation, besides collective bargaining, exist in some of these countries, though they are practised very unevenly. In Bulgaria, the Labour Code provides for two forms of representation: union and non-union, with limited rights to participate in decisions regarding the management of the firm. In Hungary, the 1993 Act on employment introduced works councils on the lines of the German model, but without the right to co-determination. In other countries, provisions regarding participation have disappeared as they were inherited from the past and are thus viewed as remnants of socialism. In the Czech Republic, the 1988 Act on state enterprises instituting works councils was abrogated in the 1990s. In Poland, the 1990 Act on the privatization of state enterprises contained no requirement for the setting up of works councils. Privatization has therefore abolished worker participation in practice, although the law entitles workers to one-third of the seats on the board of directors. Workers are also represented on boards of directors in Hungary; as in Poland, their presence is often symbolic.

In terms of content, it has been noted that the unions have moved from negotiating "patronage" (organizing sport and leisure activities, housing) to negotiating conditions of employment. A survey carried out by the ILO on local union branches in the countries of Central Europe provides more information on the content of this bargaining.[8] It appears, first of all, that wage bargaining takes place for the most part at enterprise level. In Poland, 96.5 per cent of local union branches stated that wages were negotiated at this level. The figure was 72 per cent in the Czech Republic, 65 per cent in Hungary and 60 per cent in Slovakia. Of the remaining conditions of employment, occupational safety and health topped the list – being covered in 98, 53, 83 and 97 per cent of agreements in the Czech Republic, Hungary, Poland and Slovakia, respectively. The importance accorded this issue is not surprising when it is recalled that, under the old system, the inspection of working conditions was one of the unions' official tasks. What is new, however, is the interest shown in such matters as vocational training (an average of 66 per cent of collective agreements) and job security (60 per cent). Finally, with the exception of overtime, which is much in evidence in collective agreements, the subject of flexibility (flexible working hours and contracts of employment) is seldom touched on in negotiations (28 per cent of collective agreements on an average).

It cannot be concluded from these few statistics that bargaining at enterprise level is a widespread practice, or that it assumes the same form as in the Western countries. It is virtually non-existent in the nascent private sector, taking place for the most part in state-owned enterprises. Yet the number of these large enterprises is in steady decline – and this trend will continue with the restructuring of the economy. Furthermore, while the current agreements may be the fruit of genuine negotiation, which was not the case during the communist period, the negotiators on the management side often seek to form alliances with the unions to obtain concessions from the State to help them overcome difficulties in their enterprises.[9] In these conditions, it would be rash to conclude that negotiation at enterprise level is predominant until such time as the process of privatization has reached a critical level, encouraging the emergence of a group of employers which is more homogeneous and thus better able to organize itself. Moreover, case-studies undertaken in the Czech Republic, Bulgaria (where in state enterprises the tradition of sectoral negotiation has persisted) and Hungary have shown that, if it is to develop within enterprises, collective bargaining requires the stimulus provided by national tripartite agreements.[10] This raises the problem, to which we have already referred, of building a functional link between these two levels.

Results and problems of national agreements

Observers have been tempted to regard certain tripartite agreements signed in the countries in transition as declarations of (good) intent which have yielded few practical results. In certain cases this criticism is not unconnected to the legacy of the previous planning systems, which has been perpetuated today in a form of "corporatism". The general impression at times is that the achievements of tripartite agreements are judged in the light of functions fulfilled in the past by the mechanisms of central planning, which provided detailed and (apparently) effective solutions to the largest possible number of problems. It goes without saying that if similar hopes are placed in tripartite consultations and bargaining, disappointment is bound to ensue.

In the Russian Federation, the experience of tripartite agreements has, with the exception of the settlement of the miners' strike in March 1992, been far from convincing. A Tripartite Commission for the Regulation of Labour and Social Relations was created in November 1991 and its constitution amended in 1993 and 1994. Its tasks consist of drawing up tripartite agreements, monitoring their implementation and facilitating the settlement of disputes. Regional tripartite committees have also been set up to fulfil the same functions. Agreements have in fact been signed regularly, the first in 1992 and the most recent one for the period 1996-97. But the fact remains that results have been very modest due both to conflicts among the organizations represented and to the difficulty for the Government to respect its initial financial commitments particularly with regard to the minimum wage. The role of the Commission has been further weakened with the launching by the Government in 1994 of a "Treaty on Civil Accord", which fulfils the same functions, participation having been extended to other representatives of civil society.

The case in other countries is different. Not only is it impossible, even after careful analysis of these agreements, to arrive at such a clear-cut judgement, but it must be wondered what objectives can be achieved by national negotiations taking place in such a particular context. We need hardly recall that the context is one of profound social upheaval, in which the primary objective is to maintain a minimum of social cohesion. From this point of view, tripartism has had some positive effects in the countries in transition, even though social cohesion remains very fragile, particularly in Eastern Europe. Tripartite agreements are, in addition, an integral part of the mechanisms for regulating certain conditions of employment, especially wages.

Countries such as Hungary and the Czech Republic initially set up tripartite committees and drafted agreements to forestall social conflict – which would inevitably have arisen with the application of austerity programmes. In Hungary, this initiative was actually taken during the final years of the communist regime in response to mounting political and social tension. These committees helped towards settling the major lorry drivers' dispute in Hungary in 1990 and the miners' strike in the Russian Federation in 1992. It is also significant that Bulgaria experienced an upsurge of social conflict during the periods when social dialogue was marginalized. Finally, it was under the pressure of the wave of strikes of summer 1992, that Poland embarked upon the path of tripartite dialogue.

As to the content of these agreements and their implementation, there have been some positive results, along with a number of failures. In the latter respect, the best known case is that of the Hungarian negotiations of 1994-95 on the social and economic agreement.[11] The breakdown in negotiations may be explained by the fact that the Government tried to gain support of the social partners to introduce an austerity programme without being able, on account of the economic situation, to offer any significant concessions in return. This experience clearly illustrates that tripartism cannot take the place of political institutions. Nevertheless, even though the tripartite discussions did not result in any specific achievements, they enabled major social conflicts to be defused. Moreover, this setback did not prevent the continuation of tripartite dialogue which recently led (February 1997) to the signing of a joint programme of activities (see box 6.2).

In other cases, the results of negotiations have been much more tangible. In fact, they have, in many countries, initiated profound reforms in labour law, particularly in the area of collective bargaining and social protection.[12] In Poland, for example, the tripartite pact on state enterprises in transition (February 1993) led, inter alia, to the drafting of a law to protect workers' claims in the event of their employer's insolvency (see box 6.3). In Croatia a tripartite agreement was signed in May 1997 instituting an economic and social council. Discussions on the same point are under way in Estonia, and, in Lithuania, a tripartite committee which meets regularly was set up some years ago.

In many countries, tripartite committees are also the mechanism through which wage increases are regulated. In addition to their role in the economic and political fields, one of their main activities is therefore the setting of minimum wages. The wage policies brought in during the first years after democratization impeded the exer-

Box 6.2.   Tripartism in Hungary

Hungary was the first country in the region to create a tripartite body at the national level, in 1988, under the last communist Government. The Labour Code of 1992 gave this body, known as the "National Council for Reconciliation of Interests" (NCRI), a legal foundation and broadened its sphere of competence. While it was the wish of governments that the social partners should be closely involved with the management of the very delicate process of transition, employers' organizations and trade unions saw tripartism as a powerful means of achieving recognition.

When it was created in 1988, the Council's role consisted chiefly in setting the statutory minimum wage and negotiating directives on maximum wage increases in the "non-budgetary sector" (i.e. private enterprises and public enterprises subject to privatization). With regard to the minimum wage, the Council was called upon to take decisions (so that the Government could not change the minimum wage without the agreement of the employers and workers represented on the Council). In the case of maximum wage increases, the Council's task was to negotiate directives. These directives were binding upon enterprises, but only in the sense that those firms which exceeded the maximum increases set by the Council were punished by the imposition of tough fiscal penalties. The intention was gradually to liberalize the wage policy by phasing out these penalties. In accordance with its mandate, the NCRI has regularly set minimum wages. Over the years, however, they have fallen far below the subsistence level. While the decisions of the NCRI no longer have much influence on the absolute level of the minimum wage, they are nevertheless of some practical interest in that trends in the minimum wage have an impact on the entire range of salaries. It will also be noted that, in accordance with its mandate, the NCRI has negotiated numerous directives on maximum wage increases. The fiscal penalties for exceeding these maximum levels were progressively reduced and they disappeared completely by the end of 1992. Thus, the process of wage liberalization was successfully brought to completion by the NCRI.

The NCRI has also concluded a number of agreements on aspects of economic and social policy. For the most part, these are agreements signed annually in conjunction with the drafting of the budget for the following year (and which are often known, for that reason, as "agreements on the budget"). Generally, the parties seek to reach agreement upon a package of measures, some of which are intended to promote a balanced budget and competitiveness, and others to ensure a minimum of social protection – with neither type, however, touching upon fundamental aspects of economic and social policy (such as privatization, for example). Since the negotiations usually prove to be more difficult than anticipated, the content of the agreements which are finally concluded is often fairly limited and covers a mixed bag of issues. "Agreements on the budget" were concluded in 1991, 1992, 1993 and 1994. An idea of their content might be gleaned by examining briefly the agreement of November 1992 – although it must be emphasized that it is generally considered to be more far-reaching than other agreements of this type. Firstly, the 1992 agreement resolved the thorny problem of how to divide the assets of the former official union – no small achievement. It also brought to completion the process of wage liberalization by abolishing the last remaining fiscal penalties imposed in cases where the maximum increases provided for in the agreement were exceeded. Other important measures included: increases in the minimum wage and pensions; a number of tax exemptions for workers; a reduction of the VAT on certain basic commodities; an increase in employers' and workers' contributions to unemployment insurance; the raising of the retirement age for women; compensatory measures linked to the imminent introduction of tuition fees in higher education (a concession obtained by the scientists' union which had representation on the NCRI); and a promise by the Government to consult with employers and workers on certain aspects of employment policy and on some areas of policy concerning taxation, industry and agriculture.

In the summer of 1994, the socialist-liberal Government, which had recently come to power, announced that it wished to conclude with the employers' organizations and unions an agreement considerably more ambitious than the usual "agreements on budget". In fact, it wanted to sign a "social and economic agreement" covering its four-year term of office, which would give it the green light from the employers' and workers' side for a vast economic stabilization and recovery programme and include measures to alleviate the social implications of this programme. After six months of negotiation within the NCRI, the parties were forced to admit that it was impossible to conclude such an "agreement" and had to confine themselves to an "agreement on the budget" of the usual kind.

This did not, however, signal the end of tripartism since, on 27 February 1997, a new agreement was signed within the NCRI aimed at promoting collective bargaining, facilitating the settlement of industrial disputes and strengthening the application of labour legislation. The social partners agreed upon a series of practical measures which were to be implemented to this end. This agreement provides for the enhancement of the Council's authority and of the resources at its disposal.

The experience of tripartism in Hungary has therefore by no means been entirely negative. Clearly, it has not fulfilled the ambitious tasks assigned to it, notably in connection with the agreement of 1994. But there can be no doubt that it has enabled difficult reforms to be implemented in the fields of wages, employment policy and industrial relations.

cise of this function, sometimes even superseding it, as in the Czech Republic.[13] These restrictions have now been lifted in the countries of Central Europe, but remain in place in the Russian Federation, Ukraine and Romania, in the form of a system of taxes on wage increases above a certain amount. While there has been criticism of the fact that these minimal increases are well below the level of inflation, tripartite committees undoubtedly play a role in wage regulation.

These committees therefore form, along with the enterprise, the matrix of an emerging system of collective bargaining. A final attribute of tripartite negotiations in the countries in transition is that they contribute to the organization of the social partners, without whom there can be no deeply rooted development of a democratic market economy. Much, however, remains to be done in this area. The unions clearly have a leading role in the industrial relations system today, but it is difficult for them to assume this role in the absence of a group of employers whose interests and involvement are clearly identifiable. Trade unions retain an undeniable potential for organization at enterprise level. But their efforts to reorganize at this level, though real, are still limited due, in particular, to the anarchic development of an economic set-up in which the private sector is largely informal. It is true none the less that, with its successes and failures, the progressive development of a system of social dialogue is making an undoubted contribution to the stabilization of these new democracies.

Box 6.3.   Tripartism in Poland

Tripartite consultations and negotiations of the "classic" type appeared later in Poland than in most other Central European countries. This was a result both of the Mazowiecki Government's wish to carry out "shock therapy", which was scarcely compatible with tripartite management of the transition process, and of the deep opposition between *Solidarity* and OPZZ, the old communist union. However, the worsening social situation prompted the Government, in June 1992, to offer to negotiate with the unions and employers a tripartite pact on the future of state enterprises. In fact, there were several separate rounds of negotiation, since the unions refused to sit at the same table. The negotiations were concluded in November 1992. On 22 February 1993, three separate (but virtually identical) agreements were signed with *Solidarity,* OPZZ and the seven industry-wide unions, respectively. The main aim of the pact, which was the first genuine tripartite agreement signed in Poland, was to define a series of principles which were to be put into practice subsequently by means of legislation. The pact consists of three parts dealing with the privatization of state enterprises, their financial restructuring and a certain number of social questions. With regard to the part of the pact concerning privatization, it will be noted that Poland is the only country in Central Europe to have dealt with this important question – at least with some of its aspects – in a tripartite agreement. The agreement stipulates, in particular, that, during the six months prior to the entry into force of the future law on privatization, workers may have a say in the choice of the mode of privatization, that they may acquire free shares in the privatized enterprises, and that they may be represented, on a minority basis, on the boards and management committees of the privatized enterprises. Discussions on the application of this part of the pact were long and difficult, due, in particular, to the various changes of government since its signing. They led eventually to the Act of 30 August 1996 on the commercialization and privatization of state enterprises. This Act, which was promulgated three years after the signing of the pact, in a context of rapid change, is rather different from the one initially envisaged. However, this has not led to an outcry among the signatories of the pact.

The part of the pact dealing with the financial restructuring of state enterprises includes certain provisions concerning financial assistance for these enterprises and bank credits in their favour. These provisions led to the adoption of an Act on 3 February 1993. The pact also provides for the abolition of the *popivek* (i.e. the fiscal penalties imposed when wage increases exceeded the levels set) and the establishment of links between the growth of consumption and of GNP: the growth of GNP must be accompanied by increased consumption, and, while the growth of the latter should not exceed that of GNP, neither should it be less than half that level. Currently, the *popivek* has effectively been abolished and there is a directive stipulating that the Government must ensure under its policies that the aforementioned links between the growth of consumption and GNP be maintained.

The part of the pact dealing with social questions envisages the adoption of new laws on the protection of workers' claims in the event of their employers' insolvency (a matter of great importance given the large number of bankruptcies) and the creation of works social funds (to provide workers with certain benefits, particularly in the area of "welfare"); it also foresees the amendment of the chapters of the Labour Code concerning collective agreements and health and safety issues. All these laws were passed, on 29 December 1993, 4 March 1994, 29 September 1994 and 2 February 1996, respectively; at the time the main concern was to provide the country with regulations suited to a market economy and in line with the standards of the International Labour Organization and the European Union. It is generally accepted in Poland that the part of the pact dealing with social questions has been applied in its entirety.

Finally, the pact provides for the creation of a tripartite committee to deal with economic and social issues. This was established by resolution 7/94 of the Council of Ministers. In accordance with this resolution, the committee's role consists essentially in giving opinions and making proposals on aspects of economic and social policy, particularly with regard to wages, employment, social protection and the distribution of resources between consumption and investment. In practice, although the committee has given opinions on such matters as the reform of social insurance and the drafting of the national budget, its work has focused on the periodic negotiation of wage increases. However, the figures published by the committee are intended only as guidelines; indeed they are averages and their distribution is negotiated subsequently at the appropriate levels. This, at any rate, is the case in the private sector, where these figures may be exceeded and the *popivek* has been completely abolished. In state enterprises subject to privatization, the figures in question may also be exceeded, but the manager may be called to account if his enterprise becomes insolvent and it can be proved that this would not have occurred had he not granted wage increases higher than those set by the committee. In the case of the "budgetary sector" (i.e. the civil service and public services not subject to privatization, such as education and the postal service), the committee concludes genuine wage agreements, whose provisions are binding upon the parties – although, once again, the figures negotiated in these agreements are only averages, their distribution being determined later at the appropriate levels.

Despite the difficulties which it is encountering, this country has made considerable progress in this area. The concluding of the pact on state enterprises and the important role played by the tripartite committee in wage regulation are two aspects of that progress. But they are not the only examples. A great deal of social dialogue continues to take place on an interoccupational basis, whether at the level of the country as a whole or within certain regions. Citing only regional agreements, mention must be made of those signed within the framework of development programmes, for the Walbrzych region in 1994, the Katowice district in 1995, and the Zielona Gora and Lower Silesia regions in 1996. Thus, while it is true that tripartite consultations and negotiations have not touched upon certain vital economic and social problems, neither have they been limited to matters of secondary importance.

Notes

[1] Z. Mansfeldová: "Tripartism in the Czech Republic", in R. Kyloh (ed.): *Tripartism on trial: Tripartite consultations and negotiations in Central and Eastern Europe* (Geneva, ILO, 1995), p. 74; S. Neykova: *Major problems on the collective bargaining practices in Bulgaria (1993-1995)* (Sofia, 1995), p. 5.

[2] S. Clarke, et al.: *The development of industrial relations in Russia,* document prepared for the ILO, p. 113.

[3] A. Toth: *The role of multi-employer collective agreements in regulating terms and conditions of employment in Hungary* (Budapest, 1995), p. 15.

[4] P. Vörös: *The situation of collective bargaining in Hungary* (Budapest, 1996), p. 4.

[5] P. Vörös, op. cit.

[6] J. Rusnok and M. Fassman: "The true effects of wage regulations in the Czech Republic", in D. Vaughan-Whitehead (ed.): *Reforming wage policy in Central and Eastern Europe* (Budapest, European Commission/ILO, 1995), p. 141.

[7] T. Chetvernina et al.: *Collective agreements in Russia: Current practice* (Moscow, Academy of Sciences of Russia, TACIS, ICFTU, 1995).

[8] ILO: *Trade union experiences in collective bargaining in Central Europe. A report of an ILO survey in Bulgaria, Czech Republic, Hungary, Poland and Slovakia* (Geneva, 1997).

[9] M. Sewerynski (ed.): *Evolution of Polish labour law and collective labour relations during the period of post-communist transformation* (Warsaw, Ministry of Labour and Social Policy, 1995), p. 37; J. Thirkell, R. Skase and S. Vickerstaff (eds.): *Labour relations and political change in Eastern Europe: A comparative perspective* (London, University College London Press Limited, 1995), p. 58; O.A. Kirichenko and P.M. Koudyukin: "Social partnership in Russia: The first steps", in *Economic and Industrial Democracy* (London, Sage), Vol. 14, 1993, pp. 43-54.

[10] J. Thirkell, R. Skase and S. Vickerstaff, op. cit., p. 172.

[11] L. Héthy: "Anatomy of a tripartite experiment: Attempted social and economic agreement in Hungary" in *International Labour Review* (Geneva, ILO), Vol. 134, No. 3, 1995, pp. 361-375.

[12] G. Casale: *Collective bargaining and the law in Central and Eastern Europe: Some comparative issues* (Budapest, ILO (Central and Eastern European Team), 1997), Report No. 20.

[13] D. Vaughan-Whitehead: "Wage policies in Central and Eastern Europe: In search of greater social and economic effectiveness", in D. Vaughan-Whitehead, op. cit., pp. 13-71.

7 The instruments of social dialogue in the newly industrialized and developing countries

While the growth of precarious forms of employment and joblessness in the industrialized countries has to a certain extent undermined formal systems of industrial relations, there is no comparison with the situation in the developing countries, where social protection provisions laid down by law or collective agreements in fact cover only a small section of the workforce. Not only do they apply exclusively to the formal sector, which employs a minority of the economically active population, but they only partly cover it. However, though organized industrial relations are marginal, they still deserve special attention for two reasons at least. First, it is in the formal sector that large foreign companies, with their obvious importance for national economies, become established, and industrial relations are one of the factors they take into account in their investment decisions. Second, the role of occupational organizations, and trade unions in particular, in the formulation of labour legislation – a substitute for under-developed collective agreements – is far more important than union density would lead one to expect.

Obviously, it would make little sense to speak of an industrial relations model specific to developing countries – even in the limited sector in which the term could apply. Industrial relations in these countries do, of course, have certain features in common, precisely on account of their very weakness, but most of all they are characterized by their tremendous diversity. While there is no clearly discernible uniformity among countries on the same continent, their proximity, and hence their common exposure to certain types of experience, nevertheless justifies their being presented by region here. In any event, the purpose of this chapter is to identify trends based on significant examples rather than to provide an exhaustive description of specific systems. Lastly, the inclusion in this chapter of the newly industrialized countries, some of which are members of the OECD, is warranted by the fact that industrial relations there, while evolving rapidly, have not yet attained the degree of institutionalization found in the countries with a longer history of industrialization.

Industrial relations in Latin America

The countries of Latin America vary widely in terms of size, level of economic development and extent of their formal sector. Although exposed to similar influences under colonial rule, each country's unique history has shaped its own system of industrial relations, with some countries having centralized bargaining while in others it is decentralized, and some having a unified trade union movement, as opposed to others where it is pluralistic. There is one exception to this diversity: the tradition of state intervention in the regulation of industrial relations.

This regulatory tradition, which in recent years has seen the negotiation of a number of tripartite agreements, has led to a situation similar to that in the transition countries: a lack of machinery linking centralized decision-making with that at enterprise level. It is nevertheless true that, with varying success, the recent development of tripartism in several Latin American countries has had a positive influence by bringing democratic institutions into play following lengthy periods of authoritarian rule. Tripartism has also helped design measures to adjust to the new economic conditions, at a time when social cohesion had been jeopardized by structural adjustment policies. The primacy of the legislature goes hand in hand with a weak collective bargaining system which has proved largely incapable of replacing the role of law by regulation through collective agreements. However, along with a new willingness to relax legislation which in any case applies essentially to large companies in the formal sector, these countries have seen the conclusion of a number of enterprise-level agreements that come close to European agreements in terms of the emphasis placed on maintaining jobs.

Uneven spread of enterprise-level bargaining

There are many reasons for the weakness of collective bargaining compared with legislative activity. First, most of these countries have, or have had, authoritarian or populist regimes that constrained the development of social dialogue. Sometimes using tripartite commissions with limited powers, these regimes monopolized the function of regulating the labour market; populist governments sought to gain exclusive control of workers' protection by legislative means in order to secure popular support. Thus strengthened, a legalistic tradition naturally encouraged labour organizations to act mainly at the central level. Moreover, the size of the informal sector and the proliferation of small and medium-sized enterprises in these countries has made it extremely difficult for unions to become established at grass-roots level, again militating in favour of action at the centre. And, although this was probably not a decisive factor, as shown in the previous chapter, establishing a union presence was made more difficult in countries where the law requires a minimum number of members in order for a trade union to be set up. It is also worth mentioning that the trade unions, often allied with political parties, have much greater scope for action at the national level than union density would lead one to suppose. As for employers' organizations, while their effectiveness as economic pressure groups is recognized, their role in labour matters is less important. Lastly, in a number of countries the establishment of trade unions at the national level was encouraged by authoritarian regimes which sought in this way to gain control over the workers.

Two distinctive types of collective bargaining system can be discerned in Latin

America. In the first group, which comprises fewer countries – Brazil, Argentina and Uruguay – but is important both economically and in terms of population, industry-wide bargaining predominates. Mexico may also be included in this group because, although enterprise-level agreements are the norm, company bargaining is closely controlled by industry committees that have to approve the agreements. In the other countries, industry-wide bargaining is marginal, even where expressly authorized by law, as in the Dominican Republic or Venezuela, and decentralized bargaining takes place mainly in the large enterprises. This type of decentralization is, for the most part, more a reflection of the general weakness of collective bargaining than the result of a deliberate strategy inspired by the American or Japanese models. As an explicit model, it has only really been put into practice in Chile, where the Act of June 1979 authorized the negotiation of collective agreements only by company unions. With the restoration of democracy, however, this restriction has been lifted. Only recently have some governments taken a positive view of the benefits of decentralization. Logically enough, it is in the countries with an industry-wide bargaining structure that the highest proportion of employees are covered by collective bargaining. For example, in 1995, the figure was over 70 per cent in the formal sector in Argentina. The proportion is also high – 95 per cent in 1994 – in the federal jurisdiction in Mexico. In the countries with decentralized bargaining coverage remains low, at around 15 per cent. Agreements only cover the formal sector, and are often concentrated in certain branches of activity such as banking in Paraguay or the power industry in Venezuela. So what appears here is a dichotomous model of labour regulation in which the legislative system predominates on the one hand and individual employee-employer relationships on the other.

Generally speaking, collective bargaining is neither very dynamic nor very innovative. Agreements essentially deal with traditional issues such as pay, holidays and some health and safety aspects, and as often as not merely reproduce the contents of earlier agreements. In countries where inflation has remained high, pay is clearly the dominant issue, whereas it has lost momentum in countries where inflation has been brought under control, such as Argentina and Brazil.

It is in the large multinationals that collective bargaining is most highly evolved, and here it displays features similar to those in European countries. Jobs are a priority issue for the unions. In Brazil, Ford was the first company to sign an agreement on flexible working time, in exchange for a commitment to safeguard jobs. In Argentina, flexible working time and a set of measures designed to raise productivity also featured in the collective agreements signed by the main automobile manufacturers – Ford, GM, Chrysler, Fiat and Toyota. Box 7.1 gives examples of the contents of the collective agreements signed in 13 companies in this region. The fact that some of them were concluded before the arrival of the companies is a sign of the importance the trade unions attach to jobs, but also reflects the centralized character of the trade union movement in Argentina, where enterprise-level collective bargaining remains

Box 7.1.   Innovations in enterprise agreements in Latin America

Subjects covered	Enterprises	Main agreements
A. Adaptability to changes on labour issues:		
1. Diversification of contracts	Fiat, GM, Toyota, Mina Alumb. – Argentina; Magma Tintaya – Peru	All types of fixed-term contracts
2. Workforce stability	GM, Magma Tintaya – Peru	Entreprise committed to relocate excess workers
	Nissan, Bancomer – Mexico; Fanapel – Uruguay	In the event of redundancies, employees covered by the agreements are protected: casual and temporary workers are the first to be dismissed
3. Reorganization of working time	Fiat, GM, Toyota – Argentina; Ford – Mexico	Enterprise has the right, under certain conditions, to change employees' working hours
	Fiat, GM, Toyota, Mina Alumb. – Argentina; Ford – Mexico; Magma Tintaya – Peru	Only hours actually worked are taken into account in shift work
B. Training, remuneration, productivity:		
1. Organization of work systems	GM, Toyota, Mina Alumb. – Argentina; Magma Tintaya – Peru; Tolteca – Mexico; Fanapel – Uruguay	Creation of multidisciplinary and multifaceted teams
2. Training	All enterprises mentioned	Permanent in-house training programmes
3. Remuneration	Fiat, GM, Toyota – Argentina; Telef., Tolteca – Mexico; Fanapel – Uruguay	Bourses and group awards for increased productivity Bonuses and individual awards for increased productivity
C. Worker participation:		
	Fiat, GM, Toyota, Mina Alumb. – Argentina; Magma Tintaya – Peru; Telef. – Mexico; Fanapel – Uruguay	Management-worker committees to evaluate and propose measures for improving productivity and competitiveness

Source: ILO: *News, Latin America and the Caribbean, 1996 Labour Overview* (ILO, Lima).

firmly under centralized control. This example shows that it would be rash to use this country as an illustration of a natural tendency to decentralize (or, for that matter, Chile where, as we have seen, bargaining outside the enterprise was prohibited outright until the restoration of democracy). In any event collective bargaining in Latin America remains the preserve of a limited group of employees, mainly those in large companies.

Some States have taken measures which could have the effect of giving a boost to collective bargaining, even though the results so far have been modest. For instance, new Chilean legislation allowing multi-employer bargaining should encourage the conclusion of agreements in small enterprises. This, however, remains to be seen, judging by the results of a survey conducted by the Ministry of Labour, which suggest that only a little over 20 per cent of employers and fewer than 20 per cent of trade union representatives were aware of the law.[1] In Argentina, the application of certain measures to make working conditions more flexible can only be legally implemented through collective bargaining. The same applies to the different types of work contract authorized by the 1991 Act. Similarly, Argentinian legislation on small and medium-sized enterprises allows certain exemptions from the general regulations governing work contracts (for example, relating to termination of the contract) provided they take the form of a collective agreement. So far only one agreement of this kind has been signed.

Collective bargaining, in particular at the enterprise level, is thus still in limited use as an instrument of social regulation, while structural economic reforms in these countries are exacerbating instability and social exclusion. In response, many countries, true to the tradition of centralization, have resorted to legislation and, more recently still, to national pacts drawn up through a tripartite procedure.

The influence of the legislative system and the experience of tripartism

The formal regulation of terms and conditions of employment in Latin America traditionally takes place at the central level, as has already been noted; detailed labour legislation forms the core of regulations to protect workers. In several Latin American countries centralization goes as far as including in the Constitution labour provisions which, on other continents, are laid down by legislation or collective bargaining. The Constitution of Guatemala, among others, addresses such matters as discretionary bonuses or length-of-service bonuses, and Brazil's Constitution deals with worker protection in the face of automation. But the most common method is extremely detailed labour legislation, which leaves a reduced scope for collective bargaining. This raises the question of adapting employment conditions to the new requirements of competitiveness.

Improving flexibility is a general watchword in Latin America. One may well wonder what it might mean in countries with a predominantly informal economy, where flexible employment conditions are particularly pronounced. This watchword is aimed at attracting foreign companies and is also addressed to large enterprises in the formal sector which are subject in many cases to very strict legislation. More often than not, introducing greater flexibility in conditions of employment in these countries means only one thing: amending legislation. This is true of Peru, for example, where a large number of decrees have been enacted to this end. Under these circumstances, the State would appear to have sole responsibility when it comes to introducing measures to relax conditions of employment. But this means that some governments are having to relinquish their role of protecting workers, on which their popularity has traditionally rested. Moreover, in the absence of other viable procedures for defending their interests, the general strike becomes the only means available to employees of making their voice heard. It is therefore hardly surprising that certain countries, such as Venezuela, the Dominican Republic and Paraguay, are strengthening rather than relaxing social guarantees. Others have embarked on reforms designed to introduce flexibility into labour law provisions, the best-known example being Chile before democratization. Since then, Chile has seen moves, albeit limited, in the opposite direction, especially with respect to dismissal.[2] Unless they are imposed by an authoritarian regime, these reforms must be supported by a degree of social consensus. It is this realization that has made many of these countries aware of the advantages of tripartism. And tripartite discussions have indeed been held, partly inspired by the Spanish example of a smooth transition to democracy, although there is no tradition of tripartism in most of these countries.

Although results have been mixed, tripartism has played an undeniably positive role of social stabilization in the particularly difficult economic and political context of many Latin American countries. The various agreements concluded in Mexico over the last decade are cases in point. Although there has been criticism of the formal character of consultations, the main thrust of which had at times been laid down in advance by the Government, they did make a significant contribution to the social stability of a country hit by a particularly severe economic crisis. This dialogue continued with the signing of a bipartite agreement ("Towards a new work culture") between COPARMEX, the employers' federation, and CMT, the trade union federation, which aimed to reconcile respect for workers' basic rights with the needs of production. In parallel with this, a tripartite agreement ("Alliance for economic renewal") was negotiated in October 1995, putting forward specific measures to maintain workers' purchasing power through an increase in the minimum wage and unemployment benefits, and to encourage companies to hire through tax incentives. The 1990 tripartite agreement, "Chile, an historic opportunity", and the follow-up agreements signed in 1991 and 1993 in that country also illustrate the advantages of the tripartite approach as a means of preserving social cohesion while implementing structural change (see box 7.2). It has undoubtedly facilitated Chile's peaceful transition to democracy, a process more usually accompanied by violent social conflict.

Box 7.2. Chile: Tripartism and legislative changes

In April 1990, following the restoration of democracy, a tripartite agreement entitled "Chile, an historic opportunity" was signed by the new Government, the central trade union organization and the Confederation of Production and Commerce. Apart from an increase in the minimum wage and some family allowances, the agreement contained few concrete measures, but a number of proposals. None the less, it was hailed as smoothing the transition to democracy, which in other countries has been anything but smooth: "Quite probably their true aim was to initiate a policy of dialogue which would help to ensure democratic transition without industrial conflict. On the whole this objective was achieved, in considerable contrast to the high level of industrial conflicts that has characterized democratic transition in all other countries."[1]

But the agreement also served as a catalyst for drawing up legislation which, without veering away from the principles of liberalism, strengthened social protection on many points, and was thus a marked shift away from the huge programme of deregulation implemented under the authoritarian regime. Among the amendments introduced to the previous system through four laws consolidated in the 1994 Labour Code, the following may be noted:

– a reduction in the statutory length of fixed-term contracts from two years to one year;
– enhanced protection of employment on dismissal, the reason for which must be stated explicitly. The maximum amount of compensation for unjustified dismissal was also raised from six to 11 months;
– authorization to bargain above enterprise level.

The practice of tripartism has been very sporadic since then, with the important exception of the creation in 1994 of a Forum for Productive Development. Four committees were set up within the Forum in 1996 to deal with matters relating to job security, labour relations, minimum wage and regional development. The Forum also initiated the creation in 1995 of a national tripartite centre to promote quality and productivity.

[1] A. Bronstein: "Societal change and industrial relations in Latin America: Trends and prospects", in *International Labour Review* (Geneva, ILO), Vol. 134, No. 2, 1995, pp. 163-186.

Tripartism has also produced some other very tangible results. For instance, the conclusion in March 1997 of an agreement limiting end-of-contract bonuses in Venezuela is a particularly significant result in that country. In most cases, the impact of tripartism has been felt in the legislative changes it has stimulated. In Argentina and the Dominican Republic, for example, tripartite discussions took place before new legislation was enacted. The National Employment Act of 1991 in Argentina was the culmination of two years of negotiations with the social partners. Several recent laws, such as those governing employment in small enterprises or bankruptcy, were the direct result of the tripartite framework agreement on employment, productivity and social equity signed in 1994. While consultation efforts and the desire to achieve a minimum consensus on the broad outlines were real enough, the fact remains that the provisions of legislation sometimes take considerable liberties with the conclusions reached in tripartite discussions. This is the case in Argentina where, disregarding the 1994 framework agreement, the Government has been trying since September 1996 to push through amendments of the law on employment to which the unions were vehemently opposed. In Colombia, too, in January 1997, a few months after signing a social pact to curb inflation, the Government declared an economic "state of emergency", enabling it to take austerity measures without consulting either parliament or the social partners. These few cases highlight the importance, as well as the fragility, of tripartism in practice.

Another problem is that the excessively close relationship between the legislative sphere and tripartism makes the latter appear responsible for decisions that are in fact taken by the legislative and executive powers, while tripartism's relative powerlessness is not offset by a real ability to act as a driving force at lower levels. And the implementation of legislation is inhibited by the lack of adequate means of enforcement. In other words, while dialogue at the centre should inspire government and parliamentary initiatives, it should also inspire initiatives on the part of the social and economic actors at more decentralized levels as well. In this respect, as we have seen, much remains to be done. For all that, the experience to date and emergence of tripartism are, considering the past and present situation of Latin American countries, an indication of the will, albeit not widespread, to strengthen the basic mechanisms of social dialogue. And the latter is particularly necessary as countries follow the path toward industrialization in a democratic system, as the experience of some Asian countries also shows.

Industrial relations in Asia

As in the case of Latin America, there is no such thing as an Asian model of industrial relations.[3] A distinction should be drawn between three main groups, at least: countries with a socialist system, such as China and Viet Nam; India; East and South-East Asia. There are noticeable differences even within these three groups. The countries of Asia, and especially those of South-East Asia, have attracted attention in recent years on account of their dynamism and growth. Their economic success has often been ascribed, whether explicitly or not, to the existence of fairly unrestrictive regulations on employment conditions and to decentralized collective bargaining. But quite apart from the fact that levels of development vary widely in this part of the world, the idea that there is little state intervention in the regulation of the labour market is largely erroneous, as is that of a uniform model of collective bargaining.

For a long time, authoritarian power took the place of industrial relations. With industrial development, a rise in education standards and the dawn of democracy, the need for sounder collective bargaining made itself felt in some countries. This was the case in the Republic of Korea, which will be analysed separately. The fact remains, however, that the mechanisms which facilitate social dialogue are, on the whole, still underdeveloped. Yet their development would appear essential if these countries, especially those undergoing rapid growth, are to embark under optimal conditions on the path to industrialization and democracy. The following paragraphs set out to define the place and role of collective bargaining and social dialogue at enterprise level and to assess the conditions for coordination at the national level.

Moving towards collective bargaining

Without any doubt decentralized bargaining is characteristic of many of these countries. Some also have joint committees for dialogue in the Japanese mould. However, the most prevalent feature is the lack of dynamism of the instruments of social dialogue. The proportion of employees covered by a collective agreement rarely exceeds 4 per cent in most countries of the region.

The Republic of Korea is, to a certain extent, one of the exceptions. The practice of collective bargaining at enterprise level is clearly evident, although no precise information is available on the proportion of workers covered by agreements. Some authors estimate that it is about equal to the unionization rate, which is around 17 per cent.[4] To this must be added a series of quasi-agreements negotiated within companies without any recognized trade unions. The content of the agreements, traditionally centred on pay, has been extended to include non-pay clauses, such as shorter working hours and, albeit still to a limited extent, worker participation in management (organization of work, new technologies, subcontracting). Enterprise-level agreements are all the more important in view of the fact that a substantial part of social protection is provided by the company, which offers assistance for children's education and housing, for instance. The loss of one's job can therefore have very grave consequences; and jobs are already a major bargaining issue. A recent survey indicates that employment protection clauses were contained in 36 per cent of agreements in 1995.[5] Judging from the disputes of January 1997, this issue seems destined to occupy a very prominent place, and we shall return to it below. The 1996 Act, which includes provisions relating to collective dismissals, was adopted to make up for the lack of formal regulation. This matter had been dealt with on the basis of case-law and a recommendation of the Minister of Labour to the effect that enterprises should not proceed with collective dismissals except where absolutely necessary. The new Act sought to define those conditions and called for prior consultation with workers' representatives and the authorization of the industrial relations committee. The response to the Act shows just how sensitive this issue is and how it will increasingly need to be dealt with through collective bargaining. The Act of March 1997 defers by two years the application of the new legislation relating to dismissal, and the law will be very restrictive. In particular, the enterprise will have to prove that it is experiencing very serious economic difficulties and the unions will have to be consulted.

The importance of enterprise-level agreements for the protection of employees thus gives rise to the same problems as those observed in the United States, and it is these which are at the root of the recent disputes in the Republic of Korea. They are particularly acute as the risk of job losses increases. For instance, in China, the enterprise is, and no doubt will remain, an essential level of social protection. There, the situation has been changing rapidly since the implementation in December 1978 of reforms concerning the gradual introduction of a market economy. The new Labour

Law of July 1994 does provide minimal protection in terms of working time and minimum pay, but it does away with lifelong employment for newly recruited employees ("the end of the iron rice bowl"). Yet it is the enterprise, and hence the job, which provides workers with protection in terms of health care and, in many cases, of children's education and housing. Given the overmanning in many Chinese enterprises, the country is likely in future to face a situation like the one the Republic of Korea has been through, as can already be seen in heavy industry. The new Trade Union Law enacted in April 1992 seems scarcely able to prepare the unions for such an eventuality, since it preserves the ambiguity of their dual function: representing the workers' interests as well as safeguarding those of the enterprise and the State.[6] Of course, effective industrial relations instruments are necessary above all in a democratic system. From this standpoint various stages can be envisaged. An intermediate stage would be that of Singapore. Because of the high concentration of foreign-owned firms, the employers' organization does not command a strong, institutional presence. Still, a particular "tripartite" system of fixing wages was put in place in 1972. It is considered to be effective, but at the price of strong government control over union and employers' activities.

In most of the countries and areas of the region, collective agreements are still few in number. In Taiwan, China, for example, collective bargaining covers only 2 or 3 per cent of the workforce, even though unionization levels are relatively high. There are a number of different reasons for the scarcity of collective agreements. Most of these countries have only recently become democratic or are still governed by authoritarian regimes of varying degrees of strictness and thus do not have adequate institutions of industrial relations. What is more, many of them display the classic characteristics of developing countries, as set out at the beginning of this chapter. These have the effect of severely limiting both the extent and the effectiveness of collective bargaining. In the Philippines, negotiated pay levels are very close, if not equal, to the national minimum wage, particularly in the textiles industry, where female workers are in the majority. In the rapid growth countries and areas where the jobs issue is becoming increasingly crucial as a result of restructuring and the relocation of production, the weakness of industrial relations is threatening to lead sooner or later to serious adjustment problems. Already disputes have started to flare up outside the Republic of Korea. In Taiwan, China, it is mainly the Government that is intervening to put assistance programmes in place. In Malaysia, the scope of collective bargaining is strictly regulated. The law stipulates that bargaining cannot cover a number of subjects considered to be the sole prerogative of the employer: dismissals, transfers, promotions and work organization issues.

Apart from the countries with decentralized systems, the other major category in the region is the Indian system. India has in common with the rest of South-East Asia low collective bargaining coverage, estimated at 2 per cent of the workforce (the civil service and certain areas of the public sector not being covered by collective bargaining). Hence the dominance of regulation by legislation. However, the country's complexity and size and its democratic tradition set its industrial relations system apart from the rest of Asia. Each of India's states has significant autonomy with regard to social protection. Within its federal system, it is the states that set the minimum wage, and the differences are considerable (ranging from 5 to 80 rupees in 1996), though weak enforcement is common to all of them. Similarly, where dismissals are concerned, the law requires the prior authorization of the local administrative authorities, and this is granted more readily by some states than others.

The 2 per cent of the workforce covered by collective agreements represent more than 6 million workers. Unlike Pakistan, where bargaining takes place mainly within the enterprise, in the Indian industrial sectors covered by collective bargaining, agreements are concluded at various levels. National industry-wide agreements cover the sectors dominated by public enterprises, while in the traditional sectors one finds industry-wide agreements by region, such as those concluded in the jute, textile and metallurgy industries. While the increase in enterprise agreements has been appreciable, it is not necessarily undermining coordination at industry level; in the textile branch, for instance, industry federations continue to exercise a major influence in pay negotiations. It is perfectly clear, however, that labour flexibility issues are dealt with at enterprise level and that agreements in this area, though still rare, are steadily increasing in number.[7] In the enterprises concerned one finds agreements in which job reductions are linked to a social plan including supplementary pension schemes, subcontracting clauses and exemptions from authorization for lay-offs. This is especially true in the private sector. Centralization is still the order of the day in public sector enterprises. Privatization, while still limited, has occurred in enterprises operated by some states. However, no federally operated enterprises have been privatized. For these, the Government is endeavouring to give greater autonomy in fixing wages, but it is meeting with resistance from a management ill-prepared for such responsibilities. Social dialogue on employment therefore takes place at two levels in India: at the tripartite level, which will be analysed later, and at enterprise level in the private sector. Thus, a long history of democracy has given birth to a fairly elaborate system of labour relations, its effectiveness still limited by the complexity of the country and the heterogeneity of its economic development.

Collective bargaining still plays a relatively minor role in Asia. Nevertheless, the Republic of Korea's experience shows that this mechanism for dealing with labour problems is likely to evolve as economies develop and democracy advances. Will there be participation at the national level in this development, or will it take place on an informal basis, as in Japan for example? Given the diversity of countries, there is no one answer. But at the present time, with few exceptions, there is little activity at this level, as will be seen below.

Difficulties of social dialogue at the national level

In the countries of Asia there is no legalistic tradition like the one in Latin America. Nevertheless, the very weakness of collective bargaining means that the law plays a crucial role in countries such as China and Viet Nam, of course, but also in the Philippines, Singapore, Sri Lanka and Taiwan, China. To take only one example, in India the law imposes extremely strict conditions for dismissal and even goes so far as to regulate job classifications within the enterprise. But such a degree of centralization of the regulations governing social protection, without any relegation of authority to the enterprise level, implies that the legislation in fact only protects public sector employees and those of large enterprises, that is, a small minority.

The social partners, and especially the unions, have little influence on the drafting of legislation, with few exceptions, such as Singapore (but under special conditions, as we have seen) or, to some extent, the Philippines. In some cases the unions' powerlessness to act at the national level is the result of a legal prohibition. In Malaysia, the national unions are incorporated only as "societies" to facilitate relations among workers, and have no bargaining powers, which are granted exclusively to enterprise unions. This constraint on the social partners' ability to act at national level is reflected in the practice of tripartism, which is uneven, to say the least.

While Asian countries which have no legislation establishing one or more tripartite commissions are few and far between (Thailand has more than ten), tripartism varies a great deal in practice. In Malaysia, Thailand and Sri Lanka, the role of tripartism is limited, either because the tripartite commissions seldom meet or because their conclusions have little effect. In a few countries, however, tripartism is more active. To a certain extent this applies to the Philippines, where some significant results were achieved on minimum wages at the end of the eighties. India, on the other hand, has a long history of tripartism. The first tripartite body, the Indian Labour Conference, was set up in 1942, and has been followed by many others. In the course of its history, consultations have been very sporadic and the attitude of governments inconsistent, sometimes to the point of rejecting conclusions reached unanimously. However, recent tripartite consultations initiated by a Government anxious to implement structural reforms have produced some results, albeit controversial. They have enabled a minimum consensus to be built on the need for reform while providing at least some protection for the workers affected.

There is no doubt that the weak authority of the unions over workers and the deep divisions within the trade union movement limit the impact of social dialogue at the top. There is no doubt either that tripartism is not, on its own, going to resolve complex economic crises. However, if it is to have any chance of fulfilling its function of reconciling social and economic imperatives in a democratic society, its basic principles must be respected: freedom of association and of collective bargaining. It is also essential that tripartism should not be applied ad hoc, without being integrated in a genuine system of social dialogue. The Republic of Korea's experience in this regard is highly instructive.

The country's first such experience was linked with efforts to curb inflationary pressures. After failing in its attempt to achieve pay restraint through direct recommendations to employers in 1990 and 1991, the Government shifted to a tripartite approach and urged the recognized union (FKTU) and the employers' organization (KEF) to sign a national pay agreement in 1993. But owing to the absence of mechanisms linking the national with the local level, both on the unions' and on the employers' side, and to the exclusion of an unofficial but representative union (the KCTU), actual wage increases were significantly higher than the negotiated figures. This experience led to a weakening of the FKTU (which withdrew from the discussions) to the advantage of its competitor, the KCTU.

The country's second major experience of tripartism took place against the background of the new labour law passed by parliamentary majority in December 1996. Its failure in no way diminishes its importance for the future. Originally, the legislative reform was to have reflected the outcome of discussions on industrial relations within a presidential commission, which was set up on 9 May 1996 and brought together the employers, the unions (including the not officially recognized KCTU), academics and a group representing the public interest. After some fundamental disagreements, the KCTU withdrew from the commission, and it was on the basis of a report setting out the differences that the Bill was drafted. Without entering into the details of the legislation, the failure of this experience was partly due to the contradiction between recourse to tripartism and the restrictions placed on the principle of freedom of association and of collective bargaining. The law delayed by several years the introduction of multiple unions both at national and at enterprise level, and authorized employers to replace striking workers. The new law passed in March 1997 extended freedom of association by authorizing multiple unions at the national level. At enterprise level this will have to wait another five years. Paradoxically, disputes have focused on the risk of dismissals, although the Bill's clauses on this subject (the first time that Korean law had addressed this issue) were relatively protective compared with the legislation of other OECD countries. The explanation for the workers' reaction lies in a particular sensitivity towards employment protection, while mobilization against the restrictions placed on union activities reflects the need for collective protection.

Despite the failure, the creation of a national tripartite commission prior to the drafting of the labour law constitutes a remarkable precedent in the Republic of Korea, which will surely influence the future of the country's industrial relations and those of its neighbours. Under domestic and international pressure, these countries will have to find a way of reconciling the demands of competitiveness with the observance of social protection standards.

Industrial relations in Africa

The introductory remarks at the beginning of this chapter about developing countries apply in large part to the countries of Africa. The dominance of the agricultural and informal sectors, which is greater than elsewhere, severely limits the potential impact of tripartite or bipartite negotiations. By taking part in national liberation movements, the unions have managed in many countries to become a recognized force, although as a result they have often been perceived by the political parties as competitors.[8] In the labour sphere, their influence has on the whole been limited. In recent years they have been affected, even more than on other continents, by the backlash of structural adjustment programmes whose effects have included staff reductions in the public sector, where the trade union presence was most significant. There are some exceptions. Reference is often made to the United Republic of Tanzania, where unionization rates are high and measures have been taken to promote rural unions.[9] In many countries, especially those of francophone Africa, there is a formal and fairly elaborate structure of industrial relations, but it is little used in practice. Still, some of these countries have specialized tripartite bodies, especially in the field of vocational training, which have performed satisfactorily. Lastly, the case of Africa confirms – if confirmation were needed – that the level of development of industrial relations is largely dependent on the degree of industrialization and development of democracy. In South Africa, for instance, as well as in Mauritius, tripartism and collective bargaining, aside from a few difficulties, are truly dynamic. The same cannot, however, be said of all African countries with a higher level of economic development. In Tunisia, for example, despite the recent strengthening of the functions of the Economic and Social Council and the introduction of compulsory works councils, collective bargaining is still limited in practice.

A collective bargaining system in need of rebuilding

The torpidity of tripartite consultation and negotiation at the national level is all the more damaging to social dialogue as it is probably the most relevant level in countries where the formal sector is limited and does not warrant an elaborate negotiating structure. Of course, industry agreements do exist, for example in Senegal, but they only really apply to a few companies and are not regularly renewed. In Uganda, six banks are covered by a multi-employer agreement which fixes pay, working time and procedures for individual dismissal. A similar agreement was concluded in the plantation sector. Otherwise, agreements, where they exist, are signed in a few large enterprises. Privatization of whole tracts of the state and parastatal sectors, in which collective bargaining was most highly evolved, is increasingly reducing its coverage. Even where there are institutions for social dialogue, they are often ineffectual. In Tunisia, works councils are mandatory for enterprises employing at least 50 workers.

Box 7.3. NEDLAC in South Africa

The National Economic Development and Labour Council was set up by Parliament in 1994 and on 18 February 1995 replaced the National Manpower Commission and the National Economic Forum. It is made up of representatives of employers' organizations, trade unions (with at least 200,000 members), the State and community and development organizations. It comprises four chambers: public finance and monetary policy; commerce and industry; labour market; and development.

Its functions are very broad and may be subsumed under five headings:

– the promotion of economic growth, participation in decision-making on economic affairs and social equity;

– consensus-building and the conclusion of agreements on economic and social policy issues;

– consideration of draft legislation on labour market policy before its submission to Parliament;

– promotion of coordinated policy on social and economic affairs.

Among its achievements, NEDLAC prompted the creation of an agency to promote national investment and of a fund for the development of small and micro-enterprises. It was also consulted on the adoption of the Small Business Act 1996 and plays an important role in the new system of labour relations put in place by the Labour Relations Act 1995.

But they exist in only 15 per cent of the companies in this category. In 1973, joint committees were made mandatory in enterprises with at least 20 employees but, today, they exist in only 30 per cent of the companies subject to this requirement. In view of this poor track record, a new system was put in place by the Act of 21 February 1994, which provides that enterprises with at least 40 permanent employees shall set up consultative committees whose functions cover the organization of work and productivity, company welfare, careers, training, discipline, and health and safety. It is too early to evaluate the success of this reform, but it would appear that these new committees are focusing mainly on welfare and discipline issues. Social dialogue is still centralized, including in the national commissions provided for by the law. South Africa, with a few other rare cases, is the exception. Before democratization, collective bargaining took place in some sectors and enterprises. The Labour Relations Act 1995 encouraged the spread of industry-wide bargaining in bargaining councils, in which the social partners have, initially, to define the coverage of future industry agreements under the aegis of NEDLAC (see box 7.3). A system of industrial relations close to the European model is thus being established in that country.

Given the situation prevailing in most African countries, it is likely that social dialogue, which is particularly useful in times of structural adjustment, needs government initiatives in order to develop. Some governments have realized this and steps have been taken accordingly, for example in the *Entente* countries.[10] Another positive sign is the emergence of bipartite initiatives which have sprung up here and there. In Côte d'Ivoire, the trade union confederations and employers' organizations signed a protocol of agreement in 1995 setting up a permanent independent consultation commission. In Uganda, in the wake of serious strike activity since the early nineties, the employers' federation set up a think tank, called the Industrial Relations Clinic, for its members. The unions then joined the structure, which now serves as a consultation body on issues such as collective bargaining, the settlement of disputes, and productivity. Lastly, in Madagascar, for the first time in the history of its industrial relations, employers and unions negotiated and signed in November 1996 a national agreement raising minimum wages. These trends may well be tentative, but they are paving the way for the development of social dialogue in these economically fragile countries, where the threat of social unrest is ever present.

Tripartism and structural adjustment

As we have seen in connection with the transition countries and those of Latin America, when it came to implementing difficult economic adjustments, national tripartite agreements are frequently sought. This happens much less often in Africa, despite the economic and social upheavals caused by the adjustment programmes under which many African countries have been living for years. In Burkina Faso, the privatization commission is not tripartite, and many job-creation programmes are implemented without the participation of the social partners. In Benin, although the first adjustment programme was accompanied by a certain amount of consultation, the following two were imposed unilaterally, against the advice even of the National Assembly. Furthermore, the bodies for consultation on social issues set up in many countries have generally been ineffective. A case in point is the Consultative Labour Commission in Côte d'Ivoire, which meets in accordance with its statutes, but whose debates have little effect on the decisions ultimately taken by the Government. In Uganda, the National Labour Advisory Board is fairly inactive. There are several reasons for the weakness of social consultation. Apart from the limited resources these countries have at their disposal the main factor is probably the fact that the unions have lost the power to mobilize that they had in Africa's turbulent history following decolonization. More than elsewhere, the capacity for mobilization on concrete and often complex economic objectives is weak in countries with a predominantly rural economy and where the formal sector is shrinking.

As in the case of collective bargaining, some efforts are being made to develop social consultation at the national level. In Morocco, for example, a consultative council to follow up on social dialogue was set up in 1994. In Kenya, the social partners and the Government have embarked on tripartite consultations on economic and social reform. These initiatives are still fragile, except in South Africa, where democratization has been backed by strong union involvement. In particular, it led to the creation in 1995 of the National Economic Development and Labour Council (NEDLAC), a tripartite body (but including community organizations as well) with a very broad mandate. This institution was set up as part of a regulatory framework along northern European lines in a society marked by a long history of conflict in industrial relations and politics. As often happens, the tripartite approach has been used here to ward off the dangers facing social cohesion – glaring social inequalities, and very high expectations that are difficult to meet given the lack of economic resources. Clearly, it is too early to judge the outcome of this institution. But it is these results that will determine whether other countries of the region, even those where economic conditions are very different, will follow the example.

Conclusions

Most of the countries surveyed in this chapter are undergoing far-reaching changes. In many cases, those changes arise from the implementation of major structural reforms coupled with very difficult economic conditions and accompanied more often than not by radical political transformations. But in other cases they are occurring in the context of an exceptional improvement in the economic situation, enabling some countries to achieve vigorous industrialization. The use of social dialogue to deal with these upheavals has had mixed results. In a significant number of countries it has undeniably allowed these reforms to be introduced while averting serious social unrest. In others either dialogue has been a mere formality, or else it has been ignored altogether. Whatever the case, it is worth noting that the development of industrial relations is linked to the advance of democracy and industrialization. A strong force can impose its own solutions. Conversely, without a recognized method of regulation, there is a risk that the world of work will become fragmented, with countless different groups each trying to impose its own values and interests. This risk is particularly acute in the burgeoning democracies, where a multitude of unions and interest groups are generally emerging, but where the basic framework for social dialogue still has to be put in place.

The modalities of social dialogue are obviously very diverse, though one can identify certain subregional similarities here and there. Moreover, the common traits discernible in relation to the models described in Chapter 5, for example in terms of centralization/decentralization, do not suffice for constructing similar categories for these countries. Decentralization in Malaysia does not bring the country any closer to the North American or even the Japanese model. Other aspects of industrial relations are fundamentally different, as are the social and economic conditions prevailing in each country. Lastly, the place of the informal sector and its particular forms of collective organization will be a determining factor in the role industrial relations will play in many of these countries.

Notes

[1] Ministry of Labour and Social Welfare: *Como operan las normas de negociación colectiva* (Santiago, 1994).

[2] For a summary of these reforms, see A. Bronstein: "Labour law reform in Latin America: Between state protection and flexibility", in *International Labour Review* (Geneva, ILO), Vol. 136, No. 1, 1997, pp. 5-26.

[3] A. Verma, T.A. Kochan and R.D. Lansbury (eds.): *Employment relations in the growing Asian economies* (London, Routledge, 1995).

[4] ibid.

[5] KCTU (Korean Congress of Trade Unions) and KLSI (Korean Labor Society Institute): *Trade union's participation in management* (Seoul, 1996).

[6] Y. Zhu: "Major changes under way in China's industrial relations", in *International Labour Review* (Geneva, ILO), Vol. 134, No. 1, 1995, p. 45.

[7] C.S.V. Ratnam: *Indian industrial relations,* paper prepared for the ILO (1997).

[8] J. Kraus: "Trade unions and democratization in Africa", in M. Doro (ed.): *Africa Contemporary Record 1989-90* (New York, Africana Publishing, 1994), p. A.70.

[9] T. Fashoyin and S. Matanmi: "Democracy, labour and development: Transforming industrial relations in Africa", in *Industrial Relations Journal* (Oxford, Basil Blackwell), Vol. 27, No. 1, Mar. 1996, pp. 38-49.

[10] Benin, Burkina Faso, Côte d'Ivoire, Niger and Togo.

8 Industrial relations and the informal sector

Introduction

In the previous chapters we have seen how changes in the organization of work and production, brought about as a result of rapid technological change and economic liberalization, have affected traditional industrial relations structures and actors. In particular, the growing autonomy of the firm and the rise in precarious forms of employment have led to a certain individualization of the employment relationship. Workers' organizations, which were originally designed to cater to the needs of a stable and homogeneous labour force, have found it difficult to adjust their structures and functions and respond effectively to the varied demands of an increasingly heterogeneous labour force.

Although job instability and firm autonomy are relatively new trends in today's world of work in the formal sector, they have long been common to the informal sector of many developing countries. Indeed, the informal sector is mainly comprised of non-wage and unorganized workers – and industrial relations have traditionally focused on the organized sector of the wage-earning segment of the labour force. In the informal sector, remuneration, conditions of work, and employment and income opportunities are not, unlike in the formal sector, a matter for negotiation with an employer but depend on a variety of actors; operators in this sector are obliged to be in constant contact with market institutions, local authorities, suppliers and contractors. They are engaged in work processes and arrangements which are highly precarious and to a great extent unregulated and unregistered. By definition, they are outside the net – albeit to varying degrees – of state regulations and control. Hence, traditional industrial relations principles do not extend to informal sector workers.

The question might therefore be justifiably raised of why the informal sector has been included in a discussion on industrial relations. In fact, the very same considerations which are central to industrial relations – economic integration, social cohesion and democracy – are also of concern in the case of the informal sector. This argument holds particularly true when it is considered that the informal sector is not likely to disappear in the foreseeable future but rather to continue to grow. It employs a sizeable share of the urban labour force in many developing countries, which is estimated to fluctuate between 30 and 80 per cent. However, the working and living conditions of most informal workers are precarious and unsafe, sometimes inhumane – and evidence suggests that, with the appropriate support, informal workers might cease to live from day to day and become economically stronger, thus increasing their contribution to economic growth and social integration. Finally, all workers, irrespective of their employment status, aspire to improve their employment prospects, the quality of their jobs and, ultimately, their living conditions.

Our concern here is not whether industrial relations concepts are relevant to employment conditions in the informal sector. Indeed, the scanty evidence available seems to suggest that some of the mechanisms of industrial relations are already in place in this sector. Our aim is rather to determine which institutions and processes of industrial relations are already being used to enhance the income-earning capacity, living and working conditions and bargaining power of informal sector operators – and to gauge their success. In particular, we would like to examine whether there is scope and need for the two traditional actors in industrial relations, namely employers' organizations and trade unions, to extend their activities to cover informal sector issues.

This chapter will not provide definitive answers to these questions; neither will it suggest the "extension" of industrial relations to the informal sector or the development of an alternative model of industrial relations for the informal sector. Research on the institutional aspects of the informal sector and the practical experience of industrial relations actors in this domain are as yet inadequate to allow us to put forward any clear-cut conclusions. This chapter, however, is a first attempt to address informal sector issues from an unusual – but we believe useful – perspective, i.e. that of industrial relations.

The first part of this chapter will outline briefly the characteristics of the informal sector in an attempt to identify what features, if any, it shares with the formal sector. This will help us appreciate to what extent industrial relations processes and institutions are relevant to the problems and needs of informal sector operators. In particular, emphasis will be placed on the diversity among informal sector operators in terms of productivity and observance of fiscal and labour regulations. An examination will also be made of the sector's constraints and the institutional and policy biases against it. The differing interests and problems among informal workers, which may be attributed to the variety of types of employment and labour relationships in the sector, will be reviewed. This will help us comprehend the wide range and specificity of the issues giving rise to their demands, and of the strategies required to meet them.

In the second part, attention will be paid to the rationale and extent of the organizational efforts of the informal sector operators themselves. Collective representation is not only a pillar of industrial relations. As stressed by the Director-General of the ILO in his Report on the dilemma of the informal sector,[1] it is the principal means whereby informal sector workers might bring about changes in their working and living conditions. The institutional and regulatory factors, which may facilitate or hamper their mobilization and organization as a powerful interest group, will be examined. A short analysis will also be made of the similarities and differences between informal sector workers' associations and trade unions and employers' organizations of formal sector workers.

Finally some remarks will be made concerning the role of the State and of employers' and workers' organizations in incorporating the informal sector in the mainstream of development processes.

Are industrial relations relevant to the informal sector?

In many developing countries, the vast scale and rate of growth of the informal sector presents a dilemma and a challenge for industrial relations processes and institutions. It is a dilemma because, by definition, the informal sector encompasses employment situations and labour relations which not only differ from those in the formal sector, but often infringe upon established rules and laws. And regulation is often the outcome of protracted, and sometimes bloody, struggles and negotiations conducted by the social parties with a view to achieving important equity, productivity and democracy goals.

On the other hand, the informal sector represents a challenge because the needs and problems confronting those involved in it cannot be dismissed as irrelevant or unimportant. Apart from the fact that it absorbs a large and growing fraction of the labour force in most developing countries, it provides a "safety net" for poor households and workers who find themselves excluded from the formal sector in times of economic depression.

It has been mentioned earlier in the text that the inadequate legal and social protection of informal sector workers and their restricted access to capital market and formal training institutions may be attributed to a great extent to their lack of representation and participation in decision-making. This has had negative repercussions on productivity and quality of work. We will attempt, in the first part of this chapter, to describe the specific characteristics of the informal sector, highlighting the difficulties that these entail both conceptually and in terms of statistical evidence. This will help cast a light on the factors and conditions which prevent the setting up of representative employers' and workers' organizations in this sector. The main needs and concerns of informal sector operators will then be examined to try to see whether these differ entirely from those of the formal sector, or whether some common ground can be found. In so doing, we shall assess whether the structures and modes of operation of the classical industrial relations institutions might be of use to informal sector operators; we shall also try to determine in which circumstances alternative means and strategies might be required.

Clarifying the concept

Since the term "informal sector" was first coined in the 1970s, it has gained prominence in the literature on development and employment policies. Despite the great deal of research conducted on it, its meaning and scope still remain a matter of controversy as its magnitude, nature and composition vary between regions and countries.[2] The boundaries of the informal sector and the relationship between the formal and informal economy are determined by the extent and degree of regulation and institutionalization of a country's economic activities.[3] For the purposes of this report, the term refers to a range of economic units in urban areas which are largely owned and operated by single individuals with little capital and labour, and which produce and distribute goods and services with a view to generating income and employment. Other characteristics include labour-intensive technologies, easy entry, high levels of competition, production of low-quality goods and services, limited capacity for accumulation and restricted access to assets, credit and other services. Undeclared and unprotected labour, as well as unstable relationships of production, are also important traits. These features, however, are not universal, as there are many different "informal sectors" showing different levels of productivity, labour use and remuneration, and organization.[4] Furthermore, while there is considerable overlap between poverty and the informal sector, the social and economic arrangements prevailing in this sector cut across the whole social structure.[5]

Magnitude, trends and patterns of growth

Most informal activities are unrecorded in official statistics, thus making it difficult to gauge the extent of informal production and the labour force. Furthermore, data are scattered, unreliable and out of date. The definition of what the informal sector encompasses and the methodologies employed to measure it also vary from region to region and from country to country, making any comparative analysis meaningless.

Despite these constraints, there seems to be a consensus on the steady growth of the informal sector in almost all developing countries,[6] with the exception of the newly industrializing countries (East Asia).[7]

In Latin America, for instance, 15.7 million new jobs were generated between 1990 and 1994, of which 8.4 in every ten were in the informal sector.[8] Informal sector employment grew in the region at an annual rate of 4.7 per cent, compared to 1.1 per cent in the formal sector.[9] The slow growth of formal sector employment, combined with an equally sluggish rise in the minimum wage, resulted in a reduction in the average level of incomes in the informal sector; own-account workers were the hardest to be hit.[10]

In Colombia, urban informal employment grew at 3.6 per cent per annum between 1984 and 1994, absorbing over 50 per cent of total urban employment and contributing to 18 per cent of GNP.[11] Between 1984 and 1992, women's participation in the sector rose from 40.6 per cent to 43.2 per cent. This was accompanied by a decline in the most traditional categories of informal sector employment (family workers, domestic labourers, own-account workers) to the benefit of paid labour and owners of micro-enterprises. Employment in trade and services accounted for 62.3 per cent of the sector's total employment.

In Asia, it is estimated that the informal sector absorbs between 40 and 50 per cent of the urban labour force, although significant variations may be found between the newly industrializing countries (less than 10 per cent), and countries such as Bangladesh, where the sector's employment share is as high as 65 per cent. A report on the urban informal sector[12] in Asia reveals that women's participation in this sector varies considerably between South-East Asia and South Asia. It estimates that in Bangkok, Thailand, and Manila, the Philippines, for instance, women account for over 50 per cent of the workforce. Most of them work in the tertiary sector (retail trade), although their participation in manufacturing, especially garment manufacturing, exceeds 60 per cent of those employed in that subsector. Conversely, in some cities of India and Pakistan, women's participation in this sector seems to be lower and concentrated in a few and mostly low-productive activities.

In Africa, it is estimated that the urban informal sector currently employs about 61 per cent of the urban labour force and will generate some 93 per cent of all additional jobs in this region in the 1990s.[13] In sub-Saharan African countries, the annual rate of expansion of employment in the urban informal sector was reported to be 6.7 per cent between 1980 and 1985.[14] In Ghana, this sector grew by 5.6 per cent per annum compared to less than 1 per cent in the formal sector.[15] It is estimated that the informal sector in this country absorbs 65 per cent of non-agricultural employment – accounting for about 22 per cent of GDP.[16] Women are to be found in trading (60 per cent) and, to a lesser extent, in manufacturing (about 34 per cent) and the services sector, such as the food-processing and dressmaking subsectors. In Kenya, the proportion of women engaged in the urban informal sector rose from 39 to 56 per cent between 1977 and 1986.

The expansion of employment in the informal sector has been, for the most part, linked to the slow – sometimes even negative – growth of formal sector employment in many developing countries.[17] This lack of dynamism is generally attributed to a combination of three factors: first, the rapid and significant growth in the urban labour force, determined by improved living conditions and rural-urban migration; second, economic stabilization and restructuring programmes, introduced in the early 1980s in many African and Latin American countries, which contributed to the decrease in both public sector employment and real wages and salaries; and third, the quest for increased flexibility and deregulation required on account of the growing competitiveness in the global markets, which has resulted in enhanced capital intensity and reduced labour costs.

Given the absence of alternative employment opportunities, this process has drawn many retrenched workers into the informal sector. At the same time, a large number of households participate simultaneously in the formal, informal and subsistence sectors. In fact, many formal sector workers have decided to supplement their income by working part time in the informal sector to counteract the decline in their real wages in the formal sector resulting from austerity measures. Studies on poor households in both urban and rural areas reveal the existence of intra-household earning arrangements envisaging the participation of one household member – usually a male – in the formal sector, and the engagement of another member – commonly a female – in informal sector activities.[18]

Another effect of the growing informalization of the economy has been the rise in the number of women who work.[19] According to one source, the participation rates of women in the informal sector (excluding agricultural work) are: 80 per cent in Lima, Peru; 65 per cent in Indonesia; 72 per cent in Zambia; and 41 per cent in the Republic of Korea.[20] In many countries, the public sector has traditionally been women's major formal sector employer. The contraction of the public sector and resulting job losses have affected women more than men, because of their concentration in temporary and lower level jobs.[21] Furthermore, as already noted, the decline in formal sector real wages has compelled many women, who were previously taken up exclusively by household chores and family care, to turn to remunerated work; and this has proved much easier to find in the informal than in the formal sector. This may be attributed to the discrimination and segregation they encounter in the formal labour market because they have a lower level of education and training than men and have interrupted whatever work experience they might have on account of childbearing and family responsibilities.[22] Attitudes which attach more value to the reproductive role of women rather than their productive functions, as well as cultural norms which restrict women's mobility, constitute other powerful barriers to women's entry into the labour market. As mentioned earlier, the threshold to participation in the informal sector is usually low, thus making it much easier for women to find work in this sector despite these disadvantages. Furthermore, in the informal sector, the workplace and the home are very often one and the same thing and labour relations are based largely on family and/or kinship ties. This helps ease constraints related to social and cultural values and expectations.

Constraints in organizing

Heterogeneity of activities and employment status

Many authors[23] have underscored the heterogeneity of the informal sector. Activities range, in fact, from petty trading and service repairs, to transport, construction and manufacturing. Informal sector units may encompass the self-employed working alone or with the aid of unpaid family members, as well as "micro-enterprises" employing a few hired workers and apprentices.

The informal sector employs men, women, youth and children alike. None the less, there are considerable differences in levels of income, type of activity, productivity and employment status depending on age and sex. Women tend to be concentrated in low-productivity and often unremunerated jobs. This suggests, as shown, the existence of labour market rigidities, and of cultural and social constraints, which reduce women's mobility from low to high-productive jobs.

The informal sector is also characterized by a wide variety of employment statuses and labour relationships.

Furthermore, as we have seen earlier, the emergence of new and atypical forms of employment in the formal sector has weakened trade unions and led to a decline in their membership rates. This decline has been ascribed to the fact that the organized labour movement finds it difficult to adjust its programmes and institutional structure to the rapidly changing and diversified needs of formal sector workers.

It is reasonable to suggest that, in the case of the informal sector, the problems entailed by the diversity of employment status may be even worse. Another factor preventing informal sector workers from trying to improve their working conditions and/or remuneration through organization is that family or ethnic loyalties count more than working-class solidarity. This is certainly one main reason why, despite often unsatisfactory working arrangements, working relationships in this sector are usually characterized by the absence, or low level, of conflict. This factor, coupled with the very modest scale of operation of most informal sector units and their high instability, is responsible for the low rate of unionization of workers in small enterprises.[24]

Closely associated to this aspect is the blurred distinction between informal sector associations, representing wage-earners or other types of dependent workers in an attempt to improve their wages and working conditions, and those grouping micro-entrepreneurs or own-account workers who are concerned primarily with productivity goals. Sometimes, as we shall see in the second part of this chapter, the same informal sector organization may pursue both sets of goals. This is often due to the fact that their members may change their employment status throughout the year, or combine self-employment with wage-earning types of activities. This is particularly the case of home-based production. Home-based workers may engage in paid labour in peak periods while, for the rest of the year, they may produce the same or similar goods and services for direct sale on the market.

Some six categories of workers may be identified. These comprise: own-account workers operating alone or with unpaid family members who are not paid wages but earn an income; owners or employers of micro-enterprises with a few apprentices and hired workers; wage labourers engaged in micro-enterprises, usually with no formal contracts, working on a casual or regular basis; family workers who are not remunerated; wage workers who work in a place of their own choosing, such as homeworkers; and paid domestic workers.

The relative importance of each of these categories of workers varies from country to country and in each subsector of activity. Evidence suggests, however, that the self-employed working alone or aided by unpaid employees, including both family members and apprentices, dominate the sector.[25] Surveys conducted in selected Asian cities in China, the Philippines and Thailand revealed that the vast majority of the economic units operating in the urban informal sector employ between one and four workers, including the owner – and these were mainly family members or relatives.[26] In Metro Manila, for instance, 90 per cent of all sample enterprises had four or fewer workers. In selected cities of India, this proportion was found to be much lower, as the units comprising one single person ranged between 56 and 82 per cent of the sample units.[27] In Latin America, a recent study on the urban informal sector in a few countries confirmed the predominance of self-employment and unpaid family members. The significance of the latter, however, varies between countries, being inversely related to the size of formal sector employment. In Argentina and Brazil, for instance, own-account workers operating with or without unpaid family members accounted for 48 and 43 per cent, respectively, of urban informal employment in 1994. In the same year, own-account workers represented up to 68 per cent of the sector's working population in Lima, Peru.[28] Studies carried out in Africa, Asia and Latin America confirmed that self-employment was concentrated mainly in trade and service types of activities.

The proportion of workers, including owners and paid labourers, engaged in small-scale enterprises represent around 10 per cent of the informal sector labour force in Latin America. In Argentina, micro-enterprises absorb about 11.7 per cent of the persons employed in the urban informal sector. This share declines to 9.4 per cent and 8.3 per cent in Lima, Peru and Brazil, respectively.[29] In Asia, a study confirmed the small proportion of wage labour engaged in the informal sector; however, this share increased according to the subsector and sex. In fact, manufacturing was estimated to absorb 30 per cent and 72 per cent of the urban informal labour force in Manila and Bangkok, respectively. In India, over 40 per cent of the women working in the urban informal sector were in wage employment.

A survey carried out in Dar-es-Salaam, the United Republic of Tanzania, revealed that unpaid workers represented the majority of the sector's employees, and that 40 per cent of the former were related in some way to the employer.[30] In 1994, wage labour in the urban informal sector accounted for 39.6 per cent of total employment in the sector in Argentina, 29.5 per cent in Brazil and 23 per cent in Lima, Peru.[31]

Finally, there are a number of units in the urban informal sector which are not truly independent as their freedom to take decisions is somewhat curtailed or they do not carry out entrepreneurial functions, such as taking risks, or place their goods and services on the market. These units may include operators who rent their work equipment and are therefore subject to the conditions set by the equipment's owner, or homeworkers – most of whom are women producing services and goods for pay, usually from their homes, for an employer or a contractor. Equipment may or may not be supplied by the employer or contractor and homeworkers do not take any decisions concerning the design and operation of their work. What distinguishes this form of employment from factory work is that it is carried out with very little supervision or regulation of working methods.

Small-scale activities and instability

It is well known that there is an inverse relationship between the size of a productive unit and the degree of organization of the workers engaged in it. In other words, the smaller the unit or enterprise, the more difficult it is for the workers to form a representative association.

Most informal sector operators operate on a small-scale basis, at a low level of organization, with no or little division between labour and capital. This is confirmed by the fact that the level of investment required to create a job in the informal sector is much smaller than that required in the formal sector.[32] Productivity, for instance, can be equally varied in the informal sector. Subsistence-level operators, such as shoeshiners and scavengers, exist alongside units engaged in remunerative activities which are linked to the most dynamic sectors of the economy.

In addition to their very limited scale of operation, informal sector units can be very unstable, which makes it even more difficult to set up workers' associations and sustain them. Within relatively short periods of time, many units may spring up only to disappear soon afterwards – or to change location or activity. In Manila, for instance, a study found that 47 per cent of all the units surveyed had sprung up in the preceding 12 months, and that only 14 per cent of the total had been operating for ten years.

The way in which the sector has been growing so far would seem to indicate that small-scale activities will continue to prevail in the foreseeable future. Some authors[33] concur that the general tendency for this sector has been to grow by lateral expansion, i.e. by a constant increase in the number of economic units – as opposed to the rise in the number of jobs per unit. The inflow of both new entrants to the labour force and retrenched workers has lowered the entry barriers. This has had a twofold effect of reducing the average returns per economic unit and of worsening the sector's working conditions by obliging informal sector operators and their family members to work much harder.[34] Income deterioration in informal sector ventures has also resulted in an early drop-out from school and labour market entry. Children are thus deprived of the opportunity of acquiring a better education and training – and this jeopardizes their prospects of vertical labour mobility and sets in motion the conditions for the perpetuation of poverty.[35]

There has also been a reduction in the length of apprenticeships, which constitute the main channel for transfer of skills in the sector. In the United Republic of

Tanzania, for instance, a recent ILO report[36] found that a concomitant of increased economic hardship was that apprentices tended to take up self-employment after only a few months – whereas, in the past, "graduating" into self-employment took several years. This has resulted in lower quality goods, unfair competition for the former masters, and a general decline in the sector's income levels. This trend suggests the existence of low entry barriers, although the rate of entry varies between activities, being higher in manufacturing than in trade and services. The high incidence of the latter in the informal sector of many cities in Asia, Africa and Latin America confirms the lower level of skill and capital required in these activities.

Informality/illegality and its cost

Another distinct feature of informal sector units is that they operate on the fringe, if not outside, of the legal and administrative framework. This obviously hinders the process of organization of informal sector operators. Failure to comply with existing rules and regulations obviously runs counter to the inherent objectives of any organization which claims to be representative. Many informal sector operators do not respect – or only to a limited extent – the regulations concerning registration, licensing, tax payments, occupational safety and health and working conditions. A number of studies examining the cost to informal sector operators of "abiding by the rules" suggest the existence of trade-offs between employment and regulations.

This failure to comply with laws and regulations has been ascribed to different factors. Some authors attribute it to the high cost in terms of time and money entailed by complying with these regulations.[37] Inadequate standards, lengthy and cumbersome procedures, red tape, and inefficient bureaucracies would seem to explain both the emergence of the informal sector and its low productivity.

Others maintain that informal activities are carried out beyond regulation mainly because of the inability of informal sector operators to bear the cost of regulation, due to their low revenues deriving from tight markets and resource shortage.[38] They claim that the low productivity of this sector may be explained in terms of the existence of a labour surplus which pushes down incomes and generates subsistence activities. Inability to pay taxes or observe labour laws would therefore be a structural constraint and not, or only in part, a matter of inadequate regulation.

Another reason for non-observance relates to an unawareness of the costs and benefits associated with regulation.[39] Furthermore, taxes and other levies are not regarded as a contribution to a redistributive system, but rather as an imposition by the State in return for which no benefit can be expected.[40] Ambiguous regulations which are liable to be interpreted differently by officials enforcing them also contribute to the lax enforcement of the law. In addition, the fact that there are not enough public inspectors further weakens the institutional capacity to guarantee law application.

A distinction needs, nevertheless, to be drawn between those informal sector activities which cannot afford to be "legal", because they do not generate sufficient surpluses, and those activities which could bear such a cost but which, for pecuniary or similar reasons, are carried out illegally to evade taxes and regulations. The latter type of activities, including "off-the-book" production of goods and services by established enterprises in the formal sector, the employment of clandestine workers or socially undesirable activities, including prostitution and drug-trafficking, are not regarded as being part of the informal sector.[41]

Failure to comply with regulations and laws gives rise to a number of problems which affect the well-being of informal sector workers and their productivity. The fact that they are unregistered or not included in any list deprives them any legal protection in such matters as the guarantee of property rights or the enforcement of contracts.[42] Traders and artisans operating in unauthorized locations are subjected to harassment from the police authorities. And this, apart from forcing them to spend a great deal of time and resources protecting and defending whatever assets and stocks they might have, prevents them from making any improvements in capital and technology for fear of eviction.

Disadvantages relate also to restrictions in terms of participation in public tenders (only registered businesses are allowed to compete) and access to services, such as credit, training and technical assistance, and/or infrastructure. As we shall see in the following section, income and working conditions, including safety and health, tend to suffer as well. Another inconvenience, deriving from non-observance, relates to the social stigma commonly associated with the fact of being informal.

All these factors explain why a fraction of informal sector operators seek either to register and/or to pay taxes.[43] The extent of compliance seems to be directly related to the size and number of years of operation of the unit, and to the sector of economic activity. As to the latter, units engaged in commerce and services, because of their higher "visibility", are more likely to pay registration fees and taxes than those involved in manufacturing. In all cases, however, there is a consistent failure to observe labour laws, especially those on social security.

To sum up, "invisibility" and the non- or partial observance of rules and obligations have severe repercussions on the productivity, working conditions, remuneration and social protection of informal sector operators; and these are all matters which are at the core of industrial relations. The question is therefore to ascertain which industrial relations institutions and instruments might be of relevance to address the relevant problems in the informal sector.

Despite the structural differences between formal and informal sector units, in terms of labour/capital ratios, scale of operation, returns to labour, and degree of observance of business and labour laws, they share, to a certain extent, similar concerns. In both cases, in fact, enhancement of productivity, income, and improvement of working conditions constitute fundamental goals.

Informal workers' needs and socio-economic concerns

Enhancement of income and working conditions

In view of the sector's instability and precarious nature, work processes in both micro-enterprises and self-employed ventures tend to be extremely flexible and intermittent. This flexibility has obvious repercussions on the sector's labour relations, which, as mentioned earlier, are often not subject to formal contracts on working hours, remuneration and social security coverage. A survey conducted in Dar-es-Salaam showed that employees' remuneration was determined on the basis of the productivity or income of the enterprise, rather than the number of hours worked at the workplace.[44] Studies carried out in other African and Latin American countries confirmed that workers were paid at piece rates or by the job and that hours of work were not strictly monitored.[45] Furthermore, only a small proportion of informal sector entrepreneurs paid their employees' social contributions.[46] The same finding emerged in a study covering selected countries of Latin America and the Caribbean.[47] It has also been noted that when social security contributions are paid, family members are those most likely to be covered.[48]

In the case of *de facto* dependent workers, such as homeworkers, conditions of work, productivity and the level and regularity of incomes are entirely contingent upon the subcontracting relationship, unless these operators "move" to own-account work or another form of employment. In turn, the ability of these operators to obtain satisfactory terms and conditions of work depends on the motives which compelled them to engage in subcontracting arrangements in the first place, and on the regulatory and institutional frameworks.

Informal sector operators may work on a subcontracting basis because they find it attractive (no risks and no managerial decisions to take; the possibility, especially for women, to remain at home and reconcile domestic chores with income-earning activities) or because they do not have any other choice. Indeed, they may have no other choice on account of their restricted access to capital (ability to raise funds through their own resources, state institutions or informal networks), to skills and work experience and to the market (viable locations for trade; ability to sell; understanding of market demands and fluctuations, etc.) Most homeworkers tend to be women because, as mentioned earlier, their access to well-remunerated jobs in the formal sector is restricted not only by their lower levels of education and mobility, but also by labour market occupational segregation and wage discrimination. Home work may provide the only socially and culturally acceptable opportunity for many women to earn an income. Research has underscored the disadvantages associated with this form of employment, which include: irregularity of income; poor working conditions (long working hours, exposure to toxic substances which affect the health of both the homeworkers and their families, as the place of work is at home); isolation; and lack of organization and social protection.

Evidence suggests that compliance with labour laws and safety and health standards tends to improve progressively with the expansion of informal sector businesses. However, this usually only applies to regulations and standards relating to pay and working conditions, e.g. minimum wage, holidays and working hours. Regulations concerning payment against loss of income resulting from sickness, work-related accidents or death are rarely respected even in the most successful cases;[49] this may be attributed to several factors. In the case of the entrepreneurs, they are mainly deterred by the high cost of the contributions and feel that health and safety standards are not applicable to their enterprises.[50] In the case of the employees, they do not see much point in paying regular social security contributions, particularly for pension purposes, when they do not envisage any long-term career development within the enterprise. Another important factor which might explain the non- or partial observance of labour laws within small enterprises is the paternalistic nature of the working relationships which characterize them.[51] Apprentices and wage labourers are often bound to the business owner – who, moreover, is personally involved in the work on a daily basis – by family, geographic or ethnic ties; this tends to promote non-conflictual relationships.

What should be done to improve the working conditions and the social protection of informal sector operators? Is law reform or the issuance of a special legal regime for informal sector workers the best option? Could poor and unhealthy working conditions be improved through collective bargaining by informal sector organizations themselves? Or could established formal sector employers' and workers' organizations include these issues on behalf of informal workers as part of their collective bargaining with the State?

Many authors have concluded that labour laws, apart from being costly, are, to a large extent, inadequate to regulate the relationships between employers and employees in the informal sector.[52] The principles of annual leave, sick leave, and maternity leave benefits, which are enshrined in labour legislation and based on the premise that a regular wage is being paid and that the employer has full control over working hours, are very far removed from the social context in which most micro-enterprises operate.

Consequently, it has been suggested to overhaul the existing regulatory framework to take into account the way people are employed and work in the informal sector.[53] This, it is maintained, would bring about a greater enforcement of the laws and improved working conditions – without hampering the entrepreneurs' accumulation capacity.

Others, although they acknowledge the inadequacy of the present regulatory setting, fear that the development of a special separate regime for informal sector operators would reinforce the perception of the informal sector as a peripheral segment of the economy. Furthermore, it might induce formal sector enterprises to change their structures in order to take advantage of the associated benefits. Micro-entrepreneurs' incentives to enhance their productivity and accumulation capacity would also diminish.[54] Some authors advocate a gradual and flexible approach towards laws and regulations which would take into account the state of the economy.[55] In any case, it is clear that regulations cannot be dismissed as mere constraints to entrepreneurship development in the informal sector. In many cases, and this applies in particular to safety and health standards, they have been devised not only to protect workers but also different groups and society as a whole. There are also certain basic human rights, such as freedom of association, freedom from forced labour and freedom from discrimination, and extreme forms of exploitation, such as child labour, which are fundamental to human dignity and the actual ability of informal sector workers to improve their working conditions and employment opportunities.[56]

Others have noted that, in respect of homeworkers, poor enforcement of existing rules is not so much a matter of inadequacy of the law, but rather the result of an economic system which requires the perpetuation of this type of activity.[57] In the search for solutions to these problems, it is vital therefore that these workers should organize themselves to protect their interests; there should also be a combined effort on the part of employers, trade unions and governments to recognize the necessity of homeworking, while addressing its more urgent problems.

There are some interesting cases of trade union support to informal workers' associations, in terms of advocacy for policy changes or for the extension of the existing social insurance scheme to informal sector operators to protect them against irregularity of work, and provide for income security and old age; these will be reviewed in the second part of this chapter. In Ghana, the Industrial and Commercial Workers' Union (ICWU) provides training to members of the Ghana Hairdressers' and Beauticians' Association in the area of occupational health and safety, in addition to traditional workers' educational activities.

Informal sector workers lack a credible voice to be able to present their case before the appropriate government authorities and institutions. Established trade unions can certainly act as a suitable conduit for pressure for change in the working conditions and social protection of informal sector workers. But are these to be scattered initiatives or do they reflect a new orientation amongst organized labour in the formal sector? Are there real conditions for cooperation between the two sectors? These questions will be addressed in the second part of this chapter. Nevertheless, we may venture to conclude that the informal sector workers' associations of trade union type might prove to be the most appropriate channel to press for improvement in the sector's labour conditions and working environment. Conversely, it is reasonable to argue that some form of employers' organization, such as micro-entrepreneurs' associations, might be best suited to tackle the many constraints which hamper the sector's productivity.

Improvement of productivity

The sector's low productivity may be attributed to the fact that informal sector operators have limited – indeed if any – access to productive resources, skills, markets, infrastructure, and services. They commonly obtain start-up capital or working capital through their own savings or funds raised from relatives and friends. Traditional moneylenders, suppliers and warehouses, which disburse small sums of money through very simple and expeditious procedures, constitute another important source of credit. These institutions, however, benefit the most from increased production, because of the exorbitant rates of interest they usually charge to borrowers. Traditional community-based savings and credit associations which provide financial support for both social and economic purposes also exist in many countries. The best known are the *tontines* in West Africa[58] or the *arisan* in Indonesia. However, their coverage is limited and they have little capital with which to operate; furthermore, their viability is undermined in highly inflationary contexts.

The reason why informal sector operators resort to informal credit institutions is because official financial institutions consider them "non-bankable". Lending to informal sector operators is, in fact, a costly and risky operation. The small profit margins of informal sector operators, the lack of collateral they can offer to secure their loans and the small size of the loans they need make informal sector operators unattractive to the public and commercial banking systems. The latter are, in fact, designed and administered to cater to the needs of large and medium-sized enterprises.

Informal sector operators – who generally speaking, though not always, possess little schooling to enhance their production and marketing capacity – are also held back by their lack of access to training and technology. Formal training institutions are costly and usually teach skills which bear little relevance to the situation and needs of the informal sector. These institutions are either part of the public sector and administered by regulations ill-equipped to deal with illiterate or semi-literate people, or are run by private businesses and cater to the needs of formal sector enterprises. Informal apprenticeship systems thus constitute the principal channel through which informal sector operators acquire skills.

Restricted access to both credit and training makes it impossible for informal sector operators to expand their initial endowment base, resulting in low productivity and depressed levels of income. The growth of home work and subcontracting can in part be explained by the fact that informal sector operators resort to these forms of work to try to obtain raw materials, credit, training and access to the market. This is very often the case of women whose access to both credit and training is usually more restricted than that of men on account of their lower literacy levels, their limited exposure to public transactions, customary or statutory laws on property and land rights,[59] etc.

Evidence suggests that micro-entrepreneurs' associations are not the only, or necessarily always the most effective, type of organization to overcome these constraints. Informal workers' organizations, homeworkers' associations and informal sector cooperatives – whose principles, functions and membership tend to vary considerably over time, thus making it difficult to differentiate between employers' and workers' type of organization – often mobilize to obtain credit, inputs and training at more advantageous conditions. For example, the Self-Employed Women's Association (SEWA), in India, set up a bank in 1979 which earmarked a substantial part of its urban loans to families of retrenched textile workers to enable them to take up alternative employment.

Vocational training or the periodic sharing of experiences can also successfully enhance the productivity of members of informal sector associations. In the formal sector, productivity has been significantly improved in enterprises as a result of various processes of labour-management relations, including skills upgrading. Despite the strategic importance of this function, most informal sector organizations, as we will see later, do not provide this kind of service to their members.

In many countries, the State, after years of indifference or coercion, has been more active in developing targeted interventions to overcome these various problems in the informal sector. Most efforts have focused on the sector's supply constraints, e.g. its restricted access to credit, training and technology, rather than on trying to step up demand for goods and services produced by informal sector economic units. Scant attention has been paid to the macro-environment and such factors as land tenure security, trade and fiscal policies or economic growth, which secure a good return to the investments of small-scale informal businesses.

Provision of credit, obtained by reforming financial sector policies and regulations or creating alternative sources of funding and delivery mechanisms, has been the most popular type of intervention, involving both government and non-government agencies. Despite the undisputed success of some experiences, such as the Grameen Bank in Bangladesh and the Bank Rakyat in Indonesia, the number of beneficiaries has generally been fairly limited compared with the demand. Because of financial and institutional constraints, in fact, informal sector operators displaying a higher repayment capacity have tended to benefit most.

It has also been suggested that subsequent rounds of credit to the same borrowers would result in diminishing returns from investments if no other measures were taken at the same time to try and cope with the other constraints in the sector – namely limited access to training, technology, infrastructure and services. The relatively high cost of these credit programmes has also been singled out as a major problem which undermines their sustainability, especially when many governments are under considerable pressure to cut expenditure.

Some governments have acknowledged the need to provide a more favourable macroeconomic environment for informal sector micro-businesses and have tried to reform their regulatory and policy frameworks. In Brazil and Mexico, special statutes for micro-enterprises have been adopted, with some success, to simplify registration requirements and procedures and ease tax payments. In other countries, similar attempts have encountered serious obstacles at the implementation stage. In the Philippines, for instance, the Kalakalan 20 – the legislation providing, inter alia, for the exemption of micro-businesses from a number of payments – could not be applied because it had no political support.

Most interventions targeting informal sector operators have also concentrated more on equity considerations than productivity enhancement. Indeed, credit has commonly been considered as a way of empowering the poor rather than a means of increasing productivity.

The links between micro and macro interventions have often been disregarded. Policy-makers have not deemed it necessary to coordinate the initiatives directed at the informal sector, which are often of a fragmented and scattered nature, at the micro and macro levels. At the grass-roots level, many NGOs have felt that trying to find a solution to local problems at the local level independently of both state and market institutions was the most effective guarantee against co-option or control by such institutions.[60] Through the empowerment of the poor, it was argued, local initiatives would automatically have an impact on the shaping and implementation of government policies.[61]

State-promoted interventions have seldom contemplated the participation of the potential beneficiaries in the design, implementation and evaluation of programmes directed at them. The mere channelling of inputs and services required was deemed enough in itself to create the conditions enabling informal sector operators to participate and benefit from development processes. Efforts to encourage the setting up of informal sector workers' organizations so that their needs and expectations might be reflected in national policies and programmes have often failed to bring about any substantial policy changes. In Kenya, for instance, the Federation of Juma Kali Entrepreneurs was established with government support; fora were subsequently created, involving both the Government and the Federation, to discuss and look into problems and possible solutions. However, this did not result in major improvements in the productivity or conditions of work of informal sector operators. The Federation's inherent managerial, technical and financial weaknesses in running its affairs, coupled with the inadequacy of both the organizational structure and the consultation process and procedures, severely limited the impact of the Government's initiative.

This clearly shows that interventions should not only try to tackle the resources and market constraints of informal sector operators by means of policy incentives and strategies coordinated at micro and macro level; they should also provide ample scope for self-organization and appropriate mechanisms for dialogue and negotiation. This again confirms the relevance of industrial relations processes and instruments to informal sector workers.

Problems specific to informal sector workers

There are obviously concerns which are common to both classical industrial relations and the informal sector; however, informal sector operators have to cope with a set of problems specific to the sector, of which insecurity of land tenure is one of the most flagrant. A number of studies[62] have pointed out that a large proportion of informal sector ventures do not operate in a fixed location but on the streets and in open areas; they often occupy areas over which they do not hold any right or conduct their business in inadequate premises. Many factors contribute to this state of affairs. First of all, evidence shows that the land allocated to the sector in urban areas has been declining over time.[63] Land scarcity has pushed up land prices to levels which informal sector operators cannot afford or are not ready to pay because they want to be able to count on a higher disposable income. The inability of the informal sector operator to afford the price of the land, coupled with imperfections in the land market and regulations concerning tenure and sale of land, have exacerbated the situation.[64] Furthermore, attempts to create infrastructure, such as covered markets or workshops for informal sector operators, have often met with failure because they did not satisfy the expectations of the intended beneficiaries. For instance, operators have preferred to be located in areas where demand was higher, i.e. the inner city, rather than on the outskirts of the town – where the city authorities have wanted to keep them.

As a result, many informal sector operators squat on private and/or public land, creating serious problems of congestion; and this naturally has negative repercussions on the environment and their working conditions. They are also subject to police harassment and liable to have their assets confiscated because they infringe the regulations – and are exposed to the risks of fire and theft. The fact that they occupy unauthorized areas also deprives them of access to basic services, such as water and electricity, and infrastructure, including roads and drainage, which undermines their productivity. To remedy such constraints, informal sector operators have to rely on low quality and expensive informal systems of service provision. In Cali, Colombia, for instance, the price of drinking water supplied by tank to slum areas is ten times higher than that provided by the local authorities. In Nouakchott, Mauritania, the price paid to water merchants can be 100 times higher than that supplied through piped water connections.[65] Insecurity in terms of land tenure, due to their ambiguous legal status or illegal occupation of land, also severely limits the ability of informal sector operators to improve their businesses. A number of organizations representing different categories of informal sector workers have placed the issue of land tenure security high on their agendas.

The erosion of incomes in the formal sector and the persistence of economic and demographic constraints which hinder formal sector employment growth make it necessary to upgrade the informal sector.[66] This in no way implies that enhancing the labour absorption capacity of the formal sector of the economy is no longer the most valid long-term solution to the employment problem. It simply means that the informal sector should be reinforced as it helps to cushion the adverse social impact of economic restructuring or recession by providing a source of subsistence income and making it possible to produce cheap goods and services for low-income households with no recourse to public subsidies; it also contributes to human capital formation through apprenticeship.

Efforts directed at this sector should acknowledge that it consists of both dead-end survival activities and those, more dynamic, which involve small-scale enterprises with an actual or potential advantage over formal sector enterprises.[67] As a general rule, these enterprises account for only a small proportion of the total number of informal sector operators. Their significance, however, varies across regions and countries and relates to their general level of economic development. In Latin America, for instance, dynamic informal sector operators coexist alongside subsistence-type economic units; in Africa, the latter still dominate the sector; whereas small-scale enterprises with a high potential for economic expansion are more common in the successful Asian countries.[68]

The blurred distinction between employers' and workers' associations in the informal sector and the specificity of some of the sector's constraints suggest, however, the need to make at least two adjustments in the classical system of industrial relations. These relate to the possible forms of organization and the issues to be addressed within the framework of negotiating machinery.

The scope of the adjustments required will be better understood in the light of the experiences of selected informal workers' associations in a number of developing countries.

Informal workers' organizations: Characteristics, constraints and prospects

In the previous section, we have attempted to show to what extent industrial relations processes and institutions are relevant to the problems and needs of informal sector workers. In so doing, we have tried to point out that there is scope for cooperation between informal sector workers and workers' and employers' organizations in the formal sector. But, for this to happen, changes need to be made to the structures, services provided by and modes of operation of these organizations. This is particularly true in the case of formal workers' organizations which seem increasingly to stress the strategic importance of informal sector workers.

It would be unrealistic to expect trade unions and/or employers' organizations to cover entirely the needs and demands of such an expanding and heterogeneous sector. This, coupled with the scant and often inadequate attention paid by the State to the sector, has led informal workers themselves to mobilize resources to cope with an often hostile environment.

This section will examine the motives which have prompted informal sector operators to engage in collective action, as well as the types, structures and functions of informal sector workers' organizations. In so doing, we shall seek to demonstrate how the specific circumstances and features of the sector and the State's policies and initiatives affect the scope, strategies and effectiveness of these organizations. This will help us to identify any similarities with or differences between informal and formal sector employers' and workers' organizations and to understand the nature and extent of their interaction and relationship. Consequently, we might draw some preliminary conclusions on ways in which the State, as well as employers' and workers' organizations, might encourage the promotion of informal workers' organizations and facilitate mutual understanding and dialogue. A word of caution, however, is necessary. The literature on the topic is more than limited, as are the empirical data. We have, therefore, to base our considerations on the reasons for and modes of operation of informal sector organizations on the findings of a number of case-studies conducted by a wide range of institutions; and these studies have been conducted at different stages with varying purposes and different conceptual and methodological approaches. In most cases, however, they have concentrated on the sector's productive constraints and barely examined its institutional and industrial relations aspects. This, coupled with the modest number of examples examined, prevent us from developing more sophisticated models of informal sector associations or arrangements by region or by subsector of activity.

Workers' rights and weak organizational capacity

It is the fundamental right of workers to try to improve their living standards and working conditions and protect their health and safety at work. Workers in the modern economy have pursued these goals by setting up organizations or associations of their own. Associations of informal sector workers have also sprung up for the same reason. Against all odds, workers in the informal sector are joining together to fight collectively for improved working conditions.

The value of organizations of informal sector workers and producers is apparent. Organizations provide a forum where needs and constraints can be assessed and strategies devised to cope with them. Organizations help operators to pool their resources and efforts in pursuit of common objectives, and serve as intermediaries vis-à-vis the State and/or other institutions. They can help redress market imperfections in the supply of capital goods or raw materials, or support services through collective bargaining on output prices – in the case of subcontracting; they can even help change the regulations. Organizations can bargain with other interest groups competing for the same scarce resources and services; they can lobby with other sectors to obtain recognition of and support for their claims. Organizations also help to assert their members' social identity and to contribute to social integration and regulation. Furthermore, public authorities, for practical reasons, prefer to deal with an organization acting on behalf of a group of people, rather than having to deal with an "invisible" segment of the population.

The vital importance of organizations, especially to impoverished women workers, has been amply stressed. Organizations help build ties of solidarity which transcend kinship and family boundaries, provide services which remove or reduce the obstacles hampering women's access to mobility within the labour market, and enhance women's awareness of their multiple roles and respective rights.

Despite the obvious advantages of being organized, the level of organization among informal sector operators is generally low – and the growth rate of existing organizations is sluggish. In Bogotá, Colombia, for instance, only 1 per cent of informal sector operators are estimated to belong to some type of association.[69] A study carried out in Dar-es-Salaam, the United Republic of Tanzania, calculated the level of organization in the sector, spontaneous or otherwise, to be 20 per cent.[70]

In South Asia, the unionization rate in the formal sector is 25 per cent but, if we consider the formal and informal sectors together, this decreases to 9 per cent (see statistical annex).

Informal workers' associations: Characteristics and constraints

As mentioned earlier, informal sector operators suffer from a number of constraints; they have limited access – if any – to productive assets and markets and have to cope with job precariousness and a lack of social protection, which undermine their income-earning capacity and bargaining power vis-à-vis market institutions and state agencies. We have also mentioned the heterogeneous nature of the informal sector. Each subgroup has to cope with different sets of problems and demands – which obviously has repercussions on its ability to mobilize and organize.

It is reasonable to believe that own-account workers and owners of micro-enterprises are in a relatively stronger negotiating position than casual labourers, apprentices or unpaid family workers. All dependent informal sector workers – whether paid or unpaid – are in a precarious situation and maintain a relationship with the employer which is heavily influenced by neighbourhood, family or ethnic ties. These factors severely hamper any efforts aimed at mobilizing and organizing to obtain better terms of work, because class interests are not the only or primary source of action. In the case of homeworkers, who are in a situation of labour dependency and part of a decentralized production system, it is even more difficult to organize to try and obtain improved conditions. As they are mainly women, lacking alternative income sources, being poorly educated and unskilled and earning an income combined with domestic chores, they fear for their jobs.

It may therefore come as no surprise to learn that most of informal workers' organizations usually comprise own-account workers or micro-entrepreneurs, and, that associations of homeworkers or other *de facto* dependent workers are much less developed. This does not exclude, however, the possibility of organizations which include both own-account workers and wage labourers or home-workers. The cases examined suggest that there is mixed membership either when the group, which is in a minority position, tries to change employment status in order to conform to that prevailing in the association, or when there have been recent changes in the employment status of certain members. In the latter case, persons having changed their status continue to identify with those belonging to their previous employment category. Chiangmai HomeNet, a cooperative of homeworkers' groups in Thailand, is an example of the first type of situation. The majority of HomeNet's members are home-based independent workers; however, home-based wage workers joined the organization because of the opportunity to become own-account workers.[71] Conversely, in Argentina, dismissed formal sector salaried workers, who entered the informal sector as independent labour, joined trade union-type associations comprising informal sector apprentices and wage workers.[72]

Grounds for organizing

Studies show that informal workers join together and organize for very pragmatic reasons: to address problems and demands that members cannot solve individually and/or the State is not able to meet. Evidence suggests that there is often a direct relationship between economic recession and hardship and the emergence of self-help informal workers' associations. None the less, the State's incentives and promotional policies can also act as a powerful catalyst. Informal sector operators tend to respond more positively in this case if the requirements and procedures are simple and transparent and registration is not seen as a means of increasing control and regulation rather than as a way of facilitating access to services and development opportunities. In Côte d'Ivoire,[73] a state policy to create a truly representative and functional national crafts association failed to produce the expected results because the organizational structure proposed was too bureaucratic and complex. The various layers of trade and inter-trade committees envisaged at the local, departmental and national levels contrasted, in fact, with the economic fragility of the existing crafts associations. Attempts to impose outside structures and procedures thus undermined a genuine political will to encourage the setting up of an organization capable of defending the trade's interests and taking part in policy negotiations; this is an example of a government's failure to understand the patterns and dynamics inherent in craft associations.

Workers in the informal sector usually organize to overcome business constraints. These include: high prices for inputs; low prices for the goods produced; difficulties in gaining access to credit and service; threats of eviction by city authorities; and the risk of income losses deriving from unexpected events, such as death or illness.

Organizations can also spring up in response to government or non-government programmes to deal with specific problems, such as deficient housing in urban slums or limited access to credit by particularly disadvantaged groups. This type of organization very often breaks up as soon as the reasons which gave rise to its existence are no longer valid. In fact, it is often seen as being a temporary vehicle for obtaining short-term support rather than as a means to further the broader interests of those concerned. This is illustrated by the fact that membership fees are not paid, as soon as external funding and support dries up.

The past decade has witnessed a proliferation of women's groups in the informal sector. This is certainly a reflection of the support provided by donor and development agencies to initiatives aimed at combating gender discrimination and inequalities. But it can also be ascribed to the fact that governments regard women's organizations as politically less threatening than male-dominated associations.[74] It has been observed that women's organizations are less vulnerable to corruption because, traditionally, they have been less exposed to dealing with public institutions.

Sometimes, however, organizational efforts to create solidarity ties based on gender can fail in societies with strong social-cultural hierarchies. During an ILO project to grant poor women access to land and security of tenure, in India, for instance, cohesive women's groups sprang up in areas which were more homogeneous from an ethnic and caste point of view. In the areas with a mixed caste composition, the organizational process proved more difficult, despite the fact that all women suffered from the same constraints related to gender.

Scope of informal workers' associations

Informal workers' associations vary in scope. They may be either neighbourhood or trade based or may encompass informal sector operators who, although engaged in different trades, work in the same location. Neighbourhood associations, although composite in membership, do not involve any competition for market and profit shares. As a result, they may often be more cohesive and stable than organizations pursuing production objectives. A very interesting case in point is the Apitong Neighbourhood Association (ANA) in Manila, Philippines. Established in 1987 to avail itself of the government-sponsored community mortgage programme for housing in urban areas, ANA was able to mobilize additional public and private institutional and financial support to develop the land it acquired through the mortgage programme. This not only took the form of developing road, drainage and water systems, but also included management training and the disbursement of credit to members interested in setting up small businesses. This process was not without its problems. At a certain point, internal intrigues and mistrust of leadership capabilities undermined the unity and integrity of the association. Delays in the implementation of projects occurred inter alia because of the ANA's officers' inability to reconcile their institutional obligations with their own economic activities. The association, however, was able to overcome its problems by establishing an effective mechanism for settling disputes and engaging in cost-sharing arrangements with local authorities and non-governmental organizations.

It has also been observed that in contexts where political representation is territorially based, neighbourhood organizations can influence the outcome of voting.[75] Furthermore, because they bring together informal sector operators and low-income formal workers who live in the same areas, these organizations can promote joint formal/informal workers' initiatives against policy decisions which are contrary to common interests. The riots which took place a few years ago in a number of Latin American and African cities to protest against the rise in prices of basic staple foods are a clear example of this type of alliance.

Trade-based organizations are made up of operators who share similar trade interests, who often deal with the same suppliers and middlemen, who relate to the same government institutions and have to comply with the same regulations, and who are confronted with the same constraints in terms of access to services, assets and markets. Despite being in competition with each other, there is scope for long-term cooperation. In the United Republic of Tanzania, for instance, groups of repair service businesses, including plumbers, electricians, mechanics and welders, have formed an association to provide collective guarantees. Under these guarantees, customers can expect, in the event of bad repair service, to have the additional work carried out free of charge. In view of the stiff competition from poorly qualified newcomers, and as a means to defend their market, these associations have decided to develop a codified skills profile for their trade to be able to regulate access to trade and contract negotiations on a collective basis.

Multi-trade, area-based associations are fairly cohesive. Their members do not compete for the same customers but share common concerns, such as keeping their immediate surroundings clean as a service to the clientele, thus avoiding the attention of health inspectors or trade officers, and preventing police harassment and/or theft. This suggests that local proximity and similarity of business interests are conducive to the development of organizational processes.

Ethnicities, religion and common geographic origin can also encourage the formation of solidarity groups. In certain Asian countries, for instance, access to certain occupations is restricted to groups with distinct social and cultural traits.[76] Ethnicity, through shared language, values and lifestyles, provides a social bonding to members which, in many cases, proves much stronger than class consciousness; it can also lead to political mobilization for changes in policies.[77]

Factors of instability

A characteristic common to most informal sector organizations is their fragility. They often disband even before achieving their objectives or as soon as these are reached, or pass periodically from activity to hibernation. Only rarely do they evolve into more settled, structured institutions pursuing long-term development and political objectives. This is not surprising. These associations suffer, in fact, from the same shortcomings which their members confront in their businesses, namely restricted capacity to mobilize resources, lack of managerial and technical skills, and the absence of clearly specified financial and operational rules and procedures. Members' responsibilities and tasks are also vaguely defined, their commitment irregular, and their participation in the organization's activities limited. Devoting time to the association means, in fact, reduced income at the end of the day – hence the high turnover rates which undermine the association's ability to satisfy members' demands. Several studies indicate that decision-making is often highly centralized. Due to their daily struggle for survival, members prefer to delegate the adoption of decisions and running of the organization to the highest level (the president or the executive committee), with little control from their end, as long as the officials prove capable of delivering services and satisfying members' expectations. The heavy reliance on a few persons and poor monitoring and control systems explain the ups and downs of most informal workers' associations. The image and fate of an organization is often closely linked to the performance of its executive. In Latin America, for instance, the political aspirations of many well-respected micro-entrepreneurs have resulted, paradoxically, in the weakening of the organizations over which they were presiding.[78]

The stability of an informal workers' association can also be undermined by conflicting signals given by the various levels of government. In the United Republic of Tanzania, for instance, the existence of a cooperative grouping 158 street-based watch repairers was threatened when the Ministry of Labour decided to issue special annual individual licences for the self-employed. In accordance with recently enacted legislation which stipulated that all self-employed people should have a full commercial licence as proof of gainful employment, the Ministry of Labour issued individual licences to the cooperative's members – who promptly decided to discontinue paying their fees as cooperative members.

In Nagpur, India, 15 unions of rickshaw pullers decided, with the aid of an NGO, to group themselves into one union and launched a campaign to revise the Public Vehicle Act, 1920; their aim was to prevent anyone other than pullers from owning a rickshaw. In Nagpur, as in many other Asian cities, the large majority of rickshaw pullers did not own the vehicle they used, but leased it from the owner. Consequently, no improvements were made to the design of the vehicle and the incomes of the rickshaw pullers remained low, as their daily rent was estimated to account for between 20 to 40 per cent of their earnings. The union, through extensive lobbying, succeeding in having the law amended so as to render illegal the ownership of a vehicle rickshaw, unless the owner pulled it himself. An additional victory of the rickshaw pullers' union was the establishment of a government fund releasing credits to the pullers willing to purchase their own vehicle. The rickshaw owners responded by doubling the price of the rickshaws and pressuring the courts to have the law over-turned. However, the union was able to deal with these setbacks; what really lost the union the battle, was the lack of coordination between the central and local govern-ments. The latter refused, in fact, to issue licences to the pullers, thus preventing them from obtaining the loan which would have allowed them to buy their equipment. As a consequence, ten years after the amendment to the Public Vehicle Law, the number of rickshaw pullers has nearly doubled, but only one-fifth of them are owners.

Types of associations and role of industrial relations organizations

The constraints and problems of informal workers' organizations described above clearly show that there is not one but many types of organization of informal sector operators and that no one universal form of organization is effective. Organ-izations may be formal or loose associations of workers, cooperatives, associations run on trade union lines or resembling employers' organizations, or non-governmental organizations. They may or may not have a legal personality – although this usually becomes necessary when the organization consolidates and diversifies its support services to its members. Through the acquisition of a legal personality, in fact, organ-izations not only gain access to services and facilities but also acquire rights and hence social recognition.

The choice of type of organization is based on a series of factors: the national legal framework; the social legitimacy and/or advantages associated with a certain form of organization; the purposes pursued and cultural traditions. For instance, in Argentina, Brazil and Peru, trade union-type organizations seem to prevail in the organized urban informal sector.[79] In Brazil and Peru, this may be attributed to the fact that the national legislation allows own-account workers to form or join trade unions and that organized labour (especially in Brazil) has paid attention to the self-employed in the informal sector. In fact, this category of worker represents one of the 12 branches in which the Single Central Organization of Workers (CUT) is concentrating its organizational work. Issues of relevance to own-account workers in the informal sector are also addressed within tripartite fora, such as local and state committees dealing with employment and protection of the unemployed.[80] Conversely, Argentina's legislation does not allow own-account workers to join or establish trade unions. Despite this ban, many informal sector operators have lately set up trade unions. It is worthwhile noting that a significant proportion of the members of these organizations once worked as wage labourers in the formal sector. Their familiarity with the func-tions and role of trade unions and the fact that they do not regard themselves as independent labour have certainly contributed to this state of affairs. This may also explain the mixed membership of most of these trade unions, which represent not only own-account workers, but also wage labourers and/or apprentices in the informal sector. Interestingly enough, this mixed membership is apparent in organizations which are national in scope. This is the case of the Argentinian Workers' Congress – which covers the self-employed, other categories of informal workers and the unemployed. Workers may join the Congress either individually or through an organization. As a result of the latter, the Congress cannot register as a trade union.

In the United Republic of Tanzania, cooperatives enjoy special treatment under national law, which is a legacy of the former socialist regime. Cooperatives' licences, for instance, exempt every member from individual licensing requirements and taxes. Indeed, taxes are paid on the basis of the range of transactions registered in the cooperatives' books. Consumers' cooperatives, for example, have access to a quota of basic commodities at controlled prices. These privileges have prompted many informal sector operators to opt for the legal status of cooperative, despite the fact that their mode of operation and nature of business is often different from any registered cooperative. Any inconsistencies there might be between an operation's stated objectives and actual activities are "tolerated" by lenient local authorities.

Cost in terms of time and money is another important factor which determines the choice of legal status. Recently, in the United Republic of Tanzania, a number of informal sector operators began registering as ordinary societies because, despite the limited scope of authorized activities (societies, for instance, cannot perform economic functions and cannot enter into obligations which would result in major liabilities), the registration process is easier and less costly. Conversely, in Côte d'Ivoire, cooperatives, trade associations and trade union-type organizations are new to the informal sector and are mainly confined to Abidjan. The majority of associations groups workers with a common geographic origin, or those with ethnic and family ties.[81]

In the Philippines, a recent study shows that there is a high registration rate of informal sector operators' organizations. Organizations register with different authorities at various levels, ranging from local government to the Ministry of Labour or the Cooperative Development Authority. This high rate of registration is an indicator of both the benefits which may be derived from obtaining legal personalty and the Government's proclaimed intention to "empower people". Pursuant to the commitments it made at the World Summit for Social Development in Copenhagen, the Government has launched an ambitious set of targeted programmes for disadvantaged groups – including informal sector operators – as part of its Social Reform Agenda. Tripartite summits are periodically held to consult the concerned actors on suitable policy prescriptions and participation is restricted to organized sectors. Legal recognition becomes therefore a means to gain public recognition and support.

Reference was made earlier in the text to the slow pace of growth of informal sector organizations. Studies have shown that financial, managerial and technical constraints are not always the main reason for this trend. Reduced membership is sometimes a deliberate choice to prevent unwanted competition. A case in point is the Panorama Rancho Estate Tricycle Operators and Drivers, Inc. (PARETODA), an organization in the Philippines which, since 1980, has offered membership to any tricycle operator or driver operating in the Panorama Rancho Estate. In 1990, PARETODA decided to "freeze" membership for a three-year period to prevent unwanted competition and income erosion. (Membership makes it easier to acquire a permit to operate and obtain a franchise which legitimizes its operations.)

Another reason for the slow growth of organizations in the informal sector may be that they become more careful in screening their members because, as they mature, they become increasingly aware of the structural and operational features they should incorporate to meet better their members' needs. In Thailand, for instance, the above-mentioned association Chiangmai HomeNet opted in its early days for an "open door" membership policy. As the organization grew in strength, stricter admittance criteria were introduced. Although it had initially allowed individual membership, it subsequently only admitted groups of homeworkers, on the grounds that this type of membership would be better equipped to expand and diversify its activities. In the five years since its creation, in 1990, HomeNet has set up a credit union and a cooperative.

Strategies

One way in which informal sector operators have sought to obtain better tariffs and/or financial services, or gain recognition or legal protection, has been to establish links and alliances with other informal sector trade associations or with national/international support groups to try and broaden their bargaining position. International contacts have often helped informal workers' associations gain recognition and stature within their own countries. These associations have also obtained logistic and organizational support from formal sector unions and, more recently, from employers' organizations. This has enabled them to use other industrial relations processes and services and to become active in the running of their own organizations.

The role of trade unions

As mentioned earlier in the text, a number of trade unions in the developing world are already providing capacity-building and other types of support to organizations in the informal sector. In Ghana, several informal sector associations, such as the Ghana Union of Professional Photographers (GUPP) have obtained, through the assistance of the mainstream union, agency status with the internal revenue authority to collect taxes from their members.[82] Trade unions are also developing policy initiatives to give more attention to the informal sector. In Brazil, for example, the CUT has continued to advocate favourable policies towards small-scale producers, craftsmen and other self-employed workers, to enable them to pursue income-generating and employment-promotion activities.[83]

Any initiatives taken by trade unions concerning the informal sector are not free from difficulties; this is clearly demonstrated by the debate on the role that organized labour should play with respect to informal sector issues. In some cases, trade unions still hesitate to engage in issues related to the informal sector. They fear that the nature and magnitude of the problems facing formal sector workers are such that they could not deal, in addition, with informal sector workers' concerns. They also feel that their institutional capacity is severely eroded by declining membership, which deprives them of the means to cope effectively with increasing demands. Indeed, when informal sector workers join a trade union, their membership fees are either symbolic or much lower than those paid by regular wage-earners. What is more, contributions paid by informal sector operators are often irregular due to their unstable incomes; they also sometimes claim that there is an imbalance between what they pay and what they receive in return. Furthermore, established trade unions find it difficult to obtain financial support from national and international donors to defend the interests of informal sector workers because of the competition from NGOs.

In some cases, informal sector issues are the object of specific policy statements; in others, they have been incorporated into the general discourse.[84] Interestingly enough, women trade unionists have played a leading role in bringing up the issue and pressing for the definition of a clear position in this field.[85] In general terms, international trade unions, as the following examples testify, tend to be especially open and eager to engage in activities in support of informal sector workers.

There is no doubt that the circumstances of informal sector employment pose a challenge for the trade union movement. The informalization of the economy, by encouraging the formation of small-scale and more flexible forms of economic activities on the fringe of established rules and organizational arrangements, undermines the power of organized labour in economic bargaining and social organization. As the International Confederation of Free Trade Unions (ICFTU) pointed out at its 15th World Congress in Caracas in 1992: "The increase in the number of marginalized workers threatens to undermine the acquired rights and conditions of workers in regular employment".[86, 87] Moreover, the difference between formal and informal sector workers in terms of labour arrangements and conditions, regularity of incomes, and job stability results in different needs and priorities. As a consequence, trade unions' traditional organizing strategies, functions and activities, which proved effective in addressing the demands of a full-time and regular labour force working in factories, may be unsuited to responding to the interests of precarious workers often engaged in home work and unstable production relationships. How trade unions and informal sector associations might work together to improve the working lives of this vast group of income-earners, remains an issue. Trade unions, however, are more and more convinced of the need to find a solution quickly.

In several developing countries, the prospect of trade unions increasing membership in their traditional area of recruitment is uncertain. However, as mentioned earlier in the text, there are many households belonging both to the formal and the informal sector, and cases in which workers switch between both sectors – even during the same working day. Organizing workers in the informal sector would thus appear to be a strategically appropriate option, so as to give the trade union movement a greater voice in social and economic decision-making.[88]

So far, there seem to be at least two clear-cut structural approaches which the trade union movement has adopted to try and forge a relationship with informal sector workers and their associations. The first envisages the organization of informal sector workers as part of the existing union membership. The second sets out to build alliances designed to assist informal workers who wish to form or strengthen their own organizations.

Organizing informal workers as trade union members

In a number of countries, trade union organizations are developing strategic policies to enhance the recruitment and organization of informal sector workers. In Ghana – as in some other countries – union constitutions are being revised to allow the membership of informal sector workers.

In this situation, informal workers sometime form part of a special department; in the case of women workers they might belong to what is generally referred to as the women's wing or department of the existing union. The question, however, remains as to what extent the mainstream union can efficiently represent the interests of this group of workers without changing the existing structure, which is heavily dominated or influenced by a tradition nursed by wage-earning members.

The case of SEWA is well known. It evolved as a women's wing of the Textile Labour Association (TLA) of India and eventually became an independent union – ostensibly because a women's wing was not necessarily suitable for addressing the problems of women workers in the informal sector. While the strategies for promoting the economic and social advancement of informal sector workers may be similar to those of formal sector workers, the problems facing workers in informal employment are substantially different from those encountered by workers in the formal sector. The above-mentioned example of SEWA shows that incorporating informal sector workers in traditional trade unions might meet with resistance from the people concerned. But informal sector workers would normally welcome any form of association with mainstream trade unions if this allowed them to deal with issues concerning their precarious situation and economic and social disadvantage.

Capacity-building and alliance forging

Trade unions might also create strategic and supportive links with informal sector associations by providing them with guidance and capacity-training services. Unions can forge these links through the industrial relations framework. Indeed, informal sector workers and their associations might be helped to develop organizational structures and management that would help them become effective and democratic institutions.

Another form of organizational support would be to train associations of informal workers on ways to plan and organize peaceful demonstrations, picket, lobby and engage in other trade union activities to dissuade the authorities from adopting policies and taking action detrimental to informal sector employment. Other services could include: institutional support; acting as an intermediary with financial and donor agencies; setting up programmes and schemes useful to informal sector workers; and organizing and providing credit at acceptable terms for informal sector workers.

In several developing countries, such alliances already exist. In Brazil, for example, 28 trade unions of self-employed workers, accounting for 20 per cent of such organizations, are affiliated to trade union confederations.[89] The establishment of the Cissin-Natanga Women's Association of Burkina Faso is an example of the critical role which mainstream trade unions can play in the emancipation of informal sector associations. Originally organized by a group of women attending a literacy course, the transformation of the group into an association in 1985 was inspired by the country's trade union centre, the National Organization of Free Trade Unions (ONSL). The association has built craft and literacy centres for its members, where the latter are trained in various trades – thereby improving their economic well-being.[90]

SEWA was able to affirm its own institutional status when it broke away from the TLA, thanks to the financial and legal support of international trade unions and intergovernmental agencies. By becoming a member of the International Union of Food, Agricultural, Hotel, Restaurant, Catering, Tobacco and Allied Workers' Associations (IUF), SEWA was treated as an equal partner by Indian trade unions representing workers in the formal sector. Furthermore, its relationship with the International Confederation of Free Trade Unions (ICFTU) and international development organizations secured the financial means which enabled SEWA to diversify its activities. By expanding its constituency and services, SEWA entered into close contact with the Government and was able to influence policies in support of poor self-employed women.

In Caracas, Venezuela, the Coordinating Body of Informal Sector Retail Workers (CONIVE) – an umbrella organization comprising various associations of informal sector retail traders – has sought to strengthen its bargaining position vis-à-vis local authorities by seeking international recognition. In particular, CONIVE resorted to and obtained the legal advice and political endorsement of two regional trade unions, namely the Latin American Central of Workers (CLAT) and the Latin American Federation of Retail Workers (FETRALCOS). This is a very interesting case: a number of small retail traders, street vendors and allied workers of the city capital decided to create trade associations which, eventually, joined together as a federation (CONIVE). Since 1989, the latter has been trying to negotiate with the municipal authorities to persuade them to allocate an area for a market where small retail traders might operate. More recently, CONIVE, together with CLAT and FETRALCOS, have requested the municipal authorities to withdraw a draft municipal order banning the use of the city streets by street vendors (it is estimated that more than 7,000 informal sector vendors are at present operating in the area in question). CONIVE's main argument against such an order is that it does not envisage alternative employment solutions for those potentially affected, and that street vendors have the right to work. As a counter-measure, CONIVE submitted, for the consideration of the local authorities, a set of guidelines and proposals to address the chaotic and steady growth of informal retail trade in Caracas. The lack of a public policy on the matter is deemed to be the main cause for this state of affairs.

The role of employers' organizations and the importance of alliance building

Several authors have emphasized that policies supporting the informal sector should concentrate on small-scale activities with a potential for growth and technical upgrading. Employers' organizations can certainly play a pivotal role in promoting the modernization of this segment of the informal sector, thus reinforcing its interaction with formal sector enterprises. Recent literature has shown, in fact, that the current profound changes in the organization of production have resulted in a symbiotic relationship between large and small enterprises.[91] Individual firms are no longer able to command the full range of innovations relevant to their operations; competitiveness increasingly lies in timely delivery systems and inter-firm linkages.[92] Studies show that the pace of company restructuring and reliance on subcontractors is slower in developing countries than in industrialized countries. In addition, in developing countries, decentralization of operations and outsourcing have been more concerned with achieving short-term cost reduction than long-term productive gains. Evidence indicates, however, that this trend has started reversing in some developing countries, such as Mexico and Brazil.

In addition, some employers' organizations have started to look at small and micro-entrepreneurs as potential new members. Indeed, they have begun encouraging the establishment of associations of micro and small-scale entrepreneurs and businesses. In a number of African countries, such as Kenya, Nigeria and Uganda, major associations of employers are actively involved in providing useful institutional services to informal sector businesses. These employers' organizations have established, often in cooperation with the ILO, programmes such as "Improve Your Business" and "Start Your Business" for this category of members.

Both governments and donors are increasingly viewing the private sector as a crucial conduit for micro/small enterprise development as this might generate new opportunities and financial support for the involvement of employers' organizations in micro/small enterprise promotion. However, if this is to succeed, employers' organizations need to broaden their skills and expertise and diversify the services provided. Until now, services have primarily been concerned with labour relations, e.g. disputes settlement and collective bargaining. Additional human and financial resources are needed to acquire a clear understanding of the problems and constraints confronting micro-enterprises and to promote advocacy activities in their support.

Linking up with other trade associations has often proved an effective way of increasing the bargaining power of employer-type informal workers' organizations with the local authorities, so that they might lobby for policy or legal changes or gain access to services and resources. PARETODA, the Manila-based association of tricycle operators and tricycle drivers mentioned earlier in the text, decided to join the Marikna Tricycle Operators' and Drivers' Association to be able to benefit from the experience of other transport association members (TODAs), comprising more than 60 groups. Local authorities granted PARETODA's request for a tricycle terminal, thanks to the advice and guidance given by the more experienced TODAs. At present, the various associations are considering engaging in a lobbying campaign to reduce the franchising fees and ease the traffic rules.

The Committee of Central American Micro-entrepreneurs (COCEMI) is another example of associations coming together to take concerted action. This regional NGO groups associations of micro-entrepreneurs from seven Central American countries representing a wide variety of trades. The organizational strength and ability to devise and promote initiatives to upgrade the development of micro-enterprises varies from national member to national member – reflecting the various national policies in support of micro-enterprises. Despite these differences, member associations believe that a regional network is the most effective way to take advantage of the funding opportunities and technical support available at the regional level. COCEMI wants to become a conduit of technical and financial assistance to its national member associations. Through recognition at the regional level, it hopes to help upgrade the bargaining power of its affiliates at the country level (see box 8.1).

Another strategy adopted by cooperative-type informal sector associations has been to pool resources and assets with other trade associations, to try and reinforce their productivity and bargaining power.

In Cotonou and Abomey, Benin, approximately 1,600 micro-enterprises, employing about 6,500 people, are organized in some 60 mutual savings and loan associations.[93] These associations comprise a range of trades, including food-processing, small-scale machinery repair workshops and building trades. When their

Box 8.1. Operating at regional level to improve national performance: The case of COCEMI in Central America

In the seven countries of Central America, it is estimated that about 2.7 million people work in the urban informal sector. Of these, 60 per cent are involved in own-account activities, while the rest work in micro-enterprises. Since the mid-1980s, the latter have started to attract the attention of government and non-government agencies, and of international donors. Credit has been by and large the main axis of such programmes – and individual enterprises the main target. Associations of entrepreneurs of micro-enterprises have increasingly become the focus of national and international support programmes. The decline of the State's role in the provision or channelling of public services and resources and the current process of democratization, after years of cruel war in the region, have shown the importance of considering these associations as partners in both development and the process of consolidation of democratic regimes.

The Committee of Central American Micro-entrepreneurs (COCEMI) is an example of the way a number of national associations of micro-enterprise entrepreneurs have responded at regional level. Founded in 1992 in Tegucigalpa, Honduras, COCE-MI, a non-profit-making and non-political regional organization, represents and promotes the interests of its national affiliates with national, regional and international agencies, through networking and lobbying. It is setting out to become a recognized interlocutor in national and regional decision-making concerning the development of micro-enterprises. It is for this reason that COCEMI is participating in two fora at Central American level, at which representatives of various sectors of organized Central American civil society – such as employers, workers, universities, women and indigenous peoples – discuss and express their opinions about the way Central American integration is progressing. It also intends acting as a conduit for technical and financial support to its national members' associations, consolidating the seven national committees – which comprise COCEMI – and expanding their associations at the national level.

Aware that only if it succeeds in meeting its members' needs will it continue to function, COCEMI is trying to improve services to its affiliates. A regional system of information is being introduced to help member associations take informed decisions by having access to reliable, up-to-date and complete information on market performance, and financial and technical facilities. The establishment of such a network is also intended to upgrade COCEMI's efficiency, by reducing the time and money involved when the member associations meet to organize joint activities. Furthermore, COCEMI is considering a regional trade fair to promote the products and services provided by its affiliates. There are none the less many challenges facing COCEMI. Due to its technical, managerial and financial constraints, it is still heavily reliant on the time and energy devoted by its own members. In addition, the level of economic advancement varies from country to country, as do the national policies and programmes towards micro-enterprises – with the obvious repercussions this has on economic performance. This gives rise to a wide variety of needs and demands, which might not always be easy to reconcile and translate into consistent regional strategies of action. Despite all these difficulties, COCEMI's members continue to meet and work together and to gain growing visibility and recognition. COCEMI's enterprise member associations still believe the regional path to be the most effective strategy to enhance their visibility and strength at the national level.

Source: COCEMI: *Hacía la consolidación organizativa*, IIIrd Conference of the Committee of Central American Micro-entrepreneurs (COCEMI), San José, Costa Rica, 1994 (COCEMI, 1995), and the draft version of the publication of the results of the Vth Conference of COCEMI, Tegucigalpa, Honduras, 1996.

membership is broken down by sex, it may be observed that around 50 per cent are male-only, 35 per cent are women-dominated and the rest are mixed associations. The associations combine traditional solidarity-based saving and credit practices with economic effectiveness. Apart from their high rate of recovery and observance of repayment schedules, these associations have, over time, shown a growing propensity to lend out the savings collected, thus increasing their contribution to capital formation. They have been vested with a legal personality recognized by the Ministry of Internal Affairs, and are governed by by-laws drawn up by their members. Legal recognition by the Ministry has acted as a deterrent against abusive practices by local government agencies. Local proximity and social control have proved the key to their success. A spin-off has also been the strengthening of closer neighbourly relationships. In order to consolidate their position, the 60 mutual associations have recently been examining ways to establish a partnership in order to manage their liquid assets jointly, with a view to strengthening their financial independence.

Dialogue and negotiation

Undoubtedly the major problem facing informal sector workers and their associations is their lack of defined interface with public authorities: this explains, to a great extent, their inability to gain access to the services they need to operate effectively and efficiently. The issue at stake is therefore the nature of their relationships with the government, social institutions, trade unions and employers' organizations. Related to this is the question of the recognition of informal sector associations as legal entities – which is so necessary to give them access to government authorities and services.

Trade unions and employers' associations can play an advocacy role in trying to promote public policies favourable to informal sector workers. The machinery for social dialogue which exists in many countries to deal with labour and industrial relations issues in the formal sector might be used to address informal sector-related concerns. For instance, trade unions can promote and facilitate regular consultation between informal sector associations and government authorities, for policy direction; and they can also negotiate substantive issues on behalf of informal sector workers and their associations, both for those in wage employment and non-wage income-earners.

However, in so far as interfacing with the authorities is concerned, trade unions need to work towards transforming the existing or new consultative and advisory machinery into negotiating or decision-making machinery. The National Economic Development and Labour Council (NEDLAC) of South Africa, which provides for multi-interest representation for negotiating on broad macroeconomic issues, is a true example of the role of the social partners in national policy formulation.

The participation of informal workers' organizations in mechanisms and/or fora involving government and non-governmental institutions, in order to address issues of relevance to the workers concerned, has very often helped foster mutual understanding and opened new avenues for informal sector operators. The establishment of such mechanisms can be the result of different circumstances: a favourable policy environment; the pressure of trade unions or external actors, such as international funding or development agencies; or the strong bargaining power of an informal workers' organization – or a combination of two or all of these factors.

Irrespective of the reasons giving rise to these mechanisms, they can only be effective in securing a sustained and long-term dialogue if there is coordination and consistency between macro-policies and micro-regulations and if representative and functional informal workers' organizations are promoted.

In the Philippines, the combination of sensitized policy-makers and a rapidly expanding network of homeworkers' associations, PATAMBA, led to the establishment of the National Steering Committee (NSC) on Home Work in 1991. This Committee, comprising the Department of Labor and Employment (DOLE), the Trade Union Congress of the Philippines (TUCP) and a few NGOs, paved the way for the consolidation of PATAMBA and contributed to policy and institutional changes concerning home work. As a result of its participation in the Committee, PATAMBA's visibility and public recognition has expanded. Its network of contacts with donor agencies and government institutions, such as the social security system, has broadened its access to new sources of assistance and aid. PATAMBA's capacity to deliver services to its members has consequently improved and its grass-roots support has been consolidated. Through the Committee, PATAMBA was able to take part in and influence the work of the National Tripartite Conference, which approved amendments to the implementing rules of the Labour Code provisions pertaining to home work. This resulted in the adoption of Administrative Order No. 5 which provides for the right of homeworkers to form or join organizations of their own choosing, sets the requirements by which homeworkers' associations can acquire legal personality, and covers other aspects such as time and conditions of payment, as well as duties of employers, contractors and subcontractors.

The provisions contained in Administrative Order No. 5 were largely based on the Declaration of Homeworkers' Rights and the Magna Carta of Homeworkers adopted by PATAMBA during its Founding Congress in May 1991. The effectiveness of this Order has yet to be fully tested, but evidence suggests that law enforcement is still problematic. Many homeworkers affiliated to PATAMBA have, in fact, reported cases of non-compliance of agreed terms of work by subcontractors, but have not filed complaints against them for fear of retaliation. Indeed, when complaints have been filed, DOLE's regional department has refused to consider them, arguing that they are not the competent body to deal with such matters. In a context of high unemployment, fiscal deficit, and cuts in the public sector, which undermine labour inspection services, good laws are not enough. This has convinced PATAMBA of the need to combine advocacy and legal work with improved training, marketing and credit services to its members. PATAMBA, realizing the vulnerability of homeworkers to external pressure, has also tried to create alternative forms of employment (self-employment or participation in cooperatives) for them. In an attempt to upgrade the market opportunities of cooperatives, for instance, PATAMBA has joined larger net-

---

Box 8.2.   Networking for the legal and social protection of homeworkers: The case of HomeNet International

Worldwide, home work absorbs a significant number of workers who are essentially women.

Traditionally associated with the clothing and garment industries, it has, more recently, begun to be linked to a broad range of industries and trades, from food processing or toy production to packing and assembly work and electronics. The growth of home work may be ascribed to the changes occurring in the organization of production and work in national and international enterprises, as a strategy to reduce costs and maintain trade competitiveness. Homeworkers are often at the very end of a chain of inter-enterprise relationships leading to major transnational companies. Although they may work even in small and remote villages, their pay and conditions of employment are often influenced by international forces.

One of homeworkers' main problems is "invisibility", as national statistics fail to capture them. Being unrecorded, homeworkers are deprived of legal and social protection. Where the law recognizes and protects them, enforcement is the problem.

Homeworkers often work behind closed doors, in isolation. Furthermore, women home-based producers often do not regard themselves as workers. Many of them see their main social function to be housekeepers. Performing an economic activity is thus considered to be an extension of their domestic chores or as a "help" to household incomes. This explains their vulnerability to low and irregular incomes, as well as their conditions of work.

In various parts of the world, homeworkers have started organizing, establishing contacts with homeworkers in other countries and seeking support from interested groups to overcome invisibility and improve their employment situation.

HomeNet International is a very interesting case of North-South cooperation between associations of homeworkers, such as the Self-Employed Women's Association (SEWA) in India and the Self-Employed Women's Union (SEWUI) in South Africa, and other interested groups including trade unions, such as the International Union of Food, Agricultural, Hotel, Restaurant, Catering, Tobacco and Allied Workers' Associations (IUF), cooperatives, research centres, and women's associations.

Established in 1994 and funded by the International Department of the Netherlands Trade Union Confederation (FNV), HomeNet International seeks to: (i) enhance awareness and knowledge about the working conditions and the plight of homeworkers, through the collection and dissemination of information; (ii) encourage inter-institutional contacts and exchange of experiences; (iii) raise and channel technical assistance to homeworkers; and (iv) campaign and lobby for improvements in national and international laws and policies to the advantage of homeworkers.

HomeNet and its members played an important role in promoting the adoption of the Home Work Convention, 1996 (No. 177), and its accompanying Recommendation, 1996 (No. 185), by the International Labour Conference in 1996. Recognizing that international standards would represent a major step towards gaining legal recognition and protection for these workers, it identified and tried to secure the support of key governments and trade unions participating in the International Labour Conference. As a follow-up, HomeNet is promoting a two-pronged strategy to create homeworkers' associations at the grass-roots level and to advocate and lobby for favourable national policies.

Source: *HomeNet Newsletter*, No. 1, Summer 1995, No. 3, Jan. 1996.

---

works of marketing support groups. To overcome its financial and technical constraints, PATAMBA has also joined international networks of homeworkers' associations, supportive trade unions, and other sympathetic associations, such as HomeNet International (see box 8.2). The contacts established through the NSC and the experience within this Committee, in terms of networking and lobbying, have helped PATAMBA obtain recognition and mobilize the external support required to satisfy members' demands.

In Benin, the success of the mutual savings and loan associations and the Government's interest in promoting development opportunities for craft micro-entre-preneurs[94] have led to the creation of the High Council for Handicraft Trades (CSA). This Council brings together some ten ministries, artisans, and private institutions, including chambers of commerce, industry and agriculture, employers' organizations and NGOs operating throughout the country. Although still dominated by the State, it constitutes a highly interesting attempt to forge tripartite consensus on very delicate and vital questions – ranging from the content and enforcement of regulations and the means to encourage the creation of craft associations to ways to mobilize and coordinate private and public action in this area.

Prospects

Given their limited scope, the cases reviewed in this chapter do not allow us to extrapolate general lessons. They none the less provide some tentative clues as to the specificity of informal sector operators' organizations and give us an idea of the characteristics distinguishing them from traditional industrial relations institutions – such as trade unions of formal sector workers or employers' associations. They also help us understand what it takes to foster cooperation between these institutions and informal sector workers' organizations, and between these organizations and the State.

Some preliminary comparisons may be made between formal workers' trade unions and informal workers' associations. It is important to pinpoint the similarities and/or differences between the two as this will help devise strategies which might be more conducive to a meaningful and long-term partnership.

One of the distinct features of informal workers' organizations is their loose internal organization – contrary to trade unions and employers' organizations which have well-established internal hierarchies regulated by law. As we have shown, the absence of clearly defined structures and procedures has often been a factor of organizational instability. Sometimes, however, it has allowed informal sector organizations to adjust their activities and modes of operation to changing constituencies and opportunities with relative ease.

Another expression of the institutional flexibility of these organizations is their propensity, at least at the beginning, to accept membership irrespective of occupational activity and employment status. A commonality of interests, deriving either from a shared cultural, social or economic identity, or from situations adversely affecting a wide range of informal sector operators – such as a rise in basic food prices or a law forbidding them to operate in a city area – often proves to be a strong factor of cohesion and solidarity.

It is true that, especially in the long term, an over-diversified membership, covering a wide variety of interests and needs, might jeopardize institutional effectiveness, particularly in a context of scarce financial and technical resources.

However, at the outset, this wide membership can provide the critical mass required to bring about changes to an undesirable situation or to meet members' immediate needs. Some of the cases reviewed, such as Chiangmai HomeNet, nevertheless show that a consolidation of informal sector organizations is usually accompanied by the introduction of more selective membership criteria and a diversification of member services. This is particularly true in the case of organizations controlled by women. Indeed, women's access to and mobility within the labour market are to a great extent contingent upon their ability to reconcile domestic tasks with productive functions. SEWA's success can also be ascribed to its capacity to meet – through a combination of services catering also to women's family responsibilities – the broad range of needs of poor self-employed women.

Another characteristic distinguishing informal workers' associations from formal sector employers' and workers' organizations is their coverage. While the former are mainly confined to local or regional areas, the latter are national in scope. The cases examined, however, show that as soon as an informal workers' organization achieves a certain degree of internal cohesion and stability, it starts searching for new partners. CONIVE in Venezuela and PARODA in Manila are an example of associations trying to obtain a larger constituency to increase their bargaining power or achieve a higher degree of economic self-sufficiency.

It goes without saying that, in general, informal sector trade groups are much less financially sound than formal sector trade unions and employers' organizations. Payment of membership fees is irregular because of the precariousness of informal sector workers' jobs and the absence of an effective fees-collection system. But we have observed that some organizations have been able to remedy this constraint by tapping into other sources of funding – including NGOs, government institutions or international development agencies. Obviously, the risk entailed by entering into financial arrangements with other institutions is loss of autonomy. Such a possibility is certainly high in the case of weak and loose organizations; organizations with well-defined structures and a strong social identity might be less likely to be manipulated or co-opted.

To reduce such a risk, organizations such as PATAMBA in the Philippines, SEWA in India, or CONIVE in Venezuela have, as we have seen, entered into alliances with trade unions to promote issues of direct interest to them, while simultaneously seeking financial support from other agencies. Obtaining support from an international actor has granted these organizations visibility and recognition at the national level, thus contributing to their political independence. This is another reason for co-operation between informal sector operators and the organized labour movement at various levels.

We have to acknowledge, however, that a favourable political or policy environment has been instrumental in bringing about changes in the environment affecting informal sector workers. This was certainly the case of PATAMBA, which was able to influence policy-making on home work, thanks to the strong support of the senior officials of the Department of Labor and Employment. In Benin, the successful experience of the mutual savings and loan associations of Cotonou paved the way for the establishment of a national tripartite body responsible for coordinating and orienting policy and programme interventions in support of the informal sector, because the Government was sensitive to the issues involved.

The policy of the Government of the Philippines to obtain recognition for informal workers' organizations by means of straightforward, accelerated and low-cost procedures, has undoubtedly enhanced the social legitimacy of these workers' organizations, facilitated their access to services and made them less vulnerable to police harassment or eviction.

But well-intentioned government measures do not always yield the desired results. A case in point is the Côte d'Ivoire. The Government's laudable attempt to encourage the creation of a national crafts organization able to defend and promote the trade's interests met with difficulties at the implementation stage. The institutional setting devised to enable the crafts associations to participate in consultations and negotiation with the Government at various levels did not reflect the inherent patterns and logic of association, but corresponded to a preconceived top-down organizational system. Furthermore, the registration procedures were cumbersome and complicated. The potential beneficiaries began to suspect that registration was directed at enhancing state control, rather than improving their work prospects and conditions.

A lack of consistency and coordination between government agencies at various levels sometimes creates a situation of uncertainty and instability for informal workers' organizations. Central government agencies or the legislative powers may adopt measures to upgrade the informal sector – which are then neutralized by local government authorities. The case of the rickshaw pullers who were not able to benefit fully from the reform of the Public Vehicle Act because of the local government's refusal to issue driving licences is a clear example of this point. In Venezuela, the recognition, at the highest level, of the sector's importance in terms of income-creation and employment for surplus labour, as well as of the need to promote it, was accompanied by measures to restrict informal retail trade in the streets of Caracas. In the United Republic of Tanzania, favourable credit policies for informal micro-entrepreneurs came up against the problem of city planning, which did not provide for any market or worksite for informal sector operators.

In the Philippines, a new order, issued by DOLE to provide homeworkers with greater protection from abusive practices by subcontractors and middlemen, proved difficult to enforce because DOLE's field offices regarded its application as a matter outside the scope of their jurisdiction.

Interestingly enough, in all the cases reviewed, central government agencies proved more supportive towards informal sector operators than authorities at the local level. Policy reforms at the national level did not automatically result in enhanced opportunities for informal sector operators. It may well be asked why this is the case. And we may wonder what the likely repercussions of the current process of decentralization and devolution of power and obligations to local-level government will be on informal sector workers and their organizations. Will the latter be regarded as mere sources of local revenues or as partners in development?

A great deal of literature emphasizes that decentralization and good governance – i.e. enhanced transparency on development options available to the local population and accountability of government structures to local private organizations – ensure participation of local interest groups in decisions concerning the use and allocation of resources.[95] By means of public hearings and other local-level consultations, local social groups have the opportunity to voice their concerns and priorities, debate alternatives and negotiate compensation.

Evidence suggests, however, that decentralization can, in the absence of genuinely representative and strong interest groups, perpetuate unbalanced power relationships and unfair redistributive practices. Once again, the need for a regulatory and institutional environment, which encourages the formation and operation of independent and truly representative informal workers' organizations, is apparent. But this would require: the recognition of informal sector operators through registration rules and procedures which are straightforward, quick and cheap; supportive macroeconomic policies; and government institutions and officials capable of dealing with the conditions under which the informal sector operates. Furthermore, coordination needs to be improved both vertically, namely between central government and local-level authorities, and horizontally, e.g. across sectors at both central and local levels.

Concluding remarks

The informal sector constitutes an important, if not central, aspect of the economic and social dynamics of less-developed countries. In many of these countries, this sector has expanded and is here to stay in the foreseeable future. Indeed, it owes its very existence to structural problems – including the incapacity of national economies to absorb surplus labour.

The structure and dynamics of this sector represent a challenge to traditional legal instruments and industrial relations institutions and methods, particularly collective bargaining. The informal sector units operate on a small scale; their working conditions are precarious; there are multiple intermediaries between workers and capital and a wide variety of work situations. All these factors fragment labour processes and reverse the material conditions which first ushered in the labour movement, as an organized force, in the formal economy.

Informal sector workers are involved in loose networks of activities in which ethnic, family or kinship ties and loyalties tend to prevail. This, coupled with the fact that these activities are limited in scale, dilute the potential for labour-related action.

It is also reasonable to argue that the involvement of social groups such as women, ethnic minorities, youth and children – whose participation rate in the regular labour market is usually low – also contributes to the emergence of a different labour culture. Women working in the informal sector, for instance, are not particularly inclined to mobilize and organize in order to attain higher quality work, and/or social protection or better pay. This may be attributed to their often poor educational attainments, unfriendly laws and regulations on inheritance or ownership of assets, their domestic tasks and family responsibilities, and social and cultural models which value women's reproductive role over their productive functions. They are discouraged from organizing because of their fear of retaliation, their inability to find alternative jobs, and their perception of themselves as housewives or mothers rather than as workers.

In addition, informal sector operators display a variety of working arrangements and show differing degrees of evasion/compliance with regulations on labour, safety and health, and tax payment, reflecting a range of needs and interests which cannot easily be reconciled and advanced in one and the same type of organization. All these characteristics may help to explain the low incidence of workers' organizations in the informal sector – although the instability and fragility of ventures in this sector might also act as a strong deterrent.

The mixed membership apparent in a number of informal sector organizations reviewed earlier in the text is another indicator of how the working arrangements and dynamics inherent in the sector give rise to a process of mobilization and organization which bears little resemblance to that of organizations in the formal sector. And this is only to be expected, given the lack of a clear-cut employer-employee relationship. Ironically, however, mixed membership – when it includes workers whose change in employment status from, for instance, formal sector salaried workers to informal sector self-employed is not accompanied by a change in the way they perceive their role in the world of work – may favour the creation of organizations run on trade union lines.

The specific problems encountered by a large proportion of informal sector units – namely insecurity of land tenure and lack of access to water and electricity – are also alien to those engaged in declared and regular employment, as they go beyond the labour sphere. Paradoxically, however, matters unrelated to employment can, in contexts characterized by a deterioration in living standards and increased income inequalities, act as a vehicle to bring together informal sector operators and low-wage formal sector workers.

No strong collective actor has as yet emerged in the informal sector. The existing informal sector associations tend, in fact, to have a limited geographical coverage, and their effectiveness and sustainability are undermined by the irregularity and instability of their members' employment and incomes. Their daily struggle for survival, their lack of managerial and technical skills, and their limited ability to mobilize assets from external sources limit the coverage of these associations and their range of services and activities. This, in turn, has the effect of further reinforcing members' distrust in the actual value of collective action to solve their work-related problems.

This brings us to the crucial question of the relationship between informal sector associations and workers' and employers' organizations in the formal sector. In the past few years, formal sector organizations, particularly trade unions, have paid much more attention to informal sector issues than before. Indeed, it was previously maintained that the informal sector was a transient phenomenon destined to disappear with economic modernization. What is more, the sector's precarious and unstable labour arrangements and poor working conditions were viewed by some as a threat to the rights and benefits acquired by regular labour.

More recently, the move of many workers from the formal to the informal sector and the growing casualization of labour may have helped to change this point of view. In any case, a number of trade unions have embarked on a series of initiatives in support of informal sector workers. Despite the significant differences between national and international trade unions and between sectors, the general trend has been either to promote the organization of informal sector operators as trade union members, or to support the strengthening of informal sector associations through technical assistance or lobbying and networking. In some cases, trade unions have changed their statutes and structures to allow for the participation of informal workers in decision-making bodies. Interestingly enough, the scope of their action has mainly included own-account workers – and even micro-entrepreneurs – and to a lesser extent dependent workers.

We have also seen the potential for the involvement of employers' organizations in informal sector-related matters, especially in terms of capacity-building directed at the most dynamic segment of the sector.

In view of the size and steady growth of the sector and the difficulties that the growing casualization of work in the formal economy pose to the organized labour movement, it is clear, however, that the State has a major role to play to help informal workers overcome their disadvantages.

And organizational efforts cannot be sustained in the absence of a favourable regulatory framework. The right of informal sector workers to join or create representative associations of their choosing, as well as state recognition of their role as interlocutors and/or partners in policy-making or programme implementation are, as we have seen, key enabling factors. The variety of informal sector associations that exist throughout the world is a clear indication of the ability of informal sector workers to grasp, despite their constraints, the opportunities provided by the State or the law in terms of both material support and social recognition.

The granting of institutional recognition and representation has, in some cases, also led the State to amend its regulations and change its law enforcement in areas relating to access to productive assets or taxation and to adopt a more flexible and promotional approach which is better suited to irregular and precarious work processes and labour relations. Conversely, interventions merely focused on productivity enhancement, which have tended to overlook the institutional and industrial relations aspects of the sector, have only had a partial and transitory success.

Notes

[1] ILO: *The dilemma of the informal sector,* Report of the Director-General (Part 1), International Labour Conference, 78th Session, Geneva, 1991, p. 44.

[2] ILO: *Statistics of employment in the informal sector,* Fifteenth International Conference of Labour Statisticians, Report III, Geneva, 19-28 January 1993 (Geneva, 1992), p. 7.

[3] M. Castells and A. Portes: "World underneath: The origins, dynamics and effects of the informal economy", in A. Portes et al., *The informal economy: Studies in advanced and less-developed countries* (Baltimore and London, Johns Hopkins University Press, 1989).

[4] G. Rodgers (ed.): *Urban poverty and the labour market: Access to jobs and incomes in Asian and Latin American cities* (Geneva, ILO, 1989), p. 9.

[5] D.C. Mead and C. Morrison: "The informal sector elephant", in *World Development* (Elsevier Science, Ltd., 1996), Vol. 24, No. 10, pp. 1611-1619,

[6] ILO: *World Employment 1995* (Geneva, 1995), p. 92.

[7] ILO: *The future of urban employment,* International Symposium on the Future of Urban Employment, Turin Centre, 5-7 December 1995, p. 22.

[8] C. Maldonado and M. Hurtado (eds.): *El sector informal en Bogotá: Una perspectiva interdisciplinaria* (Geneva, ILO, 1997), p. 15.

[9] ibid., p. 15.

[10] ILO: *Informa. Panorama laboral,* 95, No. 2 (Lima, 1995).

[11] Maldonado and Hurtado, op. cit., p. 16.

[12] ILO: *The urban informal sector in Asia: Policies and strategies* (Geneva, 1996), p. 16.

[13] ILO: *World Labour Report 1992,* Vol. 5 (Geneva, 1992), p. 39.

[14] ILO: *The future of urban employment,* op. cit., p. 23.

[15] S.D. Barwa: *Structural adjustment programmes and the urban informal sector in Ghana,* Issues in Development Discussion Paper No. 3 (Geneva, ILO, 1995), p. 5.

[16] ILO/JASPA: *From redeployment to sustained employment generation: Challenges for Ghana's programme of economic recovery and development* (Addis Ababa, 1989), p. 78.

[17] ILO: *World Employment 1995,* op. cit., p. 92.

[18] E.R. Bhatt: "Organizing self-employed women for self-reliance in India", in G. Kinnock et al. (eds.), *Voices for one world* (London, Fontana, 1988), pp. 143-165.

[19] ILO: *World Labour Report 1992,* op. cit., pp. 23-24.

[20] L.L. Lim: *More and better jobs for women: An action guide* (Geneva, ILO, 1996), p. 11.

[21] ibid., p. 28.

[22] S. Mitter: *Organiser les travailleurs et les travailleuses dans le secteur informel,* Report prepared by the International Confederation of Free Trade Unions (Brussels, ICFTU, 1989), pp. 7-14.

[23] S.V. Sethuraman: "The urban informal sector: Concept, measurement and policy", in *International Labour Review* (Geneva, ILO), Vol. 114, No. 1, July-Aug. 1976, pp. 69-81; G. Aryee: *Project implementation report: Summary of activities, lessons and recommendations,* Interdepartmental Project on the Urban Informal Sector, IDP INF/Report (Geneva, ILO, 1996), p. 8.

[24] V. Tokman (ed.): *Beyond regulation: The informal economy in Latin America* (Publishers Lynne Rienner, Boulder, Colorado, and London, 1992), p. 14.

[25] G. Rodgers (ed.), op. cit., p. 9; D. Tajgman: *Employment relations and labour law in the Dar-es-Salaam informal sector,* IDP INF/WP-5 (Geneva, ILO, 1996), p. 9.

[26] ILO: *The urban informal sector in Asia: Policies and strategies,* op. cit., p. 15.

[27] ibid., p. 15.

[28] S. Feldman: *La organización y representación de quienes desarrollan actividades en el sector informal en Argentina, Brasil y Perú,* document prepared for the ILO (1996), p. 11.

[29] ibid., p. 11.

[30] D. Tajgman, op. cit., p. 9.

[31] S. Feldman, op. cit., p. 11.

[32] ILO: *The urban informal sector in Asia: Policies and strategies,* op. cit., p. 19.

[33] G.C.Z. Mhone: *The impact of structural adjustment on the urban informal sector in Zimbabwe,* Issues in Development Discussion Paper No. 2 (Geneva, ILO, 1995), pp. 3 and 7.

[34] ibid., p. 7.

[35] G. Rodgers and G. Standing (eds.): *Child work, poverty and underdevelopment* (Geneva, ILO, 1981), p. 12.

[36] P. Wenga, A. Iffland and M. Schulz: *Self-help organizations in the informal sector of the Dar-es-Salaam region,* Paper prepared for the Dar-es-Salaam Seminar, 23-24 May 1995, Discussion Paper No. 5 (Geneva, ILO, 1995), p. 32.

[37] H. de Soto: *The other path: The invisible revolution in the Third World* (New York, Harper & Row, 1989).

[38] V. Tokman (ed.), op. cit., pp. 3-20; C. Maldonado: "The informal sector: Legalization or laissez-faire?", in *International Labour Review* (Geneva, ILO), Vol. 134, No. 6, 1995, pp. 703-728.

[39] J. Galindo: "Costos y beneficios de la legalización del sector informal: La perspectiva desde los trabajadores informales", in Maldonado et al., op. cit., pp. 90-110.

[40] C. Maldonado: "Building networks: An experiment in support to small urban producers in Benin", in *International Labour Review* (Geneva, ILO), Vol. 132, No. 2, pp. 245-264.

[41] ILO: *Statistics of employment in the informal sector,* op. cit., p. 9.

[42] ILO: *The dilemma of the informal sector,* Report of the Director-General, International Labour Conference, 78th Session (Geneva, 1991), p. 39.

[43] V. Tokman, op. cit., pp. 5-8.

[44] D. Tajgman, op. cit., pp. 10-11.

[45] C. Maldonado: "The informal sector: Legalization or laissez-faire?", op. cit.

[46] ibid., p. 11.

[47] V. Tokman, op. cit., pp. 14-16.

[48] S. Feldman, op. cit., p. 10.

[49] V. Tokman, op. cit., p. 13.

[50] C. Maldonado: "The informal sector: Legalization or laissez-faire?", op. cit.

[51] J.M. Servais: "Secteur informel: un avenir pour le droit du travail", in *Actualités du droit,* Revue de la Faculté de Droit de Liège (Antwerp, 1994), pp. 661-685.

[52] C. Fernando and A.M. Diaz: "Marco legal del sector informal en Bogotá: Enfoques y aplicaciones – La perspectiva desde las instituciones", in C. Maldonado et al.: *El sector informal en Bogotá: Una perspectiva interdisciplinaria,* op. cit., pp. 59-88; D. Tajgman, op. cit.; C. Maldonado: "The informal sector: Legalization or laissez-faire?", op. cit.; and V. Tokman, op. cit.

[53] D. Tajgman, op. cit., p. 35.

[54] J. Galindo in C. Maldonado et al., op. cit., p. 108.

[55] C. Maldonado: "The informal sector: Legalization or laissez-faire?", op. cit.

[56] ILO: *The dilemma of the informal sector,* op. cit., p. 39.

[57] M.L. Vega Ruiz: *Home work: A comparative analysis of legislation and practice,* Labour Law and Labour Relations Programme Occasional Paper 10 (Geneva, ILO, 1996), p. 32.

[58] C. Jacquier: *La mobilisation de l'épargne par l'économie sociale: Les nouvelles formes coopératives et mutualistes d'épargne et de crédit dans les pays en développement* (Geneva, ILO, 1994), p. 4.

[59] ILO: *Gender, poverty and employment: Turning capabilities into entitlements* (Geneva, 1995), pp. 38-39.

[60] B. Sanyal: *Cooperative autonomy: The dialectic of State-NGOs relationship in developing countries,* International Institute for Labour Studies, Research Series 100, No. 1 (Geneva, 1994), pp. 35-39.

[61] ibid., p. 39.

[62] ILO: *The urban informal sector in Asia: Policies and strategies,* op. cit., P. Wenga et al., op. cit.

[63] ILO: *The future of urban employment,* op. cit.; p. 42.

[64] P. Wenga et al., op. cit., pp. 10-13.

[65] ILO: *The future of urban employment,* op. cit., p. 41.

[66] ILO: *The dilemma of the informal sector,* op. cit., pp. 15-18; ILO: World Employment 1995, op. cit., pp. 92-93.

[67] G.C.Z. Mhone: *The impact of structural adjustment on the urban informal sector in Zimbabwe,* Issues in Development Discussion Paper No. 2 (Geneva, ILO, 1995), p. 6.

[68] ILO: *World Employment 1995,* op. cit., pp. 92-93.

[69] J.N. Cely: "Organizaciones del sector informal en Bogotá: Perfil y diagnóstico", in Maldonado et al., op. cit., pp. 111-131.

[70] P. Wenga et al., op. cit., p. 8.

[71] ILO/ROAP: *From the shadow to the fore: Practical actions for the social protection of homeworkers in Thailand* (1993), p. 9.

[72] S. Feldman, op. cit., p. 27.

[73] B. Gaufryau and C. Maldonado: *Secteur informel: Fonctions macro-économiques et politiques gouvernementales. Le cas de la Côte d'Ivoire,* ILO research document S-INF 1-13 (Geneva, ILO, 1997), pp. 18-19.

[74] B. Sanyal: "Organizing the self-employed: The politics of the informal sector", in *International Labour Review,* Vol. 130, No. 1 (Geneva, ILO, 1991), p. 47.

[75] ibid., p. 46.

[76] ibid., pp. 46-47.

[77] M. Tomei: "Indigenous and tribal peoples and trade unions: Recent initiatives", in *Labour Education,* ILO 98-1995/1 (Geneva, ILO, 1995), pp. 8-14.

[78] S. Feldman, op. cit., p. 34.

[79] ibid., pp. 17-35.

[80] ibid., p. 24.

[81] B. Gaufryau and C. Maldonado, op. cit., p. 19.

[82] F.A. Parry: *Institutional linkages between trade unions and informal sector associations in Ghana* (ILO/EAMAT, Addis Ababa, 1995), p. 5.

[83] S. Feldman, op. cit., p. 24.

[84] International Confederation of Free Trade Unions (ICFTU): *Report of the Sixteenth World Congress,* Brussels, 25-29 June 1996.

[85] M. Martens and S. Mitter (eds.): *Women in trade unions: Organizing the unorganized* (Geneva, ILO, 1994).

[86] Marginalized workers, according to the ICFTU's resolution, include working women and men who for different reasons do not form part of the regular workforce, including homeworkers, workers on contract or sub-contract, temporary workers, part-time workers, seasonal labourers, illegally employed workers, rural workers, unpaid family workers, domestic workers, migrant workers without residence rights, self-employed workers, and many other workers in the informal sector or otherwise in a precarious employment situation.

[87] ICFTU: *Draft Resolution on Strategies for the Integration of Marginalized Workers,* 15GA/11.7 (Final draft), Caracas 1992.

[88] ibid., p. 2; H. Thomas: "Challenges facing trade unions", in *Globalization and Third World Trade Unions* (1996), p. 242.

[89] S. Feldman, op. cit., p. 24.

[90] C. Mamounata: "Trade unions and workers in the informal sector in Burkina Faso", in M. Martens and S. Mitter, op. cit., pp. 145-152.

[91] M. Henriques: *Employers' organizations and small enterprise development,* MD 1-04 (Geneva, ILO, 1995), p. 3.

[92] ibid., p. 3.

[93] C. Maldonado: "Building networks: An experiment in support to small urban producers in Benin", op. cit., p. 251.

[94] ibid., p. 15.

[95] World Bank: *Development in practice. Governance – The World Bank's experience* (Washington, DC, 1994), pp. 42-43.

9 The present as a signpost to the future

The traditional channels for relations among public authorities, employers and their associations, and trade unions are being questioned everywhere. More fundamentally, the compromises – of a political nature – which had been established between economic constraints and social justice are being affected in every instance. The pressures brought to bear on the social actors by increased competition and the other factors which we have described have become greater. Wherever one looks, people are challenging what used to be taken for granted, many policies are being queried and traditional attitudes as well as the structures of social relations themselves are being shaken.

Even in the most industrialized countries, jobs and worker protection are becoming increasingly insecure. The diversity of situations and interests seriously undermines the internal cohesion of national societies, causing or risking the marginalization of sections of the population. Many key figures are expressing indignation, stating that man is not a machine – or a commodity – and emphasizing that the laws of the market, left to operate unhindered, may well give rise to a society which favours the strong and marginalizes the weak.

We must certainly guard against these dangers and ensure that development is economically profitable and acceptable in human terms. This aim underscores the importance of institutions, such as trade unions, that mediate between the individual and the market. However, it also leads us to reflect on the utility of industrial relations mechanisms, on whether these are up to date and, where not, on the need to adapt them to today's realities, including those in developing countries. To this end, we shall examine the signs of a new kind of social dynamics emerging in a broad geographical context.

New social dynamics?

The internationalization of the economy, whether as present fact or future potential, has a clear impact on industrial relations. It certainly seems to contribute, however indirectly, to the weakening of the trade union movement in several countries. The greater possibilities for transferring activities from one region to another, or from one country to another, enhance employers' arguments at the bargaining table, even if such arguments are stronger than actual transfers are frequent (which is most often the case). This globalization process combines with other factors, foremost among which are the new production and communication technologies, which are crucial in the changes taking place in the economic and social landscape.

Merely referring to the market for labour is a rather simplistic form of behavioural reasoning as far as industrial relations are concerned. The inherent risk is one of focusing attention on a purely economic – even econometric – approach to human relations. To do so would be to overlook the importance of the social dimension, cultural factors and political choices. In other words, different kinds of behavioural logic need to be distinguished.

It goes without saying that it is difficult to determine the relative importance of history and culture, the social and political environment and the economic options favoured by governments in the creation and development of national systems of industrial relations. All are agreed, however, in pointing out that in East and South-East Asia, for instance, these systems cannot be fully understood except in relation to cultural values. The extent to which the struggle against apartheid shaped collective social relations in present-day South Africa is well known. We are familiar with the current concern of Western European governments at the rise in urban violence and marginalization; their impact on collective bargaining issues can already be seen. An analysis of industrial relations would obviously be incomplete if it were restricted to a consideration of rational economic processes without sufficient attention being devoted to other social factors.

This complex blend has often been mentioned in contrasting the very different social concepts prevalent in the United States, Western European countries, such as France, Germany and Italy, as well as Japan. In particular, the European social "model" is claimed by some to be responsible for all that region's difficulties: it is supposedly too costly and a serious obstacle to economic growth and employment. By contrast, others portray this model as a shield against the risk of an intolerable growth in inequality and consequent dangers for society; they repeatedly state that we must not allow policies to be dominated by the market and that they must have a human dimension. Moreover, they add, a good social climate in Western Europe has probably helped to combat a tendency towards fatalistic attitudes among workers, to motivate and give them dynamism, as well as to increase profitability, productivity and competitiveness. All this has enabled the region to become wealthier.

Clearly, we must move beyond the entrenched camps in this debate. A brief study of the different visions which various regions of the world have of social issues and industrial relations will offer some illustration and assist in drawing conclusions. The aim is not to express any preference for one strategy over others, but to achieve a better understanding of how each one of them endeavours to resolve the long-standing search for balance between the economic and the social spheres.

Let us start with Western Europe, most recently at the centre of attention. What is meant by the European social model? Is it a specifically European way of viewing and addressing social problems or, rather, a set of common institutions and practices established at a European Union level? In reality, it is the former, and is only slowly taking concrete shape at the level of the latter, the European Union.

Admittedly, a European "social dimension" already exists, and it would be wrong to play down its importance. A Community social policy has been built up on treaties as well as on the instruments derived from them: free movement of workers and persons in general; social security for migrant workers and European citizens travelling in the European Union; promotion of equality between men and women workers; emergence of minimum social standards, or even standards leading to harmonization pure and simple (for example, on occupational safety and health); and the setting up of a social dialogue with two initial collective agreements – already mentioned – on parental leave and part-time work.

In the final analysis, however, this specifically European form of protection remains limited. Firstly, only few directives such as that on European works councils are essentially concerned with the supranational level. Furthermore, other European instruments may embody not very exacting standards which may well, for political if not legal reasons, end up weakening national regulations at one time more favourable to workers. Then there are the limits placed on the European Union's scope of action as well as its political and economic strategies.

In our view, the European social concept clearly reflects three historical realities. The first is that of social regulation based on centralized consultation and dialogue which may be bipartite or tripartite. Whatever the number of parties involved, State institutions are never indifferent to the outcome of the talks in which the social actors have participated. This practice of collective bargaining (in the broad sense) is generally furthered by a sophisticated system of industrial relations. While it is true that tripartite agreements and other forms of high-level social pacts have been, and are, observed in other regions of the world, especially in Latin American and the European countries in transition, no other region has resorted as much to dialogue, be it formal or informal, at the central level.

The second reality is what is known as the welfare State or rather, to use the German expression, the social State. Both terms imply an elaborate social security system including, where appropriate, provision of a minimum guaranteed income and other forms of labour protection (establishment of a minimum wage, for example). They also cover public services provided by the State in the social and economic spheres (industrial, commercial, etc.).

The third reality, related to the two others, is the more comprehensive implementation of Keynesian policies than in the United States, with the social partners participating in varying degrees. For many years, both sides of industry have been involved at the governments' invitation in seeking compromises among the different economic variables – the production of wealth, its distribution and job creation.

It is important that this common achievement should not be permitted to mask the clear differences which exist between countries in the region. Nevertheless, the concept of a European social model undoubtedly expresses some degree of political culture held in common: Europeans are reluctant to accept phenomena of exclusion and excessive inequality; they expect the State to act in order to remedy the social consequences of the mechanical operation of the market economy (they wish to find answers to the "social question").

If there is a distinct European social concept, its specific features must distinguish it from those of other regions. For example, the United States approach to labour and employment problems appears much less interventionist. In this field, as in others, it is much more voluntarist. The emphasis is placed on individual freedom and responsibility as well as action by local economic agents and groups, rather than on political power at the state or federal level. The law focuses more on civil liberties than on social rights (more on equality of opportunity and treatment than on any levelling of incomes).

Historically, the country's federal system has made it a complex matter for Congress in Washington to act in order to provide workers with the kind of protection granted under the laws of continental Europe. In the United States, enterprise- (or establishment)-level collective bargaining has been given preference over labour and social security legislation. In the countries of continental Europe, on the other hand, the help of the government, the administration and the legislation is expected – although in varying degrees – to improve living and working standards. Moreover, the socialist doctrine of the struggle of the classes for control of the State has practically never caught on in the United States. In the past, a trend developed there towards greater centralization of authority and to assigning greater importance to federal machinery in labour matters. These efforts to achieve greater uniformity, as well as the similarity of the objectives enshrined in President Roosevelt's New Deal and those of the ILO, finally led the United States, in 1934, to join the International Labour Organization. Although federal legislation did evolve significantly in the 1960s, it did so chiefly in the sphere of civil rights (protection of various groups from discrimination, for example).

A third approach has more recently emerged: that of Japan. The State and its officials play a very active role in that country. Their influence appears substantial, but their concerns – which once again have their historical roots – are centred on growth and productivity. Simplifying grossly, it could be said that the State deals with economics before turning its attention to social issues in the belief that resolving the former takes priority over the latter. There is no need, however, to point out that, in general terms, a great deal of attention is devoted to social problems in a country as industrialized as Japan. It was in this context that the current three pillars of the Japanese industrial relations system were erected after the Second World War: lifetime employment, the calculation of wages and social benefits based on seniority, and enterprise-level trade unionism. The Republic of Korea also appears to be moving towards a fairly similar approach.

Other countries do not really fit into these three models but often borrow from each of them in different degrees and over different periods of time. Several Latin

American, and Central and Eastern European States are currently facing social choices of this kind. Central and Eastern European countries share many social and cultural values with Western Europe. As for developing countries, they have a vast informal sector in common, in which attention is being focused not only on jobs, but also on the ability of those working in that sector to make themselves heard.

Nevertheless, all of the various models outlined above develop, react to changing times and undergo crises, especially when economic indicators remain gloomy. Like Europeans, the Japanese are now wondering about the relevance of the features which gave them their singularity. In the United States, and also in Canada, the growing insecurity of labour relations and the deepening inequalities among workers have prompted not only the attention of researchers but also that of government administrations to plan reforms and call on eminent expert groups to reflect upon them. In the United States, the Dunlop Commission published its report in 1994. Two years thereafter, a paper entitled *Seeking a balance* was prepared by Professors A. Sims, R. Blouin and P. Knopf at the request of the Canadian Government.

The development of industrial relations in enterprises is under scrutiny everywhere. The renewed desire to improve performance has led many companies to review their human resources policies and working arrangements. The choices made by the multinationals are without doubt of particular interest, in as much as their personnel management practices have an impact on traditional national institutions and the methods used by the country's major firms (sometimes, in the latter case, as a result of imitation or even fashion).

In most cases, the changes seen recently are based on the idea that cooperation between employers and workers helps increase output and productivity. Consequently, all necessary attention should be devoted to the way in which companies become part of this process and to the importance they attach to human resource development as well as to other forms of worker participation in the decision-making process. These developments are not entirely free of paradox, however, when the desire to involve workers in the decision-making process happens to coincide with less job security for some of them. Hence the re-emergence, for this reason especially, of serious industrial conflicts in such countries as France, Germany and the Republic of Korea.

In any event, it is clear that (a) managers have effectively taken the initiative in reshaping industrial relations in the workplace; (b) almost everywhere, individual firms are tending to exert greater influence in the conduct of industrial relations and in personnel management decisions, while obviously also responding to the specific demands of employees as they arise; and (c) companies must, more than ever, be seen in a supranational context. The challenge for trade unions is clear. The impact of these new practices on traditional forms of relations within the enterprise as well as on the function of unions, varies. Unions in the United States have often reproached employers for using such practices as an indirect means of reducing union influence in their companies. Frequently, however (especially in Germany and Japan), the new practices have enabled workers' organizations, directly or indirectly, to take a more active part in company life without being visibly weakened. Furthermore, these new practices appear most widespread in firms with a strong union presence.

The emergence of new types of industrial relations is nevertheless a further indication of the crisis in traditional forms of representation. The increase in the levels at which these relations are conducted raises the issue of how employers' organizations and trade union confederations are coming to terms with this growing diversity.

Undeniably, some of the decision-making authority on social matters now no longer lies with the central employers' associations which are devoting more attention to coordination activities and services to their members. This change is in line with a desire on the part of many employers to regain control of labour relations management. The only serious consequence would be if management were not to assume the responsibility for social aspects which previously fell to employers' associations. That is why there has been a revival, especially in the ILO, of discussions on companies' social responsibilities.[1] This issue is quite naturally also under scrutiny at a time when intervention by national public authorities (as well as regional institutions such as the European Commission) is facing difficulties of its own. This point has already been made. Moreover, some companies – but very few, in the final analysis – have become virtually stateless as far as their headquarters are concerned.

Given that it is taking on such responsibility, management's social obligations cannot remain the preserve of a certain number (substantial perhaps, but still limited) of enlightened company heads whilst being ignored, other than in empty declarations, by those who, by contrast, choose a policy of unrelenting cost-reduction. Many know – while others have to be persuaded – that, in addition to its ethical and social aspects, this responsibility is important in terms of image (with respect to the consumer) and motivation (with respect to workers). This is also a new perspective for employer associations.

It would be of great interest to improve our knowledge of the "state of play" in this sphere listing the specific experiences obtained by all companies, large and small. We have mentioned some examples, including the codes of conduct developed by some companies (Levi Strauss is among the best known examples) and the possibility mooted in various circles of attaching a social label to products. Sometimes, the initiative has come from management. Elsewhere, it originates with the unions and is then subject to collective bargaining. Like the organization of production itself, codes and labels may be extended to subcontractors and other commercial partners.

Workers' organizations perform functions which no other institution (and in particular no NGO) has proved able to carry out in their stead: those of an intermediate group between the individual worker and the various decision-making levels. They allow the voices of those who are working or want to work to be heard; they are involved in the search for a harmonious balance in producing and distributing the fruits of growth; and they represent an integrating factor in civil society. Based on the principles of association, they use local and national structures – which are as relevant as in the past – to support action at the international level as well. To carry out these tasks the most dynamic unions have embarked on a sometimes substantial programme of modernization and adaptation. The signs of revival are certainly plentiful, even if they are not always taken to full advantage. Additional issues are being included in action programmes, particularly in relation to defending jobs. Membership is being actively proposed to new categories of the working population. Despite all the obstacles, a transnational dimension is being opened up for negotiations. Lastly, new alliances are being envisaged and, sometimes, concluded; they involve not so much political parties but groups and associations which either basically have trade union characteristics or have been established for more specific social purposes (to defend human rights, minorities, consumers, the unemployed who are no longer entitled to benefits).

In short, success doubtless depends upon the momentum to be gained from new social dynamics provided by workers' confederations that genuinely open up to anyone who wants to work and which are movements with a true social vision for the defence and promotion of such people's interests, however varied.

Each of the two main sides involved in industrial relations, therefore, is experiencing a period of diversity (and even competition) but also adjustment to change and movement. Here, no doubt, lies one of the keys to tomorrow's social history.

We have described the broad gamut of arrangements governing labour relations. They reflect, above all, the efforts made by the main players to adapt their structures, their forms of interaction and strategies to new economic circumstances; equally they show the present limitations and flaws of some of the proposed efforts at reform.

It is also appropriate to examine how far government authorities allow market forces to determine the balance between capital and labour. The State's role as it is seen in many European countries in particular has been challenged because its room for social action, inter alia, has been curtailed – although the point should not be exaggerated. Most particularly a national Keynesian policy implied complete control by the State of the levers of the economy; that can no longer operate in a context in which nations are losing part of their power to exercise this control.

Throughout the world, however, the State is facing increasing demands upon it. It is called upon to modernize its institutions in the face of greater competition and to maintain or restore social cohesion seriously weakened by processes of exclusion. It is urged to defend jobs and guarantee a minimum income for those who do not have one or whose wages are not enough to survive on. As the end of the century approaches, therefore, the real issue in industrial relations is whether the traditional collective agreements or some other, new arrangements can help to solve the most acute current problem – unemployment and insecure employment.

Can bipartite negotiation or tripartite dialogue, however, really create jobs? There is no simple answer. In this respect, the driving force is, undeniably, economic growth and it was no doubt an illusion to believe that the great social pacts, in Europe or Latin America, could reduce unemployment. Yet negotiations on employment, at various levels, can have very positive effects. They always lend emphasis to the human dimension of industrial relations (for example, the care to avoid abrupt dismissals). In some circumstances, this bargaining also creates a climate conducive to improved economic structures (less rigid) and to non-inflationary development, the fruits of which are fairly distributed. It can even prevent job losses, or allow the setting of recruitment targets, especially when it takes on a decentralized, enterprise-level form. Above and beyond their direct effects, such negotiations often open up new approaches hitherto considered taboo (cessation of wage indexation, working time flexibility without financial compensation). Finally, especially in many Latin American and Central European countries, they contribute actively to the establishment of democratic institutions.

We have pointed out not only the multiplicity but also the growing diversity of kinds of social negotiation. New modes of dialogue have come into existence which are not always sufficiently well known. For example, local-level job creation initiatives are under way in Belgium through tripartite institutions known as local employment agencies. In South Africa (within NEDLAC), in Canada (in Quebec, at the Economy and Employment Summit in autumn 1996), in Ireland (especially with the National Economic and Social Forum, but also at the local level), an additional partner has emerged giving voice to the most disadvantaged sections of the population and the economy.

Nevertheless, no country has yet succeeded in finding wholly satisfactory solutions to the phenomena of exclusion, impoverishment and marginalization. It is at that level, however, that the real social scandal is to be found. And many consider that the ranks of their victims will swell still further and that the number of workers in stable jobs will fall. It appears improbable that the persons concerned would be able to defend their own interests alone, because they are scattered, have weak bargaining power and very little ability to take collective action. Hence the appeals for solidarity within society and a rethinking of "social citizenship"; this is all related to the concerns described above.

Almost everywhere, however, including in the informal sector of developing countries, successes have been achieved in defending and promoting the interests of the weakest sections of the population. Although such experience is not (yet?) very indicative of a new trend, it does suggest, especially when seen together with the new forms of collective bargaining which have been described above, that it may be possible to encourage the conclusion of new social contracts that are the sign of a fresh will to act together and act broadly. These contracts would not, of course, take the place of traditional collective agreements but would supplement them to benefit those who are not, or are insufficiently, covered by them. Such a step would help to promote, and provide a framework for, multiple and innovative solutions, often at the local level. It implies the recognition of spokespersons freely chosen by the parties concerned, the determination of methods of action that are both flexible yet stable, encouraging social solidarity, as well as specific measures to ensure that the objectives laid down are achieved.

Let us briefly take up each of these items. Naturally, we shall be concerned more with outlining prospects for the future than with a discussion of observable trends in the present.

We have already indicated the urgent need to overcome the representation crisis. The concept of a workers' organization, like that of an employers' organization, is a broad one. The former comprises associations established to defend the interests of the self-employed – and, for example, of the many persons working in the informal sector – as well as those with insecure jobs; employers' organizations includes groups of micro-enterprise managers. It is of little importance for the arguments being discussed here that the dividing-line between the two is blurred. What is more important is that all these industrial relations organizations should be able to conclude strategic alliances with associations pursuing similar objectives (consumer or feminist groups, cooperatives, networks of small-scale entrepreneurs) or even to establish links of co-operation with other institutions (we have already mentioned mutual aid bodies, other NGOs, social integration officers). Sometimes, even, the social partners agree to include in their ranks, in addition to representatives of the public authorities, spokespersons for other population groups. In any event, it is important for all the partners to be publicly recognized in the task which they are called upon to perform.

It is not necessary to dwell at length on methods of action. There are three main forms. The first is to seek support from public institutions (which, in the informal sector, for example, may be able to offset certain weaknesses of representation) and political bodies. The second is participation in bodies whose objectives are vocational (training centres, for instance) or social (e.g. social welfare bodies). The third, and most widespread, method is collective bargaining (in a broad sense), seeking consensus, a "social dialogue" with two, three or more than three participants and in various fora, depending on the circumstances. Social dialogue still remains the most favoured – as well as the most dynamic and democratic – instrument for fostering reflection and discovering innovative compromises between individual and collective values, economic efficiency (and the very natural profit motive) and the desire for protection (the need to share social risks and for solidarity in the distribution of the fruits of growth). In the circumstance of social dialogue when several levels of negotiation exist, articulating the links between them thus assumes new importance.

These new contracts born of an era in which jobs are rare or insecure – and we know how ubiquitous the latter aspect is – should be designed less to establish sets of elaborate rules than to lay down others better suited to the objective sought: the fight against unemployment and insecurity of income, against increased inequalities, even among salaried employees, and the risk that the gap between the winners and the losers may widen.

We have already identified collective agreements which are less regulatory than programmatic and which do not so much carry the obligation strictly to respect detailed rules as to apply specific policies to achieve certain ends. These framework agreements remain flexible as regards the choice of means and the coordination of different forms of negotiation. Where appropriate, they may lay down penalties for cases in which the parties fail to take action, or where the consensus-making machinery may have jammed, or abuses committed, rather than penalize inadequate results.

Agreements can even be imagined outlining possible career-development scenarios, made up of modules which may be combined, with alternating periods of work, retraining and leave (maternity, parental, military service).[2] These rules, which are of a different kind, would help those concerned to pass with ease from one period of development to another, while retaining some responsibility for career choices.

Such arrangements could also help to solve inevitable conflicts of interests, firstly for the worker himself, as, for example, in seeking the best possible balance between private life (family) and the world of work, and then in his or her working relations. Lastly, at the macroeconomic policy level, they could enable satisfactory compromises to be found balancing sometimes contradictory factors: security and mobility on the labour market, through social insurance measures which, whilst compulsory, encourage the beneficiary to be proactive rather than to rely on assistance; a necessary centralization of solidarity programmes, but recognition of the benefits offered by local structures in terms of new ideas and new initiatives; encouraging the hiring of workers while maintaining genuine equality of opportunity and treatment; minimum assistance to associations involved in the defence of disadvantaged groups, but the will, as one finds already, to stand at their side, in other words to help them to help themselves and to let them take their destiny into their own hands, rather than showing them the way.[3]

A broader geographic context

The economic changes described at length in this report have led States not only to adapt their structures to international competition but also to seek strategic regional alliances.[4] They have done so mainly within the structures whose emergence we have noted. Some groups, like the European Union, already existed; others, like NAFTA and MERCOSUR, have been formed more recently.

Supranational regulations have been designed to facilitate industrial relations at this level. The most sophisticated body of rules is undoubtedly that which the European Union has progressively adopted. Notable examples include the Joint Declaration of European Heads of State and Government of 9 December 1989, which constituted the Community Charter of the Fundamental Social Rights of Workers, as well as the Protocol and Agreement on Social Policy, signed at Maastricht on

7 February 1992. As we observed, few real collective agreements have been signed at the European level.

Other regional institutions have adopted social norms (the Council of Europe, for example). The United States has obtained the consent of its NAFTA partners, Canada and Mexico, to the addition to the North American Free Trade Agreement of a supplementary agreement on labour.[5] In 1976, the Organisation for Economic Co-operation and Development (OECD), a worldwide institution with, however, only a limited membership, adopted a Declaration on International Investment and Multinational Enterprises, which includes a voluntary code of conduct for such enterprises. Finally, at the world level, there are the Conventions and Recommendations adopted by the ILO and its other instruments, such as the Tripartite Declaration of Principles concerning Multinational Enterprises and Social Policy.

These legal instruments should promote the development of collective labour relations, both regional and international. Admittedly, the results so far remain limited, in spite of all the efforts made by the trade unions in particular. However, some recent developments could initiate change if others were to follow.

First of all they include the first two European collective agreements: one signed by UNICE, CEEP and the ETUC on 14 December 1995, relating to parental leave; the other, concluded by the same organizations in May 1997, addressing part-time work.

Subsequently, European works councils have been established in a large number of multinational companies operating in the European Union. Although their powers are limited to consultation and information, they clearly act as a favoured forum for conciliation whenever the parties are open to dialogue. Moreover, in at least one case, the parties have decided to go further. The Danone group, the IUF and five French trade unions embarked on a discussion regarding the operation of the European works council in that company and, on 28 March 1996, signed an agreement[6] giving it real negotiating power in the areas of employment, training, safety, working conditions and the exercise of union rights.

It is true that these examples are drawn solely from practice in the European Union. Nevertheless, the recent pluri-national social conflicts referred to above and the growing belief that trade liberalization must be accompanied by social safeguards could consolidate these changes and extend them to other regions. The agreement signed in April 1997 between major United States clothing industry firms, unions and human rights movements, with the assistance of White House experts, is a significant example.

The liberalization of trade and markets also calls for new social policies at the world level. There is a multidimensional role here for the ILO, and the Organization is conducting in-depth work in this area.[7]

Nevertheless, each country's social heritage is profoundly distinctive. Clearly, one cannot simply seek to reproduce elsewhere something that derives from another

State's history. In spite of this, everyone has an interest, more than ever before, in knowing how others respond to the everlasting issue of how one can balance economic efficiency and concern for the individual. Different countries have experimented with different approaches and there are lessons to be learned from their varied experiences. All the facts acquired form a considerable knowledge base, of vital use to each State as it designs its own approaches, adapts them to continual social change, and then begins to coordinate them with other States in the same region and, internationally, within the International Labour Organization. It is an analysis of these many facts and their import for industrial relations that the present report has sought to provide.

Notes

[1] See also, for example, Centre des jeunes dirigeants d'entreprise: *L'entreprise au XXIᵉ siècle* (Paris, Flammarion, 1996).

[2] See report of the Commission (Commissariat général du Plan) presided by Jean Boissonnat: *Le travail dans vingt ans* (Paris, O. Jacob, La documentation française, 1995); see also K. H. Ladeur: "Social risks, welfare rights and the paradigms of proceduralisation: The combining of the institutions of the liberal constitutional State and the social State", in J. de Munck, J. Lenoble and M. Molitor (eds.): *L'avenir de la concertation sociale en Europe* (Louvain, Centre de philosophie du droit, Université catholique de Louvain, 1995), p. 143.

[3] R. Plant: *The role of rural workers' organizations in economic and social development: A case study of the ILO's Convention No. 141 in Mexico and the Philippines* (Geneva, ILO, 1993), pp. 11, 20 ff. and 55-56.

[4] S. M. Jacoby: "Social dimensions of global economic integration", in S. M. Jacoby (ed.): *The workers of nations: Industrial relations in a global economy* (New York and Oxford, Oxford University Press, 1995), pp. 3 ff.

[5] As well as another on the environment.

[6] *European Works Councils Bulletin*, May-June 1996, pp. 5-7 and 16-17.

[7] ILO: *The ILO, standard setting and globalization,* Report of the Director-General, International Labour Conference, 85th Session, Geneva, 1997.

Statistical annex

Industrial relations indicators

Table 1.1. Trade union membership

	Year	Union membership (thousands)	Year	Union membership (thousands)	Change in membership (%)*
Africa					
Botswana	1995	45			
Cameroon	1995	250			
Cape Verde	1995	15			
Côte d'Ivoire	1995	300			
Egypt	1995	3 313	1985	2 721	21.8
Eritrea	1995	18			
Ethiopia	1995	152	1985	4	
Gabon	1995	5			
Ghana	1990	700			
Guinea	1995	13			
Kenya	1995	500	1985	700	−28.6
Mali	1995	103			
Mauritania	1995	15			
Mauritius	1995	106	1985	98	7.8
Morocco	1994	290			
Namibia	1995	55			
Nigeria**	1990	3 520	1982	3 000	
Senegal	1995	184			
South Africa	1995	3 154	1985	1 391	126.7
Swaziland	1995	21	1985	2	975.7
Tanzania, United Rep. of	1995	470			
Tunisia	1994	220			
Uganda	1995	63	1989	102	−38.3
Zambia	1995	273	1985	320	−14.7
Zimbabwe	1995	250	1985	162	54.4
Americas					
Antigua and Barbuda	1995	14	1985	9	60.4
Argentina	1995	3 200	1986	3 262	−1.9
Bolivia	1994	276			
Brazil	1991	15 205			
Canada	1993	4 128	1985	3 730	10.7
Chile	1993	684	1985	361	89.6
Colombia	1995	840	1985	877	−4.2
Costa Rica	1995	139	1985	139	0.0
Cuba	1995	2 772	1985	2 893	−4.2
Dominican Rep.	1995	450	1989	360	25.0
Ecuador	1995	300			
El Salvador	1995	103	1985	79	30.6
Guatemala	1994	89	1985	65	35.9
Guyana	1995	70			
Honduras	1994	106			
Mexico	1991	7 000	1989	9 500	−26.3
Nicaragua	1995	280			
Panama	1991	90			
Paraguay	1995	109			
Peru	1991	442			
United States	1995	16 360	1985	16 996	−3.7
Uruguay	1993	151	1990	222	−31.9
Venezuela	1995	1 153	1988	1 700	−32.2

Table 1.1.   Trade union membership *(cont.)*

	Year	Union membership (thousands)	Year	Union membership (thousands)	Change in membership (%)*
Asia					
Australia	1995	2 440	1985	2 793	−12.6
Bangladesh	1995	1 721	1985	1 090	57.8
China	1995	103 996	1985	85 258	22.0
Hong Kong (before 1.7.97)	1994	562	1985	368	53.0
India	1991	6 100	1980	5 917	3.1
Indonesia	1995	1 000			
Japan	1996	12 410	1985	12 418	−0.1
Jordan			1988	212	
Korea, Rep. of	1995	1 615	1985	1 004	60.8
Malaysia	1995	706	1986	606	16.6
New Zealand	1995	362	1986	680	−46.7
Pakistan	1994	984	1987	881	11.7
Philippines	1995	3 587	1985	2 117	69.4
Singapore	1995	235	1984	201	16.9
Sri Lanka	1991	1 640	1985	1 565	4.8
Taiwan, China	1995	3 146	1987	2 100	49.8
Thailand	1995	416	1985	234	77.3
Europe					
Austria	1995	1 287	1985	1 404	−8.3
Azerbaijan	1995	1 707	1985	2 522	−32.3
Belarus	1995	4 134	1985	5 355	−22.8
Belgium	1995	1 585	1985	1 499	5.8
Bulgaria	1993	1 810	1991	2 200	−17.7
Cyprus	1995	161	1985	145	11.1
Czech Rep.	1995	1 886	1990	3 820	−50.6
Denmark	1994	1 808	1985	1 730	4.5
Estonia	1995	167	1985	580	−71.2
Finland	1995	1 377	1985	1 411	−2.4
France	1995	1 758	1985	2 555	−31.2
Germany	1995	9 300	1991	11 676	−20.3
Former Germ. Dem. Rep.	1993	2 681	1991	3 428	−21.8
Former Germ. Fed. Rep.	1993	7 654	1985	8 127	−5.8
Greece	1995	500	1985	650	−23.1
Hungary	1995	1 860	1985	3 000	−38.0
Iceland	1994	94	1985	83	12.7
Ireland	1993	437	1985	449	−2.6
Israel	1995	450	1985	1 850	−75.7
Italy	1994	6 392	1985	6 860	−6.8
Luxembourg	1995	85	1987	75	13.3
Malta	1994	77	1985	53	44.8
Netherlands	1995	1 540	1985	1 290	19.3
Norway	1995	1 068	1985	971	10.0
Poland	1995	3 420	1989	6 300	−45.7
Portugal	1995	800	1986	1 434	−44.2
Romania	1993	3 700	1991	4 000	−7.5
Russian Fed.	1996	42 356			
Slovakia	1995	1 150	1990	1 920	−40.1
Spain	1994	1 606	1985	835	92.3
Sweden	1994	3 180	1985	3 341	−4.8
Switzerland	1994	740	1985	806	−8.2
Turkey**	1995	2 667	1987	1 493	
Ukraine	1995	21 850	1985	26 000	−16.0
United Kingdom	1995	7 280	1985	9 739	−25.2

* Calculations based on the exact (non-rounded) membership data.   ** The basis for calculating union membership changed over time.

Table 1.2. Trade union density (%)

	Year	Union membership as a percentage of:			Year	Union membership as a percentage of:		
		Non-agricultural labour force	Wage and salary earners	Formal sector wage earners		Non-agricultural labour force	Wage and salary earners	Formal sector wage earners
Africa								
Botswana	1995	11.5		19.3				
Cameroon	1995	14.7						
Cape Verde	1995	16.9						
Côte d'Ivoire	1995	13.0		77.9				
Egypt	1995	29.6	38.8		1985	38.9	42.7	
Eritrea	1995	7.2						
Ethiopia	1995	4.1		22.3	1985			
Gabon	1995	2.0						
Ghana	1990	25.9						
Guinea	1995	2.5						
Kenya	1995	16.9		33.3	1985	41.9		59.6
Mali	1995	13.7						
Mauritania	1995	2.7						
Mauritius	1995	25.9	29.2	36.6	1985	34.8		48.3
Morocco	1994	4.8						
Namibia	1995	22.0						
Nigeria	1990	17.2						
Senegal	1995	21.9		54.8				
South Africa	1995	21.8	40.9	51.9	1985	15.5	17.7	22.8
Swaziland	1995	19.1	22.4					
Tanzania, United Rep. of	1995	17.4		51.6				
Tunisia	1994	9.8						
Uganda	1995	3.9		6.8	1989	7.8		10.2
Zambia	1995	12.5		54.5	1985	18.8		40.0
Zimbabwe	1995	13.9		21.7	1985	11.6		15.3
Americas								
Antigua and Barbuda	1995		53.8					
Argentina	1995	25.4	38.7	65.6	1986	48.7	67.4	
Bolivia	1994	16.4		59.7				
Brazil	1991	32.1	43.5	66.0				
Canada	1993	31.0	37.4		1985	31.2	36.7	
Chile	1993	15.9		33.0	1985	11.6		
Colombia	1995	7.0		17.0	1985	11.2		
Costa Rica	1995	13.1	16.6	27.3	1985	22.9	29.1	
Cuba	1995		70.2		1985		100.0	
Dominican Rep.	1995	17.3			1989	18.9		
Ecuador	1995	9.8		22.4				
El Salvador	1995	7.2		10.7	1985	7.9	8.3	
Guatemala	1994	4.4		7.7	1985	8.1	8.2	
Guyana	1995	25.2[a]						
Honduras	1994	4.5		20.8				
Mexico	1991	31.0	42.8	72.9	1989	54.1	59.6	
Nicaragua	1995	23.4		48.2				
Panama	1991	14.2	20.1	29.0				
Paraguay	1995	9.3		50.1				
Peru	1991	7.5		18.3				
United States	1995	12.7	14.2		1985	15.0	18.0	
Uruguay	1993	11.6		20.2	1990	19.9		
Venezuela	1995	14.9	17.1	32.6	1988	25.9	29.8	44.6
Asia								
Australia	1995	28.6	35.2		1985	40.6	50.0	
Bangladesh	1995	4.3	7.5		1985	15.3		

Table 1.2. Trade union density (%) *(cont.)*

	Year	Union membership as a percentage of:			Year	Union membership as a percentage of:		
		Non-agricultural labour force	Wage and salary earners	Formal sector wage earners		Non-agricultural labour force	Wage and salary earners	Formal sector wage earners
China	1995	54.7		70.0	1985	59.4		
Hong Kong (before 1.7.97)	1994	18.5	22.4		1985	14.1	16.8	
India	1991	5.4		22.8	1980	6.6		26.5
Indonesia	1995	2.6	3.4	4.8				
Japan	1995	18.6	24.0		1985	22.6	28.8	
Jordan					1988	27.6		
Korea, Rep. of	1995	9.0	12.7		1985	8.6	12.4	
Malaysia	1995	11.7	13.4		1986	13.5		
New Zealand	1995	23.2	24.3		1986	47.1	54.1	
Pakistan	1994	5.5		29.0	1987	6.4		
Philippines	1995	22.8	38.2		1985	18.4	20.7	
Singapore	1995	13.5	15.9		1984	17.0	19.4	
Taiwan, China	1995	27.9	33.1		1987	30.2	42.9	
Thailand	1995	3.1	4.2	5.2	1985	3.3	4.3	
Europe								
Austria	1995	36.6	41.2		1985	51.7	51.0	
Azerbaijan	1995	75.4	63.8	100.0	1985	100.0	96.3	
Belarus	1995	96.1	88.0		1985	100.0	100.0	
Belgium	1995	38.1	51.9		1985	42.0	52.0	
Bulgaria	1993	51.4	58.2		1991	61.9	62.3	
Cyprus	1995	53.7	56.5		1985	62.7		
Czech Rep.	1995	36.3	42.8		1990	76.8	76.9	
Denmark	1994	68.2	80.1		1985	67.4	78.3	
Estonia	1995	26.4	36.1		1985		82.5	
Finland	1995	59.7	79.3		1985	61.4	68.3	
France	1995	6.1	9.1		1985	11.6	14.5	
Germany	1995	29.6	28.9		1991	30.7	35.0	
Former Germ. Dem. Rep.	1993	34.1	42.4		1991	41.1	46.2	
Former Germ. Fed. Rep.	1993	24.5	29.1		1985	29.5	35.3	
Greece	1995	15.4	24.3		1985	23.5	36.7	
Hungary	1995	52.5	60.0		1985	74.1	80.4	
Iceland	1994	70.7	83.3		1985	76.7	78.3	
Ireland	1993	36.0	48.9		1985	41.0	56.0	
Israel	1995	23.1	23.0		1985[b]	132.8	146.0	
Italy	1994	30.6	44.1		1985	32.9	47.6	
Luxembourg	1995	39.5	43.4		1987	48.0	53.0	
Malta	1994	57.9	65.1		1985	45.5	47.9	
Netherlands	1995	21.8	25.6		1985	23.3	28.7	
Norway	1995	51.7	57.7		1985	50.7	55.7	
Poland	1995	27.0	33.8		1989	47.1	58.8	
Portugal	1995	18.8	25.6		1986	40.6	51.4	
Romania	1993	40.7			1991	50.7	52.8	
Russian Fed.	1996	74.8						
Slovakia	1995	52.3	61.7		1990	76.8	76.9	
Spain	1994	11.4	18.6		1985	7.3	11.5	
Sweden	1994	77.2	91.1		1985	79.3	83.8	
Switzerland	1994	20.0	22.5		1985	25.4	28.8	
Turkey	1995	22.0	33.7		1987	14.1	21.0	
Ukraine					1985	100.0		
United Kingdom	1995	26.2	32.9		1985	36.0	45.5	

[a] Union membership as a percentage of the economically active population. [b] Including pensioners.

Table 1.3. Change in trade union density (%)

	Period	Union membership as a percentage of:						Trend*
		Non-agricultural labour force		Wage and salary earners		Formal sector wage earners		
		Change in density						
		In points	In %	In points	In %	In points	In %	
Africa								
Botswana								
Cameroon								
Cape Verde								
Côte d'Ivoire								
Egypt	85-95	−9.3	−23.9	−3.9	−9.1			−
Eritrea								
Ethiopia								
Gabon								
Ghana								
Guinea								
Kenya	85-95	−25.0	−59.6			−26.3	−44.2	−−
Mali								
Mauritania								
Mauritius	85-95	−8.9	−25.7			−11.7	−24.2	−−
Morocco								
Namibia								
Nigeria								
Senegal								
South Africa	85-95	6.3	40.7	23.2	130.8	29.1	127.3	++
Swaziland								
Tanzania, United Rep. of								
Tunisia								
Uganda	89-95	−3.9	−49.9			−3.4	−33.3	−−
Zambia	85-95	−6.3	−33.5			14.5	36.3	−−
Zimbabwe	85-95	2.3	20.1			6.4	41.6	++
Americas								
Antigua and Barbuda								
Argentina	86-95	−23.3	−47.9	−28.7	−42.6			−−
Bolivia								
Brazil								
Canada	85-93	−0.2	−0.6	0.7	1.8			=
Chile	85-93	4.3	37.2					++
Colombia	85-95	−4.2	−37.3					−−
Costa Rica	85-95	−9.8	−42.6	−12.5	−43.0			−−
Cuba	85-95	0.0		−29.8	−29.8			−−
Dominican Rep.	89-95	−1.6	−8.6					−
Ecuador								
El Salvador	85-95	−0.6	−8.0					−
Guatemala	85-94	−3.7	−45.6					−−
Guyana								
Honduras								
Mexico	89-91	−23.1	−42.7	−16.8	−28.2			−−
Nicaragua								
Panama								
Paraguay								
Peru								
United States	85-95	−2.3	−15.2	−3.8	−21.1			−−
Uruguay	90-93	−8.2	−41.4					−−
Venezuela	88-95	−11.0	−42.5	−12.7	−42.6	−12.0	−26.9	−−
Asia								
Australia	85-95	−12.0	−29.6	−14.8	−29.6			−−

Table 1.3. Change in trade union density (%) *(cont.)*

	Period	Union membership as a percentage of:						Trend*
		Non-agricultural labour force		Wage and salary earners		Formal sector wage earners		
		Change in density						
		In points	In %	In points	In %	In points	In %	
Bangladesh	85-95	−11.0	−71.9					−−
China	85-95	−4.6	−7.8					−
Hong Kong (before 1.7.97)	85-94	4.4	30.8	5.7	33.7			++
India	80-91	−1.2	−18.2			−3.7	−14.0	
Indonesia								
Japan	85-95	−4.0	−17.7	−4.8	−16.7			−
Jordan								
Korea, Rep. of	85-95	0.4	4.7	0.3	2.4			=
Malaysia	86-95	−1.8	−13.4					−
New Zealand	86-95	−23.9	−50.7	−29.8	−55.1			−−
Pakistan	87-95	−0.9	−13.4					−
Philippines	85-95	4.4	24.1	17.5	84.9			++
Singapore	84-95	−3.5	−20.4	−3.5	−18.1			−
Sri Lanka								
Taiwan, China	87-95	−2.3	−7.6	−9.8	−22.8			−−
Thailand	85-95	−0.2	−7.4	−0.1	−2.5			=
Europe								
Austria	85-95	−15.1	−29.2	−9.8	−19.2			−
Azerbaijan	85-95	−24.6	−24.6	−32.5	−33.7			−−
Belarus	85-95	−3.9	−3.9	−12.0	−12.0			−
Belgium	85-95	−3.9	−9.2	−0.1	−0.2			=
Bulgaria	91-93	−10.5	−17.0	−4.1	−6.6			−−
Cyprus	85-95	−9.1	−14.5					−
Czech Rep.	90-95	−40.5	−52.8	−34.1	−44.3			−−
Denmark	85-94	0.8	1.2	1.8	2.3			=
Estonia	85-95			−46.4	−56.3			−−
Finland	85-95	−1.7	−2.8	11.0	16.1			+
France	85-95	−5.5	−47.4	−5.4	−37.2			−−
Germany	91-95	−1.1	−3.5	−6.1	−17.6			−−
Former Germ. Dem. Rep.	91-93	−7.1	−17.2	−3.8	−8.3			−−
Former Germ. Fed. Rep.	85-93	−4.9	−16.8	−6.2	−17.4			−−
Greece	85-95	−8.1	−34.5	−12.4	−33.8			−−
Hungary	85-95	−21.6	−29.2	−20.3	−25.3			−−
Iceland	85-94	−6.0	−7.8	5.0	6.3			+
Ireland	85-93	−5.0	−12.3	−7.1	−12.6			−
Israel	85-95	−76.9	−76.9	−77.0	−77.0			−−
Italy	85-94	−2.3	−7.0	−3.5	−7.4			−
Luxembourg	87-95	−8.5	−17.7	−9.6	−18.1			−−
Malta	85-94	12.4	27.3	17.2	35.8			++
Netherlands	85-95	−1.6	−6.7	−3.2	−11.0			−
Norway	85-95	1.0	2.0	2.0	3.6			=
Poland	89-95	−20.0	−42.6	−25.0	−42.5			−−
Portugal	86-95	−21.8	−53.7	−25.8	−50.2			−−
Romania	91-93	−10.0	−19.8					−−
Russian Fed.								−
Slovakia	90-95	−24.5	−31.9	−15.2	−19.8			−−
Spain	85-94	4.1	56.2	7.1	62.1			++
Sweden	85-94	−2.1	−2.7	7.3	8.7			+
Switzerland	85-94	−5.4	−21.2	−6.2	−21.7			−−
Turkey								
United Kingdom	85-95	−9.8	−27.2	−12.6	27.7			−−

* Trend in union density rates is calculated for wage and salary earners. Where the union density rates for wage and salary earners are not available, the trend is calculated for non-agricultural labour force or for formal sector employment. Key for trend symbols: ++ Change in union density rates is larger than +20 per cent; + Change in union density rate is larger than +5 per cent, but not larger than +20 per cent; −− Change in union density rate is larger than -20 per cent; −Change in union density rate is larger than −5 per cent, but not larger than −20 per cent; = Change in union density rate is not larger than ±5 per cent. The trend is calculated on the basis of a 10-year period. If the number of years is shorter, trend scores are adjusted accordingly.´

Table 2. Profile of national employers' organizations (as of May 1997)

	National employers'organizations which are members of the International Organization of Employers	Number of enterprises covered	Type of enterprise	Workforce employed by associated enterprises	Direct/indirect membership of enterprises*
Africa					
Algeria	Confédération générale des opérateurs économiques algériens (CGOEA).	> 14,000	Private.	> 1,000,000 empl.	Direct.
Benin	Organisation nationale des employeurs du Bénin (ONEB).				
Botswana	Botswana Confederation of Commerce, Industry and Manpower (BOCCIM).				
Burkina Faso	Conseil national du patronat Burkinabé (CNPB).				
Burundi	Association des employeurs du Burundi (AEB).	10% of. private and parastatal sector.	Private or parastatal.	52% of private and parastatal sector.	Direct.
Cameroon	Groupement inter-patronal du Cameroun (GICAM).	117 + 13 empl. orgs.	Private.		Both.
Cape Verde	Association commerciale, industrielle et agricole de Barlavento (ACIAB). Association commerciale de Sotavento du Cap-Vert (ACS).	150	Private.		
Chad	Conseil national du patronat tchadien (CNPT).	67	Private, mixed or public.	8,000	Direct.
Congo	Union patronale et interprofessionnelle du Congo (UNICONGO).	400	Private or mixed.	25,000	Indirect.
Côte d'Ivoire	Conseil national du patronat ivoirien (CNPI).	> 500	Private or mixed.	> 100,000	Indirect.
Egypt	Federation of Egyptian Industries (FEI).	18,000	Private, cooperative public or mixed.		Indirect.
Gabon	Confédération patronale gabonaise (CPG).	220		30,000	Both.
Ghana	The Ghana Employers'Association (GEA).				Both.
Guinea	Conseil du patronat guinéen (CPG).				
Kenya	Federation of Kenya Employers (FKE).	3,000		500,000	Both.
Lesotho	Association of Lesotho Employers (ALE).	100	Private or mixed.	70% of the labour force.	Both.
Madagascar	Groupement des entreprises de Madagascar (GEM).				Both.
Malawi	The Employers' Consultative Association of Malawi (ECAM).	250		80,000	Both
Mali	Fédération nationale des employeurs du Mali (FNEM).	500		10,000	Indirect.
Mauritania	Confédération générale des employeurs de Mauritanie (CGEM).	60,800	Private.		Indirect.
Mauritius	Mauritius Employers' Federation (MEF).	600	Private.	150,000	Both.
Morocco	Fédération des chambres de commerce et d'industrie . du Maroc (FCCIM).				Indirect.
Mozambique	Associação de Empresas Privadas de Moçambique (AEPRIMO).				
Niger	Syndicat patronal des entreprises et industries du Niger (SPEIN)	45	Private or mixed.	>5,000/ 25% of the private sector.	Direct.
Nigeria	Nigerian Employers' Consultative Association (NECA).			450,000-500,000	Both.
Senegal	Conseil national du patronat du Sénégal (CNP).				
Seychelles	Federation of Employers'Associations of Seychelles.			7,500/80% of the labour force.	Both.
South Africa	Business South Africa.	80-85%		About 5,000,000/ 90% of the private sector.	Indirect.
Tanzania, United Rep. of	The Association of Tanzanian Employers (ATE).				
Togo	Conseil national du patronat (CNP).				Indirect.
Tunisia	Union tunisienne de l'industrie, du commerce et de l'artisanat (UTICA).	>150,000			Indirect.

Table 2. Profile of national employers' organizations (as of May 1997) *(cont.)*

	National employers' organizations which are members of the International Organization of Employers	Number of enterprises covered	Type of enterprise	Workforce employed by associated enterprises	Direct/indirect membership of enterprises*
Uganda	Federation of Ugandan Employers (FUE).			150,000	Both.
Zambia	The Zambia Federation of Employers (ZFE).			250,000	Both.
Zimbabwe	Employers' Confederation of Zimbabwe (EMCOZ).		Private.	>2,000,000	Both.
Americas					
Antigua and Barbuda	Antigua Employers' Federation.	115	Private or government.		Direct.
Argentina	Unión Industrial Argentina (UIA).	> 60,000	Private or mixed.		Both.
Bahamas	Bahamas Employers' Confederation (BECON).				
Barbados	Barbados Employers' Confederation (BEC).	254	Private or mixed.	25,000	Both.
Bolivia	Confederación de Empresarios Privados de Bolivia (CEPB).	18,000	Private.	450,000	Indirect.
Brazil	Confederação Nacional da Indústria (CNI).	260,000	Private.	About 7,000,000.	Indirect.
Canada	Canadian Employers' Council (CEC).		Private.	Majority.	Both.
Chile	Confederación de la Producción y del Comercio.	35,000	Private.		Both.
Colombia	Asociación Nacional de Industriales (ANDI).			70% of the industrial employment.	
Costa Rica	Unión Costarricense de Cámaras y Asociaciones de la Empresa Privada (UCCAEP).	5,000	Private or mixed.	> 200,000	Both.
Dominica	The Dominica Employers' Federation (DEF).	80	Private.	8,000	Direct.
Dominican Rep.	Confederación Patronal de la República Dominicana (COPARDOM).	400	Private or mixed	50,000	Direct.
Ecuador	Federación Nacional de Cámaras de Industrias del Ecuador.	7,000	Private or mixed.	20% of labour force of the private sector.	Indirect.
El Salvador	Asociación Nacional de la Empresa Privada (ANEP).	10,000	Private or cooperative.	200,000	Indirect.
Guatemala	Comité Coordinador de Asociaciones Agrícolas, Comerciales, Industriales y Financieras (CACIF).	200,000		2,000,000	Indirect.
Guyana	The Consultative Association of Guyanese Industry Limited (CAGI).				
Honduras	Consejo Hondureño de la Empresa Privada (COHEP).	10,000		85% of the labour force.	Indirect.
Jamaica	The Jamaican Employers' Federation (JEF).				Both.
Mexico	Confederación de Camáras Industriales de los Estados Unidos Mexicanos (CONCAMIN).	100,000	Private or mixed.	About 5,000,000.	Indirect.
	Confederación Patronal de la República Mexicana (COPARMEX).	36,000		About 2,000,000.	Indirect.
Nicaragua	Consejo Superior de la Empresa Privada (COSEP).				Indirect.
Panama	Consejo Nacional de la Empresa Privada de Panamá (CONEP).				Indirect.
Paraguay	Federación de la Producción, la Industria y el Comercio (FEPRINCO).				Indirect.
Peru	Confederación Nacional de Instituciones Empresariales Privadas (CONFIEP).				
Saint Lucia	St. Lucia Employers' Federation.	85	Private.		Direct.
Suriname	Suriname Trade and Industry Association (STIA).	285	Private or mixed.	75,000/50% of the labour force.	Indirect.
Trinidad and Tobago	The Employers' Consultative Association of Trinidad and Tobago (ECA).	230	Private.		Both.
United States	United States Council for International Business (USCIB).	300			Direct.
Uruguay	Cámara de Industrias del Uruguay (CIU).	1,500	Private.	200,000	Indirect.
	Comisión Patronal del Uruguay de Asuntos Relaciones con la OIT.	8,000			Indirect.

Table 2. Profile of national employers' organizations (as of May 1997) *(cont.)*

	National employers' organizations which are members of the International Organization of Employers	Number of enterprises covered	Type of enterprise	Workforce employed by associated enterprises	Direct/indirect membership of enterprises*
Venezuela	Federación Venezolana de Cámaras y Asociaciones de Comercio y Producción (FEDECAMARAS).	>100,000	Private or public.	>2,000,000	Indirect.
Asia					
Australia	Australian Chamber of Commerce and Industry (ACCI).	> 300,000/ 50% of total.		75% of labour force.	Indirect.
Bahrain	Bahrain Chamber of Commerce and Industry.	6,500	Private.	100,000	Direct.
Bangladesh	Bangladesh Employers' Association (BEA).	80% of employers.		85% of labour force in organized sector.	Both.
Fiji	Fiji Employers' Federation (FEF).				
India	Council of Indian Employers (CIE).			27,000,000/100% of labour force.	Direct in organized sector.
Indonesia	The Employers' Association of Indonesia (APINDO).	9,100	Private, cooperative or public.	5,000,000	Direct.
Japan	Japanese Federation of Employers' Associations (NIKKEIREN).	26,000		20,000,000	Indirect.
Jordan	Amman Chamber of Industry (ACI).	7,500		90,000/60% of labour force in private sector, exc. agriculture.	Direct.
Korea, Rep. of	Korean Employers' Federation (KEF).	4,000	Private.	2,500,000	Both.
Kuwait	Kuwait Chamber of Commerce and Industry.	46,000	Private, cooperative, public or mixed.		Direct.
Lebanon	Association of Lebanese Industrialists.				
Malaysia	Malaysian Employers' Federation (MEF).			About 1,000,000.	Both.
Nepal	Federation of Nepalese Chambers of Commerce and Industry (FNCCI).				
New Zealand	New Zealand Employers' Federation (INC).	10,000	Private, cooperative or government.	> 500,000	Indirect.
Pakistan	Employers' Federation of Pakistan (EFP).	16,782	Private, government or mixed.	>1,237,000	Both.
Papua New Guinea	The Employers' Federation of Papua New Guinea.	150 /35% of total.	Private.	54,300/25% of total labour force.	Direct.
Philippines	Employers' Confederation of the Philippines (ECOP).				Both.
Saudi Arabia	Jeddah Chamber of Commerce and Industry (JCCI).	40,000		100% of labour force.	Direct.
Singapore	The Singapore National Employers' Federation (SNEF).	1,400	Private, cooperative or mixed.	300,000	Direct.
Sri Lanka	The Employers' Federation of Ceylon (EFC).	400	Private or mixed.	About 500,000.	Direct.
Taiwan, China	Chinese National Federation of Industries (CNFI).				
Thailand	Employers' Confederation of Thailand (ECOT).				Both.
United Arab Emirates	Federation of United Arab Emirates Chambers of Commerce and Industry (FCCI).	50,000	Private, cooperative or mixed.	200,000	Indirect.
Europe					
Austria	Federation of Austrian Industry (VÖI).	2,000	Private or cooperative.	> 400,000	Direct.

Table 2. Profile of national employers' organizations (as of May 1997) *(cont.)*

	National employers' organizations which are members of the International Organization of Employers	Number of enterprises covered	Type of enterprise	Workforce employed by associated enterprises	Direct/indirect membership of enterprises*
Belgium	Fédération des entreprises de Belgique (FEB).	30,000	Private or mixed.	About 1,000,000.	Indirect.
Bulgaria	Association of the Organizations of Bulgarian Employers (AOBE).		Private.		
Croatia	Croatian Employers' Association (CEA).	2,400	Private or mixed.	220,000	Indirect.
Cyprus	Cyprus Employers' and Industrialists' Federation (OEB).	2,700	Private, cooperative, government or mixed.	65% of private sector labour force.	Both.
Czech Rep.	Confederation of Industry of the Czech Republic (SP).	1,100		> 1,000,000	Indirect.
Denmark	Danish Employers' Confederation (DA).	28,000	Private or mixed.	600,000	Indirect.
Finland	Confederation of Finnish Industry and Employers (TT).	5,700		490,000	Direct.
France	Conseil national du patronat français (CNPF).	1,500,000		14,000,000	Indirect.
Germany	Confederation of German Employers' Associations (BDA).		Private.	80% of labour force.	Indirect.
Greece	Federation of Greek Industries (FGI).	3,560/70%	Private.	80% of labour force in the private sector.	Both.
Hungary	National Association of Entrepreneurs (VOSZ).	6,000 + 50 associations.			Both.
Iceland	Confederation of Icelandic Employers (VSI).	About 2,500.			Both.
Ireland	Irish Business and Employers' Confederation (IBEC).	4,000	Private, cooperative or mixed.	300,000	Direct.
Israel	Manufacturers' Association of Israel (MAI).	1,100	Private, public or mixed.	160,000	Direct.
Italy	Confederazione Generale dell' Industria Italiana. (CONFINDUSTRIA)	130,000	Private or mixed.	About 4,000,000.	Indirect.
Latvia	Latvian Employers' Confederation (LEC).	27%			Both.
Luxembourg	Fédération des industriels luxembourgeois (FEDIL).		Private or mixed.	55,000	Both.
Malta	Malta Employers' Association (MEA).	220	Private or mixed.	20,000	Direct.
Netherlands	Confederation of Netherlands Industry and Employers (VNO-NCW).	86,000			Indirect.
Norway	Confederation of Norwegian Business and Industry (NHO).	12,000	Private, cooperative, government or mixed.	400,000	Both.
Poland	Confederation of Polish Employers (KPP).	1,000	Private, government or mixed.	350,000	Indirect.
Portugal	Confederação da Indústria Portuguesa (CIP).	38,000			Indirect.
Romania	Romanian Employers' Organisation (Patronatul Roman) (REO).	75,800	Private, public or mixed.	3,600,000/ 60% of total labour force.	Indirect.
Russian Fed.	Coordinating Council of Employers' Organizations of Russia (CCOER).				Indirect.
San Marino	Associazione Nazionale dell' Industria Sanmarinese (ANIS)	180	Private.	4,500-5,000	Direct.
Slovakia	Federation of Employers' Unions and Associations of the Slovak Republic.	70%			Indirect.
Slovenia	Employers' Organization of Slovenia (EOS).		Private, cooperative or mixed.		Direct.
Spain	Confederación Española de Organizaciones Empresariales (CEOE).	1,000,000	Private, public or mixed.	5,000,000	Indirect.
Sweden	Swedish Employers' Confederation (SAF).	42,000		1,300,000	Indirect.

Table 2. Profile of national employers' organizations (as of May 1997) *(cont.)*

	National employers' organizations which are members of the International Organization of Employers	Number of enterprises covered	Type of enterprise	Workforce employed by associated enterprises	Direct/indirect membership of enterprises*
Switzerland	Union centrale des associations patronales suisses (UCAPS).			>1,000,000	Both.
Turkey	Turkish Confederation of Employers'Associations (TISK).	1,500	Private.	>1,200,000/22.5% of total labour force.	Indirect.
Ukraine	Ukrainian League of Industrialists and Entrepreneurs (ULIE).				Indirect.
United Kingdom	Confederation of British Industry (CBI).	250,000		>10,000,000/ 75% of empl. in the private sector of industry and transport.	Both.

* In many countries enterprises are not able to become members of the national umbrella employers' organization and, therefore, they are represented by sectoral or industry-wide employers' organizations.

Table 3.1.　Collective bargaining structure in selected countries

	Bargaining levels over past 10 years	Dominant levels over past 10 years	Trend over past 10 years	
	N/S, C	N/S, C	N/S	C
Africa				
Egypt[1]	N/S, C	N/S, C	i	i
Eritrea[1]	N/S, C	N/S, C	s	d
Kenya[1]	N/S, C	N/S, C	s	i
Mali[1]	N/S, C	N/S	i	i
Mauritius[1]	N/S, C	N/S, C	i	s
South Africa	N/S, C	C	i	i
Swaziland[1]	N/S, C	C	s	d
Uganda[1]	N/S, C	N/S, C	i	i
Zambia[1]	N/S, C	C	s	i
Zimbabwe[2]	N/S, C	N/S, C	i	d
Americas				
Argentina[3]	N/S, C	N/S	s	i
Brazil[1]	N/S, C	N/S	i	i
Canada[4]	N/S, C	C	d	i
Chile[1]	C	C		i
Colombia[1]	N/S, C	N/S, C	i	i
Cuba[1]	N/S, C	N/S, C	i	i
Guyana[1]	N/S, C	C	s	i
Mexico	N/S, C	C	s	s
Nicaragua[1]	N/S, C	N/S, C	s	i
Peru	N/S, C	C	d	i
United States[1]	N/S, C	C	d	i
Uruguay	N/S, C	N/S	s	i
Venezuela	N/S, C	C	d	i
Asia				
Australia[1,4]	N/S, C	C	d	i
Bangladesh[1]	N/S, C	C	i	i
China[1]	C	C		i
India[6]	N/S, C	N/S	s	i
Japan	N/S, C	C	s	i
Korea, Rep. of	N/S, C	C		
Malaysia[7]	C	C		
New Zealand[5]	N/S, C	C	d	i
Pakistan	C	C		
Philippines[1]	C	C		i
Singapore[1]	N/S, C	C	s	s
Thailand[1]	C	C		i
Europe				
Austria[8,9]	N/S, C	N/S	s	i
Azerbaijan[1]	N/S, C	N/S, C		s
Belarus[1]	N/S, C	C		
Belgium[8,9]	N/ S, C	N/S	s	i
Bulgaria[11]	N/S, C	N/S, C	i	i
Cyprus[1]	N/S, C	N/S	i	s
Czech Rep.[11]	N/S, C	C	s	i

Table 3.1. Collective bargaining structure in selected countries *(cont.)*

	Bargaining levels over past 10 years	Dominant levels over past 10 years	Trend over past 10 years	
	N/S, C	N/S, C	N/S	C
Denmark [9]	N/S, C	N/S	s	i
Estonia [1]	N/S, C	C	i	i
Finland [9]	N/S, C	N/S, C	s	i
France [8, 9]	N/ S, C	N/S	s	i
Germany [8, 9]	N/S, C	N/S	s	i
Greece [8, 9]	N/S, C	N/S	d	i
Hungary [11]	N/S, C	C	d	i
Ireland [10]	N/S, C	C	i	s
Italy [8, 9]	N/S, C	N/S	s	i
Netherlands [8, 9]	N/S, C	N/S	s	i
Norway [12]	N/S, C	N/S		
Poland [11]	N/S, C	C	d	i
Portugal [8, 9]	N/S, C	N/S	i	i
Russian Fed. [13]	N/S, C	C	d	i
Slovakia [11]	N/S, C	C		
Slovenia [1]	N/S, C	N/S	s	s
Spain [8, 9]	N/S, C	N/S	i	i
Sweden [8,9]	N/S, C	N/S	s	i
Switzerland [8, 9]	N/S, C	N/S	i	
Ukraine [1]	N/S, C	C	i	i
United Kingdom [8, 9]	N/S, C	C	d	i

For details on numbered notes after countries, refer to the Technical Notes. N/S = National/sectoral level. C = Company/plant level. d = Decrease. i = Increase. s = Stable.

Table 3.2.   Collective bargaining coverage rates[a] in selected countries

	Year	Proportion of employees covered by collective agreements (%)
Africa		
Ghana[1]	1995	25.0
Kenya[1]	1995	35.0
Mauritius[1]	1995	40.0
Nigeria[1]	1995	40.0
Swaziland[1]	1995	25.0
Uganda[1]	1995	25.0
Zambia[1]	1995	30.0
Zimbabwe[1]	1995	25.0
Americas		
Argentina[3, b]	1995	72.9
Bolivia[4]	1995	11.1
Canada[5]	1996	37.0
Chile[6]	1995	12.7
Cuba[2]	1995	98.2
El Salvador[4]	1995	13.2
Guyana[2]	1995	27.0
Honduras[4]	1995	12.7
Nicaragua[4]	1995	38.3
Panama[4]	1995	16.0
United States[2]	1995	11.2
Uruguay[4]	1993	21.6
Asia		
Australia[1]	1995	65.0
China[2]	1995	15.1
India[8, c]	1995	< 2
Japan[9]	1994	25.0
Malaysia[10]	1995	2.6
New Zealand[7]	1995	23.1
Philippines[11]	1995	3.7
Singapore[12]	1996	18.8
Taiwan, China[13]	1995	3.4
Thailand[2]	1995	26.7
Europe		
Belarus[2]	1995	94.7
Czech Rep.[2]	1995	55.0
Denmark[14, b]	1996	55.0
France[b]	1995	90.0
Germany[15]	1996	90.0
Greece[16]	1994	90.0
Hungary[2]	1995	45.0
Ireland[16]	1994	90.0
Netherlands[17]	1996	80.0
Norway[18, b]	1996	66.0
Spain[19]	1996	82.0
Sweden	1995	85.0
United Kingdom[20]	1994	25.6

For details on numbered notes after countries, refer to the Technical Notes. [a] Collective bargaining coverage rate is the proportion of employees covered by collective agreements in the formal sector. [b] Estimate. [c] Less than 2% of the total workforce (including informal sector workers) is covered.

Table 4.1. Number of strikes and lockouts

	1980	1985	1990	1991	1992	1993	1994	1995
Africa								
Algeria			2 023	1 034	493			
Botswana[a]							7	6
Burundi	8	12						
Central African Rep.				4	13	2		
Egypt	4	2	4	1	0	3	5	8
Ghana	59	12	24	24				
Guinea			2	8	4			
Kenya		87						
Malawi	4	2						
Mali	1	1						
Mauritius			8	6	9	4	9	7
Morocco[a]	748	222	178	364	310	323		
Namibia[a]			24	8	23	5	7	
Niger[a]		6	24	3				
Nigeria	185	56	126	125	187	107	137	
Senegal[a]			26	55	19			
South Africa		389	885	600	789	784		
Tunisia		391	564	466	496	513	425	
Zambia	121	50	103	102	91			
Zimbabwe	297							
Americas								
Bahamas			0	0	0			
Barbados	7	5	17	10	12	5	2	8
Bolivia		319	30	110	40	35	42	44
Brazil[a]	81	843					576	
Canada[+]	1 028	829	579	463	404	381	375	326
Chile[a]	89	42	176	219	237	224		
Colombia		87	514	234	638	292		
Costa Rica	61	10	42	11	19	21	19	15
Ecuador	75	72	140	87	49	28	14	
El Salvador	42	54	20	26	47	36	12	42
Guatemala			19		25	35	17	17
Guyana	333	718	329	307	258	475	468	422
Haiti	2 946	1 653						
Honduras	37	14	93	23	43			47
Jamaica			65					
Mexico[a,+]	1 339	159	150	136	156	155	116	96
Nicaragua[a]			55	133	85			
Panama			0	0	1	0	1	1
Peru[+]	739	579	613	315	219	151	168	102 .
Suriname	17	9	6	2	7	27		
Trinidad and Tobago	27	45	14	16	17	24	13	14 .
United States[b]	187	54	44	40	35	35	45	31
Venezuela	195							
Asia								
Australia	2 429	1 895	1 193	1 036	728	610	560	643
Bangladesh	104	95	5	3	11	11	2	5

Table 4.1. Number of strikes and lockouts *(cont.)*

	1980	1985	1990	1991	1992	1993	1994	1995
Fiji	73	20						9
Hong Kong (before 1.7.97)[+]	37	3	15	5	11	10	3	9
India[+]	2 856	1 755	1 825	1 810	1 714	1 393	1 062	
Indonesia	198	78	61	130	228			
Japan[+]	1 133	627	284	310	263	252	230	
Korea, Rep. of	206	265	322	234	235	144	121	88
Malaysia[a]	38	25	17	23	17	18	15	13
Myanmar			0	0	0	0	0	0
New Zealand	360	383	127	68	47	50	60	61
Pakistan	59	58					25	24
Papua New Guinea	53		13	4	11	10		
Philippines[b]	62	371	183	182	136	122	93	94
Singapore	0	0	0	0	0	0	0	0
Sri Lanka[+]	227	145	116	130	103	49	233	183
Thailand	18	4	9	14	18	14	8	
Europe								
Austria	9	4	9	9	3	3	0	1
Azerbaijan			230					
Belarus			19	47	3	2	3	0
Belgium[+]			33	62	49	28	30	46
Cyprus	38	30	20	31	27	24	32	
Czech Rep.				1	2	2	3	2
Denmark[+]	225	820	232	203	151	218	240	424
Finland	2 182	833	450	270	165	125	171	112
France[+]	2 118	1 901	1 529	1 318	1 330	1 351	1 671	
Germany								
Greece	726	453	480	161	824	596	215	110
Hungary[+]				3	4	5	4	7
Iceland	14	13	1	7	4	2	11	16
Ireland[b, c]	130	116	49	54	38	46	28	34
Israel[c]	84	131	117	77	114	73	75	
Italy	2 238	1 341	1 094	791	903	1 054	861	545
Luxembourg		0	1	0	0	0		
Moldova, Rep. of[+]			0	0	701	1	0	0
Netherlands	22	45	29	28	23	12	17	14
Norway[b]	35	11	15	4	16	12	20	11
Poland						7 443	429	42
Portugal[a, +]	269	476	271	262	409	230	300	
Romania[a]					9	30	33	27
Russian Fed.[b]			260	1 755	6 273	264	514	8 856
Slovakia				21	5	1	1	0
Spain	2 103	1 092	1 312	1 645	1 360	1 209	908	883
Sweden[+]	212	160	126	23	20	33		
Switzerland[b]	5	3	2	1	3	0	8	2
Turkey			458	398	98	49	36	120
Ukraine			260	239	2 239	462		
United Kingdom							205	235

[a] Strikes only. [b] Excl. workstoppages lasting less than one day. [c] Excl. workstoppages in which less than 10 workdays not worked. [+] Refer to Technical Notes.

Table 4.2. Workers involved in strikes and lockouts (thousands)

	1980	1985	1990	1991	1992	1993	1994	1995
Africa								
Algeria								
Botswana[a, b]							1	2
Burundi	0	0						
Central African Rep.								
Egypt[b]	0	3	2	1	0	1	5	
Ghana	70	3	7	6				
Guinea			45	4	1			
Kenya		17						
Malawi	1	1						
Mali	0	0						
Mauritius[b]	7	15	2	0	2	0	1	0
Morocco[a]	67	40	21	41	31	46		
Namibia[a, b]			6	1	5	4		
Niger[a]		4	1	2				
Nigeria[b]	142	19	276	270	262	1113	1998	
Senegal[a]			4	4	4			
South Africa[b]		240	341	172	138	159		
Tunisia[b]		96	133	49	48	44	40	
Zambia	28	24	52	32	26			
Zimbabwe	91							
Americas								
Bahamas			0	0	0			
Barbados	2	1	1	1	5	0	0	0
Bolivia								
Brazil[a, b]	81	5431	14243	16805	3497		3806	
Canada[b, +]	441	162	270	253	150	102	81	124
Chile[a, b]	30	9	25	46	25	25		
Colombia[+]		10	42	18	24	10		
Costa Rica	25	11	26	4	42	43	11	74
Ecuador	16	9	24	10	8	3	2	
El Salvador[+]	12	30	4	4	127	105	4	58
Guatemala								
Guyana[b]	41	94	61	98	69	53	74	38
Haiti	4	3						
Honduras	34	1	46	64				
Jamaica			10					
Mexico[a]	43	57	49	65	91	32	27	12
Nicaragua[a]			2	29	21			
Panama[b]	18	7	0	0	0	0	1	1
Peru[+]	481	238	258	181	115	41	63	28
Suriname	3	4	1	1	2	3		
Trinidad and Tobago	8	7	4	3	6	12	2	6
United States[c, +]	795	324	185	392	364	182	322	192
Venezuela	68							
Asia								
Australia	1173	571	730	1182	872	490	265	344
Bangladesh	164	198	15	0	6	6	6	
Fiji[b]	3	6	3	1	2	3	0	

Table 4.2. Workers involved in strikes and lockouts (thousands) *(cont.)*

	1980	1985	1990	1991	1992	1993	1994	1995
Hong Kong (before 1.7.97)[b,+]	5	0	1	0	2	1	0	1
India[+]	1900	1079	1308	1342	1253	954	763	
Indonesia	22	21	31	65	228			
Japan[b,+]	563	123	84	53	109	64	49	
Korea, Rep. of[b]	49	29	134	175	105	109	104	50
Malaysia[a]	5	9	99	4	6	2	2	2
Myanmar			0	0	0	0	0	0
New Zealand	128	182	44	51	23	20	15	31
Pakistan	25	36	62	116	73		15	11
Papua New Guinea	11		6	1	2	2		
Philippines[b,c]	21	111	68	55	48	35	49	54
Singapore	0	0	0	0	0	0	0	0
Sri Lanka[b,+]	79	55	66	64	50	8	72	63
Thailand	3	1	4	10	4	5	4	

Europe								
Austria[b]	24	36	5	93	18	7	0	0
Azerbaijan			341					
Belarus			11	63	2	0	3	0
Belgium[b,+]			10	11	22	9	6	13
Cyprus	50	8	8	5	50	17	15	
Czech Rep.				5	20	3	67	2
Denmark[+]	62	581	37	38	33	59	37	124
Finland	407	170	207	128	103	23	71	127
France[+]	501	23	19	19	16	20		
Germany[b]	*8451	*781	*257	*208	*598	133	401	183
Greece	1408	786	1304	477	243	182	74	52
Hungary[+]				24	1	3	32	172
Iceland[b]	4	6	0	1	1	0	7	10
Ireland	31	169	10	18	13	13	5	32
Israel	91	474	571	39	212	462	106	
Italy	13825	4843	1634	2952	3178	4384	2614	445
Luxembourg		0	1	0	0	0		
Moldova, Rep. of[b]			0	0	26	0	0	0
Netherlands	26	23	25	42	52	21	22	55
Norway[b,c]	19	7	61	0	39	7	15	10
Poland			116	221	753	383	211	18
Portugal[a,b]	290	199	129	119	132	83	94	
Romania[a]					4	23	69	38
Russian Fed.[c]			100	238	358	120	155	489
Slovakia				21	1	0	0	0
Spain[+]	2287	1511	977	1984	5192	1077	5437	574
Sweden	747	125	73	3	18	29	22	125
Switzerland[c]	4	0	1	0	0	0	7	0
Turkey			166	165	62	7	5	180
Ukraine			131	176	182	260		192
United Kingdom[+]	834	791	298	176	148	385	107	174

*Refers to Former Fed. Rep. of Germany. [a] Strikes only. [b] Exc. workers indirectly involved [c] Exc. work stoppages lasting less than one day. [+] Refer to Technical Notes.

Table 4.3. Workdays not worked as a result of strikes and lockouts (thousands)

	1980	1985	1990	1991	1992	1993	1994	1995
Africa								
Algeria								
Botswana[a]								3
Burundi	0	0						
Central African Rep.								
Egypt	0	6	2	1	0		23	4
Ghana	197	8	7	10				
Guinea			90	8	1			
Kenya		29						
Malawi	1	0						
Mali[+]	7	0						
Mauritius	13	12	3	0	6	0	1	2
Morocco[a]	575	224	323	382	286	487		
Namibia[a]			471	18	2 592	401		
Niger[a]			0	0				
Nigeria	1 354	318	1 374	2 589	1 185	12 908	233 453	
Senegal								
South Africa		678	2 793	1 339	1 727	783		
Tunisia		125	88	50	66	60	94	
Zambia	80	66	219	258	111			
Zimbabwe	233							
Americas								
Bahamas			0	0	0			
Barbados[+]	14	5	2	1		0	0	0
Bolivia								
Brazil[a]	81	49 575	17	7	2 260		2	
Canada[+]	8 975	3 126	5 079	2 516	2 110	1 517	1 607	1 569
Chile[a]	428	132	245	731	330	312		
Colombia								
Costa Rica	427	44	159	98	5 776	3 394	159	2 531
Ecuador	508	267	428	307	320	114	74	
El Salvador[+]	44	351	154	815	1 051	463	140	396
Guatemala								
Guyana	68		244	111	127	129	90	81
Haiti	22	2 094						
Honduras								
Jamaica			31					
Mexico [a, +]	43	334	1 599	1 620	1 602	1 843	1 370	1 304
Nicaragua[a]			2	710	185			
Panama[+]	159	20	0	0	0	0	5	4
Peru[+]	2 240	1 529	1 883	1 110	290	271	242	131
Suriname	15	19	6	2	4	23		
Trinidad and Tobago	118	77	10	16	69	29	11	209
United States[b]	20 844	7 079	5 926	4 584	3 989	3 981	5 022	5 771
Venezuela[+]	315							
Asia								
Australia[+]	3 320	1 256	1 377	1 611	941	636	502	548
Bangladesh	1 160	285	28	30	20	16	3	
Fiji								21

Table 4.3. Workdays not worked as a result of strikes and lockouts (thousands) *(cont.)*

	1980	1985	1990	1991	1992	1993	1994	1995
Hong Kong (before 1.7.97)[+]	21	1	4	0	3	16	0	1
India[+]	21925	29239	24086	26428	31259	20301	15569	
Indonesia[+]	34	557	317	535	2364			
Japan[+]	1001	264	145	96	231	116	85	
Korea, Rep. of	61	64	4487	3258	1528	1308	1484	393
Malaysia[a]	25	36	302	23	16	7	6	5
Myanmar			0	0	0	0	0	0
New Zealand[+]	373	756	331	101	114	24	38	53
Pakistan	55	159	187	583	398		341	64
Papua New Guinea	21		26	1	7	5		
Philippines[b]	105	2458	1345	1140	724	710	568	584
Singapore	0	0	0	0	0	0	0	0
Sri Lanka[+]	335	170	194	109	271	21	179	294
Thailand	5	13	72	236	155	214	43	

Europe								
Austria[+]	17	23	9	58	23	13	0	0
Azerbaijan			1075					
Belarus			29	280	89	1	6	0
Belgium[+]			103	67	199	55	71	100
Cyprus	102	17	32	10	60	24	29	
Czech Rep.				2	19	0	3	2
Denmark[+]			98	70	63	114	75	197
Finland			935	458	76	17	526	869
France[+]	1523	727	528	497	359	511	521	
Germany[+]	*128	*355	*364	*154	*1545	593	229	247
Greece[+]	2907	1094	23441	5840	2830	1602	666	450
Hungary[+]				9	4	5	29	259
Iceland	31	91	0	3	0	0	97	217
Ireland[b, c]	412	418	223	86	191	61	26	130
Israel[c]	217	540	1071	98	387	1637	793	
Italy[+]	16457	3831	5181	2985	2737	3411	3374	909
Luxembourg		0	0	0	0	0		
Moldova, Rep. of			0	0	154	0	0	0
Netherlands	57	89	207	96	85	45	47	691
Norway[b]	104	66	139	3	365	34	97	51
Poland			159	518	2360	580	562	56
Portugal[+]	533	275	147	124	190	80	97	
Romania[a]					17	90	361	212
Russian Fed.[b]			208	2314	1893	237	755	1367
Slovakia				167	14	0	18	0
Spain[+]	6178	3224	2613	4537	6333	2141	6277	1457
Sweden[+]	4479	504	770	22	28	190	52	627
Switzerland[b]	6	1	4	0	1	0	14	0
Turkey			3467	3809	1154	575	243	4838
Ukraine			126	1873	866	2677		
United Kingdom[+]	11964	6402	1903	761	528	649	278	415

* Refers to Former Fed. Rep. of Germany. [a] Strikes only. [b] Exc. work stoppages lasting less than one day. [c] Exc. work stoppages in which less than 10 workdays not worked. [+] Refer to Technical Notes.

Table 5. Ratification of ILO Conventions on freedom of association and industrial relations (as of 1 June 1997)

	Freedom of Association					
	Right to Organize (No. 87)	Collective Bargaining (No. 98)	Collective Bargaining (No. 154)	Workers' Representatives (No. 135)	Rural Workers (No. 141)	Public Service (No. 151)
Africa						
Algeria	x	x				
Angola		x				
Benin	x	x				
Burkina Faso	x	x		x		
Burundi	x					
Cameroon	x	x		x		
Cape Verde		x				
Central African Rep.	x	x				
Chad	x	x				
Comoros	x	x				
Congo	x					
Congo, Dem. Rep. of		x				
Côte d'Ivoire	x	x		x		
Djibouti	x	x				
Egypt	x	x		x		
Ethiopia	x	x				
Gabon	x	x	x	x		
Ghana	x	x				x
Guinea	x	x		x		x
Guinea-Bissau		x				
Kenya		x		x	x	
Lesotho	x	x				
Liberia	x	x				
Libyan Arab Jamahiriya		x				
Madagascar	x					
Malawi		x				
Mali	x	x		x	x	x
Mauritania	x					
Mauritius		x				
Morocco		x				
Mozambique	x	x				
Namibia	x	x				
Niger	x	x	x	x		
Nigeria	x	x				
Rwanda	x	x		x		
Sao Tome and Principe	x	x				
Senegal	x	x		x		
Seychelles	x					
Sierra Leone	x	x				
South Africa	x	x				
Sudan		x				
Swaziland	x	x				
Tanzania, United Rep. of		x		x		
Togo	x	x				
Tunisia	x	x				
Uganda		x	x			
Zambia	x	x	x	x	x	x
Americas						
Antigua and Barbuda	x	x				
Argentina	x	x	x			x
Bahamas		x				
Barbados	x	x		x		
Belize	x	x				

Table 5.   Ratification of ILO Conventions on freedom of association and industrial relations (as of 1 June 1997) *(cont.)*

	Freedom of Association					
	Right to Organize (No. 87)	Collective Bargaining (No. 98)	Collective Bargaining (No. 154)	Workers' Representatives (No. 135)	Rural Workers (No. 141)	Public Service (No. 151)
Bolivia	x	x				
Brazil		x	x	x	x	
Canada	x					
Colombia	x	x				
Costa Rica	x	x		x	x	
Cuba	x	x		x	x	x
Dominica	x	x				
Dominican Rep.	x	x				
Ecuador	x	x			x	
El Salvador					x	
Grenada	x	x				
Guatemala	x	x	x		x	
Guyana	x	x		x	x	x
Haiti	x	x				
Honduras	x	x				
Jamaica	x	x				
Mexico	x			x	x	
Nicaragua	x	x		x	x	
Panama	x	x				
Paraguay	x	x				
Peru	x	x				x
Saint Lucia	x	x				
Suriname	x	x	x	x		x
Trinidad and Tobago	x	x				
Uruguay	x	x	x		x	x
Venezuela	x	x			x	
Asia						
Afghanistan					x	
Australia	x	x		x		
Bangladesh	x	x				
Fiji		x				
India					x	
Indonesia		x				
Iraq		x		x		
Japan	x	x				
Jordan		x		x		
Kuwait	x					
Lebanon		x				
Malaysia		x				
Mongolia	x	x		x		
Myanmar	x					
Nepal		x				
Pakistan	x	x				
Papua New Guinea		x				
Philippines	x	x			x	
Singapore		x				
Sri Lanka	x	x		x		
Syrian Arab Rep.	x	x		x		
Yemen	x	x		x		
Europe						
Albania	x	x				
Armenia				x		x
Austria	x	x		x	x	

Table 5.   Ratification of ILO Conventions on freedom of association and industrial relations (as of 1 June 1997) *(cont.)*

	Freedom of Association					
	Right to Organize (No. 87)	Collective Bargaining (No. 98)	Collective Bargaining (No. 154)	Workers' Representatives (No. 135)	Rural Workers (No. 141)	Public Service (No. 151)
Azerbaijan	x	x	x	x		x
Belarus	x	x				
Belgium	x	x	x			x
Bosnia and Herzegovina	x	x		x		
Bulgaria	x	x				
Croatia	x	x		x		
Cyprus	x	x	x	x	x	x
Czech Rep.	x	x				
Denmark	x	x		x	x	x
Estonia	x	x		x		
Finland	x	x	x	x	x	x
France	x	x		x	x	
Georgia		x				
Germany	x	x		x	x	
Greece	x	x	x	x	x	x
Hungary	x	x	x	x	x	x
Iceland	x	x				
Ireland	x	x				
Israel	x	x			x	
Italy	x	x		x	x	x
Kyrgyzstan	x	x				
Latvia	x	x	x	x		x
Lithuania	x	x	x	x		
Luxembourg	x	x		x		
Macedonia, FYR of	x	x				
Malta	x	x		x	x	
Moldova, Rep. of	x	x	x	x		
Netherlands	x	x	x	x	x	x
Norway	x	x	x	x	x	x
Poland	x	x		x	x	x
Portugal	x	x		x		x
Romania	x	x	x	x		
Russian Fed.	x	x				
San Marino	x	x	x			x
Slovakia	x	x				
Slovenia	x	x		x		
Spain	x	x	x	x	x	x
Sweden	x	x	x	x	x	x
Switzerland	x		x		x	x
Tajikistan	x	x				
Turkey	x	x		x		x
Ukraine	x	x	x			
United Kingdom	x	x		x	x	x
Yugoslavia	x	x		x		

Includes only ILO member States which have ratified the Convention in question.

Socio-economic indicators

Table 6.   Gross domestic product (GDP), population and poverty

	GDP per capita		Population		Population in poverty (%)			
	(in 1987 US$) 1994	Annual growth (%) 1980-1994	Total (thousands) 1996	Annual growth (%) 1980-1996	Urban		Rural	
					1980	1990	1980	1990
Afrique								
Algeria	1894	−0.8	28784	2.7	20			25
Angola			11185	3.0				65
Benin	352	0.4	5563	3.0			65	39
Botswana			1484	3.1	40	15	55	38
Burkina Faso	232[a]	1.0[a]	10780	2.8				90
Burundi	160	−0.9	6221	2.6	55	5	78	80
Cameroon	634		13560	2.8	15	13	40	24
Cape Verde	564[a]	3.2[a]	396	2.0				88
Central African Rep.	314[a]	−1.7[a]	3344	2.3			91	
Chad	160[a]	1.7[a]		2.4	30	15	56	38
Comoros			632	3.2				50
Congo	998[a]	1.3[a]	2668	3.0				80
Congo, Dem. Rep. of			46812	3.5			80	48
Côte d'Ivoire	604	−3.6	14015	3.4	30		26	
Djibouti			617	5.0			51	70
Egypt	675	2.1	63271	2.3	26	29	19	21
Equatorial Guinea	360		410	4.0				47
Eritrea			3280	2.0				
Ethiopia	143		58243	3.0	60		65	
Gabon			1106	3.0			25	41
Gambia	214	−1.2	1141	3.7			40	31
Ghana			17832	3.2	59	18	37	25
Guinea	403		7518	3.3				70
Guinea-Bissau			1091	2.0				75
Kenya	322	0.2	27799	3.3	10	29	55	46
Lesotho	266	2.6	2078	2.7	50	11	55	44
Liberia			2245	1.1	23		23	
Libyan Arab Jamahiriya			5593	3.9				
Madagascar	191	−2.5	15353	3.3	50		50	
Malawi	104	−2.5	9845	3.0	25	8	85	85
Mali	234		11134	3.1	27	7	48	42
Mauritania	439	−0.5	2333	2.6				80
Mauritius	2020	4.8	1129	1.0	12		12	
Morocco			27021	2.1	28	14	45	17
Mozambique	109	−1.1	17796	2.4	40		70	
Namibia	1433	−0.7	1575	2.7				
Niger	266[a]	−3.7[a]	9465	3.4			35	28
Nigeria	350	−1.1	115020	3.0	33		40	
Rwanda	230[a]	−2.0[a]	5397	0.3	30		60	
Senegal			8532	2.7				70
Sierra Leone	128	−1.0	4297	1.8	65		66	45
Somalia			9822	2.4	42		70	50
South Africa	1887	−1.5	42393	2.4				
Sudan			27291	2.4			85	67
Swaziland	645	0.0	881	2.9	45	12	50	36

Table 6. Gross domestic product (GDP), population and poverty *(cont.)*

	GDP per capita		Population		Population in poverty (%)			
	(in 1987 US$) 1994	Annual growth (%) 1980-1994	Total (thousands) 1996	Annual growth (%) 1980-1996	Urban		Rural	
					1980	1990	1980	1990
Tanzania, United Rep. of	148	0.1	30 799	3.2	27	43	15	19
Togo	278	−2.8	4 201	3.0	42			30
Tunisia	1 238	1.4	9 156	2.2	22	10	42	7
Uganda	495		20 256	2.8		16		24
Zambia	225	−3.1	8 275	2.3	26	45	80	87
Zimbabwe	525[a]	−0.4[a]	11 439	3.0				60
Americas								
Argentina			35 219	1.4	7	15	10	20
Bahamas			284	1.9				
Barbados	4 522[a]	−0.3[a]	261	0.3	23		23	
Belize	1 831[a]	2.1[a]	219	2.6				65
Bolivia			7 593	2.2		50	86	
Brazil	1 779	−0.3	161 087	1.8	15	43	47	63
Canada	13 534[a]	0.7[a]	29 680	1.2				
Chile	2 705		14 421	1.6	12	32	25	34
Colombia			36 444	2.0	36	38	45	68
Costa Rica	2 086[a]	1.7[a]	3 500	2.7	10	27	17	28
Cuba			11 018	0.8				35
Dominican Rep.	738		7 961	2.1	45		43	78
Ecuador	1 070[a]	−0.4[a]	11 699	2.4	40	24	65	
El Salvador			5 796	1.5		43	76	56
Guatemala	859		10 928	2.9	66	61	74	85
Guyana	451	−0.7	838	0.6				60
Haiti	222	−4.4	7 259	1.9	65		80	
Honduras	829	−0.5	5 816	3.1	14	71	55	84
Jamaica			2 491	1.0		4	51	18
Mexico	1 653[a]	−0.6[a]	92 718	2.0	36	37	54	55
Nicaragua			4 238	2.6		32	80	76
Panama	2 104[a]	0.1[a]	2 677	2.0	36	40	50	51
Paraguay	957	−0.3	4 957	2.9	19		50	
Peru			23 944	2.0	35	52	80	72
Suriname	2 823	−0.7	432	1.2				
Trinidad and Tobago	3 608	−3.9	1 297	1.1			40	
United States	18 345[a]	1.5[a]	269 444	1.0				
Uruguay			3 204	0.6	9	10	21	23
Venezuela	2 646[a]	−0.8[a]	22 311	2.5	15	31	26	53
Asia								
Afghanistan			20 883	1.7	18		36	60
Australia	12 087[a]	1.3[a]	18 057	1.4				
Bahrain			570	3.1				
Bangladesh	184		120 073	1.9	66	34	74	53
Bhutan			1 812	2.1				90
Brunei Darussalam			300	2.8				
Cambodia			10 273	2.9				
China	369		1 232 083	1.3	2	0	24	12
Fiji	1 799[a]	0.7[a]	797	1.4			30	20
Hong Kong (before 1.7.97)	10 818[a]	5.1[a]	6 191	1.3				

Table 6. Gross domestic product (GDP), population and poverty *(cont.)*

	GDP per capita		Population		Population in poverty (%)			
	(in 1987 US$) 1994	Annual growth (%) 1980-1994	Total (thousands) 1996	Annual growth (%) 1980-1996	Urban		Rural	
					1980	1990	1980	1990
India	358	3.0	944 580	2.0	40	4	51	48
Indonesia			200 453	1.8	26	17	44	14
Iran, Islamic Rep. of	2415	−1.3	69 975	3.7	13		38	30
Iraq			20 607	2.9			40	30
Japan	21 890a	2.9a	125 351	0.4				
Jordan	1 294		5 581	4.1	14		17	
Korea, Dem. People's Rep. of			22 466	1.5				20
Korea, Rep. of			45 314	1.1	10		9	
Kuwait			1 687	1.3				
Lao People's Dem. Rep.			5 035	2.9				85
Lebanon			3 084	0.9				15
Malaysia			20 581	2.5	13	7	37	19
Maldives			263	3.2				40
Mongolia	1 167		2 515	2.6				
Myanmar			45 922	1.9	40		40	
Nepal	188		22 021	2.6	55		61	
New Zealand	981a	0.6a	3 602	0.9				
Oman			2 302	4.5				6
Pakistan	335	2.8	139 973	3.1	23		30	
Papua New Guinea			4 400	2.2	10		75	
Philippines	568	−0.6	69 282	2.3	45	37	59	52
Qatar			558	5.7				
Samoa		5.7	166	0.4				
Saudi Arabia			18 836	4.3				
Singapore	11 876	6.2	3 384	2.1				
Solomon Islands			391	3.5				60
Sri Lanka	455	3.0	18 100	1.3	18	12	23	32
Syrian Arab Rep.			14 574	3.3			54	
Thailand			58 703	1.4	22	15	33	34
Turkmenistan			4 155	2.4				
United Arab Emirates	17 862a	−4.0a	2 260	5.1				
Vanuatu			174	2.5				
Viet Nam			75 181	2.1				60
Yemen			15 678	4.1				30b
Europe								
Albania			3 401	1.5				
Armenia			3 638	1.0				
Austria	15 301a	1.7a	8 106	0.4				
Azerbaijan			7 594	1.3				
Belarus			10 348	0.4				
Belgium	14 321a	1.3a	10 159	0.2				
Bosnia and Herzegovina			3 628	−0.5				
Bulgaria	1 952	−1.2	8 468	−0.3				
Croatia			4 501	0.2				
Cyprus			756	1.3	2		9	
Czech Rep.			10 251	0.0				
Denmark	18 414a	2.0a	5 237	0.1				
Estonia			1 471	0.0				

Table 6. Gross domestic product (GDP), population and poverty *(cont.)*

	GDP per capita		Population		Population in poverty (%)			
	(in 1987 US$) 1994	Annual growth (%) 1980-1994	Total (thousands) 1996	Annual growth (%) 1980-1996	Urban		Rural	
					1980	1990	1980	1990
Finland	15 068[a]	0.8[a]	5 126	0.4				
France	15 316[a]	1.4[a]	58 333	0.5				
Georgia	367		5 442	0.4				
Germany	15 883[a]	2.5[a]	81 922	0.3				
Greece	3 567[a]	0.2[a]	10 490	0.5	15		34	
Hungary			10 049	−0.4				
Iceland	17 237[a]	1.2[a]	271	1.1				
Ireland	10 993[a]	3.4[a]	3 554	0.3				
Israel			5 664	2.4				
Italy	13 262[a]	1.3[a]	57 226	0.1				
Kazakstan	858		16 820	0.8				
Kyrgyzstan			4 469	1.3				
Latvia			2 504	−0.1				
Lithuania			3 728	0.5				
Luxembourg	17 834[a]	2.0[a]	412	0.8				
Macedonia, FYR of			2 174	1.2				
Malta			369	0.8				5
Moldova, Rep. of			4 444	0.6				
Netherlands	14 889[a]	1.2[a]	15 575	0.6				
Norway	19 316	2.3[a]	4 348	0.4				
Poland			38 601	0.5				
Portugal	4 418[a]	1.9[a]	9 808	0.0				
Romania			22 655	0.1				
Russian Fed.	1 966[a]	−1.8[a]	148 126	0.4				
Slovakia	2 225		5 347	0.5				
Slovenia			1 924	0.3				
Spain	7 979[a]	1.8[a]	39 674	0.3				
Sweden	16 834[a]	0.8[a]	8 819	0.4				
Switzerland	24 981[a]	0.7[a]	7 224	0.8				
Tajikistan			5 935	2.6				
Turkey	1 607[a]	2.0	61 797	2.1				14
Ukraine			51 608	0.2				
United Kingdom	11 054[a]	1.8[a]	58 144	0.2				
Uzbekistan			23 209	2.4				
Yugoslavia			10 294	0.5				

[a] Refer to 1993, or 1980-93 period. [b] Refer to the former Yemen Arab Republic.

Table 7. Labour force structure and trends

	Labour force		Labour force participation rate (%)					
	Total (thousands)	Annual growth (%)	Total		Male		Female	
	1996	1980-1996	1980	1996	1980	1996	1980	1996
Africa								
Algeria	9061	4.0	26.0	33.7	41.1	46.5	11.1	16.0
Angola	5144	2.5	49.4	45.9	53.3	49.8	45.7	42.0
Benin	2490	2.6	47.9	45.1	51.4	47.0	44.5	42.4
Botswana	654	3.2	43.6	44.4	45.5	48.7	41.8	39.6
Burkina Faso	5419	2.3	54.6	49.3	57.7	53.8	51.6	46.7
Burundi	3337	2.4	54.9	54.5	56.9	55.9	53.1	51.1
Cameroon	5500	2.6	41.8	40.7	53.6	50.9	30.4	30.3
Cape Verde	157	3.2	32.5	41.2	46.4	51.3	20.6	29.1
Central African Rep.	1623	1.8	52.5	48.3	56.6	53.3	48.8	44.0
Chad	3145	2.3	49.9	48.4	57.4	54.3	42.6	42.3
Comoros	286	3.2	45.4	45.7	51.1	51.4	39.6	38.9
Congo	1105	2.9	42.1	41.3	49.8	47.9	34.9	35.1
Congo, Dem. Rep. of	19622	2.3	44.5	41.2	50.4	48.0	38.8	36.2
Cote d'Ivoire	5526	3.3	40.0	40.0	53.1	52.1	26.4	26.5
Egypt	23203	2.6	35.0	38.1	50.7	51.2	18.9	21.7
Equatorial Guinea	171	3.6	44.5	41.6	58.5	54.7	31.0	29.1
Eritrea	1649	1.9	51.1	50.1	54.2	53.0	48.1	47.0
Ethiopia	25392	2.8	44.9	42.9	52.4	51.2	37.5	35.7
Gabon	519	2.3	52.4	45.5	58.7	52.7	46.3	41.0
Gambia	579	3.6	51.5	50.5	57.6	56.8	45.5	45.2
Ghana	8393	3.1	47.4	47.5	46.8	46.7	47.9	47.3
Guinea	3565	2.8	51.4	47.4	54.4	50.2	48.4	45.5
Guinea-Bissau	514	1.6	50.1	46.9	61.3	57.1	39.3	37.4
Kenya	13953	3.7	47.1	51.6	50.8	54.1	43.3	46.3
Lesotho	847	2.5	41.9	41.2	53.7	52.2	30.8	29.5
Liberia	977	1.3	42.1	40.4	51.5	50.0	32.6	33.1
Libyan Arab Jamahiriya	1601	3.4	31.0	28.6	47.7	43.2	12.2	12.7
Madagascar	7199	3.1	48.7	47.2	54.0	51.9	43.6	41.8
Malawi	4807	2.8	50.3	48.1	51.4	50.0	49.3	46.8
Mali	5472	2.8	51.5	48.8	56.2	53.5	47.0	44.8
Mauritania	1072	2.3	48.1	46.2	53.5	52.0	42.8	39.9
Mauritius	478	2.1	35.5	43.2	53.5	57.8	18.0	26.8
Morocco	10488	2.6	36.0	40.0	47.7	50.7	24.1	26.9
Mozambique	9221	2.0	55.3	51.8	57.3	54.4	53.3	49.7
Namibia	650	2.4	43.3	41.2	52.7	49.3	34.3	33.5
Niger	4497	3.0	49.9	47.0	56.2	53.5	43.8	41.5
Nigeria	45565	2.7	41.5	39.6	53.6	51.0	29.7	28.3
Rwanda	3021	0.8	51.1	54.2	52.7	55.1	49.6	51.4
Senegal	3815	2.6	45.9	44.7	53.1	51.2	38.7	38.0
Sierra Leone	1610	1.6	38.6	37.2	50.8	48.3	26.9	26.5
Somalia	4291	2.1	45.8	42.8	52.4	49.6	39.3	37.2
South Africa	16635	2.7	37.5	39.7	48.9	49.3	26.2	29.2
Sudan	10652	1.5	36.6	39.9	53.4	55.5	19.7	22.4
Swaziland	315	0.8	35.7	36.7	48.2	46.8	23.7	25.8
Tanzania, United Rep. of	15793	2.2	51.2	51.4	52.2	52.6	50.2	50.1
Togo	1739	1.6	43.6	41.4	53.7	50.1	33.8	32.8
Tunisia	3459	2.7	34.3	39.6	48.0	51.7	20.1	23.5

Table 7. Labour force structure and trends *(cont.)*

	Labour force		Labour force participation rate (%)					
	Total (thousands)	Annual growth (%)	Total		Male		Female	
	1996	1980-1996	1980	1996	1980	1996	1980	1996
Uganda	10084	−0.1	51.7	49.0	54.3	52.5	49.1	47.2
Zambia	3454	3.2	41.8	42.5	46.7	46.3	37.1	37.2
Zimbabwe	5281		44.9	46.2	50.4	51.8	39.5	40.7
Americas								
Argentina	13809	1.6	38.0	40.5	55.8	54.8	20.7	24.2
Bahamas	150	3.3	42.5	54.6	48.4	57.3	36.7	48.5
Barbados	136	1.2	44.9	53.4	53.3	57.6	37.2	46.9
Belize	73	3.3	29.8	34.3	46.7	50.4	12.7	15.4
Bolivia	3057	2.6	37.6	40.7	50.9	50.7	24.7	29.9
Brazil	73733	2.8	39.2	46.8	56.2	59.9	22.2	32.0
Canada	15796	1.6	49.6	53.8	60.1	59.0	39.1	47.6
Chile	5740	2.6	34.3	40.8	51.3	54.6	17.8	25.4
Colombia	15366	3.5	33.2	43.6	49.2	53.0	17.3	31.6
Costa Rica	1369	3.5	34.7	40.0	54.5	54.2	14.6	23.7
Cuba	5323	2.3	38.4	49.6	52.1	59.5	24.4	37.1
Dominican Rep.	3379	3.0	36.9	44.0	54.7	59.0	18.5	25.4
Ecuador	4390	3.5	32.0	39.1	50.8	54.7	12.9	20.2
El Salvador	2383	2.8	33.9	43.3	50.4	54.8	17.8	28.0
Guatemala	3923	3.2	34.3	36.9	52.6	52.0	15.5	19.4
Guyana	353	2.2	32.9	43.7	49.8	57.0	16.4	27.6
Haiti	3209	1.5	47.3	43.9	53.5	51.3	41.4	37.3
Honduras	2105	3.6	33.5	37.6	49.9	50.0	17.0	22.1
Jamaica	1281	1.8	44.8	52.5	48.8	55.2	41.0	47.6
Mexico	36683	3.2	32.6	41.2	47.7	54.3	17.6	25.1
Nicaragua	1642	3.5	34.1	40.5	49.4	51.0	18.7	26.5
Panama	1095	3.0	35.0	42.2	48.2	53.2	21.2	28.3
Paraguay	1831	3.0	36.9	37.8	53.8	51.8	19.7	21.7
Peru	8652	3.0	31.3	37.8	47.3	50.9	15.0	21.5
Suriname	157	2.9	29.0	38.1	42.7	49.4	15.5	23.3
Trinidad and Tobago	549	2.8	39.1	44.7	53.5	53.5	24.7	29.7
United States	136884	1.4	48.5	51.4	58.2	56.4	39.1	45.4
Uruguay	1444	2.5	39.6	45.9	55.8	54.8	24.0	35.9
Venezuela	8785	2.5	34.2	40.9	49.5	52.0	18.5	26.6
Asia								
Afghanistan	8851	1.6	42.8	42.0	54.4	53.8	30.5	30.5
Australia	9144	2.0	45.9	51.0	58.1	58.0	33.7	43.3
Bahrain	253	3.9	39.4	45.1	60.3	62.6	10.3	20.3
Bangladesh	60374	2.4	47.1	52.8	52.7	56.6	41.2	43.5
Bhutan	888	1.8	51.5	48.0	61.9	58.4	40.9	38.9
Brunei Darussalam	131	4.0	36.0	44.8	51.8	54.7	18.0	31.5
Cambodia	5322	2.6	54.0	52.4	52.1	51.4	55.7	52.3
China	736325	1.9	54.9	59.9	60.6	63.7	48.9	55.6
Fiji	303	2.5	32.1	40.6	52.4	53.9	11.2	21.7
Hong Kong (before 1.7.97)	3210	1.6	49.2	52.9	62.2	63.6	35.2	39.6
India	411020	2.0	43.6	44.4	55.8	57.4	30.5	28.6
Indonesia	93618	2.9	39.5	48.4	51.5	56.2	27.7	37.2
Iran, Islamic Rep. of	21015	3.7	30.0	30.9	47.0	44.4	12.4	15.2

Table 7. Labour force structure and trends *(cont.)*

	Labour force		Labour force participation rate (%)					
	Total (thousands)	Annual growth (%)	Total		Male		Female	
	1996	1980-1996	1980	1996	1980	1996	1980	1996
Iraq	5 573	2.9	27.1	27.7	44.1	43.2	9.6	10.1
Japan	67 044	1.0	49.0	53.8	61.9	64.4	36.6	43.0
Jordan	1 595	5.3	23.8	29.8	39.2	43.6	7.2	13.0
Korea, Dem. People's Rep. of	11 881	2.7	43.6	52.4	48.3	59.7	38.9	46.1
Korea, Rep. of	22 399	2.3	40.8	51.1	49.5	58.3	31.9	40.4
Kuwait	656	1.7	36.2	40.5	55.0	49.9	11.1	24.3
Lao People's Dem. Rep.	2 432	2.4	51.6	47.6	56.1	51.8	47.1	44.8
Lebanon	1 031	2.0	28.3	35.1	44.5	49.3	12.6	18.7
Malaysia	8 277	2.8	38.5	41.3	50.7	50.2	26.1	30.1
Maldives	107	2.3	47.1	40.4	55.5	45.7	37.7	35.6
Mongolia	1 222	2.9	46.4	50.1	50.3	51.6	42.5	45.5
Myanmar	24 139	2.2	50.7	53.1	57.0	59.6	44.3	45.5
Nepal	10 179	2.3	48.5	46.4	57.9	54.4	38.5	37.8
New Zealand	1 780	1.9	42.5	50.1	56.1	55.8	29.1	43.2
Oman	623	3.9	29.8	26.5	51.9	43.3	4.1	8.4
Pakistan	51 292	3.4	35.4	37.5	52.2	51.8	16.9	20.3
Papua New Guinea	2 160	2.2	49.3	49.2	54.8	55.4	43.2	42.4
Philippines	28 611	2.6	39.0	42.2	50.6	51.4	27.4	31.1
Qatar	308	7.0	45.6	54.4	67.1	72.2	8.1	21.7
Samoa								
Saudi Arabia	6 187	5.0	29.5	32.9	50.5	50.6	4.9	10.1
Singapore	1 706	2.7	46.3	49.7	59.3	61.2	32.7	39.6
Solomon Islands	202	3.5	51.0	51.4	51.8	53.4	50.2	49.6
Sri Lanka	7 652	2.8	36.8	43.9	52.8	54.6	20.2	30.1
Syrian Arab Rep.	4 396	3.7	28.4	31.9	42.7	44.1	13.6	15.8
Thailand	34 916	2.7	52.2	60.6	54.8	63.8	49.5	55.2
Turkmenistan	1 750	2.5	41.4	43.4	44.6	46.5	38.2	37.9
United Arab Emirates	1 126	0.5	53.8	49.4	73.9	67.5	8.8	18.7
Viet Nam	38 291	4.6	47.7	51.5	51.1	52.5	44.5	49.4
Yemen	4 945	0.6	29.1	31.5	41.2	45.4	18.1	17.7
Europe								
Albania	1 672	2.1	45.1	49.9	53.5	56.6	36.1	41.1
Armenia	1 768	1.3	46.8	50.3	50.0	51.8	43.8	45.5
Austria	3 776	0.7	45.0	46.8	56.7	56.8	34.5	36.9
Azerbaijan	3 283	1.2	44.1	44.7	47.5	49.5	40.8	37.3
Belarus	5 351	0.3	52.8	52.6	57.0	56.5	49.2	47.6
Belgium	4 198	0.4	40.1	41.6	54.2	50.4	26.6	32.7
Bosnia and Herzegovina	1 719	0.7	39.3	46.8	53.6	57.8	25.4	34.7
Bulgaria	4 296	−0.4	51.8	50.9	56.9	53.7	46.8	47.8
Croatia	2 113	0.1	47.3	47.3	58.4	54.7	36.8	39.7
Cyprus	363	1.5	47.2	48.5	62.1	59.2	32.3	36.9
Czech Rep.	5 625	0.3	52.0	56.2	56.7	59.0	47.6	50.9
Denmark	2 935	0.5	53.1	55.1	60.3	60.9	46.1	51.4
Estonia	807	−0.1	55.4	55.6	59.1	59.4	52.2	50.7
Finland	2 603	0.5	50.5	50.4	55.9	54.5	45.4	47.4
France	26 046	0.6	44.2	45.4	54.2	51.0	34.7	38.7
Georgia	2 655	0.2	50.4	49.4	54.5	54.7	46.8	43.3
Germany	40 935	0.6	47.8	49.8	60.2	59.4	36.6	41.1

Table 7. Labour force structure and trends *(cont.)*

	Labour force		Labour force participation rate (%)					
	Total (thousands)	Annual growth (%)	Total		Male		Female	
	1996	1980-1996	1980	1996	1980	1996	1980	1996
Greece	4454	1.1	39.0	43.3	57.3	54.4	21.4	30.9
Hungary	4737	−0.5	47.8	47.9	56.0	54.7	40.1	40.2
Iceland	152	1.6	51.5	56.4	59.4	61.4	43.4	50.9
Ireland	1435	0.8	37.0	42.5	53.0	53.9	20.9	27.0
Israel	2365	3.1	37.4	43.4	49.6	50.6	25.2	33.4
Italy	25314	0.7	40.0	44.6	55.1	56.6	25.7	32.6
Kazakstan	8059	0.9	47.2	48.9	51.4	52.7	43.3	43.3
Kyrgyzstan	1885	1.2	42.7	43.2	46.1	45.7	39.4	38.6
Latvia	1363	−0.2	56.0	54.7	59.8	59.1	52.7	50.3
Lithuania	1919	0.4	52.6	51.9	56.2	56.7	49.5	46.8
Luxembourg	177	0.9	41.8	42.6	57.7	55.4	26.6	31.1
Macedonia, FYR of	997	1.6	42.8	46.8	54.1	53.8	31.3	37.9
Malta	138	1.0	36.4	38.1	58.8	55.8	15.1	19.8
Moldova, Rep. of	2181	0.2	52.3	50.3	55.0	52.9	49.9	45.6
Netherlands	7250	1.6	39.9	46.5	55.1	56.5	24.9	36.8
Norway	2238	0.9	47.5	52.0	57.0	56.3	38.2	46.8
Poland	19375	0.3	52.1	51.4	58.4	55.6	46.0	45.1
Portugal	4920	0.4	47.2	50.8	59.7	58.8	35.4	42.1
Romania	10673	−0.1	49.2	47.9	54.0	53.1	44.4	41.2
Russian Fed.	77367	0.1	54.7	53.4	60.0	57.4	50.1	47.8
Slovakia	2838	0.9	49.6	54.8	55.2	56.9	44.2	49.5
Slovenia	965	0.3	50.1	50.7	56.1	55.5	44.5	45.2
Spain	17049	1.2	37.3	44.2	54.6	55.8	20.8	30.6
Sweden	4769	2.4	50.6	54.1	57.4	57.0	44.0	51.3
Switzerland	3862	2.7	48.4	53.8	62.9	64.9	34.6	42.3
Tajikistan	2238	3.2	39.0	39.3	41.9	42.5	36.2	32.9
Turkey	28611	2.5	42.1	48.0	53.6	58.2	30.4	34.1
Ukraine	25814	4.6	52.8	50.7	57.5	55.5	48.8	45.3
United Kingdom	28967	1.3	47.8	50.1	60.0	57.6	36.3	42.4
Uzbekistan	9504	3.4	40.4	42.4	42.8	44.3	38.2	37.6
Yugoslavia	4858	3.1	46.2	47.9	57.2	54.6	35.4	39.8

Table 8. Employment and unemployment

	Total employment (thousands)	Unemployment as a percentage of the labour force	
	1995	1980	1995
Africa			
Algeria	4 465		
Egypt		5.2	
South Africa			4.5
Americas			
Argentina	4 157[a]	2.3	18.8
Barbados	110[b]		
Belize	63		
Bolivia	1 257[b, c]		3.6
Canada			9.5
Chile	5 026[b]	10.4	4.7
Costa Rica		5.9	5.2
El Salvador	1 973	12.9	7.7
Honduras	1 806[c]		3.2
Jamaica		27.3	
Mexico	33 881		4.7
Panama	868		13.7
Paraguay		4.1	
Peru	2 901[d]		7.1
Trinidad and Tobago	432	10.0	17.2
United States	124 900[b]	7.0	5.6
Uruguay	1 206[c]		10.2
Venezuela	7 670[b]	5.9	10.3
Asia			
Australia	8 235[b]	6.1	8.5
China		4.9	
Fidji			5.4
Hong Kong (before 1.7.97)	2 971[b]		3.2
Japan		2.0	3.2
Korea. Rep. of	20 377[b]		2.0
Malaysia	7 645[b]		2.8
New Zealand	1 633[b]		6.3
Pakistan		3.6	
Philippines	25 698[b]	4.8	8.4
Singapore	1 701		2.7
Sri Lanka	5 316		12.5
Thailand		0.8	
Europe			
Albania		5.6	
Belarus			2.7
Belgium			9.3
Bulgaria	3 311		11.1
Cyprus	285[b]		
Czech Rep.	5 102		2.9
Denmark	2 607		7.0
Finland		4.7	17.4

Table 8.   Employment and unemployment *(cont.)*

	Total employment (thousands)	Unemployment as a percentage of the labour force	
	1995	1980	1995
France	22296	6.4	11.6
Germany	36048		12.9
Greece	3824		10.0
Hungary	3679		10.3
Iceland	142[b]		4.9
Ireland	1268		12.2
Israel		4.8	6.9
Italy	19942	7.6	
Kyrgyzstan	1641		
Latvia	1189		6.6
Lithuania			7.3
Macedonia, FYR of			35.6
Moldova, Rep. of	1673[b]		1.0
Netherlands	6835		7.1
Norway	2079	1.7	4.9
Poland	14771		13.1
Portugal		7.8	
Romania	11152		8.0
Russian Fed.	67100		8.3
Slovakia	2147[b]		13.1
Slovenia	882		7.4
Spain	12041	11.4	22.9
Sweden	3986	2.0	7.7
Switzerland	3733[b]		3.3
Turkey	21378[b]		6.6
United Kingdom			8.5
Uzbekistan	8158		0.4

[a]Gran Buenos Aires. [b]Civilian labour force employed. [c]Urban areas. [d]Lima.

Industrial relations indicators

Tables 1.1., 1.2. & 1.3.   Trade union membership data and trade union density rates[1]

Sources

Various methods have been used to collect the data. An ILO questionnaire on union membership, union density and collective bargaining trends was sent to governments, employers and union representatives. Trade union profiles obtained through the ILO trade union network have been used as an additional source. For many countries in Africa, Latin America, and Central and Eastern Europe the data on trade union organization and employment were provided by the ILO Regional Offices. Furthermore, use has been made of data from special reports and research notes on Argentina, Brazil, India, Malaysia, Peru, Poland, the Russian Federation, South Africa and Uganda, prepared specifically for the Task Force. In total, the above ILO sources gave union membership data covering 64 countries. Absolute figures on union membership and employment are used in all cases in order to ensure that the density rates are calculated in the same way (see below).

A database established by J. Visser and published in OECD: *Employment Outlook* (Paris, 1991) provided data covering the 1980s for 24 member States of the Organisation of Economic Co-operation and Development. For the purpose of this report, the material has been updated to the mid-1990s, employing the same sources and methods as in the original report. An additional ten countries have been added on the basis of national sources, statistical yearbooks, government reports and published research, including case-studies on countries in Africa, Asia, Latin America and Central and Eastern Europe.

Data were available for 1994 or in respect of 1995 nearly all countries. For more than 70 countries a comparison with an earlier period (mainly the mid-1980s) is made.

In some cases, difficulties have been encountered with regard to the quality and comparability of the data. However, comparability over time is not a major cause for concern, except in a few cases (i.e. transitional economies). Comparability across countries, especially between countries in different regions, is more problematic.

Unions and union membership

In order to calculate union membership, two preliminary questions are addressed: What is a trade union? and: Who do we count as a union member? The Australian Bureau of Statistics suggests: *"an organization, consisting predominantly of employees, the principle activities of which include the negotiation of pay and conditions of employment for its members"*[2] as a definition of a trade union. The definition includes workers' organizations and professional associations, even when collective bargaining is not their main activity. This might be explained either by the fact that some groups have other

---

[1] These technical notes are drawn from J. Visser: *Global trends in unionization* (ILO, Geneva, 1997).

[2] J. Visser: "Trends in trade union membership", in *Employment Outlook* (OECD, Paris, 1991), p. 99.

means of promoting and defending the employment and income interests of their members, or because employers do not negotiate with them. The first condition most often applies to professional groups and it is not always clear whether a particular professional association should have been included under the above definition of a union. The widest coverage, in this particular sense, is found in Europe. In Northern Europe, professional groups such as artists, doctors, architects, lawyers or even football players form their own employee associations. These associations may, or may not, have negotiated collectively on behalf of their members. They do, however, express the employment and income interests of those members. Such organizations are included in our statistics in accordance with national practice. However, self-employed members are excluded.

Recognition as a collective bargaining agent by employers and governments is a common problem for many unions. In Western and Northern Europe bargaining coverage is usually much wider than union coverage, whereas in most other countries bargaining coverage is lower than union coverage (when union coverage is calculated as a proportion of all wage and salary earners in employment). Organizations which are not recognized by the employer are not excluded from our statistics on union representation. Only if a workers' organization has no intention of representing the employment interests of its members and is not even minimally involved in the expression of workers' grievances is its inclusion in the statistics seriously questioned.

An advantage of this rather comprehensive definition of a trade union is that it recognizes that a union's central purpose is the representation of the employment and wage interests of workers, but that it is neutral with regard to the methods applied or the organizational form adopted by a union. Methods and forms of collective action vary widely across countries and over time. General, industrial, craft, occupational, enterprise unions or professional employee associations whose activities involve collective bargaining, pressure on legislators or public authorities, strikes, working-to-rule, petitioning, demonstrations or legal action are all included in the database. Those employee associations "who are dependent on employers, who reject collective in favour of individual representation, do not seek a role in negotiations, or consist mainly of self-employed persons"[1] are excluded. Legally or voluntarily established works councils; "in house" and "company unions" which depend on the employer for their survival or finance; professional societies which mainly further the educational interests of their members; and unions of tenant farmers, shopkeepers or mainly self-employed persons are not included.

The application of these criteria requires careful consideration in each case. Where information is available on all trade unions in a particular country, for instance through a survey or register of associations, it is possible to decide which organization is or is not a trade union for the purposes of the above definition. If the data are based on reports or estimates, it is assumed that all affiliates satisfy the criteria of a trade union.

Compiling membership statistics

There are two main methods of compiling membership statistics. The first is to carry out a household, enterprise or labour force *survey*. This method has clear advantages for calculating detailed union density rates by sex, employment status, industrial branch, enterprise size, educational attainment, level of earnings or other characteristics. The survey method gives better results when it is clear to respondents what is meant by a union and membership, and if problems of statistical sampling are solved. Data based on household, population or labour force surveys are now available on a fairly continuous, annual or biennial basis for the United States (from 1973 onwards), Canada (from 1984), Australia (from 1976), South Africa (from 1985), Great Britain (from 1989), Sweden (from 1987) and the Netherlands (from 1992). In Japan (from 1980), an enterprise survey exists; and in Great Britain (from 1980), a survey of establishments with more than 25 employees is available. This is our only source for the United States; for the other countries there is additional information.

---

[1] J. Visser: "Trends in trade union membership", in *Employment Outlook* (OECD, Paris 1991), pp. 99.

The second method is a compilation of membership statistics from questionnaires completed by individual unions or trade union federations. In many countries this task is undertaken by an official registrar, a government office, a central statistical bureau, or one or more trade union federations. In some cases such data are compiled by independent researchers, either on the basis of unpublished registers, government surveys or even their own surveys. This kind of data offers advantages for a study of membership developments in relation to union type, membership concentration, inter-union competition, union politics and union ideology.

One of the main difficulties with the second method is statistical coverage or the identification of unions (i.e. not so much whether an organization should be considered as a "trade or labour union", but simply locating and identifying the existence of small, new unions). This constitutes a problem in the case of unaffiliated unions as well as in countries where there is no obligation for a union to register. Official registration is not always useful either because it is sometimes used, with denial of recognition, as a means to hinder the formation of newly emerging unions (examples are found in Indonesia, the Republic of Korea, and Thailand as well as in Latin America before democratization: see Brazil) or because unions fail to return their membership or financial files to the registrar (e.g. India).

Under-reporting of non-affiliated and non-registered trade unions constitutes a problem in many countries but in the absence of surveys, elections, and independent press reports it is difficult to estimate its size.[1] It relates less to making comparisons within countries over time than to those drawn between countries. In general, statistical coverage has increased – especially in western countries.

Many figures are based on self-reporting, i.e. membership claims made by the unions. These claims are checked with those of other unions, reports by researchers and experts who have greater insight into the industrial relations and union affairs in a particular country. Nevertheless, self-reporting of membership remains a starting-point for many of the estimates.

Self-reporting of membership reflects different administrative and political practices and may yield incomparable and unreliable results. Unions may have reasons to overstate or understate their membership figures in reports to the press, public agencies, political parties, employers or competitors. They may apply different norms regarding who is to be considered as a "member in good standing" and may be slow to remove those who have left or no longer pay their contributions. Unions may include people who no longer consider themselves as members. Comparison with survey data suggests that some overstatement in reported membership is general but, in most cases, small.

Union density and labour force statistics: three denominators

As a measurement of relative rather than absolute size, union density rates are better suited to making comparisons, especially across countries, than absolute membership figures. Union density expresses union membership as a proportion of the eligible workforce. Ideally, groups who are not legally permitted to join a union should be excluded from the calculation of union density statistics. In many countries, senior civil servants, the armed forces, police officers, security staff, teachers or domestic servants are not permitted to join a union. However, as Chang and Sorrentino (1991)[2] rightly observe, the eligibility to join a union shifts over time and across countries, and the strict application of such a criterion for calculating union density rates would make comparison across countries extremely difficult if not impossible.

Therefore, a common denominator is applied to permit comparison. Given the definition of a trade union, and the self-declared purpose and domain of most unions, this common denominator is

---

[1] Some of the main problems of statistical coverage, in this sense, are found in Cameroon, India, Indonesia, Mauritania, Namibia, Thailand and, in a minor sense, relating to small unaffiliated and mostly non-manual employee organizations or company staff unions, in Belgium and France.

[2] C. Chang and C. Sorrentino: "Union membership statistics in 12 countries", in *Monthly Labour Review* (Washington, Department of Labor), Dec. 1991, pp. 46-53.

defined as all people who earn their living on wages or salaries, including those who are employed in the public sector or work in government service. Normally, union density rates are standardized by calculating union membership as a proportion of the wage and salary earners in the same year (preferably on the basis of some annual average, or end-of-year data). Such data is directly comparable with household or labour force survey data. This method was used for calculating standardized annual union density rates between 1970 and 1989 for the OECD countries and is also one of the baselines in the ILO report. Although many unions, at least in Europe, retain membership of unemployed workers and those that have retired from the labour force (i.e. through reduced contribution rates or by offering special benefits), the calculation of standardized density rates requires their number to be subtracted from the "active membership". This is possible, mostly with the help of surveys, financial data or on the basis of estimates from some unions in most OECD countries and in a small number of other countries. Where possible, the union membership data in this report exclude self-employed, unemployed and retired workers. Their number varies from 46% in Italy, 36% in Belgium, 19% in Sweden, 18% in the Netherlands, Austria or the Czech Republic to 6% in France and 5% in Swaziland. Generally, the share of retired and unemployed workers is higher if the union is "older", if the union is organized in a declining sector (for example, manufacturing) and if the union is involved in the provision of benefits for such members. These conditions are more likely to apply in Europe (West and East) than, for instance, in Southeast Asia or Africa. Therefore, standardized or net rates have been calculated for European countries.

The major difficulty inherent in calculating union density rates on the basis of wage and salary earners in employment arises from the fact that, in many developing countries, the necessary employment data are missing. In many of these countries the line between employment, underemployment and unemployment, or between self-employment and employment for wages, is not easily drawn. In order to broaden the orbits of comparison, two more baselines for the calculation of union density rates are presented. One is connected to the concept of the non-agricultural labour force, the other to the formal wage sector.

The size of the non-agricultural labour force is estimated on the basis of ILO, OECD and World Bank data. The non-agricultural labour force is often regarded as the unions' main domain. As a rule, the number of union members in agriculture should be subtracted before union density rates are calculated. However, as it is rare for unions to organize any significant number of farm workers, this calculation has not been performed. Unionized farm workers are found only where there is a plantation system (i.e. in Malaysia)[1] or where unions have established a tradition of providing social security benefits. In the few countries where union density in agriculture is very high, for instance in the Scandinavian countries, the agricultural wage sector becomes so small (less than 5% of overall employment) that their number in the aggregate is ignored, without comparability being impaired.

The main advantage of using the non-agricultural labour force as the denominator for calculating union density rates is that data is available for almost all countries. The disadvantage is that many groups (such as the self-employed and unpaid family workers, especially in construction and in commercial, personal and household services) which do not belong to the target population of trade unions are also part of the non-agricultural labour force. The number of wage-earners is generally much smaller than the whole non-agricultural labour force – also because the latter includes the unemployed in industry and services.

Finally, in some countries – in particular Africa, South Asia and parts of Latin America – employment data are only available for the formal wage sector. Thus, this sector constitutes the third common denominator the calculation of union density rates. Following the ILO (PREALC) approach in Latin America and the 1972 ILO Kenya Employment Mission Report, the informal sector is estimated by an addition of numbers from such occupational and status categories as employers, the self-employed, unpaid family workers, farm workers and domestic workers; with an estimation of the

---

[1] W. Galenson: *Trade union growth and decline: An international study* (New York, Praeger, 1994).

number of people earning less than the minimum wage; of the size of employment in small firms, usually with less than ten workers; and of the number of workers employed on irregular contracts or working only a few hours a week. The estimates take account of the fact that many of these categories overlap.

Table 2.   Profile of national employers' organizations

This table provides an overview of national employers' organizations which are members of the International Organization of Employers (IOE).

Table 3.1.   Collective bargaining structure in selected countries

This table includes three indicators of collective bargaining structures: level of bargaining, dominant level, and trend in bargaining levels. National level and sectoral level bargaining are combined in the table to emphasize the importance of collective bargaining outside the enterprise.

Table 3.2.   Collective bargaining coverage rates in selected countries

The collective bargaining coverage rate shows the proportion of employees covered by collective agreements. The sources of the data differ and therefore caution is necessary when comparing data across countries. Collective bargaining coverage rates only concern the formal sector.

Tables 4.1., 4.2. & 4.3.   Number of strikes and lockouts, workers involved and workdays not worked

Generally speaking, strikes and lockouts are temporary work stoppages wilfully effected by one or more groups of workers and temporary closures of one or more places of employment by one or more employers with a view to enforcing or resisting a demand or expressing a grievance. However, national definitions of strikes and lockouts may differ from country to country depending on the source of the statistics. The data presented in these tables may come from several sources, including strike notices, newspaper reports and direct inquiries addressed to employers or to workers' organizations. The data cover strikes and lockouts together, as most countries do not distinguish between those two type of action in their statistics. Information on the differences in the scope, definition and methods used compiling the statistics presented in tables 4.1, 4.2 and 4.3 are given below (and indicated in the tables by the symbol +). Countries which do not have data are not included.

Africa

Mali   Workhours not worked.

Americas

Barbados   Computed on the basis of an eight-hour working day.
                                           1993, 1994: Excludes data not available for one strike in the hotel industry.
                                           1991: Excludes information for one strike lasting three days.

Canada	Strikes lasting at least half a day with more than ten days lost.
Colombia	Includes *"paros"* (public service and illegal stoppages).
El Salvador	1980: Jan.-Jun.
Mexico	Excludes enterprises covered by local jurisdiction.
Panama	Computed on the basis of an eight-hour working day. 1986: Excludes data concerning general strike, Conato.
Peru	From 1994: Strikes only; private sector. Before 1994: Computed on the basis of an eight-hour working day.
United States	Excludes work stoppages involving fewer than 1,000 workers.
Venezuela	Computed on the basis of an eight-hour working day.

Asia

Australia	New industrial classification. Excludes work stoppages in which fewer than ten workdays were not worked.
Hong Kong (before 1.7.97)	Excludes public sector. Includes stoppages involving fewer than ten workers or lasting less than one day if more than 100 workdays not worked.
India	Excludes political and sympathy strikes. Excludes work stoppages involving fewer than ten workers.
Indonesia	Computed on the basis of a seven-hour working day.
Japan	Excludes work stoppages lasting less than half a day.
New Zealand	Prior to 1988, excludes public sector stoppages. Computed on the basis of an eight-hour working day. Excludes work stoppages in which fewer than ten workdays were not worked.
Sri Lanka	Excludes work stoppages involving fewer than five workers. Includes work stoppages lasting less than one day if more than 50 workdays not worked.

Europe

Austria	Computed on the basis of an eight-hour working day.
Belgium	Excludes public sector.
Denmark	Excludes work stoppages in which fewer than 100 workdays were not worked.
France	Excludes agriculture and public administration. Localized strikes (i.e. the call to strike concerns only one establishment).
Germany	Excludes public administration. Includes work stoppages lasting less than one day if more than 100 workdays not worked.
Greece	Computed on the basis of an average number of workhours per day.
Hungary	Work stoppages in which at least 800 hours were not worked.
Italy	Computed on the basis of a seven-hour working day.
Moldova, Rep. of	One strike represents one establishment on strike.
Spain	Prior to 1990, strikes only; excludes the Basque country. 1980, 1985: Excludes Catalonia. Data from Catalonia and the Basque

country includes in total except where otherwise indicated. Data for Catalonia and the Basque country excludes from major divisions.
Table 4.1: Monthly average of workers involved in strikes in progress each month.

Sweden   From 1994: Work stoppages in which at least eight hours not worked.

United Kingdom   Excludes political strikes. Includes stoppages involving fewer than ten workers or lasting less than one day if more than 100 workdays not worked.

Table 5. *Ratification of ILO Conventions on freedom of association and industrial relations*

This table presents each country's record of ratification of ILO Conventions on freedom of association and industrial relations. These Conventions are international legal instruments that impose on ratifying States binding obligations, compliance with which is subjected to regular international supervision.

Socio-economic indicators

Table 6. *Gross domestic product (GDP), population and poverty*

The gross domestic product measures the total output of goods and services for final use produced by residents and non-residents, regardless of the allocation to domestic and foreign claims. The figures for 1994 are calculated according to the US dollar value in 1987.

The population data for the year 1996 and the annual growth of the population between 1980 and 1994 are United Nations estimates. The poverty rates are derived from a host of studies, mostly country studies that used a common methodology and similar poverty lines. They are, therefore, generally comparable over time, and between rural and urban areas, but possibly not between countries.

Table 7. *Labour force structure and trends*

The labour force and its annual growth rate are based on the ILO's most recent labour force estimates and projections. The economically active population is defined as: all persons of either sex who furnished the supply of labour for the production of goods and services during a specified time-reference period. National practice varies between countries as regards the treatment of groups such as the armed forces, members of religious groups, persons seeking their first job, seasonal workers or persons engaged in part-time economic activities. In certain countries all or some of these groups are included among the economically active, while in others they are considered to be inactive. However, the data on economically active populations do not include students, persons occupied solely in domestic duties in their own household, members of collective households, inmates of institutions, retired persons, persons living entirely on their own means, and persons wholly dependent upon others. The labour force participation rate is defined as the percentage of economically active children and adults in the 10 to 14 and 15 to 64 age groups respectively.

Table 8. *Employment and unemployment*

Statistics on unemployment refer, in principle to all persons of working age who during the reference period are without work, are available for work and are seeking work. These statistics are generally collected through labour force sample surveys. Where possible, the table shows the ILO estimates of unemployment rates as these are more comparable than the raw survey data.

Sources

Tables 1.1., 1.2. & 1.3.   *Trade union membership data and trade union density rates*

Africa

Botswana	Reported by the Botswana Federation of Trade Unions (BFTU).
Cameroon	Reported by the Confédération syndicale des travailleurs du Cameroun (CSTC).
Cape Verde	Reported by the União Nacional dos Trabalhadores de Cabo Verde Central Sindical (UNTC-CS).
Côte d'Ivoire	Reported by the Union générale des travailleurs de Côte d'Ivoire (UGTCI)
Egypt	Reported by the Federation of Egyptian Trade Unions (FETU); does not include self-employed, unemployed and retired workers.
Eritrea	Reported by the government; does not include self-employed, unemployed and retired workers.
Ethiopia	Reported by the Confederation of Ethiopian Trade Unions (CETU).
Gabon	Reported by the Coordination des syndicats du Gabon (COSYGA) in 1995.
Ghana	This figure represents only dues-paying members and has remained steady for several years.
Guinea	Reported by the Union syndicale des travailleurs de Guinée (USTG), which broke away from the Confédération nationale des travailleurs de Guinée (CNTG); it claims to be the most representative federation in Guinea.
Kenya	Estimate made by the Government; the figure includes the membership of the Teachers' Union.
Mali	Reported by the Union nationale des travailleurs du Mali.
Mauritania	Reported by the Confédération générale des travailleurs de Mauritanie (CGTM), which broke away from the Union des travailleurs de Mauritanie (UTM) in 1993.
Mauritius	Reported by the Mauritius Confederation of Workers and the Mauritius Labour Congress (MLC).
Namibia	Reported by the National Union of Namibian Workers (NUNW), which is the national centre. However, the membership of some unaffiliated unions is not included.
Nigeria	Reported membership of the unions who belong(ed) to Nigerian Labour Congress. The figure does not include staff associations for supervisors and junior and middle management employees.

Senegal	Estimate.
South Africa	Reported membership in registered unions (Dept. of Labour figures). 1995 figure includes non-registered unions in agriculture, public and domestic services,[1] corrected for 4 per cent overestimation.[2]
Swaziland	Reported membership in registered unions by the government; does not include unemployed, retired and student members (–5%).
Tanzania, United Rep. of	Reported by the Tanzania Federation of Trade Unions (TFTU), which is the umbrella organization for all affiliates.
Uganda	Reported membership of the National Organization of Trade Unions (NOTU), to which all national unions are affiliated.
Zambia	Reported by the Government; does not include self-employed, unemployed, retired workers, students or other persons who are not currently employed.
Zimbabwe	Reported by the Zimbabwe Congress of Trade Unions (ZCTU), which is the national centre.[3]

Americas

Antigua and Barbuda	Reported by the government; does not include self-employed, unemployed, retired workers and students (–28%).
Argentina	Estimates by Prof. Goldín based on data reported by the trade unions to the Ministry of Labour and Social Security.
Bolivia	Membership officially reported by trade unions.
Brazil	Estimated membership, based on data reported by the unions.
Canada	All unions, annual survey; based on Corporations and Labor Unions Returns Act; also presents data from household surveys for 1984-90.[4]
Chile	All unions, annual survey; includes membership outside the Central Unitaria de Trabajadores (CUT).
Dominican Rep.	Estimated membership, based on data reported by the unions; figure of 1989 is from various independent sources.
Ecuador	Estimated membership, based on data reported by the unions.
El Salvador	Estimated membership, based on data reported by the unions.
Guatemala	Membership officially reported by trade unions.
Honduras	Membership officially reported by trade unions.
Mexico	Estimated membership, based on data reported by the unions.
Nicaragua	Membership officially reported by trade unions.
Panama	Membership officially reported by trade unions.

---

[1] G. Standing, J. Sender and J. Weeks: *Restructuring the labour market: The South African challenge* (ILO Geneva, 1996).

[2] J. Baskin: "The social partnership challenge: Union trends and the industrial relations challenge", in J. Baskin (ed.): *Against the current. Labour and economic policy in South Africa* (Johannesburg, Raven Press, 1996), p. 27.

[3] F. Schiphorst: "The emergence of civil society: The new place of unions in Zimbabwe", in H. Thomas (ed.): *Globalization and Third World trade unions: The challenge of rapid economic changes* (London, Zed Books, 1995).

[4] D. Galarneau: "Unionized workers", in *Statistics Canada – Perpectives,* Spring 1996, pp. 43-52.

Paraguay	Membership officially reported by trade unions.
Peru	Estimated membership, based on data reported by the unions.
United States	Annual survey, based on survey of current population; only wage and salary earners in employment.
Uruguay	Estimated membership, based on data reported by the unions.
Venezuela	Officially reported membership by trade unions.

Asia

Australia	Membership in dependent employment, survey data and financial membership.
Bangladesh	Bangladesh Employers' Association and membership reported to Dept. of Labour; includes self-employed and retired workers.
China	Membership of the All-China Federation of Trade Unions (ACFTU).
Hong Kong (before 1.7.97)	All unions, annual survey (Central Statistical Office).
India	Reported membership in registered trade unions.
Indonesia	Reported membership of officially recognized federation, Indonesia Workers' Union (SPSI).
Japan	All unions, annual survey (Central Statistical Office).
Korea, Rep. of	Includes industry, craft and regional unions, as well as non-recognized unions affiliated with Korean Trade Union Congress.
Malaysia	Some "in-house" unions in industry and public sector included.
New Zealand	All unions, annual survey; union membership is reported as full-time equivalent union members.
Pakistan	Reported membership in registered trade unions.
Philippines	All unions, annual survey.
Singapore	All unions, annual survey.
Sri Lanka	Reported membership in registered trade unions.
Taiwan, China	All unions, annual survey; includes retired members.
Thailand	Reported membership by the government, private sector only.

Europe

Austria	Annual survey, affiliates of Austrian Confederation of Trade Unions (ÖGB); excludes retired members (–18.7%).
Azerbaijan	Reported membership by the Government; excludes self-employed, unemployed, retired workers and students (–19%).
Belarus	Reported membership by the government; excludes retired members (–11%).
Belgium	Annual data, corrected membership reported by three major federations; excludes self-employed, retired and unemployed members (–36.1%).
Bulgaria	Estimated membership on basis of data reported by main federations.
Cyprus	Annual survey, all unions.

Europe

Azerbaijan	Armed forces.
Hungary	Armed forces.
Turkey	Police, prison officers, armed forces and senior civil servants.
United Kingdom	Armed forces.

Table 2. Profile of national employers' organizations

International Organization of Employers (IOE): *Profile of IOE Members* (Geneva), June 1996.

Table 3.1. Collective bargaining structure in selected countries

[1] ILO: *Questionnaire on trade union membership and collective bargaining coverage* (Geneva, 1996).

[2] L. Madhuku: "Worker participation in a developing country: The case of Zimbabwe", in *Comparative Labour Law Journal* (Philadelphia, University of Pennsylvania), No. 17, April 1996, pp. 603-612.

[3] A. Goldín: *Las relaciones industriales: el caso argentino,* document prepared for the ILO (Geneva, 1996).

[4] OECD: *Employment Outlook* (Paris, OECD, 1994), pp. 174-175.

[5] A. Honeybone: *Overview of the changes in the labour relations systems in New Zealand under the Employment Contracts Act,* working paper (ILO, Geneva, 1991), pp. 11-15.

[6] Estimate by C. S. Venkata Ratnam, International Management Institute, New Delhi, 1996.

[7] D. Ayadurai: "Malaysia", in S. Deery and R. Mitchell (eds.): *Labour law and industrial relations in Asia: Eight country studies* (Melbourne, Longman Cheshire, 1993), p. 83.

[8] J. Visser: *Trends and variations in European collective bargaining,* research paper No. 96/2, Centre for Research on European Societies and Industrial Relations (CESAR), Amsterdam University, Feb. 1996, pp. 11-15.

[9] P. Burgess (ed.): *European management guides: Industrial relations and collective bargaining* (London, Incomes Data Services, Institute of Personnel and Development, 1996).

[10] G. Fajertag (ed.): *Collective bargaining in Western Europe 1995-1996* (Brussels, European Trade Union Institute, 1996), pp. 139-147.

[11] P. Aro and P. Repo: *Trade union experiences in collective bargaining in Central Europe. A report of an ILO survey in Bulgaria, Czech Republic, Hungary, Poland and Slovakia* (ILO, Geneva, 1997).

[12] K. H. Sivesind: "Bargaining and participation in Norway", in Workplace Europe – *New forms of bargaining and participation,* 4th European Regional Congress of the International Industrial Relations Association (IIRA), Helsinki, 24-26 August 1994, pp. 153-174.

[13] S. Clarke: *The development of industrial relations in Russia,* document prepared for the ILO (Geneva, Dec. 1996), pp. 120-137.

Table 3.2. Collective bargaining coverage rates in selected countries

[1] ILO estimate for 1995 (Harare, ILO/SAMAT), 1997.

[2] ILO: *Questionnaire on trade union membership and collective bargaining coverage* (Geneva, 1996).

[3] Estimates for 1995 by A. Goldín (University of Buenos Aires), 1996.

[4] ILO estimates for 1993, 1994 and 1995 (Lima, Regional Office for Latin America and the Caribbean), 1996.

[5] Industrial Relations Information Service (Ottawa), 1997.

[6] Ministry of Labour, Chile, 1996.

[7] Calculated from data in: R. Harbridge and A. Honeybone (eds.): *Employment contracts: Bargaining trends and employment law update 1995-1996* (Wellington, Industrial Relations Centre, Victoria University of Wellington, 1996), p. 7.

[8] Estimate by C. S. Venkata Ratnam for 1995, International Management Institute, New Delhi, 1996.

[9] *Yearbook of Labour Statistics 1992* (Ministry of Labour, Japan, 1993), p. 317, table 187.

[10] *Yearbook of Statistics 1996* (Department of Statistics, Malaysia, 1996), p. 220.

[11] *Collective bargaining: An update* (Bureau of Labor and Employment Statistics, Philippines, 1996).

[12] Calculated from data provided by Ministry of Labour, Singapore, 1997.

[13] Y.C. Hwang and C.K. Chiao: "The transformation of industrial relations under democratization in Taiwan, 1987-1996", in *Proceedings,* Vol. 1, 3rd Asian Regional Congress of the International Industrial Relations Association (IIRA), Taiwan, China, 30 Sep.-4 Oct. 1996, p. 83.

[14] "Denmark: Collective bargaining round begins", in *European Industrial Relations Review* (London, Eclipse Group), Feb. 1997, p. 277.

[15] Ministry of Labour, Germany, 1996.

[16] J. Visser: *Trends and variations in European collective bargaining,* op. cit., p. 32.

[17] Ministry of Labour, Netherlands, 1996.

[18] Ministry of Labour, Norway, 1996.

[19] Ministry of Labour, Spain, 1996.

[20] "Trade union membership and recognition: 1994 labour force survey data", in *Employment Gazette* (London), May 1995, p. 198.

Table 4.1., 4.2. & 4.3.   Number of strikes and lockouts, workers involved and workdays not worked

ILO: LABORSTA database (Geneva).

Table 5.   Ratification of ILO Conventions on freedom of association and industrial relations

ILO: *Lists of ratifications by Convention and by country,* Report III (Part 2), International Labour Conference, 85th Session, Geneva, 1997.

Table 6.   Gross domestic product (GDP), population and poverty

World Bank: *World Data 1995* (Washington, DC).

United Nations: *World population prospects 1950-2050: The 1996 revision* (New York, 1997).

H. Tabatatai: *Statistics on poverty and income distribution: An ILO compendium of data* (ILO, Geneva, 1996).

Table 7. *Labour force structure and trends*

ILO: *Economically active population 1950-2010,* 4th edition (Geneva), Dec. 1996.

Table 8. *Employment and unemployment*

ILO: LABORSTA database (Geneva).